INTRODUCTION

BY JOAQUIM PAULO

This is a love story. About a love for music, for composers, for the great singers and all those visionaries who, at a certain moment in time, broke free. It's about love for all the great record-producers who took a thousand and one elements, put them together, recorded them on tape, and transformed them into the music that stays with us throughout our lives and then outlives us all.

I can't tell you exactly when my love story began. It simply happened. And it came in various guises. Buying records – on vinyl, of course – was part of my DNA. It's a demanding business, discovering music of different genres and from different places, exploring, losing myself amid the vast numbers of discs recorded in every imaginable corner of the globe. It requires patience, it means traveling many miles in search of record shops, spending hour after hour going through endless, dusty record-racks, all the time waiting for that very special moment when you discover something rare among the "trash". That moment makes the sometimes physically grueling search worthwhile. Add to this the satisfaction of finding a rarity at a ridiculously low price. Result? Happiness!

I started buying records back in the 1980s, going against the current trends. While my friends listened to punk, I was going around with records by Stevie Wonder, Donny Hathaway (my favorite singer), Funkadelic, Curtis Mayfield, or Marvin Gaye tucked under my arm. Marvin (I call him by his first name) was the one most responsible for my love of that kind of music, especially *What's Going On* (one of my all-time favorites). From then on in, I was hooked for life. On music and records. On vinyl. Starting with soul and funk I went in search of jazz and psychedelia which I only half understood. I traveled to Africa and to Brazil – itself an ever-recurring theme. Music leads you simultaneously into the fields of literature, art, and politics. It encourages you to study and understand social change.

In fact, a vinyl disc is also a work of art. It has a life, a concept, and a form. Picking up a record is a long and never-ending ritual. Taking hold of the cover, removing the vinyl disc with something approaching reverence, looking at the circular groove that will produce extraordinary music, placing it on the turntable and, once again, picking up the cover and reading the technical specifications and the lyrics and analyzing all this information. Think of the delight that designers and photographers can give to countless musicians by producing a record cover worthy of the name. Creating a cover for a vinyl disc is not the same as designing a minuscule CD cover which in most cases is no more than a plastic box. The difference is huge.

Marvin Gaye's *What's Going On* takes on a whole new meaning when you listen to it with the record cover in hand. The sheer power of the photograph gives it a different dimension. The music that I explore, search for, buy, and listen to is glorious. It's mine, and that's enough. Size also matters. So does the look and feel of the surface. Am I an obsessive? A vinyl freak? Sure I am, and much more. And that is why I have brought together (only) a few of my favorite records in this book. As starting points, I used the rarity, the historical importance, the visual impact of the record cover, and, of course, the fact that I love the record. And that's where the hard work began. For instance, how can you possibly choose between recordings by an artist like Marvin Gaye? Believe me, it's very difficult.

One of those I interviewed, David Ritz, friend of Marvin Gaye and a brilliant biographer (author of biographies such as *Divided Soul*), told me he never lets a day pass without listening to Marvin Gaye. It's a huge pleasure to be able to talk to people like David Ritz and hear their stories, but it's also comforting to know that I am not alone in my obsession. But I *was* alone in choosing which records to include in the book. It was a mixture of passion, of recapturing memories of moments in my life that are linked, as if by an umbilical cord, to the purchase of a certain record at a certain time. And of the despair I felt whenever I was forced to exclude many discs before arriving at the final selection.

On the floor of my house I spread them out in rows according to category. Now the book was beginning to take shape. Its visual footprint was becoming clearer in my mind as I sifted through the amazing covers that came with Blaxploitation culture and its compelling music, the brutally powerful imagery of these records reflecting the turbulent 1970s. Magnificent covers for mind-blowing records. And, obviously, I couldn't overlook the original "groove" that came out of Africa. (Thank you, Fela.) I also wanted to show that the French are funky. That Brazilians live and breathe soul and funk. And that there's even funk from Turkey – no, there's nothing weird about it, it's authentic and very good. And lastly the Brits, who are funky people. They revere this music and helped me discover great, famous musicians as well as countless other musical heroes whose names still remain, quite undeservedly, virtually unknown. My thanks to them.

Finally, part of my passion for soul and funk was passed on to me by friends with whom I shared records. DJs that I truly respect for their unconditional love of this music, thoughtful critics, and collectors with their marvelous stories of discovery. My deepest appreciation goes to all those musical archeologists at the head of record companies whose mission is to discover rarities and re-record music lost in the mists of time. On vinyl.

Being able to put together books about music is a tremendous privilege. Apart from its distinctive sound, a record is also a work of art created by designers and photographers. It is a reflection of its times, capable of influencing generation after generation of musicians and creative artists. Putting together a book of this nature is not only a massive responsibility but also great fun. This is no encyclopedia. It is a book that can and should serve as a starting point on a journey to discover more and more music. You're going to have problems tracking down some of these records. But finding them is part of the fun. This is the world of collectors. My world. And part of it is in this book.

EINLEITUNG

VON JOAQUIM PAULO

Dies ist eine Liebesgeschichte. Es geht dabei um die Liebe zur Musik, zu Komponisten, zu großartigen Sängerinnen und Sängern und zu all den Visionären, die in bestimmten Momenten der Geschichte ihre große Stunde hatten. Es geht um die Liebe zu all den fantastischen Plattenproduzenten, die unzählige Parameter bündelten und aufzeichneten und in jene Musik verwandelten, die uns unser ganzes Leben lang begleiten und uns nicht alle überleben wird.

Ich kann euch nicht genau sagen, wann meine Liebesgeschichte begann. Sie passierte mir einfach. Platten zu kaufen (aus Vinyl natürlich), steckt mir in den Genen. Es ist eine echte Herausforderung, Musik aus unterschiedlichen Genres und von verschiedenen Orten zu entdecken – ununterbrochen zu forschen und sich selbst in der unendlichen Menge an Platten zu verlieren, die in allen Ecken der Welt aufgenommen wurden. Das erfordert Geduld: Man legt auf der Suche nach Plattenläden viele Kilometer zurück, wühlt und gräbt stundenlang in endlosen, verstaubten Plattenregalen – die ganze Zeit in Erwartung jenes besonderen Moments, in dem man unter all dem »Müll« etwas total Seltenes entdeckt. Dieser Moment macht die manchmal körperlich aufreibende Suche erst wertvoll. Man stelle sich dann noch die Befriedigung vor, eine Rarität zu einem lächerlich geringen Preis zu finden. Das Ergebnis? Pures und tiefes Glück!

Ich begann in den 80er Jahren Platten zu kaufen und schwamm damals gegen den aktuellen Trend. Während meine Freunde Punk hörten, lief ich mit Platten von Stevie Wonder, Donny Hathaway (meinem Lieblingssänger), Funkadelic, Curtis Mayfield oder Marvin Gaye unter dem Arm herum. Vor allem Marvin (ich nenne ihn beim Vornamen) war verantwortlich für meine Liebe zu dieser Musik, insbesondere durch *What's Going On* (einer meiner absoluten Favoriten). Danach war ich für den Rest meines Lebens süchtig – nach Musik und Platten, aber nur aus Vinyl. Ich fing mit Soul und Funk an und fuhr fort mit Jazz und psychedelischer Musik, die ich kaum begriff. Ich reiste nach Afrika und Brasilien, was schon an sich eine einmalige Erfahrung ist. Die Musik führt einen gleichzeitig in die Bereiche von Literatur, Kunst und Politik. Sie ermuntert einen, soziale Veränderungen zu studieren und zu verstehen.

Tatsächlich ist die Vinylplatte auch ein Kunstwerk. Sie hat Leben, Konzept und Form. Eine Platte in die Hand zu nehmen, ist ein langes und nie endendes Ritual. Man ergreift das Cover und nimmt mit an Ehrehrbietung grenzender Zuneigung die Vinylscheibe heraus, schaut sich die spiralförmige Einkerbung an, die so außergewöhnliche Musik entstehen lässt, legt sie auf den Plattenteller und nimmt wieder das Cover in die Hand, um die Texte zu lesen. Designer und Fotografen schenken unzähligen Musikern grenzenloses Entzücken, wenn sie ein Plattencover produzieren, das seines Namens würdig ist. Das Cover für eine Vinylscheibe zu schaffen, ist nicht das Gleiche wie das Gestalten einer winzigen CD-Hülle, die in den meisten Fällen nicht mehr ist als ein kleiner Plastikschuber. Der Unterschied ist riesig.

What's Going On von Marvin Gaye bekommt eine völlig neue Bedeutung, wenn du es mit dem Cover in der Hand anhörst. Die kraftvolle Ausstrahlung des Fotos verleiht ihm eine andere Dimension. Die Musik, nach der ich forsche, die ich suche, kaufe und mir anhöre, ist herrlich. Sie gehört mir, und das reicht. Mir kommt es auch auf die Größe der Platte an – ebenso auf den sinnlichen Eindruck, den die Oberfläche vermittelt. Bin ich besessen? Ein Vinyl-Freak? Ganz bestimmt, aber nicht nur das. Dies ist der Grund, warum ich in diesem Buch (nur) ein paar meiner Lieblingsplatten versammelt habe. Als Ausgangspunkt achtete ich auf ihre Seltenheit, die historische Bedeutung, die visuelle Wirkung der Plattenhülle und natürlich auf die Tatsache, dass ich diese Platte liebe. Und genau hier fing die harte Arbeit an: Wie kann man sich beispielsweise aus den Aufnahmen eines Künstlers wie Marvin Gaye eine Auswahl anmaßen? Glaubt mir, das ist echt schwer.

Ich habe David Ritz interviewt. Dieser Freund von Marvin Gaye ist ein brillanter Biograf und Autor von Büchern wie *Divided Soul* und gestand mir, dass er jeden Tag etwas von Marvin hört. Es ist eine unglaubliche Freude, mit Menschen wie David zu sprechen und ihre Geschichten zu hören. Es ist auch beruhigend, dass ich mit meiner Obsession nicht alleine bin. Doch ich war alleine, als es um die Wahl der Platten für dieses Buch ging. Es war eine Mischung aus Leidenschaft und der Erinnerung an Momente meines Lebens, die mit dem Erwerb einer bestimmten Platte zu einer bestimmten Zeit verknüpft sind, verbunden wie durch eine Nabelschnur. Und dann meine Verzweiflung, sobald ich gezwungen war, viele dieser Scheiben auszuschließen, bevor ich meine endgültige Auswahl getroffen hatte.

Ich habe alle Alben auf dem Boden ausgebreitet und geordnet. Die Form des Buches kristallisierte sich heraus, als ich die Cover durchging, die zusammen mit der Blaxploitation-Kultur und deren packender Musik erschienen waren. Wie brutal kraftvoll die Bildgebung dieser Platten war, wie sie die turbulenten 70er Jahre widerspiegelten! Herrliche Hüllen für atemberaubende Aufnahmen. Und natürlich konnte ich den originalen »Groove« nicht übersehen, der aus Afrika stammt (danke, Fela!). Ich wollte außerdem zeigen, dass die Franzosen auch funky sein können. Dass Brasilianer Soul und Funk leben und atmen. Und dass es sogar Funk aus der Türkei gibt – nein, daran ist nichts komisch: Er ist authentisch und sehr gut. Und nicht zuletzt die Briten – echt funkige Leute! Sie verehren diese Musik und halfen mir, großartige und berühmte Musiker zu entdecken, aber auch zahllose andere musikalische Helden, deren Namen unverdienterweise immer noch praktisch unbekannt sind. Mein Dank gilt ihnen allen!

Einen Teil meiner Leidenschaft für Funk und Soul habe ich von Freunden geerbt, mit denen ich Platten getauscht habe: DJs, denen ich für ihre bedingungslose Liebe zu dieser Musik größten Respekt entgegenbringe, aufmerksame Rezensenten und Sammler mit ihren fabelhaften Entdeckergeschichten. Meine größte Anerkennung gilt jenen musikalischen Archäologen in verantwortungsvollen Positionen bei Plattenfirmen: Ihre Mission ist es, Raritäten zu entdecken und Musik, die im Nebel der Geschichte verloren zu sein schien, neu aufzulegen. Und zwar auf Vinyl.

Dass ich Bücher über Musik zusammenstellen darf, ist ein Privileg. Abgesehen von ihrem markanten Klang sind Schallplatten auch Kunstwerke, die von Designern und Fotografen geschaffen wurden. Sie spiegeln ihre Zeit und können Generationen von Musikern und Gestaltern beeinflussen. An einem Buch wie diesem zu arbeiten, ist nicht nur eine große Verantwortung, sondern macht auch riesigen Spaß. Dies ist keine Enzyklopädie. Es ist ein Buch, das als Ausgangspunkt einer Reise dienen kann und soll, um auf eigene Faust mehr und mehr Musik zu entdecken. Ihr werdet bei einigen dieser Aufnahmen wahrscheinlich Schwierigkeiten haben, sie zu finden. Doch das gehört zum Spaß, dass man sich auf die Suche macht und die eine oder andere Rarität findet. Dies ist die Welt der Sammler. Meine Welt. Und ein Teil davon befindet sich nun in diesem Buch.

INTRODUCTION

DE JOAQUIM PAULO

Ceci est une histoire d'amour. Amour de la musique, des compositeurs, des grands chanteurs et de tous les visionnaires qui, à un certain moment, ont brisé les barrières. Amour de tous les grands producteurs de disques qui ont pris mille et un ingrédients, les ont rassemblés, enregistrés, et transformés en musique, une musique qui nous accompagne tout au long de notre vie, puis qui nous survit à tous.

Je ne saurais pas vous dire à quel moment exactement mon histoire d'amour a commencé. Elle est arrivée toute seule. Et sous plusieurs formes. Acheter des disques, des vinyles, bien entendu – faisait partie de mon ADN. C'est une activité exigeante, de découvrir de la musique de différents genres et de différents endroits, d'explorer, de se perdre dans les vastes quantités de disques enregistrés dans tous les recoins du monde. Cela requiert de la patience, il faut parcourir des kilomètres et des kilomètres à la recherche de magasins de disques, passer des heures et des heures à fouiller dans des bacs poussiéreux et sans fond, espérant l'arrivée de ce moment très spécial de la découverte d'un disque rare au milieu de la « camelote ». C'est ce moment qui donne toute sa valeur à la recherche, parfois éreintante. Ajoutez à cela la satisfaction de trouver une rareté à un prix ridiculement bas. Résultat ? Le bonheur !

J'ai commencé à acheter des disques dans les années 1980, et j'allais à contre-courant des tendances de l'époque. Pendant que mes amis écoutaient du punk, je me promenais avec des disques de Stevie Wonder, Donny Hathaway (mon chanteur préféré), Funkadelic, Curtis Mayfield ou Marvin Gaye sous le bras. Marvin (je l'appelle par son prénom) a été le plus grand responsable de mon amour pour ce genre de musique, surtout à travers *What's Going On* (l'un de mes grands favoris). C'est à partir de ce moment-là que je suis devenu accro. À la musique et aux disques. Au vinyle. En commençant par la soul et le funk, je suis parti à la recherche de jazz et de musique psychédélique que je ne comprenais qu'à moitié. Je suis allé en Afrique et au Brésil – un thème qui se répète à l'infini. La musique mène simultanément à la littérature, à l'art et à la politique. Elle encourage à étudier et à comprendre les changements de la société.

En fait, un vinyle est aussi une œuvre d'art. Il a une vie, un concept, et une forme. La manipulation d'un disque est un rituel interminable. Prendre la pochette en main, en extraire le disque en vinyle avec une sorte de vénération, contempler le sillon circulaire d'où jaillira une musique extraordinaire, le poser sur la platine et, une fois encore, revenir à la pochette et lire les caractéristiques techniques, les paroles, et analyser toutes ces informations. Pensez au plaisir que les graphistes et les photographes peuvent donner à d'innombrables musiciens en leur offrant une pochette digne de ce nom. Créer une pochette pour un vinyle, ce n'est pas du tout la même chose que créer une minuscule pochette de CD, qui dans la plupart des cas n'est rien d'autre qu'une boîte en plastique. Il y a un monde de différences.

What's Going On de Marvin Gaye prend une tout autre signification quand on l'écoute avec la pochette entre les mains. La photographie possède un pouvoir qui lui donne une autre dimension. La musique que j'explore, que je recherche, que j'achète et que j'écoute est merveilleuse. C'est la mienne, et c'est suffisant. La taille est aussi importante. Ainsi que l'aspect et la texture de la surface. Suis-je un obsédé ? Un fou du vinyle ? Oui, je suis tout ça, et bien plus encore. Et c'est pour cela que j'ai rassemblé quelques-uns (seulement) de mes disques préférés dans ce livre. J'ai pris comme points de départ la rareté, l'importance historique, l'impact visuel de la pochette et, bien sûr, le fait que j'aime le disque. Et c'est là que ça devient corsé. Par exemple, comment peut-on faire un choix parmi les enregistrements d'un artiste tel que Marvin Gaye ? Croyez-moi, c'est très difficile.

L'une des personnes avec qui j'ai eu un entretien, David Ritz, brillant photographe et ami de Marvin

Gaye (et auteur de plusieurs biographies, notamment *Divided Soul*), m'a dit qu'il ne se passe jamais une journée sans qu'il n'écoute du Marvin Gaye. C'est un plaisir immense de pouvoir parler à des gens comme lui et d'écouter leurs histoires, mais c'est également réconfortant de savoir que je ne suis pas seul dans mon obsession. Mais j'*étais* seul pour choisir les disques à mettre dans ce livre. C'était un mélange de passion, d'évocation de souvenirs liés, comme par un cordon ombilical, à l'achat d'un certain disque à un certain moment de ma vie. Il y a aussi eu du désespoir, quand j'ai été forcé d'exclure des disques avant d'arriver à la sélection finale.

Je les ai étalés sur le sol, chez moi, en rangées et par catégorie. Le livre commençait à prendre forme. Son empreinte visuelle devenait plus claire dans mon esprit au fur et à mesure que je passais en revue les superbes pochettes amenées par la culture de la Blaxploitation et sa musique fascinante, les images brutales et puissantes de ces disques évoquent la turbulence des années 1970. Des pochettes magnifiques pour des disques à couper le souffle. Et, bien sûr, je ne pouvais pas négliger le « groove » original qui est arrivé d'Afrique (merci, Fela). Je voulais aussi montrer que les Français sont funky. Que les Brésiliens vivent et respirent à travers la soul et le funk. Et qu'il y a même du funk en Turquie – et non, ce n'est rien de bizarre, c'est authentique et c'est très bon. Et enfin les Britanniques, un peuple très funky. Ils adorent cette musique, et m'ont aidé à découvrir de grands musiciens célèbres ainsi que d'innombrables autres héros de la musique dont le noms restent inconnus, à tort. Je les remercie.

Enfin, une partie de ma passion pour la soul et le funk m'a été transmise par des amis avec qui j'ai partagé des disques. Des DJ que je respecte énormément pour leur amour inconditionnel de la musique, des critiques inspirés et des collectionneurs, avec leurs merveilleuses histoires de découverte. Je ressens une grande gratitude pour tous les archéolo-gues de la musique qui officient dans les maisons de disques, et dont la mission consiste à découvrir des raretés et à réenregistrer de la musique qui s'était perdue dans les limbes du temps. Sur du vinyle.

C'est un immense privilège que de pouvoir faire des livres sur la musique. Un disque, c'est aussi une œuvre d'art créée par des graphistes et des photographes. C'est un reflet de son époque, capable d'influencer des générations de musiciens et d'artistes. La réalisation d'un livre de ce genre représente une responsabilité colossale, mais aussi une grande joie. Ceci n'est pas une encyclopédie. C'est un livre qui peut et qui doit servir de point de départ à un voyage de découverte de la musique, un voyage sans fin. Vous aurez du mal à trouver certains de ces disques. Mais la recherche fait aussi partie du plaisir. C'est le monde des collectionneurs. Mon monde. Et ce livre en contient une partie.

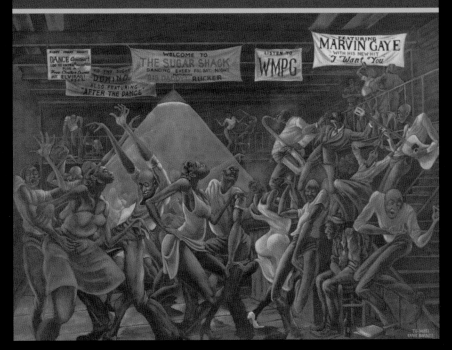

MARVIN GAYE
title **I WANT YOU** / *year* **1976** /
label Tamla Motown / *art direction*
Frank Mulvey / *illustration* Ernie
Barnes

DAVID RITZ

David Ritz is the well-known author of the best-selling biography *Divided Soul: the life of Marvin Gaye*, and the co-author of many autobiographies of great Soul music legends such as Smokey Robinson, Etta James, B.B. King, and Ray Charles. David Ritz is a good listener and endlessly passionate about music, especially Soul music, as well as being a devotee of all the idols who create such great music. The book *Rhythm and the Blues*, written with Jerry Wexler, won the Ralph J. Gleason prize in 1993 for the Best Music Book of the Year. David Ritz has written some notable songs, including Marvin Gaye's "Sexual Healing", and won a 1992 Grammy for writing liner notes for Aretha Franklin.

David Ritz ist der bekannte Autor des Bestsellers *Divided Soul: the Life of Marvin Gaye* und Mitautor vieler Autobiografien von großen Legenden der Soulmusik wie Smokey Robinson, Etta James, B.B. King und Ray Charles. Er kann gut zuhören, liebt Musik, vor allem Soul, und verehrt alle großen Idole, die diese Musik machen. Zusammen mit Jerry Wexler verfasste er das Buch *Rhythm and the Blues*, das 1993 mit dem Ralph J. Gleason-Preis für das beste Musikbuch des Jahres ausgezeichnet wurde. David Ritz ist außerdem ein namhafter Songwriter: Er schuf gemeinsam mit Marvin Gaye den Song »Sexual Healing« und gewann 1992 einen Grammy für seine Liner Notes für Aretha Franklin.

David Ritz est le célèbre auteur du best-seller *Divided Soul: the Life of Marvin Gaye*, et le coauteur de nombreuses biographies de grandes légendes de la soul comme Smokey Robinson, Etta James, B.B. King et Ray Charles. David Ritz est quelqu'un qui sait écouter. Il est infiniment passionné de musique, en particulier de la soul, et admire sans réserve tous les grands artistes qui la créent. Le livre *Rhythm and the Blues*, écrit avec Jerry Wexler, a remporté le prix Ralph J. Gleason du Meilleur livre de musique de l'année en 1993. David Ritz a montré ses talents de parolier avec la chanson *Sexual Healing* de Marvin Gaye, et a remporté un prix Grammy en 1992 pour les notes d'accompagnement qu'il avait écrites pour Aretha Franklin.

My first impressions about you and your work when I first read **Divided Soul** *were that you are, first of all, a great listener, which is a key factor when co-writing a great autobiography.*

It's kind of a spiritual journey because part of being a good autobiographer is that your own ego has to come down enough to understand that it is not your book so much as the artist's book, and people are really more interested in hearing Marvin Gaye or B.B. King or Ray Charles or Smokey Robinson talk about themselves. So the reason I think autobiography is a kind of spiritual journey is because, as a writer, you're really serving another person and not your own glorification, when most writing is about your vision and your voice. In this kind of work I do, you really have to learn to shut up and listen to other people and I have the privilege of living and traveling and being with them, and what I want to do is take you along on my journey with me and that means I have got to take the spotlight off me and keep it on them. It's not about you, it's about letting the world know who Marvin Gaye really is or was.

You had the privilege to live with all these legends. Is it difficult to get the more intimate details from them?

It depends on the individual. In Marvin Gaye's case, he was very candid and spoke openly and easily about himself because he was very autobiographical, very introspective, and so he was not a difficult man to get to speak intimately about difficult areas of his life. Other people have been difficult, and you don't start the tough questions for maybe a month or two, or three or four, and you just talk about music and easier things. You wait until they trust you and the relationship is established and until they understand that I love them and want to honor them and want to try to get to the mystery behind the genius.

Whose was the most difficult musician's mind to get into?

There's been a lot. I don't want to betray their trust but the ideal ones were Marvin, B.B. King was very open… Actually I can tell you that Ray was difficult, he's dead so I don't have to worry about him getting angry at me. Ray was difficult in the

beginning because I was scared of him. It was my first book and I remember asking him a question in the studio when he was recording and he turned toward me and said "Don't ever ask me a question when I'm working!" And once, on the airplane, I was sitting next to him on a trip between LA and NY and I turned to him and said, "Oh God we have five and a half hours for us to talk", and he turned to me and said, "I wouldn't talk to my mother now if she came out of the grave." I felt horrible for the next several hours and he just took a nap all the time. It took me a long time to figure out what the etiquette was and how I should behave in his presence, but once I did he was fine.

Returning to **Divided Soul**, *I felt like all Marvin Gaye's good and bad spirits and feelings were in this book. It was kind of a psychic experience, very open-hearted. What is your most vivid memory about Marvin Gaye?*

Of all artists and experiences I love the most it's those with Marvin, because – it isn't because I don't love Ray and Aretha and Etta and these people – but Marvin was the most complicated literary character and real character I have ever met. He's in his own category on two different levels. One level is the seductive nature of his art, because the harmony of his voice always draws me into his aural world, the world of sound that he creates, and I just want to live there. I want to hear those harmonies, those grooves, the voices, the pain, the healing, all that. But then on a personal level when I met him he *was* his music. He's very sweet, very charismatic, very spiritual, very conflicted, very confused, and very intellectual, and not only do you want to listen to his music all the time you want to be with him all the time! Even in the genre of Rhythm & Blues and Soul music which I love – I love James and Bobby Womack, Wilson Pickett, and a million people who I love, I love, I love! – but Marvin is off all that genre, he remains in the genre but he takes it to an incredible deep level and becomes the expression of at one and the same time an enormous pain and an enormous joy.

So we live between the tension of the pain and the joy and we're always going back and forward. But in terms of telling stories, probably the greatest moment is when we were in Ostend, Belgium, in a kind of strangely isolated situation and in his heart he was willing to come back to America, he wanted a hit but his hit, I knew, had to be autobiographical and so – if you listen to the lyric, it's nearly ghost-writing to him, in other words it was him writing a story – that was a creative moment, very, very meaningful for me; and then of course when I heard he was killed it was very, very, very strange and I met his mother and I met his father... It was only about five years that I was with him but I remember every detail of every time I was with him because I was aware of the fact that I was with an artist of the caliber of Mozart and as much as I love Mozart I don't listen to him every day the way I listen to Marvin Gaye!

"I want to hear those harmonies, those grooves, the voices, the pain, the healing, all that."

Do you have a favorite record or a favorite tune of Marvin's?

It's probably *Here, My Dear* because... I love them all, I love *What's Going On*, I love *Let's Get It On*, I love *I Want You*... I wouldn't say *Here, My Dear* is the best, maybe because when *What's Going On* came out I heard it fourteen million times in the beginning of 1971 and *Here, My Dear* came out 5 or 6 years later, I think it was undervalued.

I presume you lived through all the transformations of Soul music in the '70s with the Philadelphia sound, the Stax sound, the Motown sound, and the Disco sound. What do you like the most from the '70s?

I can go through a lot of things. First of all I loved early Al Green. He was the reconfirmation of the vitality of a kind of roots of R&B – *Still In Love With You*, *Let's Stay Together* – and I love Willie Mitchell's arrangements – they're very sparkling – and I love Teddy Pendergrass, I love Archie Bell and the Drells; of course I love early Stevie, *Music of My Mind* or

Talking Book, and of course Aretha, and I loved Bill Withers and we haven't even talked about the O'Jays, who were fantastic! It was a particularly rich time as R&B evolved and morphed into Disco.

Do you know the new Soul revivals like Sharon Jones and the Dap-Kings?

Sure! I don't know them personally but I love the music. She's kind of like James Brown. I like the music and I think certain genres are going to be there forever, such as the trumpet-saxophone rhythm-section line of Bebop or the string quartet, or even the kind of James Brown-hype Soul band is going to be there forever, as first developed by Ike Turner and Ray Charles and later improved by James Brown and so forth – that's going to be there forever! Because it is good! Like there will always be a great band in a Jazz format because it is just powerful. I like The Roots very much, I like Lil' Wayne very much.

Als ich Divided Soul zum ersten Mal las, war mein erster Eindruck von dir und deiner Arbeit, dass du vor allem ausgezeichnet zuhören kannst. Das ist ein wesentlicher Faktor, wenn man gemeinsam eine großartige Autobiografie verfasst.

Es ist eine Art spirituelle Reise, denn es gehört zu einem guten Autobiografen, das eigene Ego zurückzunehmen. Ich gehe davon aus, dass dies nicht in erster Linie mein eigenes Buch ist, sondern das des Künstlers, und die Leute wollen mehr davon hören, wie Marvin Gaye, B.B. King oder Ray Charles oder Smokey Robinson über sich selbst sprechen. Das ist der Grund, warum ich eine Autobiografie für eine Art spirituelle Reise halte. Bei den meisten schriftstellerischen Werken geht es um die eigene Vision und die eigene Stimme, aber hier diene ich als Schreiber tatsächlich einer anderen Person und lege es nicht darauf an, selbst im Mittelpunkt zu stehen. Bei meiner Art Arbeit muss man einfach lernen, die Klappe zu halten und anderen zuzuhören. Hinzu kommt, dass ich so privilegiert bin, mit diesen Menschen zu leben und zu reisen und viel Zeit mit ihnen zu verbringen. Also will ich die Leser auf meine Reise mitnehmen, und das bedeutet, dass ich mich selbst zurücknehme und die Künstler, über die ich schreibe, in den Mittelpunkt rücke. Es geht nicht um mich selbst, sondern darum, dass die Welt erfährt, wer Marvin Gaye wirklich ist oder war.

»Ich will diese Harmonien und Grooves hören, die Stimmen, den Schmerz, die Heilung – all das.«

Du sprichst vom Privileg, mit all diesen Legenden leben zu dürfen. Ist es schwer, von ihnen intimere Details zu bekommen?

Das hängt vom Einzelnen ab. Was Marvin Gaye angeht, der war wirklich sehr ehrlich und sprach offen und unkompliziert über sich selbst, weil er sehr autobiografisch war und schon viel über sich

nachgedacht hatte. Also war es nicht sonderlich schwer, mit diesem Mann eingehend über schwierige Bereiche in seinem Leben zu sprechen. Bei anderen war es schwerer, aber ich fange mit den heikleren Fragen auch nicht gleich in den ersten ein, zwei Monaten, oder sagen wir in den ersten drei oder vier Monaten, an, sondern spreche erst mal über Musik und einfachere Sachen. Ich warte, bis es eine vertrauensvolle Basis gibt und die Beziehung gefestigt ist, also bis sie begriffen haben, dass ich sie liebe und verehre und mir daran gelegen ist, das Geheimnis hinter ihrem Genie zu lüften.

Bei welchem Musiker war es am schwersten, hinter seine Gedanken zu kommen?

Da gab es eine ganze Menge. Ich will ihr Vertrauen nicht missbrauchen, aber bei Marvin war es ideal, und auch B.B. war sehr offen … Ich muss zugeben, dass es mit Ray ziemlich kompliziert war. Er lebt nicht mehr, also muss ich mir keine Sorgen darüber machen, ob er sauer auf mich wird. Ray war am Anfang schwierig, weil ich Muffensausen vor ihm hatte. Es war mein erstes Buch, und ich weiß noch, wie ich ihn bei einer Aufnahme im Studio mal was gefragt habe, und er dreht sich zu mir um und sagt: »Wehe, du fragst mich noch mal was, wenn ich arbeite!« Und einmal saßen wir im Flugzeug nebeneinander auf einer Reise zwischen Los Angeles und New York, und ich dreh mich zu ihm um und sage: »Toll, wir haben jetzt fünfeinhalb Stunden Zeit, um miteinander zu reden«, und er meinte: »Ich würde jetzt nicht mal mit meiner Mutter reden, auch wenn sie von den Toten auferstehen würde.« Die nächsten Stunden fühlte ich mich schrecklich, aber er hat einfach die ganze Zeit gedöst. Ich habe sehr lange gebraucht, bis ich raushatte, wie mit ihm umzugehen ist und wie ich mich in seiner Gegenwart zu verhalten habe. Aber als ich das kapiert hatte, war's ganz prima mit ihm.

Noch einmal zu Divided Soul: Ich hatte das Gefühl, in diesem Buch all die dunklen und hellen Stimmungen und Gefühle von Marvin Gaye zu finden. Es war wie eine übersinnliche Erfahrung, als ob er sein Herz ganz geöffnet hätte. Was ist deine lebendigste Erinnerung an Marvin Gaye?

Von allen Erfahrungen mit Künstlern liebe ich diejenigen am meisten, die ich mit Marvin machen durfte. Nicht, dass ich Ray und Aretha und Etta und all die anderen nicht auch lieben würde. Aber Marvin war die komplizierteste Person, die ich je getroffen habe – sowohl als Kunstfigur als auch im wahren Leben. In zweierlei Hinsicht bildet er eine ganz eigene Kategorie: Einmal ist da seine verführerische Kunst, seine harmonische Stimme, die mich immer in ihren Bann zieht, die Klangwelt, die er schafft und die süchtig macht. Ich will diese Harmonien und Grooves hören, die Stimmen, den Schmerz, die Heilung – all das. Aber als ich ihn persönlich traf, merkte ich, dass er seine Musik *war*. Er ist sehr nett, sehr charismatisch, sehr spirituell, sehr konfliktreich, sehr konfus und sehr intellektuell. Man will nicht nur dauernd seine Musik hören, sondern einfach die ganze Zeit am liebsten mit ihm verbringen! Sogar in dem Genre Rhythm & Blues und Soul, an dem mein ganzes Herz hängt – ich liebe James und Bobby Womack, Wilson Pickett und noch eine Million anderer Leute, ich liebe sie alle so sehr! –, aber Marvin sprengt das ganze Genre. Er bleibt in diesem Genre, aber durchdringt es und bringt es zu einer unglaublichen Tiefe. Er schafft es, in ein und demselben Moment einen unglaublichen Schmerz zusammen mit einer unglaublichen Freude auszudrücken.

Also leben wir in der Spannung zwischen Schmerz und Freude und wechseln immer vom einen zum anderen. Aber bezogen auf das Erzählen von Geschichten war wahrscheinlich der größte Moment überhaupt, als wir in Ostende, Belgien, mal in einer merkwürdig isolierten Situation waren. Er war im Herzen zutiefst bereit, nach Amerika zurückzukehren. Er wollte einen Hit, aber der Hit, das wusste ich, sollte autobiografisch sein, und so – wenn man genau auf den Liedtext achtet, war das beinahe wie Ghost-Writing, also anders gesagt war er es, der eine Story schrieb – war dies der kreative Moment, der für mich außerordentlich bedeutsam war. Als ich dann hörte, dass er getötet worden war, war es natürlich sehr, sehr, sehr seltsam. Ich traf seine Mutter und seinen Vater ... ich hatte nur fünf Jahre mit ihm verbracht, aber ich erinnere mich noch an jedes Detail meiner Begegnungen mit ihm, weil mir völlig bewusst war, dass ich es hier mit einem Künstler zu tun habe, der vom Kaliber eines Mozart ist. Und so sehr ich Mozart auch liebe, höre ich seine Musik doch nicht so, wie ich die von Marvin höre!

Gibt es für dich unter den Platten oder Songs von Marvin einen besonderen Favoriten?

Vielleicht *Here, My Dear*, weil ... ich liebe sie alle, zum Beispiel *What's Going On* oder *Let's Get It On*, ich liebe *I Want You* ... Ich würde nicht sagen, dass *Here, My Dear* das beste ist, vielleicht weil ich *What's Going On* ungefähr 14 Millionen Mal gehört habe, als es Anfang 1971 herauskam. *Here, My Dear* erschien fünf oder sechs Jahres später, ich finde, es wurde unterschätzt.

Ich gehe mal davon aus, dass du all die Soul-Transformationen der 70er mit durchlebt hast: den Phillysound, den Sound von Stax und Motown und Disco. Welche Musik aus den 70ern magst du am liebsten?

Da kann ich eine Menge Dinge aufzählen. Zunächst einmal habe ich den jungen Al Green echt geliebt. Er war die erneute Bestätigung dafür, wie vital eine bestimmte Wurzel von R&B ist, mit seinen Stücken *Still in Love With You* und *Let's Stay Together*. Außerdem bin ich begeistert von den Arrangements von Willie Mitchell – die sprudeln nur so. Ich finde Teddy Pendergrass klasse und auch Archie Bell & The Drells. Natürlich liebe ich auch den jungen Stevie mit *Music of My Mind* oder *Talking Book*, klar, auch Aretha und Bill Withers, ganz zu schweigen von den O'Jays, die einfach fantastisch waren! Das war eine ganz besonders vielfältige und erfüllte Zeit, als sich R&B weiterentwickelte und in Disco verwandelte.

Kennst du die neuen Soul-Revivals wie Sharon Jones and the Dap-Kings?

Na klar! Ich kenne sie nicht persönlich, aber ich liebe ihre Musik. Sie hat was von James Brown. Ich finde ihre Musik toll. Manche Genres wird es meiner Meinung nach immer geben, z. B. beim Bebop die Rhythm Section mit Trompete und Saxophon oder das Streichquartett. Auch so was wie den Hype um James-Brown-mäßige Soulbands wird es immer geben, so wie das zuerst von Ike Turner oder Ray Charles entwickelt wurde und was James Brown später verbessert hat. Das wird es immer geben, weil es einfach gut ist! So wie es immer großartige Bands in einem Jazz-Format geben wird, weil dieses Format einfach unglaublich viel Power hat. Ganz klasse sind The Roots, und ich finde auch Lil' Wayne sehr toll.

Lorsque j'ai lu **Divided Soul**, *ma première impression sur vous et votre travail était que vous étiez avant tout quelqu'un qui sait vraiment écouter, ce qui est une qualité essentielle quand on veut coécrire une bonne autobiographie.*

C'est une sorte de voyage spirituel, car pour être un bon autobiographe il faut savoir faire taire son égo et comprendre que ce livre n'est pas le vôtre, mais celui de l'artiste. Ce qui intéresse les gens, c'est d'entendre Marvin Gaye, B.B. King, Ray Charles ou Smokey Robinson parler d'eux-mêmes. C'est pour cela que je pense que l'autobiographie est une sorte de voyage spirituel, parce que, en tant qu'écrivain, vous êtes au service de quelqu'un d'autre, et non de votre propre glorification, alors qu'en général on écrit pour raconter sa propre vision, et faire entendre sa propre voix. Dans le genre de travail que je fais, il faut vraiment apprendre à se taire et à écouter les autres. J'ai le privilège de vivre, de voyager et de passer du temps avec eux, et je veux vous embarquer avec moi. Ce qui veut dire que je dois rester dans l'ombre et maintenir les feux de la rampe braqués sur mes sujets. Ce n'est pas de moi qu'il s'agit, mais de faire comprendre au monde ce que Marvin Gaye est ou a été en réalité.

Vous avez eu le privilège de vivre avec tous ces personnages légendaires. Est-ce difficile d'obtenir qu'ils vous livrent des confidences ?

Cela dépend de la personne. Dans le cas de Marvin Gaye, il était très franc, il parlait de lui ouvertement et facilement parce qu'il était très autobiographique, très introspectif. Ce n'était pas compliqué de le faire parler à un niveau intime de sujets sensibles pour lui. D'autres ont été plus réservés. Dans ce cas, j'évite les questions sensibles pendant peut-être un mois ou deux, ou trois ou quatre, et je ne parle que de musique et de sujets plus faciles. J'attends qu'ils me fassent confiance, que la relation se mette en place et qu'ils comprennent que je les aime, que je veux leur rendre hommage et essayer de comprendre le mystère caché derrière le génie.

Qui sont les musiciens dont vous avez eu le plus de mal à pénétrer l'esprit ?

Ils ont été nombreux. Je ne veux pas trahir leur confiance, mais avec Marvin c'était l'idéal. B.B. King était aussi très ouvert … En fait, je peux vous dire que Ray était difficile, il est mort, donc je n'ai pas à avoir peur qu'il m'en veuille. Ray était difficile au début, parce que j'avais peur de lui. C'était mon premier livre, et je me souviens lui avoir posé une question au studio lorsqu'il était en train d'enregistrer. Il s'est tourné vers moi et m'a dit « Ne me pose jamais de question lorsque je travaille ! » Et une fois, dans l'avion, j'étais assis à côté de lui pour un vol de Los Angeles à New York et je lui ai dit : « Oh mon Dieu, nous avons cinq heures et demie devant nous pour parler tranquillement », m'a répondu : « Là tout de suite, je ne parlerais même pas à ma mère si elle revenait d'entre les morts ». Je me suis senti très mal pendant les heures suivantes, et il a dormi pendant tout le voyage. J'ai mis longtemps à comprendre comment je devais me comporter en sa présence, mais une fois que j'ai compris, ça s'est bien passé.

Pour en revenir à **Divided Soul**, *j'ai eu l'impression que toutes les humeurs et tous les sentiments de Marvin Gaye, bons ou mauvais, se trouvaient rassemblés dans ce livre. C'était un peu comme une expérience psychologique à cœur ouvert. Quel est votre souvenir le plus marquant sur Marvin Gaye ?*

De tous les artistes et de toutes les expériences, celles que je préfère sont celles avec Marvin. Ce n'est pas que je n'aime pas Ray, Aretha ou Etta, et tous les autres, mais Marvin était le personnage littéraire et réel le plus complexe que j'aie jamais rencontré. Il est dans une catégorie à part, pour deux raisons différentes. La première est la séduction de son art, parce que l'harmonie de sa voix m'a toujours attiré dans son monde sonore, où j'ai tout simplement envie de m'installer pour toujours. Je veux entendre ces harmonies, ces rythmes, les voix, la douleur, la guérison, tout ça. Et puis, à un niveau personnel, lorsque je l'ai rencontré, il *était* sa musique. Il est très charmant, très charismatique, très spirituel, très contradictoire, très déconcerté, et très intellectuel, et non seulement on veut écouter sa musique tout le temps, mais on veut aussi être avec lui tout le temps ! J'adore le rhythm and blues et la soul (j'adore James Brown et Bobby Womack, Wilson Pickett, et il y a un million d'autres personnes que j'adore, j'adore, j'adore !), mais Marvin est au-delà du genre. Il reste dans le genre, mais il lui donne une profondeur incroyable et devient l'expression même d'une énorme douleur et d'une énorme joie, les deux à la fois.

Alors on vit dans la tension entre douleur et joie, et on est sans cesse en train de faire le va-et-vient. Mais en termes d'histoires à raconter, le plus grand moment a sans doute été lorsque nous étions en Belgique, à Ostende, dans une situation étrangement isolée. Il voulait revenir aux États-Unis, il voulait un tube, mais je savais que ce tube devait être autobiographique et, lorsqu'on écoute les paroles, il était en train d'écrire une histoire, c'était un moment créatif qui m'a beaucoup, beaucoup touché. Et puis, bien sûr, quand j'ai appris qu'il avait été tué, c'était très, très étrange, et j'ai rencontré sa mère, et son père ... Je n'ai été avec lui que 5 ans, mais je me souviens de chaque détail et de chaque instant passé en sa compagnie, parce que je savais que j'étais avec un artiste du calibre de Mozart, et autant que je puisse apprécier Mozart, je ne l'écoute pas tous les jours comme j'écoute Marvin Gaye !

« Je veux entendre ces harmonies, ces rythmes, les voix, la douleur, la guérison, tout ça. »

Avez-vous une préférence pour un disque ou un morceau de Marvin ?

C'est probablement *Here, My Dear* parce que ... Je les aime tous, j'aime *What's Going On*, j'aime *Let's Get It On*, j'aime *I Want You* ... Je ne dirais pas que *Here, My Dear* est le meilleur, peut-être parce que, lorsque *What's Going On* est sorti, je l'ai entendu quatorze millions de fois au début de l'année 1971. *Here, My Dear* est sorti 5 ou 6 ans plus tard, je pense que ce morceau a été sous-estimé.

Je suppose que vous avez vécu toutes les transformations de la soul dans les années 1970 avec le son de Philadelphia, le son de Stax, le son de Motown et le son disco. Qu'est-ce que vous avez préféré dans les années 1970 ?

Je pourrais citer beaucoup de choses. Tout d'abord, j'ai beaucoup aimé les débuts d'Al Green. Il était la reconfirmation de la vitalité de certaines racines du R&B – *Still In Love With You*, *Let's Stay Together* –, et j'aime beaucoup les arrangements pétillants de Willie Mitchell. J'aime Teddy Pendergrass, j'aime Archie Bell and the Drells ; bien sûr, j'aime les débuts de Stevie, *Music of My Mind* ou *Talking Book*, et évidemment Aretha et j'adorais Bill Withers, sans parler des O'Jays qui étaient fantastiques ! L'évolution et la transformation du R&B en disco a donné une époque particulièrement riche.

Vous vous intéressez au renouveau de la soul, avec par exemple Sharon Jones et les Dap-Kings ?

Bien sûr ! Je ne les connais pas personnellement, mais j'aime leur musique. Elle me fait un peu penser à James Brown. J'aime la musique et je pense que certains genres ne mourront jamais, comme la section de rythme avec trompette et saxophone du be-bop, ou les quartettes de cordes, ou mêmes les groupes de soul à la James Brown, qui seront toujours dans les parages, du genre inventé par Ike Turner et Ray Charles, puis amélioré par James Brown, etc. Ça ne disparaîtra jamais, parce que c'est trop bon ! Tout comme il y aura toujours un grand groupe de jazz, parce que c'est tout simplement très puissant. J'aime beaucoup les Roots, j'aime beaucoup Lil' Wayne.

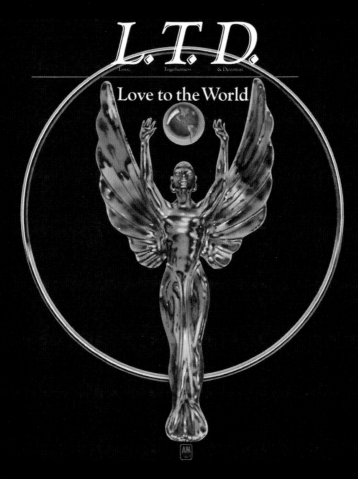

L.T.D.
title **LOVE TO THE WORLD** / *year*
1976 / *label* A&M / *design* Brian Zick/
Star Studios / *photography* Christian
Micoine / *art direction* Roland
Young / *illustration* Brian Zick/Star
Studios

LARRY MIZELL

Larry Mizell became well known with the work he developed for Donald Byrd, earning him a Grammy nomination for the album *Black Byrd*. As a consequence of such success, the Mizell brothers founded Sky High Productions, which was responsible for legendary albums by many different artists, such as Bobbi Humphrey, L.T.D., A Taste of Honey, and the Blackbyrds. While most people may not be familiar with the name of Mizell, all the music fans that dig vinyl records always look for this name in the technical listings of an album as a guarantee of quality. The Mizell family is legendary. In fact, they stamped music in such a way that they will never be forgotten. Larry Mizell is the man who placed together side by side a sophisticated Jazz-Funk with Soul music, full of genius arrangements and luxurious orchestrations, not to say an irresistible Groove which can only be achieved as the result of innovative synthesizer experiments.

Larry Mizell wurde durch seine Arbeit bekannt, die er für Donald Byrd entwickelte und die ihm eine Grammy-Nominierung für das Album *Black Byrd* einbrachte. Als Konsequenz dieses Erfolgs gründeten die Mizell-Brüder die Produktionsfirma Sky High Productions, die für legendäre Alben von vielen unterschiedlichen Künstlern wie Bobbi Humphrey, L.T.D., A Taste of Honey und den Blackbyrds verantwortlich zeichnete. Zwar ist den meisten Leuten der Name Mizell nicht so geläufig, aber alle Musikfans achten bei ihrer Suche nach Vinylplatten immer auf diesen Namen: Er garantiert die hohe technische Qualität eines Albums. Die Mizell-Familie ist legendär: Tatsächlich haben die Mizell-Brüder der Musik ihren unverwechselbaren Stempel aufgedrückt. Larry Mizell ist der Mann, der anspruchsvollen Jazzfunk neben Soulmusik stellt, angereichert mit genialen Arrangements und opulenten Orchestrierungen, ganz zu schweigen von einem unwiderstehlichen Groove, der nur das Ergebnis innovativer Experimente mit dem Synthesizer sein kann.

Larry Mizell s'est fait connaître avec le travail qu'il a réalisé pour Donald Byrd, qui lui a valu une nomination aux prix Grammy pour l'album *Black Byrd*. C'est grâce à ce succès que les frères Mizell ont créé la société Sky High Productions, qui a produit des albums légendaires de nombreux artistes, par exemple Bobbi Humphrey, L.T.D., A Taste of Honey et les Blackbyrds. Le nom des frères Mizell n'est peut-être pas très connu du grand public, mais les amateurs de musique qui fouillent les bacs de vinyles recherchent toujours ce nom dans les crédits techniques d'un album, car c'est pour eux un gage de qualité. La famille Mizell est légendaire. Elle a laissé une empreinte profonde dans le monde de la musique et ne sera jamais oubliée. Larry Mizell est l'homme qui a su réunir jazz-funk sophistiqué et musique soul, avec une abondance d'arrangements magistraux et d'orchestrations éblouissantes, sans parler d'un groove irrésistible qui ne peut être que le résultat d'expériences novatrices au synthétiseur.

What was your major influence when starting to listen to music and getting to love and play music?

I would have to say it was my parents. They were big music fans, they collected a lot of the string bands and we listened to a lot of Duke Ellington and Count Basie. I also had a great uncle who was a successful song-writer, Andy Razaf, and he wrote "Ain't Misbehavin'" and even Glen Miller's hit song "In The Mood", so we had a great musical influence. My grandmother, who lived next door, had a piano and also my brother Fonce and I started to play trumpet with the school band.

> # "We started from what we liked to call 'a groove' and we basically put the artist on top."

But it was when you and your brother went to Howard University that you started playing more...

Yes, more and more! We continued to play. I majored in Electrical Engineering in College and Fonce started off majoring in Pharmacy and then we switched to music and I spent a lot of time at the music building playing piano and doing some acting and we – myself and my brother and a few other fellows, Freddy Perry, and John Butler – had a singing group, the Van Lords.

You met Donny Hathaway at University. What memories do you have of him?

Donny was younger than us. I believe he was one or two years younger. When we met him he was a very accomplished piano player but he only played, really wanted to play, religious music. He came from a church family and we asked him to play piano for us and eventually he decided he would. I remember one time we came out on stage to sing on the Talent Show at Howard's and somehow the lead singer started singing in the wrong key while we were practicing and when we were coming on stage

Donny was able to figure out the key in a matter of seconds and we all started and nobody knew the difference, but I do remember that.

Your first project with Donald Byrd was Black Byrd. Was it at this point that Fonce began working full time with you?

Yes, yes! When I moved to LA, I believe it was '71, Fonce and I did some work... He had of course done his work with Michael and The Jackson 5 and I wrote some songs and played some session work at a motel for Marvin Gaye, and the Miracles, Four Seasons, and the Jackson 5, and then he and I started our own production company and we were living in Hollywood and Donald Byrd came by one evening. He was in town from NY, and he was cutting a recording session the next day so we played a few things and he said, "Let's cut them tomorrow!" and that's how Black Byrd got started.

Going back to your Motown days, did you have any involvement with the writing of "I Want You Back" by the Jackson 5?

No, that was strictly Fonce. I didn't do any writing for the Jackson 5 until '71. I started writing and working at Motown for Fonce but he and my room-mate from college, Freddy Perry, had already written "I Want You Back", and "ABC", "The Love You Save", the first three hits of the Jackson 5, and I came along in '71.

Were those good days at Motown?

Yes! Good memories, very good time! We were both big fans of Motown when we were in college. When I was working with them it was great! Good studio work. I had a lot of fun. Good experience!

I feel that Soul & Funk is the driving force of your music and then, on top of that, you put Jazz. Is this correct or is it the other way round?

You're correct. We started from what we liked to call "a groove" and we basically put the artist on top – we were dealing with instrumental artists with flute, sax, and trumpets – and we let them do their thing on top of the groove that we laid down.

From the end of '73 to '75, Sky High Productions produced several albums for different

record labels, which was not very usual at the time. You and Fonce were extremely prolific but by the beginning of the '80s you slowed down. Why?

We did a lot of albums. In fact after '75 we went on to do some things like Jeffrey Osborne, L.T.D., A Taste of Honey, we got a Grammy for "Boogie Oogie Oogie"; we had a production with Fantasy Records and we did Roger Glenn, we did Gary Bartz, we did a Spiritual album with Rance Allen Group and we did numerous singles. From the time I came out to about '81 or '82 we had worked our entire time with music and we built up a decent enough publishing company. We just took vacations from the music business. I did a lot of traveling. We had royalties coming in so we just continued to have fun!

Can we talk about your work in progress? Do you have any secrets?

We were very much focused on the drums and the bass and the keyboards, the chords, the chords chain, but we really had to have a good drummer and when we did our mixes we always wanted to emphasize the drums. We used regular guys on our sessions and when we did other projects like Taste of Honey we had to work with Wade Marcus to get that sound. With L.T.D. we worked with them and we just brought our intake to each project to the table, our love for music in general!

You recorded with Marvin Gaye. Is there any album work or material to follow **What's Going On?**

Yes, there was supposed to be. They were looking for a follow-up to *What's Going On* and they called in a lot of writers and producers to submit songs to the follow-up, and so we did three songs for Marvin and one was supposed to be the sequel to "What's Going On" and it ended up with nothing being released at all. One of the songs called "Where Are We Going" was released about eight years ago, I think, by Universal on three Marvin Gaye collections and they all did pretty well with *Gold*. We loved *What's Going On* so the opportunity of being in the running to get a follow-up was a great feeling at the time.

Do you have a favorite record session?

I'd qualify that by saying the favorite part of the recording process, and that was recording the first rhythm tracks on any session, particularly the Blue Note sessions when we'd record initial rhythm tracks. That was the most electric and fun part. The second-most fun part of the process was when we were using a live string orchestra. That was great as well… Recording the rhythm tracks was definitely the craziest part.

What is your all-time favorite Soul music record and musician?

That's a hard one! We listen to everything from Straight-Ahead Jazz to Funk to Classic and Gospel and we generally love them all but *What's Going On* would be at the top of my list and also Minnie Riperton's album, *Come to My Garden*.

Welches waren die wichtigsten Einflüsse, als du anfingst, Platten zu hören, die Musik zu lieben und zu spielen?

Ich würde sagen, das waren meine Eltern. Sie waren große Musikfans, sammelten eine Menge Stringbands, und wir hörten oft Duke Ellington und Count Basie. Ich hatte auch einen Großonkel namens Andy Razaf, der ein erfolgreicher Songwriter war. Er schrieb »Ain't Misbehavin'« und sogar den Hit »In The Mood« von Glenn Miller. Also hatten wir tolle musikalische Vorbilder. Meine Großmutter, die neben uns wohnte, hatte ein Klavier, und mein Bruder Fonce und ich fingen in der Schulband mit Trompete an.

> **»Wir fingen immer mit etwas an, was wir den ‚Groove' nannten, und dann packten wir im Grunde die Musiker obendrauf.«**

Aber dein Bruder und du, ihr habt ja erst mehr Musik gemacht, als ihr beide zur Howard University gegangen seid…

Ja, das wurde immer mehr! Wir haben mit der Musik einfach weitergemacht. Am College hatte ich Elektrotechnik als Hauptfach und Fonce Pharmazie. Dann wechselten wir zur Musik und ich verbrachte im Fachbereich Musik viel Zeit damit, Klavier zu spielen und ein wenig zu schauspielern. Außerdem hatten wir, also mein Bruder und ich mit ein paar Kumpels wie Freddy Perry und John Butler, eine Gesangsgruppe, die Van Lords.

An der Uni hast du Donny Hathaway getroffen. Welche Erinnerungen hast du an ihn?

Donny war jünger als wir, ein oder zwei Jahre, glaube ich. Als wir ihn trafen, war er ein sehr versierter Klavierspieler, machte aber nur religiöse Musik und wollte auch nichts anderes spielen. Er stammte aus einer kirchlichen Familie. Wir fragten ihn, ob er

für uns Klavier spielen würde, und schließlich hat er mitgemacht. Ich weiß noch, wie wir bei der Talentshow an der Howard University auf die Bühne gingen, um dort zu singen. Irgendwie hatte der Leadsänger bei den Proben wohl in der falschen Tonart gesungen, aber als wir auf die Bühne kamen, fand Donny die Tonart in wenigen Sekunden heraus. Wir fingen an und keiner merkte den Unterschied, aber ich weiß das noch ganz genau.

Dein erstes Projekt mit Donald Byrd war Black Byrd. Hat Fonce ab diesem Zeitpunkt mit dir Vollzeit gearbeitet?

Ja, richtig! Als ich nach L.A. zog, ich glaube, das war 1971, hatten Fonce und ich jeweils unsere eigenen Projekte … Klar, er hat seine Arbeit mit Michael und den Jackson 5 gemacht, und ich habe ein paar Songs geschrieben und für Marvin Gaye, die Miracles, Four Seasons und die Jackson 5 in einem Motel bei ein paar Sessions mitgespielt. Dann gründeten wir beide zusammen unsere eigene Produktionsfirma. Wir lebten in Hollywood, und Donald Byrd kam eines Abends vorbei, als er von New York in die Stadt kam. Er wollte am nächsten Tag eine Aufnahmesession schneiden. Also spielten wir ein paar Sachen, und er meinte: »Hey, das mischen wir morgen aber ab!«, und so fing's mit *Black Byrd* an.

Noch einmal zurück zu deinen Tagen bei Motown: Hast du irgendwie beim Schreiben von »I Want You Back« von den Jackson 5 mitgemacht?

Nein, das war absolut die Sache von Fonce. Ich habe für die Jackson 5 erst 1971 etwas geschrieben. Ich fing bei Motown an, für Fonce zu schreiben und zu arbeiten, aber er hatte schon mit Freddy Perry, meinem Mitbewohner vom College, »I Want You Back«, »ABC« und »The Love You Save« geschrieben, die ersten drei Hits der Jackson 5. Ich kam erst 1971 dazu.

War das bei Motown eine gute Zeit?

Ja! Tolle Erinnerungen, eine sehr gute Zeit! Wir waren beide Riesenfans von Motown, als wir auf dem College waren. Als ich dort arbeiten konnte, war es einfach großartig! Klasse Arbeit im Studio. Das hat mir unheimlich viel Spaß gemacht. Eine super Erfahrung!

Meinem Gefühl nach sind Soul und Funk die treibende Kraft deiner Musik, und dann setzt du mit Jazz noch eins obendrauf. Stimmt das oder ist es andersherum?

Stimmt genau. Wir fingen immer mit etwas an, was wir den »Groove« nannten, und dann packten wir im Grunde die Musiker obendrauf. Wir arbeiteten mit Instrumentalisten, Flöte, Saxophon und Trompete, und dann ließen wir sie mit ihren Sachen auf unseren Groove-Teppich los.

Von Ende 1973 bis 1975 produzierte Sky High Productions mehrere Alben für verschiedene Labels, was damals nicht sehr üblich war. Du und Fonce, ihr wart extrem produktiv, aber Anfang der Achtziger hast du Tempo rausgenommen. Warum?

Wir haben eine Menge Alben gemacht. Tatsächlich haben wir nach 1975 mit ein paar Sachen wie Jeffrey Osborne, L.T.D. und A Taste of Honey weitergemacht. Wir bekamen einen Grammy für »Boogie Oogie Oogie«, wir haben was mit Fantasy Records produziert und Roger Glenn rausgebracht und auch Gary Bartz. Wir haben ein Spiritual-Album mit der Rance Allen Group gemacht und außerdem viele Singles. Von dem Zeitpunkt an, als ich auf den Markt kam, bis etwa 1981 oder 1982 haben wir die ganze Zeit mit Musik gearbeitet und einen wirklich anständigen Musikverlag aufgebaut. Wir wollten dann vom Musikgeschäft mal Urlaub machen. Ich bin viel gereist. Wir bekamen weiterhin unsere Tantiemen, und so konnten wir einfach weiter Spaß haben!

Lass uns über deine aktuellen Projekte sprechen. Gibt es da irgendetwas, was du uns verraten kannst?

Wir haben uns auf Drums, Bass und Keyboards konzentriert, die Akkorde, die Akkordfolge, doch wir brauchten unbedingt einen guten Drummer, und als wir alles abgemischt hatten, wollten wir die Drums speziell betonen. Bei unseren Sessions haben wir mit Stammmusikern gearbeitet, und als wir andere Projekte wie A Taste of Honey gemacht haben, mussten wir mit Wade Marcus arbeiten, um diesen Sound hinzukriegen. Bei L.T.D. haben wir mit ihnen gearbeitet, und wir brachten bei jedem Projekt unser ganzes Fachwissen und unsere Liebe zur Musik ein!

Du hast Stücke mit Marvin Gaye aufgenommen. Gibt es Alben oder Material, das an What's Going On anschließen wird?

Ja, das sollte eigentlich der Fall sein. Man hatte nach einem Nachfolger für *What's Going On* gesucht und eine Menge Autoren und Produzenten eingeschaltet, die dafür Songs liefern sollten. So kam es dazu, dass wir drei Songs für Marvin gemacht haben, und einer davon sollte die Fortsetzung von »What's Going On« sein. Aber zum Schluss lief es darauf hinaus, dass gar nichts veröffentlicht wurde. Einer der Songs hieß »Where Are We Going« und erschien vor etwa acht Jahren, ich glaube bei Universal, und zwar auf drei Collections von Marvin Gaye, und alle bekamen dann Gold. Wir liebten *What's Going On*, und deswegen war es damals ein tolles Gefühl, dass wir beim Nachfolger mit im Spiel waren.

Gibt es eine Aufnahmesession, die du besonders gut findest?

Ich würde das etwas einschränken auf meinen Lieblingsteil beim Aufnahmeprozess. Das war immer die Aufnahme der ersten Rhythmusspuren bei jeder Session, vor allem bei den *Blue Note*-Sessions, als wir die ersten Rhythmusspuren aufnahmen. Dieser Teil hat mich am meisten elektrisiert und mir total viel Spaß gemacht. Auf Platz zwei kommen dann die Aufnahmen, die wir mit einem richtigen Streichorchester gemacht haben. Das war auch absolut großartig ... die Aufnahme der Rhythmusspuren war definitiv der verrückteste Teil.

Hast du einen absoluten Favoriten unter den Soul-Alben und Soul-Musikern?

Das ist ganz schwer zu sagen! Wir hören uns alles Mögliche an, von schnörkellosem Jazz über Funk bis zu Klassik und Gospel, und wir lieben generell alles, aber ganz oben auf meiner Liste würde *What's Going On* stehen und auch das Album *Come to My Garden* von Minnie Riperton.

Quelle a été votre plus grande influence lorsque vous avez commencé à écouter de la musique, à l'aimer et à en jouer ?

Je dois dire que cela a été mes parents. Ils étaient très amateurs de musique, ils collectionnaient des disques de groupes d'instruments à cordes et nous écoutions beaucoup de Duke Ellington et de Count Basie. J'ai aussi un grand-oncle qui était un très bon compositeur, Andy Razaf. Il a écrit *Ain't Misbehavin'* et même le grand succès de Glenn Miller, *In The Mood*, alors nous avions une excellente influence musicale. Ma grand-mère, qui habitait juste à côté de chez nous, avait un piano, et mon frère Fonce et moi-même avons commencé à jouer de la trompette dans l'orchestre de l'école.

Mais c'est lorsque vous et votre frère êtes allés à l'université Howard que vous avez commencé à jouer plus sérieusement…

Oui, de plus en plus ! Nous avons continué à jouer. J'ai eu mon diplôme d'électrotechnique à la fac, et Fonce a commencé des études de pharmacie, puis nous avons décidé d'étudier la musique, et j'ai passé beaucoup de temps dans le bâtiment de musique à jouer du piano et à pratiquer un peu l'art dramatique, et puis nous (moi, mon frère et des amis, Freddy Perry et John Butler) avons créé un groupe de chant, les Van Lords.

Vous avez rencontré Donny Hathaway à l'université. Quel souvenir avez-vous de lui ?

Donny était plus jeune que nous. Je crois qu'il avait un ou deux ans de moins. Lorsque nous l'avons rencontré, c'était un très bon pianiste, mais il ne jouait que de la musique religieuse, c'est tout ce qui l'attirait vraiment. Il venait d'une famille très pratiquante, et nous lui avons demandé de jouer du piano pour nous, et finalement il a accepté. Je me souviens qu'une fois nous sommes montés sur scène pour chanter dans le spectacle de l'université, et le chanteur principal s'est mis à chanter dans la mauvaise tonalité pendant que nous répétions. Lorsque nous sommes montés sur scène, Donny a réussi à trouver la tonalité en quelques secondes, on l'a tous suivi, et personne ne s'est aperçu de rien, mais je me souviens de ça.

Votre premier projet avec Donald Byrd était Black Byrd. C'est à ce moment que Fonce a commencé à travailler avec vous à plein temps ?

Oui, oui ! Quand j'ai déménagé à Los Angeles, je crois que c'était en 1971, j'ai travaillé un peu avec Fonce… Bien sûr, il avait travaillé avec Michael et les Jackson Five, et j'avais écrit quelques morceaux et joué quelques sessions à un motel pour Marvin Gaye, et les Miracles, Four Seasons, et les Jackson Five. Puis nous avons monté notre société de production tous les deux ensemble. Nous vivions à Hollywood, et Donald Byrd est passé un soir, il habitait à New York, mais il faisait un séjour dans le coin, et il avait une session d'enregistrement le lendemain, alors on a joué un peu et il a dit : « Il faut qu'on enregistre ça demain ! », et c'est comme ça que *Black Byrd* a vu le jour.

Pour revenir à votre époque chez Motown, avez-vous participé à l'écriture de I Want You Back des Jackson Five ?

Non, c'était Fonce. Je n'ai rien écrit pour les Jackson Five jusqu'à 1971. J'ai commencé à écrire et à travailler chez Motown pour Fonce, mais lui et mon camarade de chambre de l'université, Freddy Perry, avaient déjà écrit *I Want You Back*, *ABC* et *The Love You Share*, les trois premiers succès des Jackson Five. Je suis arrivé en 1971.

C'était la belle époque de Motown ?

Oui ! De bons souvenirs, de très bons moments ! Nous étions de grands fans de Motown lorsque nous étions à l'université. C'était génial de travailler pour eux ! On faisait du bon travail en studio. Je me suis beaucoup amusé. C'était une très bonne expérience !

J'ai l'impression que la soul et le funk sont les forces motrices de votre musique, et que vous y avez ajouté le jazz ensuite. Est-ce correct, ou bien est-ce l'inverse qui s'est produit ?

Vous avez raison. Nous partions de ce que nous appelions un « groove », puis nous y ajoutions les artistes (des instrumentistes, flûte, saxo et trompettes) et nous les laissions jouer sur le groove que nous avions préparé.

De la fin de l'année 1973 jusqu'à 1975, Sky High Productions a produit plusieurs albums pour différents labels de disques, ce qui n'était pas très courant à l'époque. Vous et Fonce étiez extrêmement prolifiques, mais vous avez ralenti au début des années 1980. Pourquoi ?

Nous avons fait beaucoup d'albums. En fait, après 1975 nous avons continué avec quelques projets pour Jeffrey Osborne, L.T.D., A Taste of Honey, nous avons eu un prix Grammy pour *Boogie Oogie Oogie* ; nous avons eu une production avec Fantasy Records et nous avons travaillé avec Roger Glenn, avec Gary Bartz, nous avons fait un album de spiritual avec le Rance Allen Group et de nombreux singles. Depuis mes débuts jusqu'à 1981 ou 1982, nous avions passé tout notre temps à travailler dans la musique, et nous avions mis sur pied une maison de disques qui tenait la route. En fait, nous avons pris des vacances loin du monde de la musique. J'ai beaucoup voyagé. Nous avions des royalties qui tombaient régulièrement, alors on a pris du bon temps !

> **« Nous partions de ce que nous appelions un ‹ groove ›, puis nous y ajoutions les artistes. »**

Pouvons-nous parler de vos projets en cours ? Avez-vous des secrets ?

Nous étions très concentrés sur les percussions, la basse et les claviers, les accords, les enchaînements d'accords, mais il nous fallait vraiment un bon batteur, et lorsque nous faisions nos mixages, nous voulions toujours mettre les percussions en valeur. Pour nos sessions nous avions l'habitude de travailler toujours avec les mêmes personnes, et pour d'autres projets comme Taste of Honey nous avons dû travailler avec Wade Marcus pour obtenir ce son. Pour notre travail avec L.T.D., nous avons simplement apporté notre contribution à chaque projet, et notre amour de la musique en général !

Vous avez enregistré avec Marvin Gaye. Y avait-il quelque chose de prévu comme suite à What's Going On, et en reste-t-il quelque chose ?

Oui, il devait y avoir quelque chose. Ils cherchaient à donner une suite à *What's Going On* et ils ont demandé à de nombreux auteurs et producteurs de proposer des chansons, alors nous en avons fait trois pour Marvin et l'une d'elles devait être la suite de *What's Going On*, et finalement il n'y a rien eu du tout. L'une des chansons, intitulée *Where Are We Going*, est sortie il y a environ huit ans, je crois, chez Universal, sur trois compilations de Marvin Gaye, et elles ont toutes bien marché avec *Gold*. Nous aimions beaucoup *What's Going On*, alors, à l'époque, l'opportunité d'être dans la course pour une suite à cet album nous a vraiment enthousiasmés.

Avez-vous une session d'enregistrement préférée ?

Je répondrai à ça en vous parlant de ma partie préférée du processus d'enregistrement. C'était l'enregistrement des premières pistes de rythme, pour n'importe quelle session, particulièrement les sessions de Blue Note. C'était le moment le plus intéressant et le plus électrisant. La partie que je préférais après ça, c'était quand nous utilisions un orchestre de cordes en direct. C'était génial aussi… Enregistrer les pistes de rythme était sans aucun doute la partie la plus dingue.

Quel est votre disque et votre musicien de soul préféré ?

C'est une question difficile ! Nous écoutons de tout, du straight-ahead jazz, du funk, du classique et du gospel, et on aime tout en général, mais *What's Going On* est tout en haut de ma liste, ainsi que l'album de Minnie Riperton, *Come to My Garden*.

STEREO COMPATIBLE DAP-012

SHARON JONES &

T H E DAP-KINGS

100 DAYS 100 NIGHTS

LET THEM KNOCK • NOBODY'S BABY
SOMETHING'S CHANGED • TELL ME
WHEN THE OTHER FOOT DROPS,
UNCLE • BE EASY • HUMBLE ME
KEEP ON LOOKING • ANSWER ME

**SHARON JONES &
THE DAP-KINGS**
title **100 DAYS, 100 NIGHTS** / *year*
2007 / *label* Daptone / *photography*
Dulce Pinzón / *design* David Serre &
Ann Coombs

GABRIEL ROTH

Gabriel Roth is a 35-year-old composer, bass player, and sound engineer. He is also a partner in the well-known label Daptone Records. Roth is truly a music-industry outsider. He claims he never listens to music that was recorded after 1974. He is a lover of raw and dirty funk from the '60s and '70s and a passionate student of these recordings. Roth is a musical puritan, always faithful to analog recording equipment despite living in a digital era. Amy Winehouse is one of the great music characters who have recorded in his studio in Brooklyn. In fact, Roth is hugely responsible for the Soul revival, but his main career project is the big Daptone family and, particularly, singer Sharon Jones and the Dap-Kings, a group of nine black, white, Latin, young and not-so-young musicians whose mission is to find the perfect Groove.

Gabriel Roth, 35, ist Komponist sowie Tontechniker und spielt Bass. Er ist außerdem Mitinhaber des bekannten Labels Daptone Records. Roth ist in der Musikbranche wirklich ein Außenseiter. Er behauptet, dass er keine Musik hört, die nach 1974 aufgenommen wurde. Er liebt rohen, dreckigen Funk aus den 60ern und 70ern und studiert diese Aufnahmen mit Leidenschaft. Als musikalischer Puritaner vertraut Roth stets den analogen Aufnahmegeräten, obwohl er im digitalen Zeitalter lebt. Amy Winehouse ist eine der großen Musikerpersönlichkeiten, die in seinem Studio in Brooklyn gearbeitet haben. Roth ist in vielerlei Hinsicht für das Soul-Revival verantwortlich, doch das wichtigste Projekt seiner Karriere ist die große Daptone-Familie, insbesondere die Sängerin Sharon Jones mit ihren Dap-Kings. Die Mission dieser Gruppe von neun jungen und nicht mehr ganz so jungen schwarzen, weißen und Latino-Musikern besteht darin, den perfekten Groove zu finden.

Gabriel Roth est un compositeur, bassiste et ingénieur du son de 35 ans. Il est également l'un des associés du célèbre label Daptone Records. Roth est un véritable franc-tireur dans le monde de la musique. Il déclare ne jamais écouter de musique enregistrée après 1974. C'est un amant du funk brut et abrasif des années 1960 et 1970, et il étudie passionnément ces enregistrements. C'est un puritain de la musique, toujours fidèle à l'équipement d'enregistrement analogique, même en pleine ère du numérique. Amy Winehouse est l'une des grandes personnalités de la musique qui ont enregistré dans son studio à Brooklyn. En fait, Roth a joué un très grand rôle dans le renouveau de la soul, mais son principal projet professionnel est la grande famille de Daptone et, en particulier, la chanteuse Sharon Jones et les Dap-Kings, un groupe de neuf musiciens noirs, blancs et hispaniques, jeunes et moins jeunes, dont la mission est de trouver le groove parfait.

What is your earliest memory that got you interested in Soul-Funk?

I always loved Blues and Soul music since I was a child, but when I was about sixteen I came to New York to visit my sister who was going to college here, and a friend of hers named Nate Greene made me a cassette of old Meters and J.B.'s stuff. I wore that tape out on my walkman for the next few years. I even remember ducking down in the back of the classroom in high-school classes so I could put my headphones on and listen to it. It really blew my mind. After that I was smitten. I started buying compilations of rare stuff, and soon began digging for old 45s and LPs myself.

Who were your first big musical heroes?

The first was probably James Brown. He really was the greatest architect of funk. He was musically an innovator whose influence on music around the world cannot be measured. His influence on me surely cannot. Later The Meters, Eddie Bo, Willie Mitchell, Otis Redding, and all the rest became heroes of mine. Smokey Robinson may be my biggest hero. As a writer, producer, and performer, he cannot be matched.

Do you remember the first record that you bought?

Probably a children's record. I don't know. I definitely bought *Thriller* when it came out, like everybody else. I remember an old 45 of "Disco Duck" that we had as kids. Later I bought a bunch of pop 45s. By the time I was fifteen, I was really into Blues records. I would buy the rawest, roughest records I could find. I remember one of my favorites was a recording of a guy who had a wire nailed to a two-by-four and played it by sliding a fifth of gin up and down it while he crooned along. He called himself One-String Jones. I guess it was kind of a weird record for a kid that age to be into.

How did your involvement with Daptone happen?

I kind of fell into it by accident. Back in 1996, when I was still in college, I hooked up with a guy named Phillip Lehman who had been running Pure Records out of Paris. Pure put out re-issues and compilations of really rare funk stuff. He and I started making records for fun, and later formed Desco Records. In 2000, Desco closed down and I started Daptone with saxophonist Neal Sugarman.

There are some points of contact between Daptone and the old labels like Motown, Stax... There is a family spirit. Is that true?

Not as much as I would like. Sharon sang some shows with Booker T and the MG's, so I had the honor of meeting those guys, but beyond that, we haven't really crossed paths. Of course, their music and family-oriented business approach is obviously a heavy inspiration for us. I have had the honor of meeting up with the great Willie Mitchell (legendary writer, producer, arranger, engineer for Hi Records, Al Green, Syl Johnson, Ann Peebles, etc.) at his Royal Studios which is still up and running in Memphis. He told me the only equipment you need to make a great record is a heart and a good pair of ears. That stuck with me.

> **"Eliminating computers from the recording process forces the engineer, producer, arranger, and most importantly the musicians to really be competent in their craft."**

Which professional musicians would you have liked to work with if you had lived in the '60s?

Otis Redding, Tina Turner, Al Jackson, Eddie Bo, James Black, Marvin Gaye, James Brown, Sam and Dave, Smokey, Syl Johnson, the Five Royales, Sam Cooke... I could go on forever.

I read in an interview that you only listen to Soul-Funk records from the '60s and '70s. Is that true?

I listen to a lot of Blues, gospel, and R&B from the '50s, and some African music and reggae from the late '70s, but for the most part, the overwhelming majority of music I enjoy is definitely from the '60s and early '70s. It's not out of any disdain for modern music. Everybody has their own tastes. I think that if you openly consider all of the music that has been recorded all over the world in the last hundred years, and the vast body of music written and transcribed over the centuries before, I think it's pretty closed-minded to accept what's on the radio right now as the best music you can find.

Are you a record collector?

Not a major one. I don't have the time and money to be a heavy collector. But I do have a lot of records I really love. I used to dig a lot more when I was younger.

Any "Holy Grail" in your record collection?

I have a few rare things. Honestly, I think the real gems are often not the rare ones. I don't have any records that are better than Otis Redding's *Dock of the Bay*, Al Green's *Back Up Train*, or James Brown's *Mother Popcorn*.

Your recording studio is like revisiting the first studios of Motown. Is it all analog? Why?

Recording equipment is just a tool. Like anything else. Some people use a screwdriver, some people use a drill. Some people use a computer, I use a tape machine. I like the sound and the feel of the equipment we use. My approach to recording is comfortable for me. It feels good. It's fun. That's what music should be about anyway. Computers just allow people more chances to undo things they shouldn't have done in the first place. Eliminating computers from the recording process forces the engineer, producer, arranger, and most importantly the musicians to really be competent in their craft.

There's a wave of musicians that produce a sound that is heavily influenced by '60s Soul, such as Amy Winehouse, Mark Ronson, and so on, but you were the pioneer…

I would never really consider myself a pioneer. I think the thing most revolutionary we are doing is that we are doing something traditional and simple.

Obviously we were a big part of Winehouse's sound, but I don't think any of us were pioneers.

What are your favorite records ever?

Jesse Boone & the Astros *No Particular One*, The Five Royales *Faith*, Sam Cooke *That's Where It's At*, Syl Johnson *Is It Because I'm Black*, Holland & Dozier *Don't Leave Me*, Irma Thomas *Two Winters Long*, Lee Fields *Could Have Been*, Smokey Robinson *You've Really Got A Hold On Me*, Fela Kuti *Confusion*, Little Willie John *Person to Person*.

Who is your favorite producer?

Willie Mitchell, Allen Toussaint, Syl Johnson, Eddie Bo.

Who's the musician you'd love to produce the most or who's the musician who you loved to produce the most?

Tina Turner. Let her know if you see her.

Durch welche ganz frühen Erinnerungen wurde dein Interesse für Soul und Funk geweckt?

Als ich noch ganz klein war, habe ich schon Blues und Soul geliebt. Als ich dann ungefähr 16 war, habe ich meine Schwester in New York besucht, die dort aufs College ging. Ein Freund von ihr namens Nate Greene nahm mir eine Kassette mit alten Sachen von den Meters und J.B. auf. Dieses Band habe ich dann in den folgenden Jahren auf meinem Walkman regelrecht abgenudelt. Ich weiß noch, wie ich mich in der Highschool hinten im Klassenzimmer geduckt habe, damit ich über Kopfhörer Musik hören konnte. Das hat mich einfach total umgehauen, es hat mich richtig erwischt. Ich kaufte mir alle möglichen Compilations mit seltenen Sachen und fing schon bald an, selbst nach alten Singles und LPs zu graben.

Wer gehörte zu deinen ersten großen musikalischen Helden?

Der erste war wahrscheinlich James Brown. Er war wirklich der größte Architekt des Funk. Er war ein musikalischer Erfinder mit einem unermesslichen Einfluss auf die Musik weltweit, und ich kann gar nicht sagen, wie sehr er mich beeinflusst hat. Später kamen die Meters, Eddie Bo, Willie Mitchell, Otis Redding und all die anderen hinzu – das waren echt meine Helden und Smokey Robinson vielleicht mein größter. Als Autor, Produzent und Performer ist er jedenfalls einzigartig.

Kannst du dich noch an die erste Platte erinnern, die du gekauft hast?

Wahrscheinlich eine Kinderplatte. Keine Ahnung. Auf jeden Fall habe ich wie alle anderen *Thriller* gekauft, als es rauskam. Ich weiß noch, dass wir als Kinder eine alte Single mit »Disco Duck« hatten. Später habe ich eine Menge Pop-Singles gekauft. Als ich etwa 15 war, fuhr ich total auf Bluesplatten ab. Ich habe immer nach Platten mit möglichst rohen, ungeschliffenen Aufnahmen gesucht. Ich weiß noch, dass eine meiner Lieblingsscheiben eine Aufnahme von einem Typen war, der Draht auf ein Kantholz genagelt und darauf slidemäßig mit einer Ginflasche gespielt hat, während er dazu summte. Er nannte sich One-String Jones. Ich glaube, das war schon eine merkwürdige Platte für ein Kind in diesem Alter.

Wie bist du zu Daptone gekommen?

Das war eigentlich eher Zufall. Als ich 1996 noch auf dem College war, traf ich jemanden namens Phillip Lehman. Er leitete Pure Records von Paris aus und veröffentlichte Neuauflagen und Compilations von wirklich seltenen Funk-Sachen. Wir taten uns zusammen, brachten aus reiner Spaß an der Freud Platten heraus und gründeten später Desco Records. Desco wurde 2000 geschlossen, und mit dem Saxophonisten Neal Sugarman gründete ich Daptone.

Es gibt einige Kontaktpunkte zwischen Daptone und den alten Labels wie Motown und Stax ... Da herrscht ein familiärer Geist. Stimmt das?

Nicht so sehr, wie ich es gerne gehabt hätte. Sharon hat bei ein paar Shows mit Booker T. and the MG's gesungen. Also kam ich zu der Ehre, diese Leute zu treffen, aber darüber hinaus sind wir uns nicht wirklich über den Weg gelaufen. Natürlich ist ihre Musik und ihre familiäre Art, ihre Geschäfte zu machen, offensichtlich eine sehr wirksame Inspiration für uns. Ich hatte die Ehre, den großen Willie Mitchell zu treffen (der legendäre Autor, Produzent, Arrangeur und Tontechniker für Hi Records, Al Green, Syl Johnson, Ann Peebles etc.), und zwar in seinen Royal Studios, die in Memphis immer noch in Betrieb sind. Er meinte zu mir, dass man für großartige Aufnahmen nur ein Herz und ein Paar gute Ohren braucht. Das blieb bei mir hängen.

Mit welchen Profimusikern hättest du gerne gearbeitet, wenn du in den 60ern gelebt hättest?

Otis Redding, Tina Turner, Al Jackson, Eddie Bo, James Black, Marvin Gaye, James Brown, Sam and Dave, Smokey, Syl Johnson, die Five Royales, Sam Cooke ... Das könnte ich endlos so fortsetzen.

Ich habe in einem Interview gelesen, dass du nur Soul- und Funk-Scheiben aus den 60ern und 70ern hörst. Stimmt das?

Ich höre mir eine Menge Blues, Gospel und R&B aus den 50ern an und ein wenig afrikanische Musik und Reggae von Ende der 70er, doch ich höre vor allem Musik aus den 60ern und frühen 70ern. Daher kommen meine Sachen meistens. Das liegt nicht daran, dass ich moderne Musik ablehne. Jeder hat so seinen eigenen Geschmack. Ich finde, wenn man sich ganz offen mit all der Musik beschäftigt, die in den letzten hundert Jahren in der ganzen Welt aufgenommen wurde, und mit all der unglaublich vielen Musik, die in den Jahrhunderten davor geschrieben und transkribiert wurde, dann ist es meiner Ansicht nach sehr engstirnig zu akzeptieren, dass das, was jetzt so im Radio gespielt wird, die beste Musik sein soll, die man finden kann.

Bist du ein Plattensammler?
Kein besonders großer. Ich habe weder Zeit noch Geld, was ich in eine umfangreiche Sammlung stecken könnte. Doch ich habe eine Menge Platten, die ich wirklich liebe. Als ich jünger war, war ich noch viel mehr auf der Jagd.

»Wenn man Computer aus dem Aufnahmeprozess ausschließt, werden Toningenieure, Produzenten und Arrangeure, aber vor allem die Musiker dazu gezwungen, bei ihrem Handwerk wirklich kompetent zu sein.«

Gibt es einen »Heiligen Gral« in deiner Schallplattensammlung?
Ich habe ein paar seltene Sachen. Ehrlich gesagt finde ich, dass die wahren Perlen oft nicht die seltenen sind. Ich habe keine Platten, die besser sind als *Dock of the Bay* von Otis Redding, *Back Up Train* von Al Green oder *Mother Popcorn* von James Brown.

Wenn man in dein Studio kommt, ist es, als würde man die ersten Motown-Studios besuchen. Ist das alles analog? Warum?

Die Aufnahmegeräte sind einfach nur Werkzeuge wie alles andere. Manche Leute arbeiten mit einem Schraubendreher, andere lieber mit einem Bohrer. Manche nehmen einen Computer, ich habe halt eine Bandmaschine. Mir gefällt der Sound und das Feeling der Geräte, mit denen wir arbeiten. So wie ich diese Aufnahmen angehe, fühle ich mich einfach wohl. Es macht Spaß. Das ist sowieso die Hauptsache bei Musik. Mit Computern können die Leute einfach mehr Sachen rückgängig machen, die sie eigentlich gar nicht erst hätten machen sollen. Wenn man Computer aus dem Aufnahmeprozess ausschließt, werden Toningenieure, Produzenten und Arrangeure, aber vor allem die Musiker dazu gezwungen, bei ihrem Handwerk wirklich kompetent zu sein.

Es gibt eine musikalische Strömung, die einen stark vom Soul der 60er beeinflussten Sound produziert, z. B. Amy Winehouse, Mark Ronson usw., aber du warst der Pionier ...
Ich würde mich selbst nie als Pionier betrachten. Ich bin der Meinung, das Revolutionärste, was wir machen können, ist, dass wir etwas ganz traditionell und einfach machen. Offensichtlich haben wir viel zum Sound von Amy Winehouse beigetragen, aber ich halte keinen von uns für einen Pionier.

Welches sind deine absoluten Lieblingsaufnahmen?
Jesse Boone & the Astros *No Particular One*, The Five Royales *Faith*, Sam Cooke *That's Where It's At*, Syl Johnson *Is It Because I'm Black*, Holland & Dozier *Don't Leave Me*, Irma Thomas *Two Winters Long*, Lee Fields *Could Have Been*, Smokey Robinson *You've Really Got A Hold On Me*, Fela Kuti *Confusion*, Little Willie John *Person to Person*.

Wer ist dein Lieblingsproduzent?
Willie Mitchell, Allen Toussaint, Syl Johnson und Eddie Bo.

Mit welchem Musiker würdest du am liebsten eine Produktion machen oder mit wem hast du am liebsten etwas produziert?
Tina Turner. Sag ihr Bescheid, wenn du sie triffst.

D'après vos souvenirs, quelle est la première chose qui a suscité votre intérêt pour la soul et le funk ?

J'ai toujours aimé le blues et la soul depuis mon plus jeune âge, mais vers seize ans je suis allé rendre visite à ma sœur à New York, elle étudiait là-bas, et l'un de ses amis, qui s'appelait Nate Greene, m'a fait une cassette de vieux morceaux des Meters et de J.B. J'ai usé cette cassette dans mon walkman pendant plusieurs années. Je me souviens même avoir plongé plusieurs fois sous ma table au fond de la classe au lycée pour mettre mes écouteurs et l'écouter. Ça m'a vraiment soufflé. Ensuite j'étais mordu. J'ai commencé à acheter des compilations de raretés, et je me suis vite mis à chercher de vieux albums et 45 tours par moi-même.

> **« En éliminant les ordinateurs du processus d'enregistrement, l'ingénieur, le producteur, l'arrangeur et, surtout, les musiciens sont obligés de vraiment savoir ce qu'ils font. »**

Qui ont été vos premiers héros musicaux ?

Le premier a sans doute été James Brown. Il a vraiment été le plus grand architecte du funk. C'était un novateur qui a eu une influence incommensurable sur la musique partout dans le monde. Et sur moi. Ensuite, il y a les Meters, Eddie Bo, Willie Mitchell, Otis Redding, et tous les autres, qui sont devenus mes héros. Smokey Robinson est peut-être le plus grand pour moi. En tant qu'auteur, producteur et interprète, il n'a pas son pareil.

Vous souvenez-vous du premier disque que vous avez acheté ?

Sans doute un disque pour enfants. Je ne sais pas. Je sais que j'ai acheté *Thriller* quand l'album est sorti, comme tout le monde. Je me souviens d'un vieux 45 tours de *Disco Duck* que nous avions quand nous étions petits. Plus tard, j'ai acheté pas mal de 45 tours de pop. À 15 ans, je m'intéressais beaucoup aux disques de blues. J'achetais les disques les plus intransigeants et les plus authentiques que je pouvais trouver. Je me souviens que l'un de mes préférés était l'enregistrement d'un type qui avait cloué un morceau de fil de fer sur une planche et faisait glisser une bouteille de gin dessus pour en tirer de la musique pendant qu'il chantait. Il s'était donné le nom de « One-String Jones ». Je suppose que c'était un drôle de disque pour l'âge que j'avais.

Comment votre histoire avec Daptone a-t-elle commencé ?

Je suis tombé dedans par hasard. En 1996, quand j'étais encore à l'université, j'ai rencontré un certain Philippe Lehman, qui dirigeait Pure Records depuis Paris. Pure sortait des rééditions et des compilations de morceaux de funk très rares. Nous avons commencé à faire des disques ensemble pour nous amuser, et par la suite nous avons créé Desco Records. Desco a fermé boutique en 2000 et j'ai créé Daptone avec le saxophoniste Neal Sugarman.

Il y a des points de contact entre Daptone et les vieux labels comme Motown, Stax... Il y a un esprit de famille. Est-ce exact ?

Pas autant que j'aimerais. Sharon a chanté en concert avec Booker T and the MG's, donc j'ai eu l'honneur de les rencontrer, mais à part ça, nos chemins ne se sont pas vraiment croisés. Bien sûr, leur manière de travailler très familiale et très axée sur la musique est évidemment une inspiration importante pour nous. J'ai eu l'honneur de rencontrer le grand Willie Mitchell (auteur, producteur, arrangeur et ingénieur légendaire pour Hi Records, Al Green, Syl Johnson, Ann Peebles, etc.) à ses studios Royal, qui sont toujours en activité à Memphis. Il m'a dit que le seul équipement nécessaire pour faire un bon disque, c'est un cœur et une bonne paire d'oreilles. Ça m'a marqué.

Avec quels musiciens professionnels auriez-vous souhaité travailler si vous aviez vécu dans les années 1960 ?

Otis Redding, Tina Turner, Al Jackson, Eddie Bo, James Black, Marvin Gaye, James Brown, Sam and Dave, Smokey, Syl Johnson, the Five Royales, Sam Cooke... Je pourrais continuer à l'infini.

J'ai lu dans un article que vous n'écoutez que des disques de soul et de funk des années 1960 et 1970. Est-ce exact ?

J'écoute beaucoup de blues, de gospel et de R&B des années 1950, et un peu de musique africaine et de reggae de la fin des années 1970, mais, dans la musique que j'aime, la majorité écrasante appartient sans aucun doute aux années 1960 et au début des années 1970. Ce n'est pas par dédain de la musique moderne. À chacun ses goûts. Je pense que, si l'on considère toute la musique qui a été enregistrée dans le monde entier pendant les cent dernières années, et le vaste patrimoine musical écrit et transcrit au cours des siècles précédents, il faudrait être assez obtus pour accepter que ce qui passe à la radio en ce moment soit la meilleure musique que l'on puisse trouver.

Êtes-vous un collectionneur de disques ?

Pas un grand collectionneur. Je n'ai ni le temps ni l'argent pour m'y consacrer vraiment. Mais j'ai beaucoup de disques que j'aime énormément. Je fouillais beaucoup plus dans les bacs quand j'étais plus jeune.

Y a-t-il un « Saint-Graal » dans votre collection de disques ?

J'ai quelques raretés. Franchement, je pense que, souvent, les vraies perles ne sont pas forcément rares. Je n'ai aucun disque qui surpasse *Dock of the Bay* d'Otis Redding, *Back Up Train* d'Al Green, ou *Mother Popcorn* de James Brown.

Dans votre studio d'enregistrement, on se croirait en train de visiter les premiers studios de Motown. Est-ce que tout est analogique ? Pourquoi ?

L'équipement d'enregistrement n'est rien de plus qu'un outil. C'est comme tout. Certains utilisent un tournevis, d'autres utilisent une perceuse. Certains utilisent un ordinateur, moi j'utilise un magnéto-phone. J'aime le son et les sensations que me donne l'équipement que nous utilisons. Mon approche de l'enregistrement est la plus confortable pour moi. Je me sens bien. C'est agréable. C'est cela qui devrait compter, dans la musique. Les ordinateurs permettent tout simplement d'effacer plus facilement ce qu'on n'aurait pas dû faire de toute manière. En éliminant les ordinateurs du processus d'enregistrement, l'ingénieur, le producteur, l'arrangeur et, surtout, les musiciens sont obligés de vraiment savoir ce qu'ils font.

Il y a une vague de musiciens dont le son est très influencé par la soul des années 1960, comme Amy Winehouse, Mark Ronson, etc. Mais vous étiez le pionnier dans ce domaine...

Je ne me considèrerai jamais vraiment comme un pionnier. Je pense que ce que nous faisons de plus révolutionnaire, c'est de travailler avec une approche traditionnelle et simple. Bien sûr, nous avons joué un grand rôle dans le son de Winehouse, mais je ne pense pas que qui que ce soit chez nous soit un pionnier.

Quels sont vos disques préférés de tous les temps ?

Jesse Boone & the Astros *No Particular One*, The Five Royales *Faith*, Sam Cooke *That's Where It's At*, Syl Johnson *Is It Because I'm Black*, Holland & Dozier *Don't Leave Me*, Irma Thomas *Two Winters Long*, Lee Fields *Could Have Been*, Smokey Robinson *You've Really Got A Hold On Me*, Fela Kuti *Confusion*, Little Willie John *Person to Person*.

Qui est votre producteur préféré ?

Willie Mitchell, Allen Toussaint, Syl Johnson, Eddie Bo.

Quel artiste aimeriez-vous le plus produire, ou quel artiste avez-vous le plus aimé produire ?

Tina Turner. Dites-le-lui si vous la croisez.

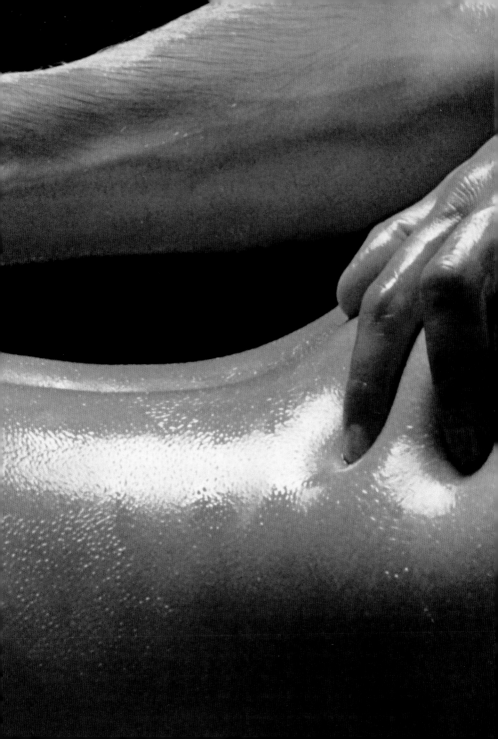

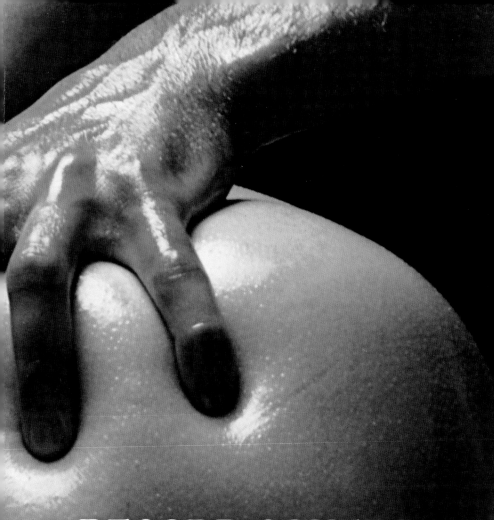

RECORD COVERS
A-Z

F-9476

The 3 Pieces

Vibes of Truth

Fantasy

THE 3 PIECES
title **VIBES OF TRUTH** / *year* **1975** / *label* Fantasy /
art direction Phil Carroll

Recorded at the height of Fantasy Records' soul-jazz
supremacy, this obscure release from The 3 Pieces received
a signature sheen from trumpeter Donald Byrd. Not unlike
Byrd productions for label-mates the Blackbyrds, *Vibes of
Truth* contains sturdy grooves, respectable soloing, occa-
sional vocals, but, ironically, no vibraphone. **O**
Diese obskure Veröffentlichung von The 3 Pieces wurde
auf der Höhe der Soul-Jazz-Vormachtstellung von Fantasy
Records aufgenommen, und der Trompeter Donald Byrd

verlieh ihr seinen charakteristischen Touch. Nicht anders
als bei Byrd-Produktionen für die Label-Kollegen von den
Blackbyrds enthält *Vibes of Truth* handfeste Grooves, res-
pektable Solos, gelegentlichen Gesang, aber ironischerweise
kein Vibraphon. **O**
Enregistré au moment de la suprématie de Fantasy Records
sur le genre de la soul-jazz, cet album obscur des 3 Pieces
est rehaussé d'un éclat unique par le trompettiste Donald
Byrd. À l'instar des productions de Byrd pour ses compagnons de label les Blackbyrds, *Vibes of Truth* renferme des
grooves solides, des solos respectables, quelques parties
vocales, mais, bizarrement, aucun vibraphone.

7th WONDER

title **THUNDER** / *year* **1980** / *label* Casablanca /
design Leo McIntyre/Gribbitt! / *illustration* Jeff Wack /
cover concept Little Boo

7th Wonder always stood in the shadow of Earth, Wind &
Fire. Besides the musical groove they also shared a fascination with ancient Egypt. The nine-member group took the
concept to obsessive heights and would often wear Egyp-
tian costumes on stage. Jeff Wack's hyper-representational
style suited the band's enthusiasm well with this mystical
and highly detailed cover painting. **O**
7th Wonder stand stets im Schatten von Earth, Wind &
Fire. Neben ihrem gemeinsamen musikalischen Groove

waren sie ebenfalls vom alten Ägypten fasziniert. Die neun-
köpfige Truppe setzte dieses Konzept in obsessivem Aus-
maß um und trat auch auf der Bühne oft mit ägyptischen
Kostümen auf. Jeff Wacks mystisches und detailreiches Co-
vergemälde in seinem hyper-gegenständlichen Stil passte
gut zur Ägyptenbegeisterung der Band. **O**
7th Wonder a toujours été dans l'ombre d'Earth, Wind &
Fire. Les deux groupes partageaient le même style de
groove, mais aussi une fascination pour l'Égypte ancienne.
Ce groupe de neuf membres a poussé le concept jusqu'à
l'obsession, et portait souvent des costumes égyptiens sur
scène. Sur cette pochette mystique et très détaillée, le style
hyperfiguratif de Jeff Wack convenait à l'enthousiasme du
groupe.

THE 9th CREATION

title **BUBBLE GUM** / *year* **1975** / *label* Rite Track / *design* William A. Smith / *art direction* J. D. Burrise / *illustration* Grayling Williams

The colorful depiction of bubble gum stuck to the bottom of the cartoon platform sole on the cover of this Bay Area funk outfit's debut LP mimics their bouncy jazz-funk sound. The title-cut and the atmospheric "Rule of Mind" have been popular sample fodder for many hip-hop groups. This album also contains the R&B chart-topper "Falling in Love", a gorgeous synth-washed ballad. ◘

Das Cover des Debütalbums von The 9th Creation zeigt farbenprächtig und comicmäßig ein unter einer Plateau-sohle klebendes Kaugummi, was dem munteren Jazzfunk-Sound dieser Funk-Band aus der Bay Area genau entspricht. Das Titelstück und das atmosphärische »Rule of Mind« waren für viele Hiphop-Gruppen ein beliebtes Samplefut-ter. Dieses Album enthält auch die hinreißende Synthiebal-lade »Falling in Love«, in den R&B-Charts ein Überflieger. ◘

Les couleurs vives de ce dessin de chewing-gum collé à la semelle d'une chaussure à plateforme illustrent très bien le son jazz-funk enlevé du premier album de ce groupe de la baie de San Francisco. Le morceau-titre et l'évocateur *Rule of Mind* ont fourni des samples à de nombreux groupes de hip-hop. Cet album contient également le numéro un des classements de R&B *Falling in Love*, une magnifique ballade inondée de nappes de synthétiseur.

100% PURE POISON

title **COMING RIGHT AT YOU** /
year **1974** / *label* EMI / *design*
Peter Shepherd / *photography* Bill
Richmond / *cover concept* Little Boo

THE 24-CARAT BLACK

title **"GHETTO: MISFORTUNE'S WEALTH"** /
year **1973** / *label* Stax / *photography* Frederick Toma /
art direction Ron Gorden & David Hogan

This curiosity from the Stax catalog is unlike anything issued from the straight-shooting Memphis label. Although Dale Warren arranged several epic pieces for Stax, including Isaac Hayes' "Walk On By", this socially conscious body of instrumentals and short pieces would constitute his most meaningful body of work on Stax or elsewhere. ◗
Diese Kuriosität aus dem Stax-Katalog ist anders als alles, was sonst so bei dem schnörkellosen Label aus Memphis erscheint. Dale Warren arrangierte für Stax eine Reihe epischer Werke, z. B. »Walk On By« von Isaac Hayes. Dieses sozialkritische Werk mit seinen Instrumentalstücken und anderen kurzen Tracks bildet allerdings insgesamt seine bedeutsamste Arbeit. ◗
Cette curiosité du catalogue de Stax ne ressemble à aucune autre production de ce label de Memphis, qui avait l'habitude de suivre une ligne dénuée de toute fioriture. Dale Warren a arrangé plusieurs morceaux épiques pour Stax, notamment *Walk On By* d'Isaac Hayes, mais cet album de morceaux instrumentaux et courts allait être son œuvre la plus importante jamais réalisée, chez Stax ou ailleurs.

A TASTE OF HONEY

title **A TASTE OF HONEY** / *year* **1978** / *label* Capitol /
design Ken Anderson / *photography* Dick Zimmerman /
art direction Roy Kohara

Produced by funky brothers Larry and Fonce Mizell,
A Taste of Honey's self-titled debut showcased a broad
range of funky soulful song-writing, as well as encasing the
ubiquitous disco classic "Boogie Oogie Oogie". Here, bassist
Janice Marie Johnson and guitarist Carlita Dorhan stand
back to back, their respective instruments to hand. **O**
Das Debüt gleichen Namens von A Taste of Honey wurde
von den Funk-Brüdern Larry und Fonce Mizell produziert.

Die Gruppe stellt hier ihre große Bandbreite an Soul-Songs
vor, nicht zu vergessen den allgegenwärtigen Disco-Klassiker »Boogie Oogie Oogie«. Hier lehnen sich die Bassistin
Janice Marie Johnson und die Gitarristin Carlita Dorhan mit
den Instrumenten in der Hand rücklings aneinander. **O**
Produit par les frères du funk Larry et Fonce Mizell, le premier album éponyme de A Taste of Honey présentait une
écriture funk et soul très variée, et contenait le grand classique du disco *Boogie Oogie Oogie*. Ici, la bassiste Janice
Marie Johnson et la guitariste Carlita Dorhan se tiennent
dos à dos, leurs instruments respectifs en main.

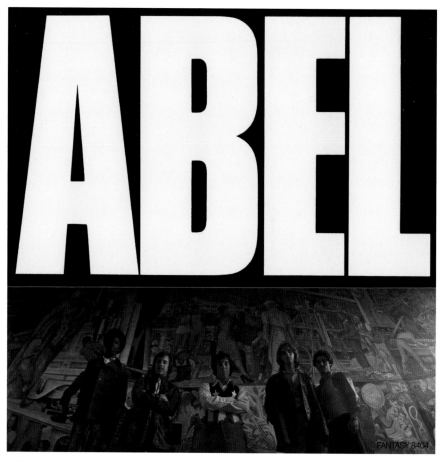

FANTASY 8404

ABEL

title **PLEASE WORLD** / *year* **1971** / *label* Fantasy /
design Tony Lane / *photography* Tony Lane

After spending several years shooting album covers for San
Francisco's Fantasy Records, Tony Lane would become Art
Director for *Rolling Stone*. During his time at the magazine,
he would employ the same design elements that made his
albums and rock posters so successful: large, yet simple
fonts, and alluring band photos. **O**

Nachdem Tony Lane einige Jahre damit verbracht hatte,
Coverfotos für Fantasy Records aus San Francisco zu schie-
ßen, wurde er Art Director beim *Rolling Stone*. Während
seiner Zeit bei diesem Magazin setzte er die gleichen Ge-
staltungselemente ein, die seine Alben und Rockplakate so
erfolgreich machten: große, aber einfache Schriften und
faszinierende Bandfotos. **O**

Après avoir passé plusieurs années à prendre des photos
pour les pochettes d'album de Fantasy Records à San Francisco, Tony Lane allait devenir directeur artistique pour
Rolling Stone. Au magazine, il allait utiliser les mêmes éléments graphiques qui avaient fait le succès de ses albums
et de ses affiches de rock : des lettres grandes et simples, et
des photos de groupe captivantes.

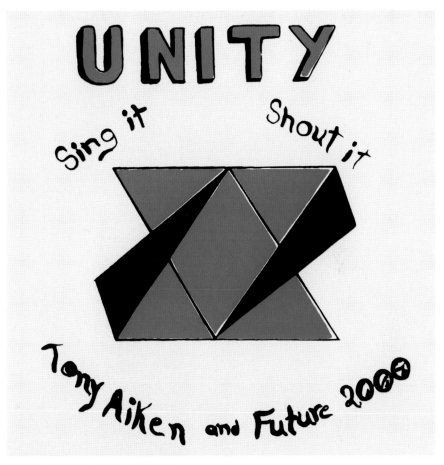

TONY AIKEN AND FUTURE 2000

title **UNITY, SING IT, SHOUT IT** / *year* **1976** /
label Kimsha / *design* Jimmy Smalls

Tony Aiken's fantastic New York-based band mixed
Afro-Caribbean sounds with a tight disco-funk groove to
dizzying results. The homemade quality of the cover
graphics is indicative of the music contained within. There
is an overriding sense of joy that comes through the whole
affair as the group jams its way through this set of soulful
dance-floor originals. ○
Tony Aikens fantastische Band aus New York mischt afro-
karibische Klänge mit einem dichten Groove aus Disco-

Funk und sorgt so für schwindelerregende Ergebnisse. Die
hausgemachte Qualität der Covergrafik ist bezeichnend für
die Musik, die sich dahinter verbirgt. Ein überbordendes
Gefühl der Freude durchströmt die ganze Angelegenheit,
während sich die Gruppe ihren Weg durch diesen Set
souliger Dancefloor-Originale jammt. ○
Le fantastique groupe new-yorkais de Tony Aiken mélan-
geait des sons afrocaribéens et un groove disco-funk serré
avec des résultats étourdissants. L'aspect « fait maison » de
l'illustration de la pochette est dans la lignée de la musique
qu'elle représente. On ressent une joie débordante en écou-
tant cet album, qui n'est qu'une grande jam-session de soul
dansante.

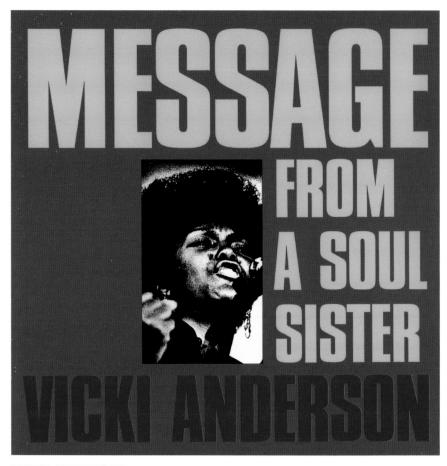

MESSAGE FROM A SOUL SISTER
VICKI ANDERSON

VICKI ANDERSON
title MESSAGE FROM A SOUL SISTER /
label Famous Flame

Born Myra Barnes, Vicki Anderson was the female vocalist for the James Brown revue during the late '60s and early '70s. Her tough as nails funk style opened the doors for many women who came after her. Unfortunately, she was never given an official full-length release. This collection, issued in the early 1990s, includes a handful of singles she recorded for Brown during her tenure. **O**
Vicki Anderson (geboren als Myra Barnes) war Ende der 60er und Anfang der 70er Jahre Sängerin bei der James Brown Revue. Ihr beinharter Funk öffnete die Pforten für

viele Frauen, die nach ihr kamen. Bedauerlicherweise wurde sie nie mit einer offiziellen LP in voller Länge gewürdigt. Diese Sammlung kam Anfang der 90er heraus und enthält ein paar Singles, die sie während ihrer Zeit bei James Brown aufnahm. **O**
Née Myra Barnes, Vicki Anderson a été la chanteuse de la James Brown Revue de la fin des années 1960 au début des années 1970. L'intransigeance de son funk a ouvert les portes pour de nombreuses femmes après elle. Malheureusement, on ne lui a jamais donné l'occasion d'enregistrer un véritable album. Cette compilation sortie au début des années 1990 comprend une poignée de singles qu'elle a enregistrés pour Brown à l'époque de la Revue.

AQUARIAN DREAM

title **FANTASY** / *year* **1978** / *label* Elektra / *design* Johnny Lee & Mary Francis / *art direction* Ron Coro / *illustration* Cynthia Marsh

Art Director Ron Coro's vision was to create a more afro-centric version of *The Dream* by painter Henri Rousseau. Cynthia Marsh set to the task in her Los Angeles studio, layering found and hand-drawn images of assorted flora and fauna over a photographic foundation of studio portraiture. She then silkscreened layers of brilliant colors and used offset lithography to achieve photographic detail. ❍

Die Vision des Art Directors Ron Coro war, eine afrikanische Version des »Traums« des surrealistischen Malers Henri Rousseau zu schaffen. Cynthia Marsh machte sich in ihrem Studio in Los Angeles an diese Aufgabe und arrangierte Fotos sowie handgemalte Bilder mit unterschiedlicher Flora und Fauna über einem Studioporträt als fotografische Grundlage. Dann fügte sie im Siebdruckverfahren mehrere Schichten mit leuchtenden Farben hinzu und arbeitete mit Offset-Lithografie, um eine fotorealistische Detailgenauigkeit zu erreichen. ❍

La vision du directeur artistique Ron Coro était de créer une version africanisante du *Rêve* d'Henri Rousseau. Cynthia Marsh s'est attelée à la tâche dans son studio de Los Angeles, en superposant des couches d'images trouvées ou dessinées à la main sur un portrait photographié en studio. Puis elle a sérigraphié des couches de couleurs vives et a utilisé la lithographie offset pour obtenir un niveau de détails de qualité photographique.

AQUARIAN DREAM

title **NORMAN CONNORS PRESENTS AQUARIAN DREAM** / *year* **1976** / *label* Buddah / *illustration* Carole Jean / *packaging* Milton Sincoff

Educated at both his hometown institution of Temple University and the Juilliard, Philadelphia native Norman Connors drummed alongside several heavies before making educated waves in the R&B pantheon. A Pisces himself, Connors produced two immense collections of highly focused disco-jazz for this seemingly anonymous group of session musicians before parting ways with the ensemble three years later. ○

Der aus Philadelphia stammende Norman Connors absolvierte seine Ausbildung sowohl an der Temple University seiner Heimatstadt als auch an der New Yorker Juilliard School. Er trommelte neben verschiedenen musikalischen Schwergewichten, bevor er auch das R&B-Pantheon in gebildete Schwingungen versetzte. Er selbst wurde im Sternbild Fische geboren und produzierte zwei umfangreiche Sammlungen mit sehr gehaltvollem Disco-Jazz für diese anscheinend anonyme Truppe von Sessionmusikern, bevor er sich drei Jahre später vom Ensemble verabschiedete. ○

Norman Connors a étudié à l'université Temple de Philadelphie, sa ville natale, ainsi qu'à la Juilliard School. Il a joué de sa batterie aux côtés de quelques poids lourds avant de faire ses propres vagues au panthéon du R&B. Né sous le signe du Poisson lui-même, Connors a produit deux immenses collections de disco-jazz très pointu pour ce groupe de musiciens de studio apparemment anonymes avant de se séparer de l'ensemble trois ans plus tard

ASHFORD & SIMPSON

title **SEND IT** / *year* **1977** / *label* Warner Bros. / *design* Andrea Ross & Sherman Weisburd / *photography* Sherman Weisburd

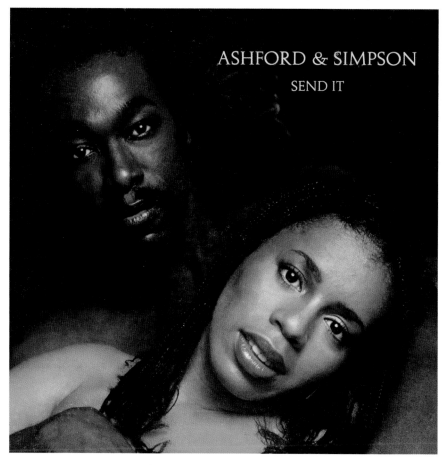

MULATU OF ETHIOPIA

ETHIOPIAN
AIRLINES
Going to great lengths to please

MULATU ASTATKE

title **MULATU OF ETHIOPIA** / *year* **1972** / *label* Worthy

Mulatu Astatke is the father of Ethio-Jazz, a hybrid of western jazz and traditional Ethiopian folk melodies that combine to create a funky, psychedelic mix of sounds that are quite unique. Born in Ethiopia, he studied music in London, New York City, and later would become the first African student at Berklee College of Music in Boston. **O** Mulatu Astatke ist der Vater des Ethio-Jazz, ein Konglomerat aus westlichem Jazz und traditionellen äthiopischen Volksmelodien. Kombiniert ergibt das einen funkigen, psychedelischen Klangmix, der wirklich einzigartig ist. Astatke wurde in Äthiopien geboren und studierte u. a. in London und New York City Musik. Später wurde er der erste afrikanische Student am Berklee College of Music in Boston. **O** Mulatu Astatke est le père de l'éthio-jazz, un hybride de jazz et de mélodies éthiopiennes traditionnelles qui forme un mélange de sons funky et psychédéliques tout à fait unique. Né en Éthiopie, il a étudié la musique à Londres et à New York, et allait par la suite devenir le premier étudiant africain du Berklee College of Music de Boston.

DONALD AUSTIN
title **CRAZY LEGS** / *year* **1973** /
label Westbound / *photography*
Fred F. Carter / *art direction* Neil
Terk

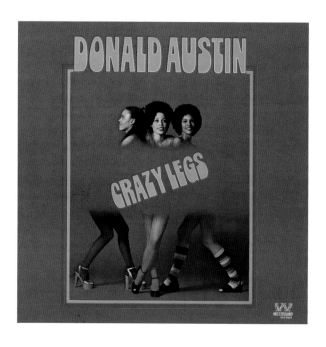

PATTI AUSTIN
title **LEAVE A LITTLE LOVE** /
year **1966** / *label* Coral

AVERAGE WHITE BAND

title **THE BEST OF AWB** / *year* **1981** / *label* RCA
International / *design* Laurence Hoadley / *photography*
Duffy

Although the Scottish group had long used an illustrated
posterior to represent the middle initial in their often-
abbreviated name, this refined collection of choice cuts
finally personifies the picturesque silhouette fans had come
to admire. Though AWB has many greatest hits compilations to its name, each contains the instrumental classic
"Pick Up the Pieces", undoubtedly the group's greatest
contribution to funk music. **O**
Die schottische Gruppe setzte schon seit Langem das Bild
eines verlängerten Rückens ein, um die mittlere Initiale ihres
oft abgekürzten Namens zu repräsentieren – auf dieser

raffinierten Sammlung ausgewählter Stücke fand sich end-
lich jene malerische Silhouette, die von Fans schon lange
verehrt wurde. AWB veröffentlichte viele Zusammenstellungen mit Greatest Hits, und sie alle enthalten den Instru-
mentalklassiker »Pick Up the Pieces«, zweifelsohne der
wichtigste Beitrag dieser Truppe zum Funk. **O**
Cela faisait déjà longtemps que le groupe écossais utilisait
un postérieur stylisé pour représenter la deuxième initiale
de leur nom, souvent abrégé, mais cette belle compilation
de morceaux de choix donne enfin une version en chair et
en os de la silhouette que les fans admiraient tant. Il existe
de nombreuses compilations d'AWB, mais chacune d'entre
elles comporte le grand classique instrumental *Pick Up the
Pieces*, sans aucun doute la plus grande contribution de ce
groupe au funk.

THE HARVEY AVERNE DOZEN

title **VIVA SOUL** / *year* **1968** / *label* Atlantic /
design Izzy Sanabria / *photography* Berne Greene

Izzy Sanabria, aka Mr. Salsa, was the go-to designer for all things funky and Latin. He had a knack for iconographic imagery whether it was through drawing or photos. For this, Averne's debut as a bandleader, Sanabria's urban chic lends an air of mystery and cool to this set of smoking-hot Latin soul. **O**

Izzy Sanabria (alias Mr. Salsa) war als Designer der Pflichtkontakt für alles, was irgendwie nach Funk und Latin roch.

Er hatte ein gutes Händchen für symbolträchtige Bildgestaltungen, egal ob als Zeichnung oder mit Fotos. Avernes Debüt als Bandleader mit dieser Sammlung von kochend heißem Latin Soul bekommt durch Sanabrias urbanen Chic ein Flair von Geheimnis und Coolness. **O**

Izzy Sanabria, également connu sous le nom de Mr. Salsa, était le graphiste de référence pour tout ce qui touchait au funk et à la musique latine. Il avait le don de créer des images emblématiques, que ce soit au moyen du dessin ou de la photo. Pour les débuts d'Averne comme leader de groupe, le chic urbain de Sanabria prête à cet album de soul latine torride une aura mystérieuse et branchée.

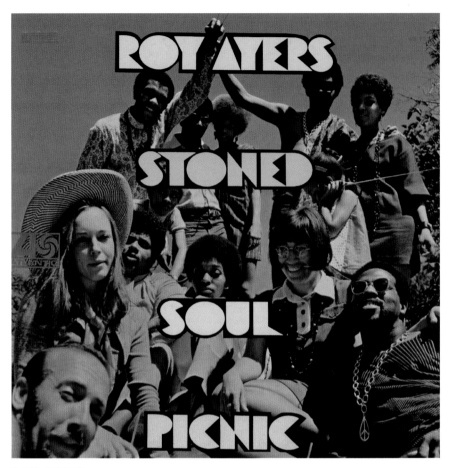

ROY AYERS
title **STONED SOUL PICNIC** / *year* **1968** / *label* Atlantic /
design Marvin Israel / *photography* Lee Friedlander

Lee Friedlander's work is world renowned. He began his
career in the late 1950s as a commercial photographer
shooting jazz musicians, but won numerous Guggenheim
grants and a MacArthur Fellowship to focus on his fine-
arts photography. He is a gifted interpreter of the modern
world, as is evident from his cover for this groovy Roy Ayers
soul-jazz session from 1968. **❍**
Lee Friedlander kam mit seinen Arbeiten zu Weltruhm.
Er begann seine Karriere Ende der 50er Jahre als Werbefoto-
graf, der Jazz-Musiker ablichtete, und gewann verschiedene
Guggenheim-Stipendien sowie ein MacArthur Fellowship,

dank derer er sich auf seine künstlerische Fotografie
konzentrieren konnte. Er ist ein begnadeter Interpret der
modernen Welt, wie auf dem Cover für diese groovige
Soul-Jazz-Session von Roy Ayers aus dem Jahre 1968 ersichtlich wird. **❍**
L'œuvre de Lee Friedlander est connue partout dans le
monde. Il a commencé sa carrière à la fin des années 1950
comme photographe commercial, en prenant des clichés
de musiciens de jazz, mais a gagné plusieurs bourses
Guggenheim et une bourse MacArthur pour se consacrer
à sa photographie artistique. C'est un interprète talentueux
du monde moderne, comme le montre la photo qu'il a
réalisée pour cette session groovy de soul-jazz que Roy
Ayers a enregistrée en 1968.

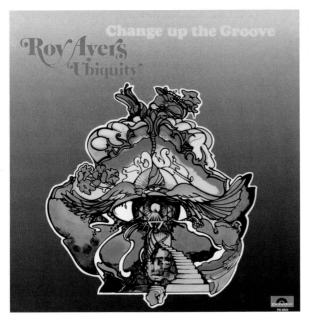

**ROY AYERS
UBIQUITY**
title **CHANGE UP THE
GROOVE** / *year* **1974** / *label*
Polydor / *design* Harrit Millman /
art direction Harrit Millman

**ROY AYERS
UBIQUITY**
title **STARBOOTY** / *year* **1978** /
label Elektra

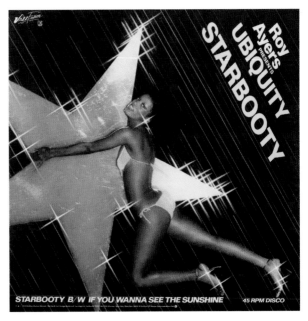

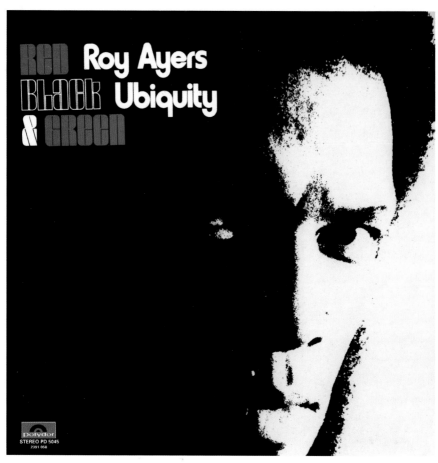

ROY AYERS UBIQUITY

title **RED BLACK** & **GREEN** / *year* **1973** / *label* Polydor /
photography Minoru Aoki / *art direction* Kats Abe

A long-time favorite of the hip-hop community, this is an
essential acid jazz disc. Roy Ayers started his career as a
vibraphonist on the West Coast scene in the early '60s. This
album captures the moment when funk and jazz could
co-exist with dizzying results. Minoru Aoki's stark, iconic
black & white image of Ayers supports the dichotomy of
grit and beauty held within. **○**
Diese essenzielle Acid-Jazz-Aufnahme ist schon seit langer
Zeit ein Favorit der Hiphop-Community. Roy Ayers begann
seine Karriere als Vibraphonist in der Westcoast-Szene der
frühen 60er Jahre. Dieses Album hält den Moment fest, in
dem Funk und Jazz mit schwindelerregenden Resultaten
nebeneinander existieren konnten. Minoru Aokis nüchter-
nes und symbolträchtiges Schwarzweißfoto von Ayers
unterstützt die Gegensätzlichkeit von Grobkörnigkeit und
der darin verborgenen Schönheit. **○**
Ce disque essentiel d'acid jazz fait partie des favoris de la
communauté du hip-hop depuis longtemps. Il saisit le
moment où le funk et le jazz ont pu cohabiter et produire
des résultats qui donnent le tournis. Roy Ayers a débuté
comme vibraphoniste sur la scène du West Coast au début
des années 1960. Le portrait emblématique et sévère
d'Ayers en noir et blanc, réalisé par Minoru Aoki, reprend la
dichotomie entre réalisme et beauté que le disque véhicule.

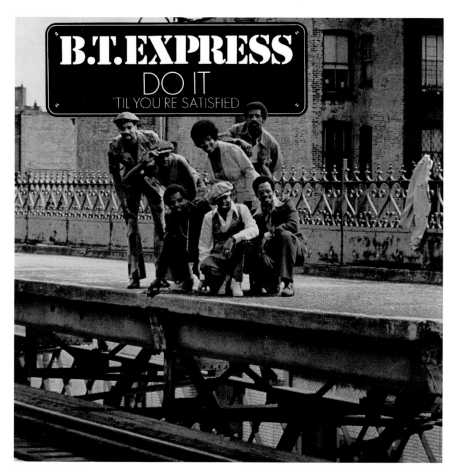

B.T. EXPRESS

title **DO IT 'TIL YOU'RE SATISFIED** / *year* **1974** / *label* Scepter / *design* Michael Mendel / *photography* Gene Ward / *art direction* Sid Maurer

Short for Brooklyn Trucking Express, the group posed atop one of New York's many elevated train platforms for their 1974 album on Scepter Records. It is most likely that this photograph was taken at the Nostrand Avenue stop of the Long Island Rail Road line in the Bedford-Stuyvesant neighborhood of the group's namesake borough. **O**
Das Kürzel steht für Brooklyn Trucking Express, und die Gruppe posierte hier für ihr Album von 1974 bei Scepter

Records auf einem der vielen Hochbahnsteige in New York. Höchstwahrscheinlich wurde dieses Foto an der Haltestelle Nostrand Avenue der Long Island Rail Road in Bedford-Stuyvesant aufgenommen, in der Nachbarschaft des Bezirks von New York, der Pate für den Gruppennamen stand. **O**
Pour leur album de 1974 chez Scepter Records, le groupe, dont le nom signifie Brooklyn Trucking Express, a posé sur le quai de l'une des nombreuses stations du métro aérien de New York. Cette photo a sans doute été prise à la station de Nostrand Avenue sur la ligne de Long Island, dans le quartier de Bedford-Stuyvesant de la circonscription homonyme du groupe.

BAND OF THIEVES
title **BAND OF THIEVES** /
year **1976** / *label* Ovation /
design Herb Bruce

BANDA BLACK RIO
title **MARIA FUMAÇA** /
year **1977** / *label* Atlantic /
design Gang / *photography*
Sebastião Barbosa

BAR-KAYS

title **SOUL FINGER** / *year* **1967** / *label* Volt /
design Loring Eutemey

Soul Finger serves as one of the rare examples of this Memphis group's classic incarnation: all but two of the original Bar-Kays would perish in the plane crash that also claimed the life of soul luminary Otis Redding. ◐

Soul Finger dient als ein seltenes Beispiel für die klassische Inkarnation dieser Formation aus Memphis: Nur zwei der ursprünglichen Bar-Kays überlebten den Flugzeugabsturz, der auch das Leben des Soul-Gestirns Otis Redding forderte. ◐

Soul Finger est l'un des rares exemples de la formation classique de ce groupe de Memphis : tous les membres de Bar-Kays, sauf deux, allaient périr dans l'accident d'avion qui a aussi emporté le génie de la soul, Otis Redding.

BAR-KAYS

title **AS ONE** / *year* **1980** /
label Mercury

FANIA (S)LP #378
STEREO

RAY BARRETTO

title **TOGETHER** / *year* **1969** / *label* Fania / *design* Izzy Sanabria / *photography* Marty Topp

The grand master of Latin record cover design delivered another classic with Ray Barretto's *Together*. Marty Topp's photos of the groovy Nuyorican brothers are balanced with the high-contrast profile of their leader. Salsa was coming into its own on the streets of New York and this record was one of the cornerstones of the movement with its mix of Latin soul and jazz. ⚪

Der Großmeister der Covergestaltung für Latin-Scheiben lieferte hier bei Ray Barrettos *Together* den nächsten Klassiker ab. Marty Topps Fotos der groovigen Nuyorican-Brüder stehen dem kontrastreichen Profil ihres Bandleaders gegenüber. In den Straßen von New York setzte sich Salsa mehr und mehr durch, und diese Aufnahme mit ihrem Mix aus Latin Soul und Jazz war einer der Grundsteine für die Bewegung. ⚪

Le grand maître du graphisme des pochettes de disque de musique latine a encore créé un grand classique avec l'album *Together* de Ray Barretto. Les photos que Marty Topp a prises des frères Nuyorican sont mises en équilibre avec le profil haut en contraste de leur leader. La salsa perçait dans les rues de New York et ce disque, avec son mélange de soul latine et de jazz, a été l'une des pierres angulaires du mouvement.

PAULA LPS 2213 / STEREO

fontella bass
FREE

FONTELLA BASS

title **FREE** / *year* **1972** / *label* Paula /
photography Larry Block

St. Louis native Fontella Bass is best known for her enduring
hit "Rescue Me", released in 1965 for the Chess label and its
subsidiary Checker. After spending three years in Paris with
the Art Ensemble of Chicago, Bass returned to the States,
recording *Free* with producer and long-time collaborator
Oliver Sain for the Shreveport, Louisiana indie, Paula. **O**
Die aus St. Louis stammende Fontella Bass ist besonders
bekannt für ihren Dauerbrenner »Rescue Me«, der 1965 bei
der Plattenfirma Chess und deren Schwesterlabel Checker
erschien. Nachdem sie mit dem Art Ensemble of Chicago
drei Jahre in Paris verbracht hatte, kehrte Bass in die Staaten
zurück und nahm mit dem Produzenten und langjährigen
Mitarbeiter Oliver Sain für das Indie-Label Paula aus
Shreveport, Louisiana, die Scheibe *Free* auf. **O**
Fontella Bass, native de Saint-Louis, est surtout connue
pour son succès impérissable *Rescue Me*, sorti en 1965 chez
le label Chess et sa filiale Checker. Après avoir passé trois
ans à Paris avec l'Art Ensemble de Chicago, Bass est retour-
née aux États-Unis et a enregistré *Free* avec son collaborateur de longue date, le producteur Oliver Sain, pour le label
indépendant Paula à Shreveport, en Louisiane.

JOE BATAAN

title **SALSOUL** / *year* **1973** / *label* Mericana /
design Quin Graphic Productions

Raised in East Harlem, Joe Bataan had exposure to both the
salsa music of his Latino community and the soul music of
the black community. It is no surprise that Bataan, born
to an African-American mother and Filipino father, would
cross-pollinate the two sounds, spawning the genre of
Salsoul, and soon establishing a label of the same name. **O**
Joe Bataan wuchs in East Harlem auf und lernte sowohl
die Salsamusik seiner Latino-Nachbarn kennen als auch

die Soulmusik der Black Community. So wundert es nicht,
dass sich bei Bataan als Kind einer afroamerikanischen
Mutter und eines philippinischen Vaters die beiden Klang-
welten gegenseitig befruchteten. Daraus erwuchs das Genre Salsoul, und bald schon entstand das Label gleichen
Namens. **O**
Pendant son enfance à East Harlem, Joe Bataan a été expo-
sé à la salsa de sa communauté hispanique et à la soul de
la communauté noire. Il n'y a donc rien de surprenant à ce
que ce fils d'une Afro-Américaine et d'un Philippin ait croi-
sé les deux sons et fait naître la salsoul, nom qu'il donna à
son label.

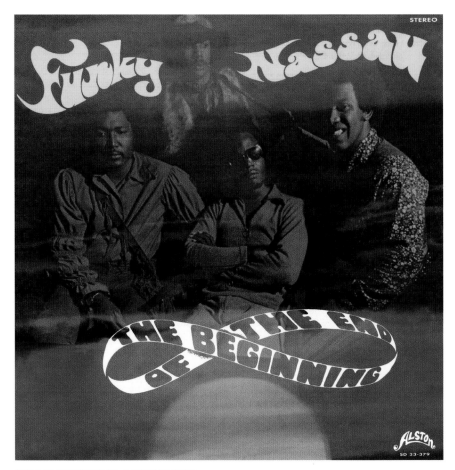

THE BEGINNING OF THE END

title **FUNKY NASSAU** / *year* **1971** / *label* Alston /
design Drago / *photography* Freddy Maura

Soaking up soul sounds from the States, this band of Bahamian brothers incorporated the strongest elements of
Caribbean music into their unique sound, one that has yet
to be duplicated. Cover artist Freddy Maura's island photographs can be found in a recent book on the history of the
Bahamas' annual Junkanoo festival. ○
Diese Band mit Brüdern von den Bahamas saugt den Soulsound der USA auf und baut die stärksten Elemente karibi-

scher Musik in ihren unverwechselbaren Sound ein, der erst
noch darauf wartet, kopiert zu werden. Die Inselfotos des
Coverkünstlers Freddy Maura kann man in einem aktuellen
Buch über die Geschichte des jährlich stattfindenden
Junkanoo-Festivals auf den Bahamas finden. ○
Ce groupe de frères bahamiens a absorbé les sons de la soul
américaine et y a incorporé les éléments les plus marquants
de la musique caribéenne pour créer un son qui est resté
unique jusqu'aujourd'hui. Les photos d'îles de Freddy
Maura, l'auteur de la pochette, sont rassemblées dans un
livre paru récemment sur l'histoire du festival Junkanoo,
qui a lieu tous les ans aux Bahamas.

BEGINNING OF THE END

ALSTON 4403

THE BEGINNING OF THE END

title **BEGINNING OF THE END** / *year* **1976** /
label Alston / *photography* Roland Rose

The Beginning of the End's second album was a surprising
departure from the stripped-down island fare found on
their debut, *Funky Nassau*. The Bahamian group's self-titled
follow-up added heaped helpings of Afro-rock and searing
synthesizer to the already rich stew of Caribbean rhythms
and stone soul vocals that made the band's sound so impressive. **O**
Das zweite Album von The Beginning of the End war ein
überraschender Abschied von der abgegessenen karibischen

Kost, die man auf ihrem Debüt *Funky Nassau* fand. Auf dem
Nachfolgealbum dieser Formation von den Bahamas mit
seinem Afro-Rock und den sengenden Synthesizern bekam
man haufenweise Nachschlag aus dem bereits reichhaltigen
Eintopf karibischer Rhythmen und erdigen Soul-Gesangs,
der für den eindrucksvollen Sound der Band sorgte. **O**
Le deuxième album de The Beginning of the End représentait un virage surprenant par rapport au ticket pour les îles
qu'était leur premier album dépouillé, *Funky Nassau*. Cette
suite éponyme du groupe bahamien ajoutait des rations
d'afro-rock et des synthétiseurs fulgurants au mélange déjà
riche de rythmes caribéens et de voix soul qui rendait le
son du groupe si impressionnant.

WILLIAM BELL

title **PHASES OF REALITY** /
year **1972** / *label* Stax / *design* Ron
Canagata / *art direction* David Krieger/
The Graffiteria / *illustration* Don
Brautigan

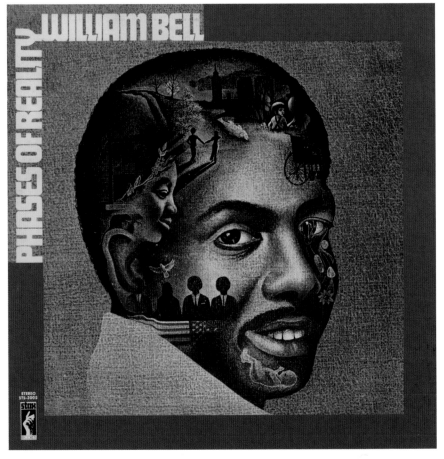

ARCHIE BELL & THE DRELLS

title I CAN'T STOP DANCING / *year* **1968** / *label* Atlantic / *design* Loring Eutemey / *photography* V. Bennett

A music-hall illustration in mid-pirouette is quite a cover curiosity for the Atlantic label, which had famously formal cover concepts in the '50s and '60s. Loring Eutemey, a graduate of New York City's Cooper Union, was largely responsible for initiating the new design standard at Atlantic, employing bold typefaces, high-resolution photographs, and heavy gloss for each cover. **O**
Diese Music-Hall-Illustration einer Tänzerin in Pirouette ist ein ganz schön kurioses Cover für das Label Atlantic, das in den 50er und 60er Jahren für seine formalen Coverkonzep-

te berühmt war. Loring Eutemey machte seinen Abschluss an der Cooper Union in New York City und war hauptsächlich dafür verantwortlich, den neuen Designstandard bei Atlantic umzusetzen. Er arbeitete bei Covern mit fetten Schriften, hochaufgelösten Fotos und viel Glanz. **O**
Cette illustration d'une danseuse de music-hall en pleine pirouette est une curiosité pour le label Atlantic, qui était connu pour ses pochettes conservatrices dans les années 1950 et 1960. Loring Eutemey, diplômé de la Cooper Union de New York, a été l'initiateur principal de la nouvelle ligne graphique d'Atlantic, en employant des caractères gras, des photographies en haute résolution et du papier très brillant pour chaque pochette.

BEN & THE PLATANO GROUP

title **PARIS SOUL** / *year* **1971** / *label* Barclay /
art direction Jacques Lubin

A very rare and very impressive album from this French
ensemble, *Paris Soul*'s simplistic depiction of the French
capital juxtaposes a colorful cityscape with an oddly
duo-chromatic rainbow, framing the Eiffel Tower and the
circular sun as one ascends from, and one sets into, a
densely populated Paris. **O**
Ein sehr kostbares und sehr beeindruckendes Album dieses
französischen Ensembles: Auf dem Cover von *Paris Soul* mit

der simplifizierten Darstellung der französischen Haupt-
stadt überspannt ein eigenartig zweifarbiger Regenbogen
ein farbenprächtiges Stadtbild und rahmt den Eiffelturm
und die kreisrunde Sonne ein. Der Turm erhebt sich aus
dem dicht bevölkerten Paris, in das die Sonne versinkt. **O**
Sur l'excellent et très rare album de cette formation française, une représentation naïve de la capitale française jux-
tapose un paysage urbain coloré et un drôle d'arc-en-ciel à
deux couleurs, qui encadre la tour Eiffel et le soleil circulaire
qui se lève et se couche sur la ville densément peuplée.

THE BILLION
DOLLAR BAND

title **THE BILLION DOLLAR BAND** /
year **1978** / *label* Epic / *design* Frank
Schulwolf / *photography* Panuska

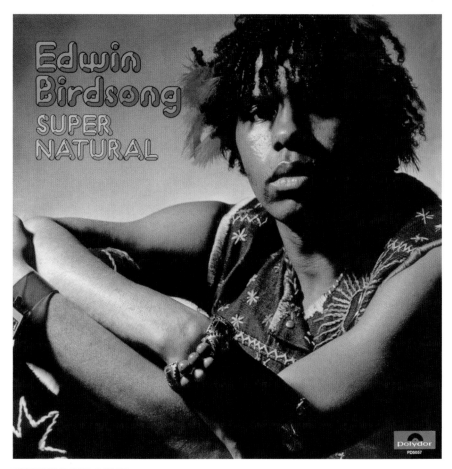

EDWIN BIRDSONG
title **SUPER NATURAL** / *year* **1973** / *label* Polydor /
design Kats Abe / *photography* Tack Kojima / *art direction*
Kats Abe

A member of the Roy Ayers jazz-funk franchise, keyboardist Edwin Birdsong penned a number of compelling compositions that pushed the boundaries of his composite
genre, perhaps hastening the emergence of the black
rock movement as well. Kats Abe, who worked almost
exclusively with Ayers, took a simple portrait of the Los
Angeles native, seen here in his early twenties. **O**
Der Keyboarder Edwin Birdsong gehörte zur Jazz-Funk-
Franchise von Roy Ayers und schuf eine Reihe bestechen-

der Kompositionen, die die Grenzen seines kombinierten
Genres erweiterten und möglicherweise auch das Entstehen der Black Rock Bewegung beschleunigten. Kats Abe,
der fast exklusiv für Ayers arbeitete, verwendete ein simples
Porträt des in Los Angeles geborenen Musikers, der zu dem
Zeitpunkt Anfang 20 war. **O**
Membre de la franchise jazz-funk de Roy Ayers, le claviériste Edwin Birdsong est l'auteur d'un bon nombre de
compositions fascinantes qui ont repoussé les limites de
ce genre hétéroclite, et ont peut-être aussi précipité
l'émergence du mouvement du black rock. Kats Abe,
qui a travaillé presque exclusivement avec Ayers, réalise ici
un portrait sobre de ce natif de Los Angeles, que l'on voit
âgé d'à peine plus de vingt ans.

BLACK HEAT
title **NO TIME TO BURN** /
year **1974** / *label* Atlantic / *design*
Dennis Lavarato & Lewis Tanner /
illustration Dennis Lavarato

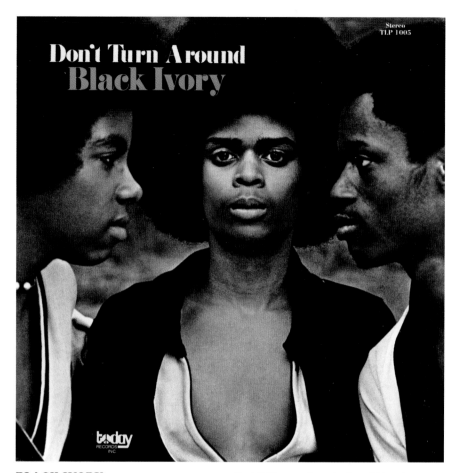

BLACK IVORY

title **DON'T TURN AROUND** / *year* **1972** / *label* Today

Black Ivory featured, from left to right, vocalists Russell Patterson, Stuart Bascombe, and Leroy Burgess. The group was managed by future disco pioneer Patrick Adams, who left his executive role at Perception Records mid-decade to forge his own inventive sound. Before his departure, Adams collaborated with Burgess frequently, helping craft numerous intricate ballads for the Harlem trio. ◗

Zu Black Ivory gehörten (von links nach rechts) die Sänger Russell Patterson, Stuart Bascombe und Leroy Burgess. Die Gruppe wurde vom späteren Disco-Pionier Patrick Adams gemanagt, der Mitte des Jahrzehnts seinen Job als Geschäftsführer von Perception Records hinwarf, um seinen eigenen einfallsreichen Sound zu schmieden. Vor seinem Abschied arbeitete Adams häufig mit Burgess zusammen und half dabei, zahlreiche komplexe Balladen für das Trio aus Harlem zu komponieren. ◗

Les membres de Black Ivory étaient, de gauche à droite, les chanteurs Russell Patterson, Stuart Bascombe et Leroy Burgess. Le groupe était dirigé par le futur pionnier du disco Patrick Adams, qui a quitté son rôle de directeur chez Perception Records au milieu de la décennie pour inventer son propre son. Avant son départ, Adams a fréquemment travaillé avec Burgess et l'a aidé à composer de nombreuses ballades délicates et complexes pour ce trio de Harlem.

BLACK MERDA

BLACK MERDA

title **BLACK MERDA** / *year* **1970** / *label* Chess /
photography Peter Amft

Following a formula forged by Jimi Hendrix on his seminal
Are you Experienced?, these Detroit soulmen left their posts
backing Edwin Starr to make powerful contributions to the
house of Motor City rock. Photographer Peter Amft led a
rich and storied career in his native Chicago, where his
immersion in the music scene made him one of the Windy
City's most valuable documentarians. ❂

Einer Formel folgend, die von Jimi Hendrix auf seinem
bahnbrechenden Album *Are You Experienced?* entwickelt
wurde, verließen diese Detroiter Soulmen ihren Posten als
Backingband von Edwin Starr, um kräftig am Haus des
Motor City Rock mitzuschaffen. Der Fotograf Peter Amft
führte in seiner Heimatstadt Chicago ein erfülltes und
sagenumwobenes Leben, und sein Engagement in der dortigen Musikszene machte ihn zu einem der wertvollsten
Dokumentaristen der Windy City. ❂

Suivant une formule que Jimi Hendrix avait inventée sur son
monumental album *Are you Experienced?*, ces soulmen de
Detroit ont déserté leurs postes d'accompagnateurs d'Edwin
Starr pour apporter leur contribution à la scène rock de la
ville du moteur. Le photographe Peter Amft a mené une
carrière riche et légendaire dans sa ville natale de Chicago,
où son immersion dans le monde de la musique a fait de
lui l'un des documentaristes les plus précieux de la ville.

THE BLACKBYRDS

title **CITY LIFE** / *year* **1975** / *label* Fantasy /
art direction Phil Carroll / *illustration* Stewart Daniels

Judging by the skyline, the metropolis portrayed in Stewart Daniels' playful illustration is most likely not modeled after the Blackbyrds' Capital City, but a fictional city where the men are bald, the women are outnumbered, and everyone's eyes are closed, accounting for the traffic. The blackbird-patterned wallpaper is a sure selling-point to anyone looking to purchase real estate in this whimsical urban center. ○

Geht man nach der Skyline, dann nimmt sich die in Stewart Daniels' verspielter Illustration porträtierte Metropole höchstwahrscheinlich nicht die Capital City der Blackbyrds zum Vorbild, sondern eine fiktive Stadt, in der Männer glatzköpfig und Frauen in der Minderheit sind und bedingt durch den Verkehr alle die Augen geschlossen haben. Die Tapete mit dem Amselmuster ist für Leute, die in diesem skurrilen Stadtzentrum nach Wohnungen suchen, sicher ein Verkaufsargument. ○

D'après la ligne de toits, la ville représentée sur l'illustration humoristique de Stewart Daniels n'est sans doute pas la capitale des Blackbyrds, mais une cité fictive où les hommes sont chauves, les femmes sont en minorité et où tout le monde a les yeux fermés, ce qui explique l'état de la circulation. Le papier peint à motif corbeaux (« blackbird ») est un argument de vente infaillible pour ceux qui cherchent un logement à acheter dans ce centre-ville fantaisiste.

THE BLACKBYRDS
title **FLYING START** / *year* **1974** / *label* Fantasy

When Donald Byrd came to teach at Howard University, he began scouring campus for talented youngsters he could direct on record. Although the cover captures the sextet getting major air, the back becomes a blooper reel when the group's collective landing gear malfunctions to humorous effect. **O**

Als Donald Byrd an der Howard University einen Lehrauftrag bekam, begann er, auf dem Campus nach talentierten jungen Leuten zu suchen, die er für Plattenaufnahmen anleiten konnte. Das Cover zeigt, zu welchen Luftsprüngen das Sextett fähig ist, doch die Rückseite zeigt das Desaster, als die kollektive Landung der Gruppe auf humorvolle Weise schiefgeht. **O**

Lorsque Donald Byrd est allé enseigner à l'université Howard, il a commencé à arpenter le campus à la recherche de jeunes talents qu'il pourrait diriger en studio. La couverture de la pochette présente le sextuor en plein vol, mais le verso montre un bêtisier hilarant des accidents d'atterrissage lors de la séance de photo.

DON BLACKMAN
title **DON BLACKMAN** / *year* **1982** / *label* GRP

A member of the Jamaica, Queens jazz-funk royalty in New York, keyboardist Don Blackman's self-titled release was the first on GRP Records after the imprint's secession from Arista. With the keyboardist's name partitioned in such a manner as to accentuate ethnicity and gender, the head-dress of beads and cowry shells, both symbolic in African culture, affirms Blackman's afrocentric identity. **O**
Der Keyboarder Don Blackman gehörte zum New Yorker Jazz-Funk-Königreich in Jamaica/Queens. Das Album, das seinen Namen führt, war das erste auf GRP Records nach der Abspaltung von Arista. Der Nachname erscheint ge-

trennt und akzentuiert auf diese Weise ethnische Zugehörigkeit und Geschlecht, während der Kopfschmuck aus Perlen und Kaurischnecken, beides Symbole der afrikanischen Kultur, die Identität von Blackman betont. **O**
Don Blackman fait partie de la noblesse du jazz-funk du quartier de Jamaica, dans la circonscription new-yorkaise du Queens. L'album éponyme de ce claviériste était son premier chez GRP Records après que le label se fut séparé d'Arista. Sur la pochette, la présentation de son nom, coupé en deux de façon à souligner son appartenance ethnique et son sexe, et les tresses ornées de perles et de coquillages, deux éléments très symboliques dans la culture africaine, affirment l'identité afrocentrique de Blackman.

BOBBY BLAND

title **GET ON DOWN** /
year **1975** / *label* ABC / *photography*
Jim McCrary / *design* Martin Donald

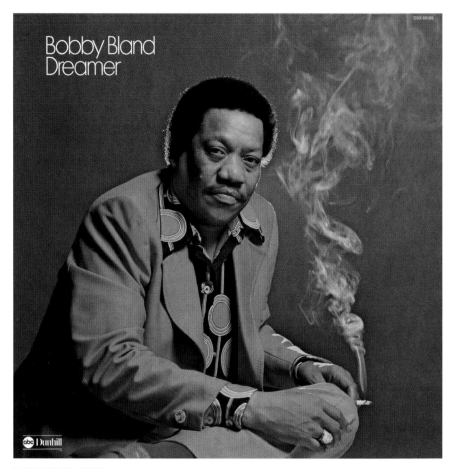

DISX-50169

Bobby Bland
Dreamer

abc Dunhill

BOBBY BLAND
title **DREAMER** / *year* **1974** / *label* ABC/Dunhill /
design Earl Klasky / *photography* Ken Veeder

Photographer Ken Veeder photographed some of Capitol
Records' biggest stars; he coaxed Nat King Cole on to a
roller-coaster for *Wild is Love* and took the Beach Boys out
to sea for *Summer Days*. Despite trends in music photography, Veeder aspired to share something about the artist
with the listener, once saying: "A group standing on a rock
doesn't say anything about the music." ●
Der Fotograf Ken Veeder lichtete einige der größten Stars
von Capitol Records ab. Er überredete Nat King Cole für
Wild is Love, sich in die Achterbahn zu setzen, und fuhr mit

den Beach Boys für *Summer Days* aufs Meer hinaus. Aktuellen Trends in der Musikfotografie zum Trotz trachtete
Veeder danach, dem Hörer etwas über den Künstler mitzu-
teilen. Er meinte einmal: »Eine Truppe, die auf einem Felsen
steht, sagt überhaupt nichts über ihre Musik aus.« ●
Ken Veeder a photographié quelques-unes des plus
grandes stars de Capitol Records. Il a réussi à faire monter
Nat King Cole sur un grand huit pour *Wild is Love* et a emmené les Beach Boys en mer pour *Summer Days*. En marge
des tendances de la photographie de musique, Veeder
aspirait à communiquer au public quelque chose sur l'artiste. Il a déclaré un jour : « Un groupe posant sur un rocher
ne dit rien de particulier sur la musique. »

BLUE MAGIC

title **THIRTEEN BLUE MAGIC LANE** / *year* **1975** /
label Atco / *design* Abie Sussman / *illustration* Ed Soyka

With songs like "Born on Halloween", "Haunted (By Your
Love)", and "The Loneliest House on the Block", Philly
combo Blue Magic set a spooky course with *Thirteen Blue
Magic Lane*. Atco befittingly assigned Ed Soyka to the case,
whose portfolio contained countless scenes for science-
fiction novels, and several covers for *Analog*, a periodical
dedicated to the world of science fiction. **O**
Mit Songs wie »Born on Halloween«, »Haunted (By Your
Love)« und »The Loneliest House on the Block« schlug die

Philly-Combo Blue Magic mit *Thirteen Blue Magic Lane*
einen gruseligen Kurs ein. Atco beauftragte passenderweise
Ed Soyka mit diesem Fall. Dessen Portfolio enthielt unzählige Szenen für Science-Fiction-Romane und viele Cover für
Analog, eine Zeitschrift für die Welt der Science-Fiction. **O**
Avec des morceaux comme Born on Halloween, Haunted
(By Your Love) *et* The Loneliest House on the Block, *le groupe
de Philadelphie a choisi la route de l'épouvante pour son
album* Thirteen Blue Magic Lane. *Atco a eu la bonne idée
de confier la pochette à Ed Soyka, dont le portfolio contenait d'innombrables scènes destinées à des romans de
science-fiction et plusieurs couvertures pour* Analog, *un
magazine consacré au monde de la science-fiction.*

WILLIE BOBO

title **HELL OF AN ACT TO FOLLOW** / *year* **1978** / *label* Columbia / *design* Tony Lane / *photography* Tony Lane

Tony Lane wore many hats as former Art Director for *Rolling Stone*, Sony Music, and Fantasy Records, among others. His work as a designer always informed his photographs with a highly graphic quality. The multiple-exposure image of Willie Bobo for this cover seizes on the percussionist's vivacious personality. ⊙

Tony Lane kannte sich als ehemaliger Art Director, u. a. bei *Rolling Stone*, Sony Music und Fantasy Records, in vielen Rollen aus. Dank seiner Arbeit als Gestalter waren seine Fotografien immer von einer hohen grafischen Qualität. Die Mehrfachbelichtung für dieses Cover greift die lebhafte Persönlichkeit des Perkussionisten Willie Bobo auf. ⊙

Tony Lane a porté de nombreuses casquettes en tant qu'ancien directeur artistique pour *Rolling Stone*, Sony Music et Fantasy Records, entre autres. Son travail de graphiste a toujours complété ses photographies avec une qualité impeccable. Sur cette pochette, l'image à expositions multiples de Willie Bobo saisit la vivacité du percussionniste.

WILLIE BOBO AND THE BO-GENTS

title **DO WHAT YOU WANT TO DO...** / *year* **1968** / *label* Sussex / *photography* Norbert Jobst/Maurer Productions

ANGELA BOFILL

title **ANGIE** / *year* **1978** / *label* Arista / *photography* John Ford / *art direction* Donn Davenport

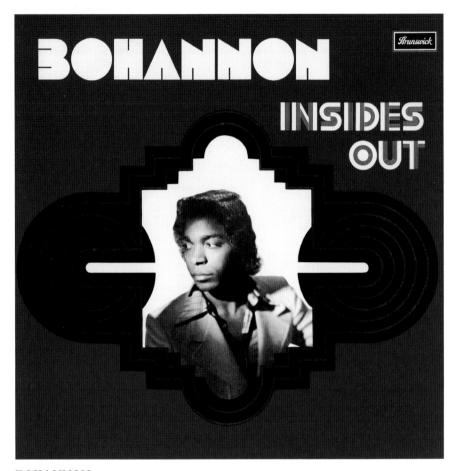

BOHANNON

title **INSIDES OUT** / *year* **1975** / *label* Brunswick /
design Artie Patrick

Hamilton Bohannon's peculiar, yet profound brand of
self-produced disco made him a legend and an anomaly,
yielding a body of work that stands as some of the most
innovative of the genre. Framed by a varnished labyrinth
of parallel lines and concentric circles, the Georgia native
dons one of his famously asymmetrical hairstyles for this
eccentric relic of soul music. ⬡

Hamilton Bohannons sonderbare und doch hintergründige
Marke einer selbstproduzierten Discomucke machte ihn
zur Legende und Ausnahmeerscheinung und führte zu

einem Gesamtwerk, das zum Innovativsten des ganzen
Genres gehört. Eingerahmt von einem ausgeschmückten
Labyrinth paralleler Linien und konzentrischer Kreise trägt
der aus Georgia stammende Bohannon für dieses exzentrische Relikt der Soulmusik eine seiner berühmten asym-
metrischen Frisuren. ⬡

Le style particulier mais profond du disco autoproduit de
Hamilton Bohannon a fait de lui une légende et une anomalie. Son œuvre est l'une des plus innovantes du genre.
Encadré par un labyrinthe de lignes parallèles et de cercles
concentriques, ce natif de la Géorgie arbore l'une de ses
célèbres coiffures asymétriques sur la pochette de cette
relique excentrique de la musique soul.

BOOGALOO COMBO
title **COM MUITO RITMO** /
year **1972** / *label* Epic

NAPPY HEAD (Tema de "GHETTO MAN"). AIN'T THAT LOVING YOU. WAY BACK HOME. EBONY EYES. GOZA NEGRA. IF YOU COULD READ MY MIND. HOT PANTS ROAD. PUT IT WHERE YOU WANT IT. SUAVECITO. UN RAYO DE SOL. ROCK AND ROLL LULLABY. THEME FROM THE MUSIC LOVERS

BOOTSY'S RUBBER BAND

title **THIS BOOT IS MADE FOR
FONK-N** / *year* **1979** / *label* Warner
Bros. / *design* Larry Legaspi & Me /
illustration Archie Ivy

BOOTSY'S RUBBER BAND
title **BOOTSY? PLAYER OF THE YEAR** / *year* **1978** /
label Warner Bros. / *design* M. Doud / *photography*
L. DuPont / *art direction* M. Doud / *illustration* B. Hickson

Parliament-Funkadelic bassist Bootsy Collins had become
as big a player as any of his peer passengers on the Mothership by the time *Bootsy? Player of the Year* was released in
1978. As a party favor to all Funkateers, the inner sleeve of
Bootsy? includes a perforated pop-out pair of cardboard star
glasses. **O**

Bootsy Collins, der Bassist von Parliament/Funkadelic, war
zu der Zeit, als *Bootsy? Player of the Year* 1978 erschien, bereits wie alle anderen Insassen des Mothership selbst ein
großer Player. Als Partygeschenk für alle Funkateers befand
sich in der Innenhülle von *Bootsy?* eine perforierte, stern-
förmige Brille aus Karton zum Herausnehmen. **O**
Lorsque *Bootsy? Player of the Year* est sorti en 1978, Bootsy
Collins, le bassiste du collectif Parliament-Funkadelic, jouait
sur un pied d'égalité avec ses autres compagnons passagers
du « vaisseau mère ». En cadeau festif pour tous les funkateers, la pochette intérieure de *Bootsy?* renfermait une paire
de lunettes étoilées détachables.

BOSCOE

title **BOSCOE** / *year* **1973** /
label Kingdom of Chad

BOTH WORLDS

title **DON'TCHA HIDE IT** / *year* **1974** / *label* TPI / *photography* Reginald Wickham / *art direction* Clinton Cowels

While working at an offset-printing press in New York City, photographer Reginald Wickham had an arsenal of design elements at his disposal, giving him an edge over fellow freelancers. While registering color separations Wickham accidentally achieved this moiré effect, which he immediately made a contact print from for this fusion funk oddity. ○

Während seiner Arbeit in einer Offsetdruckerei in New York City stand dem Fotografen Reginald Wickham ein ganzes Arsenal an Gestaltungselementen zur Verfügung, was ihm einen Vorsprung gegenüber seinen freiberuflichen Kollegen sicherte. Beim Ausrichten der Farbauszüge unterlief Wickham zufällig ein Moiré-Effekt, von dem er für diese schräge Fusionfunk-Platte sofort Kontaktabzüge machte. ○

Lorsqu'il travaillait dans une imprimerie offset de New York, le photographe Reginald Wickham avait à sa disposition un arsenal d'outils de graphisme qui lui donnait un avantage sur les autres photographes freelance. C'est en travaillant sur la séparation des couleurs que Wickham a obtenu par accident cet effet moiré, dont il fit immédiatement un tirage contact pour cette curiosité du funk fusion. ○

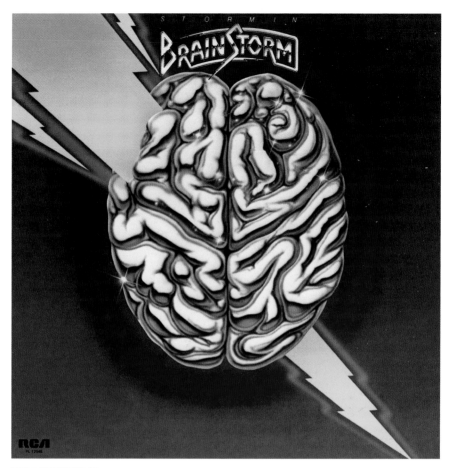

BRAINSTORM

title **STORMIN** / *year* **1977** / *label* RCA Victor /
design Tim Bryant/Gribbitt! / *art direction* Acy Lehman

A most literal interpretation was used for the cover of this
Detroit combo's 1977 outing. RCA's veteran Art Director
Acy Lehman uses a Thor-grade lightning bolt to bisect this
chrome-plated brain, giving the concept of brainstorming
a new meaning with his imaginative analysis of the compound word. **O**

Für das Cover dieser Combo aus Detroit wurde 1977 der
Titel ganz wörtlich interpretiert: Der Art Director und RCA-
Veteran Acy Lehman nahm einen Blitz, der des Donner-
gottes Thor würdig gewesen wäre, um ein verchromtes
Gehirn zu zerteilen. So verlieh er dem Begriff eine ganz
neue Bedeutung, indem er das Kompositum *Brainstorm*
fantasievoll neu interpretierte. **O**

Une illustration des plus littérales a été choisie pour la
pochette de l'album de 1977 de cette petite formation musicale de Detroit. Le directeur artistique vétéran de RCA,
Acy Lehman, y utilise un éclair digne de Thor traversant un
cerveau chromé, et donne au concept du brainstorming
une nouvelle signification grâce à son analyse créative de ce
mot composé.

BRASS CONSTRUCTION

title **BRASS CONSTRUCTION** / *year* **1975** / *label* United Artists / *photography* Jeremiah Bean / *art direction* Michael Mendel/Maurer Productions

Certainly not intending to pass for construction workers, this Brooklyn ensemble did manage to put together some of the most inventive disco of the day. Art Director Michael Mendel would mimic this same construction motif for the group's third album, *Brass Construction III*, by making a Brass Construction-brand hard hat the cover's singular subject. ◗

Dieses Brooklyn-Ensemble hat es sicherlich nicht darauf angelegt, als Bauarbeiter durchzugehen, aber sie haben es geschafft, ein paar besonders einfallsreiche Disco-Stücke zu konstruieren. Der Art Director Michael Mendel sollte für das dritte Album der Band das Baustellenmotiv erneut aufgreifen. Auf *Brass Construction III* machte er einen Schutzhelm mit dem Logo von Brass Construction zum Blickfang des Covers. ◗

Bien loin de vouloir se faire passer pour des ouvriers du bâtiment, ce groupe de Brooklyn a réussi à créer quelques-uns des morceaux de disco les plus inventifs de l'époque. Le directeur artistique Michael Mendel allait décliner cette idée pour le troisième album du groupe, *Brass Construction III*, en décorant la pochette d'un grand casque de chantier marqué du nom du groupe.

BRASS CONSTRUCTION

title **ATTITUDES** / *year* **1982** /
label Liberty / *design* Jim O'Connell /
photography Solomon Roberts Jr. /
art direction Solomon Roberts Jr.

BREAKWATER

title **BREAKWATER** / *year* **1978** / *label* Arista /
design Gerard Huerta / *photography* Gary Gross

Designer Gerard Huerta adds Breakwater's aquatic branding to a portfolio of logos that include ubiquitous emblems
for Nabisco, Pepsi, and HBO. Photographer Gary Gross, on
the other hand, spent most of the '80s embroiled in legal
disputes with Brooke Shields regarding reproduction rights
to a series of nude photos he took of the prepubescent
model/actress earlier in the decade, effectively ending his
career. **◒**

Der Gestalter Gerard Huerta fügt die aquatische Break-
water-Marke seinem Portfolio von Logos hinzu, zu dem
auch allgegenwärtige Embleme wie die von Nabisco, Pepsi
und HBO gehören. Der Fotograf Gary Gross war hingegen
in den 80er Jahren die meiste Zeit in rechtliche Auseinandersetzungen mit Brooke Shields verwickelt, wobei es um
die Wiedergaberechte einer Serie von Aktfotos ging, die er
Anfang des Jahrzehnts von dem vorpubertären Model bzw.
der Schauspielerin gemacht hatte. Das bedeutete de facto
das Aus für seine Karriere. **◒**

Le graphiste Gerard Huerta ajoute l'identité de marque
aquatique de Breakwater à un portefeuille de logos qui
comprend notamment les emblèmes omniprésents de
Nabisco, Pepsi et HBO. L'auteur de la photographie, Gary
Gross, a quant à lui passé la plus grande partie des années
1980 enchevêtré dans des querelles juridiques avec Brooke
Shields sur les droits de reproduction de photos de nu qu'il
avait prises de l'actrice / mannequin prépubère quelques
années plus tôt, ce qui finit par mettre un terme à sa carrière de photographe.

THE BRECKER BROTHERS

title **HEAVY METAL BE-BOP** /
year **1978** / *label* Arista / *photography*
Owen Brown & Ed Caraeff /
art direction Donn Davenport

BRICK

title **BRICK** / *year* **1977** / *label* Bang / *design* Jeff Blue / *photography* Jeff Blue

This Atlanta group took their synthesis of disco and jazz so seriously they established the genre of dazz, giving the art form an anthem, "Dazz", on their 1976 debut, *Good High*. The following year, Brick followed it with this self-titled collection of dance-floor friendly compositions, including the band's classic "Ain't Gonna Hurt Nobody". ⊙
Diese Truppe aus Atlanta nahm ihre Synthese von Disco und Jazz so ernst, dass sie ein neues Genre namens Dazz erfand und dieser Kunstform auf ihrem Debüt *Good High* von 1976 eine gleichnamige Hymne mitgab. Im folgenden Jahr legte Brick mit dieser Sammlung Dancefloor-kompatibler Kompositionen gleichen Namens nach, die auch den Bandklassiker »Ain't Gonna Hurt Nobody« enthält. ⊙
Ce groupe d'Atlanta a pris sa synthèse de disco et de jazz tellement au sérieux qu'il a créé le « dazz », et a donné un hymne à ce nouveau genre, *Dazz*, sur son premier album de 1976, *Good High*. L'année suivante, Brick est revenu à la charge avec cet assortiment éponyme de compositions pour les pistes de danse, où l'on trouve le grand classique du groupe, *Ain't Gonna Hurt Nobody*.

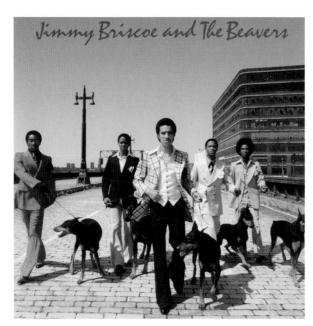

JIMMY BRISCOE
AND THE BEAVERS

title **JIMMY BRISCOE AND THE
BEAVERS** / *year* **1977** / *label* T.K.
Productions / *design* Richard Roth/
Queens Graphics / *photography*
Chris Callis / *art direction* Richard
Roth/Queens Graphics

JOHNNY BRISTOL

title **HANG ON IN THERE
BABY** / *year* **1974** / *label* MGM /
design Dave Wiseltier/Kameny
Associates / *photography* Earl
Miller

PF 21506   STEREO

SOPHISTICATED FUNK
julius brockington

LET'S STAY TOGETHER
IF YOU REALLY LOVE ME
OLD FASHIONED LOVE SONG
SINCE I FELL FOR YOU
ROCK STEADY
COLD WATER
DO YOUR THING
GOT TO BE THERE

STEREO
Perception

JULIUS BROCKINGTON

title **SOPHISTICATED FUNK** /
year **1972** / *label* Perception /
photography Bob Demchuck

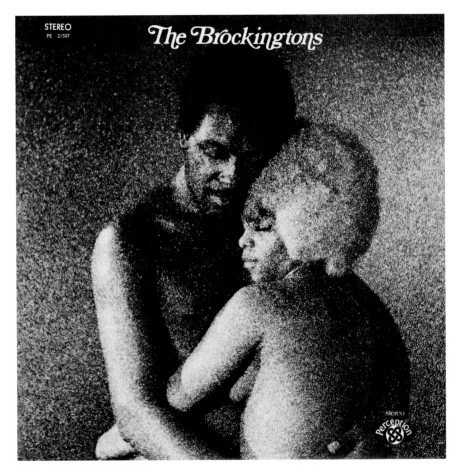

STEREO
PE 21507

The Brockingtons

stereo
Perception

THE BROCKINGTONS

title **THE BROCKINGTONS** / *year* **1971** /
label Perception / *design* James Martin Stulberger /
photography Reginald Wickham

Produced by a young gun named Patrick Adams, who
would go on to leave a serious mark on the worlds of soul,
funk, disco, and rap, this early effort from Julius Brockington
shows off his funky, gospel-inflected piano-playing. James
Martin Stulberger and Reginald Wickham were responsible
for the bulk of covers for Today Records and Perception.
They had a great feel for creating evocative images as they
did with this achingly beautiful black & white portrait. **O**
Produziert von Patrick Adams, der später den Welten von
Soul, Funk, Disco und Rap seinen Stempel aufdrücken soll-

te, protzt dieses frühe Werk von Julius Brockington mit
einem funkigen Pianospiel mit Gospel-Einsprengseln. James
Martin Stulberger und Reginald Wickham waren für den
Großteil der Cover von Today Records und Perception
verantwortlich. Sie hatten ein großartiges Gespür für sinnträchtige Bilder, wie ihnen auch hier ein quälend schönes
Schwarzweiß-Porträt gelang. **O**
Produit par une jeune star du nom de Patrick Adams, qui
allait laisser une empreinte profonde dans les mondes de la
soul, du funk, du disco et du rap, cet album du début de la
carrière de Julius Brockington met en valeur son jeu au
piano, légèrement bancal et teinté de gospel. James Martin
Stulberger et Reginald Wickham s'occupaient de la majorité
des pochettes de disque de Today Records et Perception. Ils
avaient le don de créer des images évocatrices

HUGH BRODIE
title **HUGH BRODIE AND THE
REAL THING** / *year* **1975** / *label*
Kheba / *design* Guy Hamilton /
photography Alleta Vett

BROTHER TO BROTHER

title **SHADES IN CREATION** /
year **1977** / *label* Turbo / *design*
Dudley Thomas / *photography*
O. Paccione / *art direction* Dudley
Thomas

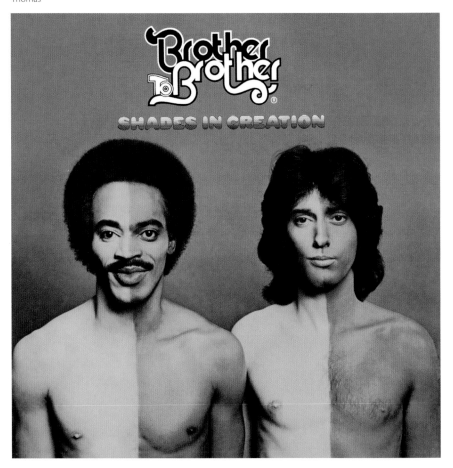

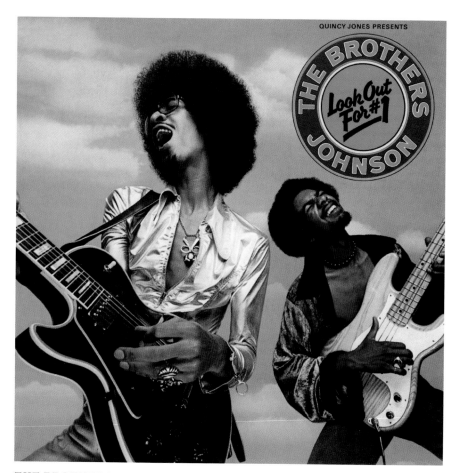

QUINCY JONES PRESENTS

THE BROTHERS JOHNSON

Look Out For #1

THE BROTHERS JOHNSON

title **LOOK OUT FOR #1** / *year* **1976** / *label* A&M /
photography Roderick Young / *art direction* Roland Young

After featuring the brothers on a pair of his own LPs,
Quincy Jones would produce a string of albums for the
Los Angeles duo, starting with 1976's *Look Out For #1*.
Photographer Roderick Young is best known for his work
in cinema, serving as a director of cinematography for a
series of culturally significant documentaries, *Wattstax,
When We Were Kings*, and most recently, *Soul Power*. ⊙
Nachdem er die Brothers auf ein paar seiner eigenen LPs
vorgestellt hatte, produzierte Quincy Jones eine Folge von
Alben für das Duo aus Los Angeles, beginnend mit *Look*

Out For #1 von 1976. Der Fotograf Roderick Young wurde
vor allem bekannt durch seine filmische Arbeit. Als Regis-
seur sorgte er für eine Reihe kulturell bedeutsamer Doku-
mentarfilme wie *Wattstax, When We Were Kings* und erst
kürzlich *Soul Power*. ⊙
Après avoir utilisé les talents de ces frères sur deux de ses
propres albums, Quincy Jones allait produire une série
d'albums pour le duo de Los Angeles, tout d'abord avec
Look Out For #1 en 1976. Le photographe Roderick Young
est surtout connu pour son travail dans le cinéma. Il a été
directeur de la photographie pour une série de documen-
taires culturels importants, *Wattstax, When We Were Kings*
et, plus récemment, *Soul Power*.

BROTHERS UNLIMITED

title **WHO'S FOR THE YOUNG** /
year **1970** / *label* Capitol /
photography Bill Speer

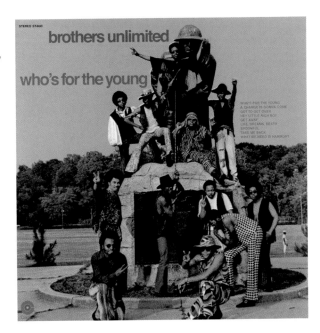

GENIE BROWN

title **A WOMAN ALONE** /
year **1973** / *label* Dunhill /
design Earl Klasky /
photography Al Kramer

**CHUCK BROWN
AND THE SOUL
SEARCHERS**

title **LIVE – D.C. BUMPIN'
Y'ALL** / *year* **1987** / *label* Rhythm
King / *design* Slim Smith /
illustration Fiona Hawthorne

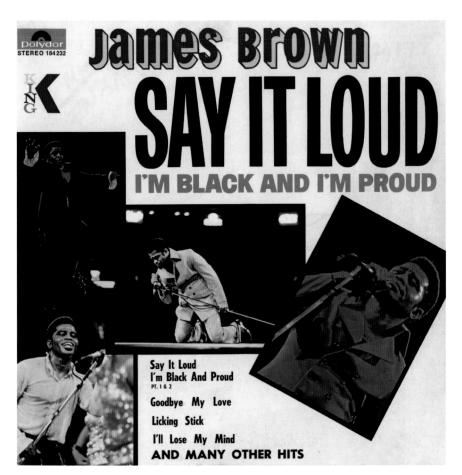

JAMES BROWN

title **SAY IT LOUD I'M BLACK AND I'M PROUD** /
year **1969** / *label* Polydor / *design* Mitchell Kanner

While *Say It Loud I'm Black and I'm Proud*'s rebellious title-
track set the tone for the Black Power movement, it cost
James Brown a portion of his crossover audience. Designer
Mitchell Kanner served as Art Director for PolyGram and
Elektra, but had an important role designing the disco-era
trade periodical, *Record World*. ◑
Der rebellische Titelsong von *Say It Loud I'm Black and
I'm Proud* stimmte auf die Black-Power-Bewegung ein, was

James Brown einen Teil seines Crossover-Publikums kostete.
Der Designer Mitchell Kanner war als Art Director für Poly-
Gram und Elektra zuständig, spielte aber auch bei der
Gestaltung der Zeitschrift *Record World* aus der Disco-Ära
eine wichtige Rolle. ◑
Le morceau-titre rebelle de *Say It Loud I'm Black and I'm
Proud* a donné le ton au mouvement Black Power, mais a
coûté à James Brown tout un pan de sa large audience.
Le graphiste Mitchell Kanner a été directeur artistique chez
PolyGram et Elektra, mais a joué un rôle important dans la
conception du magazine professionnel de l'époque du
disco *Record World*.

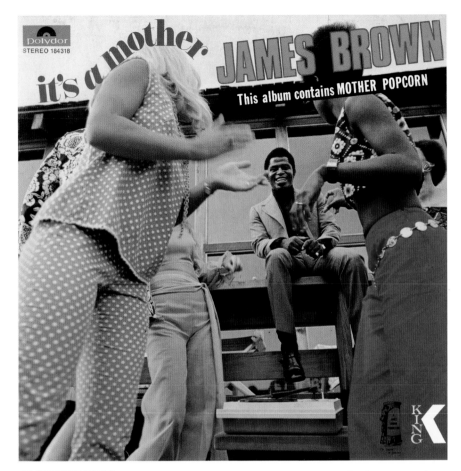

JAMES BROWN

title **IT'S A MOTHER** / *year* **1970** / *label* Polydor /
design Dan Quest Art Studio

Start-to-finish funk from James Brown, this record combined many of the two-part singles released on 45, allowing
many of the Godfather's compositions to be heard in their
entirety. Whether the subject was Brown himself, or god-
daughters of soul Marva Whitney or Marie Queenie Lyons,
Dan Quest Studio's work is done in a classic style, identified
by bold-colored traditional fonts, laid over engaging photos of the musical subject. **O**

Lupenreiner Funk von Anfang bis Ende: Auf dieser Scheibe
von James Brown werden viele der zweiseitigen Singles
kombiniert, die als 45er erschienen waren. So können die
Kompositionen des Godfather of Soul in Gänze gehört

werden. Egal ob James Brown selbst das Motiv war oder
seine »Patenkinder« des Soul wie Marva Whitney oder
Marie Queenie Lyons, die Arbeit von Dan Quest Studios
wurde im klassischen Stil erledigt, was man an den kräftig
kolorierten, traditionellen Schriften erkennt, die auf die
ansprechenden Fotos der musikalischen Motive gelegt
wurden. **O**

Du funk et rien que du funk signé James Brown, ce disque
combinait un grand nombre des singles en deux parties
sortis en 45 tours, permettant d'écouter les compositions
du Parrain de la soul dans leur intégralité et sans interrup-
tion. Que le sujet ait été Brown lui-même, ou ses filleules
dans la soul Marva Whitney ou Marie Queenie Lyons, le
travail de Dan Quest Studios affiche un style classique,
identifié par des lettres de forme traditionnelle et de couleurs vives arrangées sur des photos engageantes de l'artiste.

JAMES BROWN

title **GET ON THE GOOD
FOOT** / *year* **1972** / *label* Polydor /
photography James Spencer

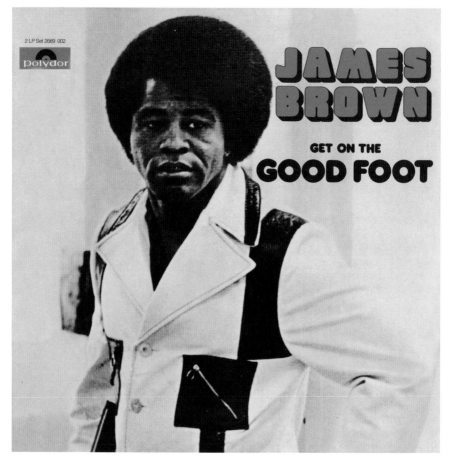

ODELL BROWN

title **FREE DELIVERY** / *year* **1970** / *label* Cadet /
photography Peter Amft / *art direction* Dick Fowler

Odell Brown was flying solo from his group The Organizers by the time this great Chicago organ-funk LP came out. He is backed by some of the top Cadet musicians here including guitarist Phil Upchurch, bassist Louis Satterfield, and drummer Morris Jennings. Cover photographer Peter Amft was better known for his up-close and personal black and white portraits of blues and rock greats. **o**
Odell Brown startete aus seiner Gruppe The Organizers heraus seine Solokarriere, als diese großartige LP mit funkiger Orgelmusik aus Chicago erschien. Er wird von einigen der besten Musiker von Cadet begleitet, z. B. von dem Gitarristen Phil Upchurch, dem Bassisten Louis Satterfield und dem Drummer Morris Jennings. Der Coverfotograf Peter Amft war bekannt durch seine sehr persönlichen Schwarzweiß-Porträts von Blues- und Rockgrößen in Nahaufnahmen. **o**
À la sortie de ce superbe album de funk de Chicago, chargé à l'orgue, Odell Brown s'était détaché de son groupe The Organizers et menait sa carrière en solo. Il y est accompagné par quelques-uns des meilleurs musiciens de Cadet, notamment le guitariste Phil Upchurch, le bassiste Louis Satterfield et le batteur Morris Jennings. Le photographe de la pochette, Peter Amft, était plus connu pour ses portraits intimes en noir et blanc des grands du blues et du rock.

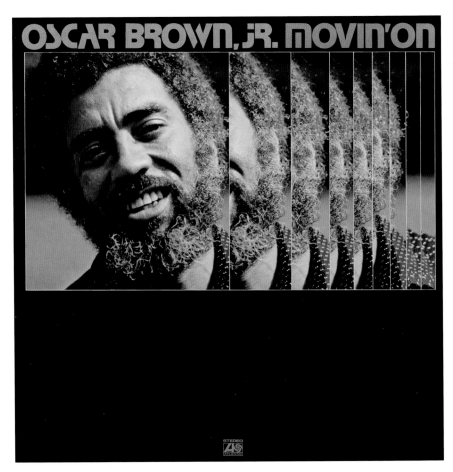

OSCAR BROWN, JR.

title **MOVIN' ON** / *year* **1972** / *label* Atlantic /
design Stanislaw Zagorski / *photography* Jim Cummins

The great Polish designer Stanislaw Zagorski began working
for Atlantic Records in the 1950s. His penchant for whimsical designs and bold use of typography meshed well with
the psychedelic era when he worked on covers for artists
like Cream and The Velvet Underground. This approach
also worked well with the new jazz sounds that were
coming out at the time. Zagorski's use of a repeated image
represents the motor-mouthed proto-rap of singer Oscar
Brown, Jr. impeccably. **O**
Der große polnische Designer Stanislaw Zagorski begann in
den 50er Jahren mit seiner Arbeit für Atlantic. Seine Nei-
gung für skurrile Entwürfe und ungewöhnliche Typografie

passte sehr gut zur psychedelischen Ära, in der er Cover für
Bands wie Cream und Velvet Underground gestaltete. Dieser Ansatz passte auch sehr gut zu den neuen Jazzklängen
jener Zeit. Dass Zagorski mit einem sich wiederholenden
Bild arbeitet, versinnbildlicht den »Proto-Rap« des Sängers
Oscar Brown Jr., der wie ein Wasserfall reden konnte. **O**
Le grand graphiste polonais Stanislaw Zagorski a commencé à travailler pour Atlantic Records dans les années 1950.
Son penchant pour les compositions imaginatives et les
typographies originales s'accordait bien à l'époque psychédélique durant laquelle il a travaillé sur les pochettes de
groupes comme Cream et le Velvet Underground. Cette
approche fonctionnait également avec les nouveaux sons
de jazz qui faisaient leur apparition à l'époque. La répétition
de l'image représente à la perfection le proto-rap turbopro-
pulsé du chanteur Oscar Brown.

WOMAN TO WOMAN

SHIRLEY BROWN

SHIRLEY BROWN

title **WOMAN TO WOMAN** / *year* **1974** / *label* Stax / *photography* Gerald Hearn

The title single of this LP would be Stax Records' last #1 hit on the R&B charts. Brown's debut showcases her gospel roots with its deep soulful cuts. The Memphis native's rich voice fits perfectly with the laidback groove set down by the Stax house-band. **O**

Der Titelsong dieser LP sollte der letzte Platz-Eins-Hit von Stax Records in den R&B-Charts werden. Shirley Browns Debüt-Album offenbart mit den tief reichenden, souligen Einsprengseln ihre Wurzeln im Gospel. Brown stammt aus Memphis, und ihre volle und facettenreiche Stimme passt perfekt zu dem lässigen Groove-Teppich, den die Hausband von Stax ausrollt. **O**

Le morceau-titre de cet album allait être le dernier numéro un de Stax Records dans les classements de R&B. Le premier album de Brown met en valeur ses racines gospel avec des morceaux profonds et expressifs. La voix chaude de cette chanteuse originaire de Memphis trouve parfaitement sa place dans le groove décontracté du groupe résident de Stax.

TOM BROWNE

title **LOVE APPROACH** / *year* **1980** /
label Arista

DISCO SOCCER

BUARI

title **DISCO SOCCER** / *year* **1979** / *label* Makossa International / *design* Churchmouse / *photography* Stan Keitt & Harry Delauney

Alhaji Sidiku Buari is one of the most influential figures in modern African music. Aside from his adventurous disco output, of which *Disco Soccer* is a prime example, he has devoted much of his career to improving the infrastructure of the Ghanaian music industry, establishing musicians' unions and helping to impede the pervasive piracy that plagues his country's recording artists. **O**

Alhaji Sidiku Buari ist eine der einflussreichsten Persönlichkeiten der modernen afrikanischen Musik. Abgesehen von seinem abenteuerlichen Disco-Output, für das *Disco Soccer*

ein hervorragendes Beispiel ist, opferte er einen Großteil seiner Karriere dafür, die Infrastruktur der ghanaischen Musikbranche zu verbessern. Er baute Musikergewerkschaften auf und half dabei, die allgegenwärtige Raubkopiererei einzudämmen, von der alle Künstler geplagt sind, die in seinem Land Platten aufnehmen. **O**

Alhaji Sidiku Buari est l'un des personnages les plus influents dans la musique africaine moderne. Outre ses aventures audacieuses dans le disco, dont cet album est un exemple de premier choix, il a consacré une bonne partie de sa carrière à améliorer les infrastructures du monde de la musique ghanéenne, en créant des syndicats de musiciens et en aidant à combattre la piraterie envahissante qui frappe les artistes de son pays.

VERNON BURCH

title **STEPPIN' OUT** / *year* **1980** /
label Chocolate City / *photography*
Scott Hensel / *art direction* Hy Fujita/
Gribbitt!

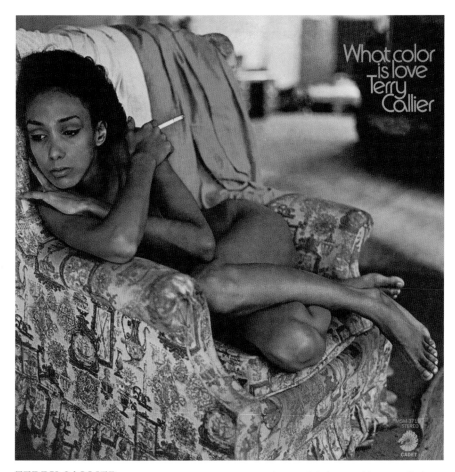

On image: What color is love Terry Callier

TERRY CALLIER

title **WHAT COLOR IS LOVE** / *year* **1972** / *label* Cadet /
photography Joel Brodsky / *art direction* David Krieger

Joel Brodsky's evocative photo embodies the wistful air of
the masterpiece contained within. Charles Stepney's multi-
layered production swirls around Terry Callier's rich voice
and sensitive folk-guitar playing to create a dizzying blend
of soul and jazz that stands toe-to-toe with the best of
Callier's childhood friend, Curtis Mayfield, as a Chicago
classic. ❍
Das suggestive Foto auf dem Cover von Joel Brodsky
verkörpert das sehnsüchtige Flair des darin enthaltenen
Meisterwerks. Die vielschichtige Produktion von Charles
Stepney wirbelt um die facettenreiche Stimme von Terry
Callier und sein sensibles Folkgitarrenspiel. Das schafft eine
schwindelerregende Mischung aus Soul und Jazz, die als
Klassiker aus Chicago mit dem Besten von Curtis Mayfield,
Calliers Freund aus Kindertagen, gleichzieht. ❍
La photo évocatrice de Joel Brodsky incarne la mélancolie
du chef-d'œuvre qu'elle illustre. La production complexe de
Charles Stepney dessine des volutes autour de la voix
chaude de Terry Callier et du jeu sensible de la guitare folk
pour créer un mélange étourdissant de soul et de jazz qui
n'a rien à envier au meilleur travail de l'ami d'enfance de
Callier, Curtis Mayfield, au rayon des classiques de Chicago.

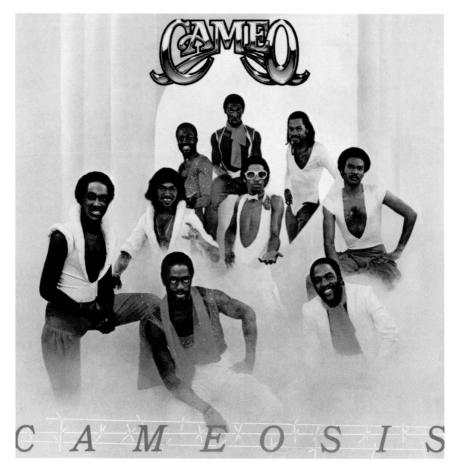

CAMEO

title **CAMEOSIS** / *year* **1980** / *label* Casablanca / *design* Stephen Lumel/Gribbitt! / *photography* Bernard Vidal

Casablanca Records founder Neil Bogart allotted a generous portion of his company's budget design to ensure that his covers had a uniform feel, and that each jacket reflected the nature of each recording's unique contents. He contracted Christopher Whorf's design firm, Gribbitt!, to provide album art for Casablanca's entire roster, with the exception of KISS. **O**
Neil Bogart, der Gründer von Casablanca Records, bewillig-te eine großzügige Portion seines Etats für Covergestaltung,

um sicherzustellen, dass seine Cover einheitlich aussehen und dass jede Hülle ihren jeweiligen Inhalt widerspiegelt. Er nahm Christopher Whorfs Designagentur Gribbitt! unter Vertrag, um für den Gesamtkatalog von Casablanca – mit Ausnahme von KISS – die Coverentwürfe zu liefern. **O**
Neil Bogart, le fondateur de Casablanca Records, a dépensé une généreuse portion du budget de graphisme de sa société pour s'assurer que ses pochettes aient un air de famille et que chaque jaquette reflète la nature individuelle de chaque enregistrement. Il a eu recours à la société de graphisme de Christopher Whorf, Gribbitt!, pour illustrer les albums de toute l'équipe de Casablanca, à l'exception de KISS.

CANDIDO
title **BEAUTIFUL** / *year* **1970** /
label Blue Note / *design* Ron Wolin /
photography Joel Brodsky

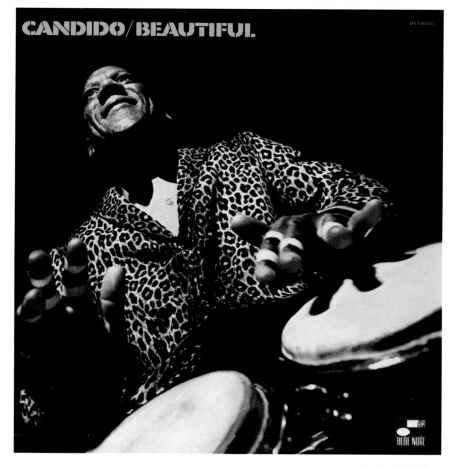

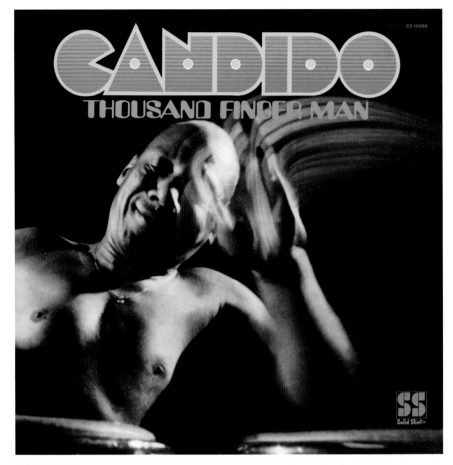

CANDIDO

title **THOUSAND FINGER MAN** / *year* **1970** /
label Solid State / *photography* Chuck Stewart /
art direction Frank Gauna

Photographer Chuck Stewart captured the look of jazz,
harnessing the subtlety and spontaneity of some of the
genre's greatest practitioners. With subjects ranging from
Charles Mingus to Wynton Marsalis, *Chuck Stewart's
Jazz Files* pairs evocative imagery with engaging storytelling
to gracefully document thirty-five of jazz music's most
industrious years. ◐
Der Fotograf Chuck Stewart hielt den Look von Jazz fest
und machte sich die Subtilität und Spontaneität von

einigen der größten Fachleute dieses Genres zunutze.
Seine Motive reichen von Charles Mingus bis zu Wynton
Marsalis. In seinem Buch *Chuck Stewart's Jazz Files* stellt er
seine bewegenden Bilder neben spannende Geschichten
und dokumentiert so 35 Jahre, in denen der Jazz besonders
fruchtbar war. ◐
Chuck Stewart a capturé l'esprit du jazz dans ses photos, il
a apprivoisé la subtilité et la spontanéité de quelques-uns
des plus grands personnages du genre. Avec des sujets tels
que Charles Mingus ou Wynton Marsalis, les *Chuck
Stewart's Jazz Files* allient des images évocatrices à une nar-
ration captivante pour documenter avec élégance trente-
cinq des années les plus productives du jazz.

CAPTAIN SKY
title **THE RETURN OF CAPTAIN SKY** / *year* **1981** / *label* AVI /
design Bob Wynne

CARL CARLTON
title **CARL CARLTON** /
year **1981** / *label* 20th Century
Fox / *design* Roland Young /
photography Michael Hashimoto

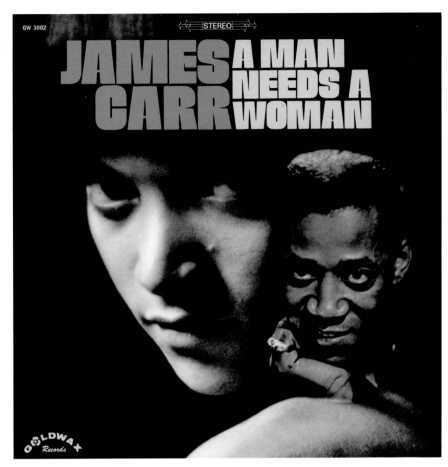

GW 3002

STEREO

JAMES CARR A MAN NEEDS A WOMAN

GOLDWAX Records

JAMES CARR

title **A MAN NEEDS A WOMAN** / *year* **1977** /
label Goldwax / *design* Forlenza Venosa Assoc.

Founded in 1964 by a former Hi Records exec and a
Memphis pharmacist, Goldwax would launch the careers
of the Ovations, O.V. Wright, and James Carr. The firm of
Forlenza Venosa Associates was a relatively new entity
when they merged these disparate images for *A Man Needs
a Woman*, pairing Carr's black-and-white likeness with a
full-color feminine stock photograph. ◗
Bei Goldwax sollte die Karriere der Ovations, von O.V.
Wright und James Carr beginnen. Dieses Label wurde 1964
von einem ehemaligen Geschäftsführer der Hi Records

und einem Apotheker aus Georgia gegründet. Die Firma
Forlenza Venosa Associates war am Markt relativ neu, als
sie diese ungleichen Bilder für *A Man Needs a Woman* ver-
schmolz. Hier wurde ein Schwarzweißbildnis von Carr mit
dem farbigen Agentur-Foto einer femininen Schönheit
gekoppelt. ◗
Fondé en 1964 par un ancien directeur de Hi Records et un
pharmacien de Memphis, Goldwax allait lancer les carrières
des Ovations, d'O.V. Wright et de James Carr. La société
Forlenza Venosa Associates était relativement jeune
lorsqu'elle a fusionné ces images disparates pour *A Man
Needs a Woman*, associant un portrait en noir et blanc de
Carr avec une photographie de femme en couleur issue
d'une banque d'images.

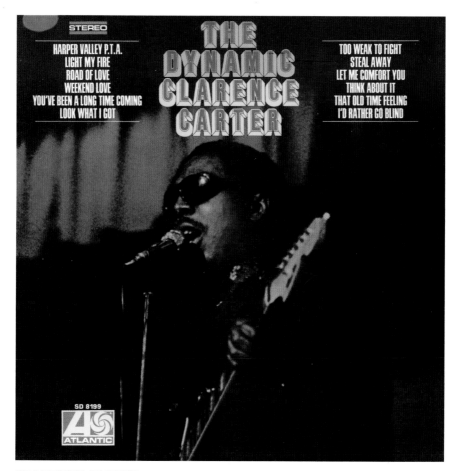

STEREO

HARPER VALLEY P.T.A.
LIGHT MY FIRE
ROAD OF LOVE
WEEKEND LOVE
YOU'VE BEEN A LONG TIME COMING
LOOK WHAT I GOT

THE DYNAMIC CLARENCE CARTER

TOO WEAK TO FIGHT
STEAL AWAY
LET ME COMFORT YOU
THINK ABOUT IT
THAT OLD TIME FEELING
I'D RATHER GO BLIND

SD 8199
ATLANTIC

CLARENCE CARTER

title **THE DYNAMIC CLARENCE CARTER** / *year* **1969** /
label Atlantic / *design* Haig Adishian / *photography* David
Patterson

Blind bluesman Clarence Carter endured several climate
changes over the course of his musical career, pioneering
blues-funk, surviving disco, and later having his catalog
reinvented by a rising generation of hip-hop producers.
Carter's output covers a range of emotions, from the serious, illustrated in the tear-jerking biography "Patches", to
the explicit, best portrayed by the whimsical "Strokin'". ○
Der blinde Bluesmann Clarence Carter überstand im Laufe
seiner musikalischen Karriere mehrere Klimawechsel. Er war
ein Pionier des Blues-Funk, überlebte die Discozeit, und

später hauchte eine neu aufkommende Generation von
Hiphop-Produzenten seinem Katalog neues Leben ein.
Carter deckt in seinen Werken eine ganze Bandbreite an
Emotionen ab: vom Ernsthaften, wie es in der auf die Trä-
nendrüse drückenden Biografie »Patches« illustriert wird,
bis zum Eindeutig-Zweideutigen, am besten porträtiert im
neckischen „Strokin'". ○
Le bluesman aveugle Clarence Carter a traversé plusieurs
changements de climat au cours de sa carrière musicale.
C'est un pionnier du blues-funk, un survivant du disco, et il
a vu son catalogue réinventé par la génération montante
des producteurs de hip-hop. La musique de Carter couvre
tout un éventail d'émotions, depuis la gravité, illustrée dans
la biographie poignante *Patches*, jusqu'à la sensualité explicite, avec le curieux *Strokin'*.

CASSIANO
title **APRESENTAMOS NOSSO**
CASSIANO / *year* **1973** / *label*
Odeon / *design* Joselito

THE JIMMY CASTOR BUNCH

title **IT'S JUST BEGUN** / *year* **1972** / *label* RCA Victor /
design Frank Mulvey / *art direction* Acy Lehman /
illustration Corrigan

Born on the Gemini/Cancer cusp, Castor's "egocentric,
intellectual, and airy" Gemini traits are represented by his
unconcealed face atop a torso, dubbed "the musical tree".
A tube runs from Castor's brain to a small patch of clouds,
indicating airiness. His introverted and intuitive Cancer
tendencies are illustrated by Castor's partially hidden face,
and its close proximity to his heart. **O**

An Jimmy Castors Geburtstag wechselte das Sternbild der
Zwillinge gerade in den Krebs. Castors Zwillings-Charakte-
ristika »egozentrisch, intellektuell und luftig« werden von
seinem unverhüllten Gesicht über dem als »musikalischer

Baum« bezeichneten Torso repräsentiert. Schläuche laufen
aus Castors Kopf in ein paar Wolkenflecken, was auf Unbe-
kümmertheit und Leichtigkeit verweist. Seine introvertier-
ten und intuitiven Neigungen als Krebs werden von Castors
teilweise verdecktem Gesicht und dessen räumlicher Nähe
zu seinem Herzen illustriert. **O**

Castor est né à la limite entre les signes des Gémeaux et
du Cancer, et ses traits de caractère appartiennent aux
Gémeaux, « égocentrique, intellectuel et aérien », sont
représentés par son visage découvert posé sur un torse
surnommé « l'arbre musical ». Un tube va du cerveau de
Castor à un petit nuage, pour indiquer l'élément aérien.
Ses tendances à l'introversion et à l'intuition, liées au signe
du Cancer, sont illustrées par le visage partiellement dissi-
mulé, tout proche de son cœur.

CATALYST

title **CATALYST** / *year* **1972** / *label* Cobblestone /
design Spencer Zahn / *photography* Spencer Zahn

Philadelphia's Spencer Zahn provided cover art for both
of Catalyst's Cobblestone releases, but was best known
around town for his collectible concert posters. Whether
it was the Chambers Brothers at Philly's legendary Electric
Factory or the Grateful Dead in nearby Lancaster, Zahn's
detailed screen-printings often necessitated half-tone
processing, used here for Catalyst's self-titled debut. **O**
Spencer Zahn aus Philadelphia lieferte die Cover für beide
Veröffentlichungen von Catalyst bei Cobblestone, aber in
der Stadt wurde er vor allem bekannt für seine unter
Sammlern heiß begehrten Konzertplakate. Die detaillierten

Siebdruckarbeiten von Zahn erforderten oft eine Halbton-
verarbeitung, so wie sie hier beim Debütalbum von Catalyst eingesetzt wurde. Er arbeitete auch für die Chambers
Brothers, die in der legendären Electric Factory in Philadelphia auftraten, und für die Grateful Dead im nahegelegenen Lancaster. **O**
Spencer Zahn, natif de Philadelphie, s'est chargé de l'illustration des deux disques de Catalyst sortis chez Cobblestone,
mais était plus connu en ville pour ses affiches de concert,
véritables articles de collection.. Qu'il s'agisse des Chambers
Brothers à la légendaire Electric Factory de Philadelphie, ou
des Grateful Dead dans la ville voisine de Lancaster, les séri-
graphies détaillées de Zahn nécessitaient souvent un traitement en demi-teintes, comme ici pour le premier album
éponyme de Catalyst.

CHAIRMEN OF THE BOARD

title **SKIN I'M IN** / *year* **1974** / *label* Invictus /
design Teresa Alfieri / *art direction* Mirella Ricciardi

Best represented by their 1970 single "Give Me Just a Little
More Time", the Chairmen of the Board still attract audiences in the south, a perk afforded by the Detroit group's
involuntary status as icons in the genre. *Skin I'm In* is a
psychedelic deviation from their dependable feel-good
formula; Parliament-Funkadelic players Eddie Hazel and
Bernie Worrell may be to blame. **◗**

Die Chairmen of the Board, am besten repräsentiert durch
ihre Single »Give Me Just A Little More Time« von 1970,
ziehen im Süden immer noch eine Menge Leute an. Diese
Gunst ist dem unfreiwilligen Status der Detroiter Gruppe
als Ikone des Genres geschuldet. *Skin I'm In* ist eine
psychedelische Abschweifung von ihrem verlässlichen
Wohlfühlrezept, was man wohl den Musikern Eddie Hazel
und Bernie Worrell von Parliament/Funkadelic ankreiden
könnte. **◗**

Le morceau qui représente le mieux les Chairmen of the
Board est leur single de 1970, *Give Me Just a Little More
Time*. Le groupe attire toujours le public du Sud, un avantage dû au statut involontaire d'icône du genre dont jouit
ce groupe de Detroit. *Skin I'm In* est une dérogation
psychédélique à sa formule habituelle pleine de bonne
humeur. Les joueurs de Parliament-Funkadelic, Eddie Hazel
et Bernie Worrell, en sont sans doute responsables.

CHAIRMEN OF THE BOARD

title **BITTERSWEET** / *year* **1972** / *label* Invictus / *photography* Richard Rankin / *art direction* John Hoernle

CHAKA KHAN

title **CHAKA** / *year* **1978** / *label* Warner Bros. /
design Drennon Design / *photography* Scott Enyart /
art direction John Cabalka

Chaka was recorded in true Atlantic fashion, with Arif
Mardin producing and arranging the sessions, while a
cornucopia of prolific jazz players executed Mardin's
sophisticated charts. Although Khan was often the visual
focus of most Rufus covers, this album befittingly features
a solitary Chaka relishing her solo debut. ◗
Chaka wurde in echter Atlantic-Atmo aufgezeichnet. Dabei
produzierte und arrangierte Arif Mardin die Sessions, wäh-

rend eine Fülle besonders produktiver Jazzmusiker Mardins
ausgefeilte Arrangements umsetzte. Auf den meisten
Rufus-Covern war Khan optisch im Fokus, doch dieses
Album zeigt Chaka passenderweise ganz allein, wie sie ihr
Solodebüt genießt. ◗
Chaka a été enregistré dans le plus pur style Atlantic, avec
Arif Mardin produisant et arrangeant les sessions tandis
qu'une pléthore de jazzmen prolifiques exécutaient ses
plans sophistiqués. Khan était souvent le centre de gravité
visuel sur la plupart des pochettes de Rufus. Ici, elle apparaît seule, savourant le début de sa carrière en solo.

THE CHAMBERS
BROTHERS

title **NEW GENERATION** / *year*
1971 / *label* CBS / *design* Abdul
Mati Klarwein

RAY CHARLES
title **CRYING TIME** / *year* **1966** /
label EMI / *design* George S.
Whiteman / *illustration* William
Alexander

THE CHEQUERS

title **CHECK US OUT** / *year* **1970** / *label* Creole /
design Dave & Alan Field / *photography* Patrick Watters

Coming in a fairly generic package, this album is actually
quite a treat from an obscure British group of Afro-
Caribbean musicians with impeccable taste and a knack for
melding island sounds with heavy dance-floor funk and
disco. The standout is a very funky cover of Bob Marley's
"Get Up, Stand Up". ○
Diese Platte steckt zwar in einer recht gewöhnlichen Hülle,
ist aber tatsächlich ein ganz schöner Leckerbissen einer

britischen Gruppe afrokaribischer Musiker mit unfehl-
barem Geschmack und einem Händchen dafür, karibische
Klänge mit mächtigem Dancefloor-Funk und Disco zu
verschmelzen. Hervorstechend ist eine äußerst funkige
Coverversion von Bob Marleys »Get Up Stand Up«. ○
Malgré sa pochette plutôt générique, cet album est en fait
une belle surprise. Les Chequers est un obscur groupe
britannique de musiciens afro-caribéens, dotés d'un goût
impeccable et d'un talent certain pour fusionner les sons
des îles avec du funk et du disco faits pour marquer les
pistes de danse. À noter, une version très funky de *Get Up
Stand Up* de Bob Marley.

CHIC

title **RISQUÉ** / *year* **1979** / *label* Atlantic /
photography Ken Ambrose / *art direction* Carin Goldberg

A graduate of New York's Cooper Union School of Art,
Carin Goldberg conceived this sepia-toned vignette of the
influential disco ensemble in 1920s gangster-chic attire.
Although an unknown piano-player appears to have been
killed in cold blood by founder and co-producer Nile
Rogers, his partner in crime Bernard Edwards seems to be
sharing a laugh with the presumably coherent victim. **O**
Carin Goldberg machte ihren Abschluss an der Cooper
Union School of Art in New York. Sie entwickelte diese

sepiagetönte Vignette des einflussreichen Disco-Ensembles
im Gangsterchic der 20er Jahre. Obwohl der Gründer und
Koproduzent Nile Rogers diesen unbekannten Pianospieler
offenbar kaltblütig umgelegt hat, schmunzelt sein Gano-
venkollege Bernard Edwards mit dem vermeintlichen Opfer
wie über einen gemeinsamen Witz. **O**
C'est Carin Goldberg, diplômée de la Cooper Union School
of Art de New York, qui a conçu ce portrait sépia du grand
groupe disco en tenue de gangsters des années 1920. Il
semble qu'un pianiste inconnu ait été tué de sang-froid par
le fondateur et coproducteur du groupe, Nile Rogers, mais
son complice Bernard Edwards semble partager un sourire
de connivence avec la victime.

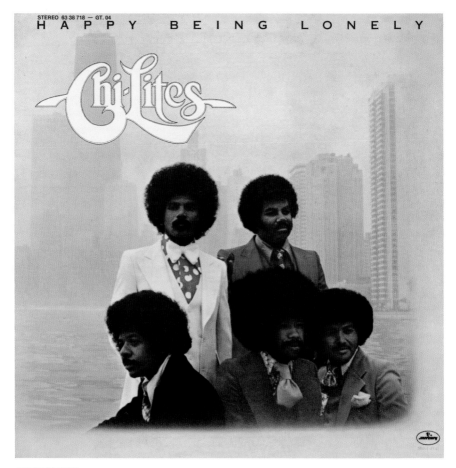

STEREO 63 38 718 — GT. 04

H A P P Y   B E I N G   L O N E L Y

CHI-LITES

title **HAPPY BEING LONELY** / *year* **1977** / *label* Mercury

Thick coats of orchestral accompaniment ensconce these lady-centric compositions, much like the veil of fog that rises over Lake Michigan, nearly obscuring from view the afroed quintet's home city. No doubt suffering from the recent departure of their principal songwriter Eugene Record, only the title track from *Happy Being Lonely* would chart, spurring a brief dispersal of the wounded group. **O**

Dicke Schichten orchestraler Begleitung umhüllen diese Lady-zentrierten Kompositionen, ähnlich dem Nebel, der sich aus dem Michigansee erhebt und den Blick auf Chicago fast verdeckt: Von dieser Stadt hat die Truppe mit den schönen Afros ihren Namen. Zweifellos litt die Gruppe

darunter, dass sich Eugene Record, ihr wichtigster Songlieferant, kurz zuvor verabschiedet hatte, und darum schaffte es nur das Titelstück »Happy Being Lonely« in die Charts, was bei der Gruppe für Betroffenheit und kurze Auflösungserscheinungen sorgte. **O**

Ces compositions centrées sur les femmes sont enveloppées d'une orchestration dense qui rappelle la brume se levant sur le lac Michigan et engloutissant presque la ville qui a donné son nom au quintette à coiffures afro. Le groupe semble avoir souffert du départ récent de son compositeur principal, Eugene Record, et seul le morceau-titre *Happy Being Lonely* est entré dans les classements. Cette déconfiture a provoqué une brève dispersion du groupe blessé.

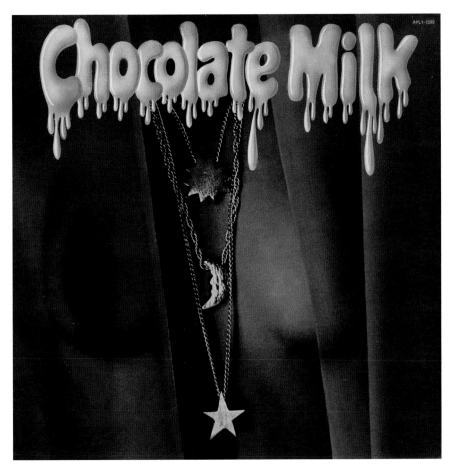

CHOCOLATE MILK

title **CHOCOLATE MILK** / *year* **1976** / *label* RCA Victor / *photography* Nick Sangiamo / *art direction* Acy Lehman

RCA's Grammy award-winning Art Director Acy Lehman was once quoted as saying, "Covers are designed to accomplish a single purpose – to get you to pick the re-cord off the rack." He most certainly achieved his goal with Chocolate Milk's self-titled release, pairing veiled breasts with a complimentary set of sun and moon pendants. **O**

Vom preisgekrönten Art Director von RCA, Acy Lehman, stammt das Zitat: »Cover werden gestaltet, um einen einzi-gen Zweck zu erfüllen: Dass man aus dem Regal gerade dieses Album wählt.« Ganz sicher erreichte er dieses Ziel mit der Platte von Chocolate Milk, indem er aus einem Umhang lugende Brüste durch Anhänger mit Sonne und Mond ergänzte. **O**

On a pu entendre le directeur artistique primé de RCA, Acy Lehman, déclarer : « Les pochettes n'ont qu'un seul but, celui de vous décider à prendre le disque dans le rayon du magasin. » Il a sans aucun doute atteint son objectif pour l'album éponyme de Chocolate Milk, avec ces seins voilés ornés de pendentifs du soleil et de la lune.

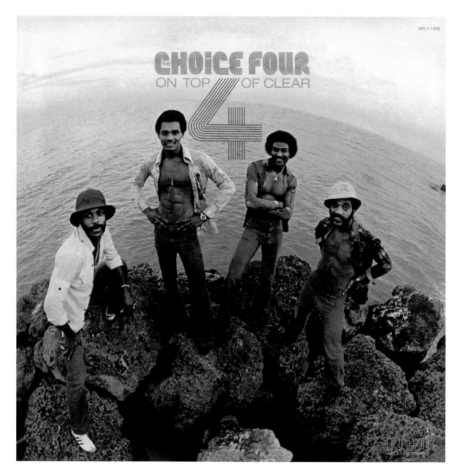

THE CHOICE FOUR
title **ON TOP OF CLEAR** / *year* **1976** / *label* RCA

The Choice Four were a soul group from Washington, D.C. Their gorgeous harmonies, led by Bobby Hamilton's pure vocals and produced by Van McCoy's skillful hands, resulted in some stirring moments, helped further by a couple of deep dance-floor mixes from Tom Moulton. The use of a fish-eye lens for the cover shot turned a portrait of four dudes standing on some rocks into an image of perpetual cool. ⭘
The Choice Four waren eine harmonische Soul-Gruppe aus Washington, D.C. Ihre hinreißenden Harmonien wurden von Bobby Hamiltons reiner Stimme angeführt und von

Van McCoys geschickten Händen produziert. Das führte zu einigen anrührenden Momenten, denen die satten Dance-floor-Mixes von Tom Moulton noch unter die Arme greifen. Die Fischaugenlinse für das Coverfoto verwandelt das Bild einiger Typen, die auf Felsen stehen, in das Porträt ewiger Coolness. ⭘
Les Choice Four étaient un groupe de sweet soul de Washington, D.C. Leurs superbes harmonies, emmenées par la voix pure de Bobby Hamilton et produites avec talent par Van McCoy, ont fait naître des moments grisants, amplifiés par deux ou trois mixages de Tom Moulton destinés aux pistes de danse. Sur la pochette, l'utilisation d'un objectif fish-eye transforme le portrait de quatre types debout sur des rochers en véritable icône du cool éternel.

THE CHOICE FOUR

alice clark

362

ALICE CLARK

title **ALICE CLARK** / *year* **1972** / *label* Mainstream /
design Maurer Productions / *photography* Raymond Ross

The person responsible for capturing this intimate portrait
is respected and revered music photographer Raymond
Ross, whose work straddled New York's big band, avant-
garde, and soul scenes over his lengthy photographic
career. When he passed away in 2004, the octogenarian left
behind tens of thousands of photographs, spanning sixty
years of musical immersion. **O**

Für dieses intime Porträt verantwortlich ist der geschätzte
und verehrte Musikfotograf Raymond Ross, dessen Arbeiten im Laufe seiner langjährigen Karriere viele Szenen mit
New Yorker Bigbands, Avantgarde- und Soulmusikern
einfingen. Als er 2004 starb, hinterließ der Achtzigjährige
Zehntausende Fotos aus über sechzig Jahren seiner Be-
schäftigung mit Musik. **O**

L'auteur de ce portrait intimiste est le grand photographe
de musique Raymond Ross, dont la longue carrière s'est
partagée entre les scènes new-yorkaises du big band, de
l'avant-garde et de la soul. Lorsqu'il est décédé en 2004, cet
octogénaire a laissé derrière lui des dizaines de milliers de
photographies qui reflètent soixante ans d'immersion dans
le monde de la musique. **O**

Merry Clayton Gimme Shelter

MERRY CLAYTON
title **GIMME SHELTER** / *year* **1970** / *label* A&M / *design*
Rod Dyer & Paul Bruhwiler / *photography* Guy Webster

Photographer Guy Webster had shot rock stars, movie
stars, and even presidents. Merry Clayton seemed always
to be in the shadow of fame as a backing singer. Webster's
high-contrast photo of Clayton for her debut LP is
bold, and coupled with the German Bauhaus-inspired
design work from Rod Dyer and Paul Bruhwiler the cover
announces the soulful singer as a force to be reckoned
with. ◗
Der Fotograf Guy Webster hat Stars aus Rock und Film und
sogar Präsidenten abgelichtet. Merry Clayton stand als
Backgroundsängerin scheinbar stets im Schatten des Ruh-
mes anderer. Das kontrastreiche Foto für ihre Debüt-LP ist
mutig, und in Verbindung mit der vom Bauhaus inspirier-
ten Gestaltung von Rod Dyer und Paul Bruhwiler kündigt
das Cover diese Sängerin als eine Soulgröße an, mit der
man rechnen muss. ◗
Guy Webster avait photographié des stars du rock, des
vedettes de cinéma et même des présidents. Merry Clayton
semblait toujours rester dans l'ombre réservée aux choristes. Pour son premier album, Webster a fait d'elle un
portrait audacieux au contraste très prononcé. Avec le graphisme de Rod Dyer et Paul Bruhwiler inspiré du Bauhaus
allemand, la pochette présente cette chanteuse expressive
comme une force que l'on ne peut ignorer.

GEORGE CLINTON

title **YOU SHOULDN'T-NUF BIT FISH** / *year* **1983** / *label* Capitol / *design* Pedro Bell/Splankwerks / *illustration* Pedro Bell with the Splankagraphic All Stars, G. "Sir Lance" Everett, Turtel Onli & Bruse A. Bell

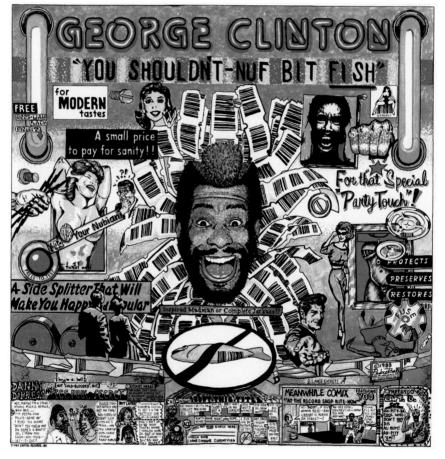

ATMOSPHERE STRUT/CLOUD ONE

P&P 1001

P&P Records

CLOUD ONE

title **ATMOSPHERE STRUT** / *year* **1976** / *label* P&P /
design Chic-Art / *photography* Patrick Adams / *art direction*
Chico Alvarez

Patrick Adams, along with co-conspirator Peter Brown,
added a new dimension to the discotheques of NYC
through their self-named P&P Records, creating high-
fidelity disco anthems from a pastiche of synthetic sounds
and live instrumentation. Famously involved in all aspects
of his company, Adams even shot the ethereal photograph
featured on the aptly-titled *Atmosphere Strut.* ○
Patrick Adams schuf zusammen mit seinem Mitstreiter
Peter Brown mittels der nach ihnen benannten Plattenfirma P&P Records für die Diskotheken von New York City

neue Dimensionen. Dort ließen sie aus einem Pastiche
synthetischer Klänge mit Live-Instrumentierungen Hifi-
Discohymnen erklingen. Adams rühmte sich, an allen
Aspekten seiner Firma beteiligt zu sein, und nahm sogar
das ätherische Foto für das treffend benannte Album
Atmosphere Strut auf. ○
Patrick Adams et son compère Peter Brown ont ajouté une
nouvelle dimension aux discothèques de New York avec
leur label P&P Records, en créant des hymnes disco haute
fidélité à partir d'une combinaison de sons synthétiques et
d'instruments joués en direct. Adams est connu pour se
mêler de tous les aspects de son label, et est même l'auteur
de la photographie éthérée de la pochette d'*Atmosphere
Strut.*

DENNIS COFFEY

title **FINGER LICKIN GOOD** / *year* **1975** /
label Westbound / *photography* Joel Brodsky

It may come as little surprise to funk aficionados that the same photographer who arranged this suggestive situation also concocted the evocative scenarios found on the Ohio Players' notorious albums *Ecstasy*, *Pleasure*, *Pain*, and the remaining four releases in that groundbreaking series. Regardless, Brodsky is perhaps best known for the iconic photograph of a messianic Jim Morrison that graces the cover of The Doors' *Best of* record, released in 1985. **O**
Für Funk-Kenner ist es keine große Überraschung zu erfahren, dass der gleiche Fotograf, der solch suggestive Situationen arrangieren kann, auch die eindeutigen Szenarien ausgeheckt hat, die man auf den berüchtigten Alben *Ecstasy*, *Pleasure* und *Pain* und den verbleibenden vier LPs dieser bahnbrechenden Serie der Ohio Players zu sehen bekommt. Ungeachtet dessen wurde Brodsky wahrscheinlich vor allem durch sein symbolträchtiges Foto eines messianischen Jim Morrison bekannt, das das Cover des *Best of*-Albums der Doors von 1985 ziert. **O**
Les aficionados du funk ne seront pas surpris d'apprendre que le photographe qui s'est chargé de cette scène suggestive a également concocté les scénarios évocateurs que l'on trouve sur *Ecstasy*, *Pleasure* et *Pain*, ainsi que sur les quatre autres albums de cette série révolutionnaire. Mais Brodsky est peut-être plus connu pour la photo emblématique et messianique de Jim Morrison qui orne la pochette du *Best of* des Doors, sorti en 1985.

MUSIC SCORE COMPOSED AND PERFORMED BY

DENNIS COFFEY AND
LUCHI DE JESUS

ORIGINAL MOTION PICTURE SOUNDTRACK

BLACK BELT JONES

 7771

DENNIS COFFEY
AND LUCHI DE JESUS

title **BLACK BELT JONES** / year **1974** /
label Weintraub-Heller

These full-contact silhouettes of Black Belt Jones (Jim "Dragon" Kelly) and Sydney (Gloria Hendry) only represent a fraction of the action. The pair must defeat countless goons and henchmen in a karate-chopping struggle to save Pop Byrd's karate school. Psychedelic soul pioneer Dennis Coffey and soundtrack veteran Luchi De Jesus collaborated on this dynamic score, which many consider the finest of the era. ⊙
Diese Silhouetten von Black Belt Jones (Jim »Dragon« Kelly) und Sydney (Gloria Hendry) im Vollkontakt repräsentieren nur einen Bruchteil der Handlung. Das Paar muss in Karate-

kämpfen unzählige Schurken und Handlanger besiegen, um die Karateschule von Pop Byrd zu retten. Der Pionier des psychedelischen Soul Dennis Coffey und der Soundtrack-Veteran Luchi De Jesus arbeiteten gemeinsam an dieser dynamischen Filmmusik, die von vielen als beste ihrer Ära betrachtet wird. ⊙
Ces silhouettes de Black Belt Jones (Jim « Dragon » Kelly) et Sydney (Gloria Hendry) en pleine séance de full-contact ne représentent qu'un petit fragment de l'action. Le duo doit rosser une ribambelle d'hommes de main pour sauver l'école de karaté de Pop Byrd. Dennis Coffey, pionnier de la soul psychédélique, et Luchi De Jesus, vétéran des bandes originales, ont travaillé ensemble sur cette musique de film dynamique que beaucoup considèrent comme la meilleure de son époque.

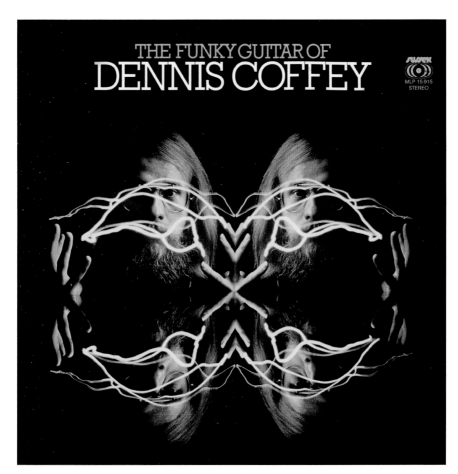

THE FUNKY GUITAR OF
DENNIS COFFEY

MLP 15.915
STEREO

DENNIS COFFEY AND
THE DETROIT GUITAR BAND
title **THE FUNKY GUITAR OF DENNIS COFFEY** /
year **1972** / *label* Sussex

Released as *Electric Coffey* in the United States, *The Funky Guitar of Dennis Coffey* encapsulates the eccentric session man at his finest. Always one to give the drummer some, fellow Funk Brothers Jack Ashford, Eddie "Bongo" Brown, and Andrew Smith make stunning rhythmic statements on the abounding breaks featured herein. **O**
In den USA kam diese Platte als *Electric Coffey* heraus, und *The Funky Guitar of Dennis Coffey* verkörpert diesen exzen-

trischen Sessionmusiker aufs Beste. Er war stets bereit, den Schlagzeuger so richtig zu fordern. Die Kollegen Jack Ashford, Eddie »Bongo« Brown und Andrew Smith von den Funk Brothers treffen erstaunliche rhythmische Statements über die hier im Überfluss vorgestellten Breaks. **O**
Sorti sous le titre *Electric Coffey* aux États-Unis, *The Funky Guitar of Dennis Coffey* présente ce musicien de studio excentrique au sommet de son art. Les Funk Brothers Jack Ashford, Eddie « Bongo » Brown et Andrew Smith font des prouesses rythmiques sur les improvisations qui fourmillent dans cet album.

THINK *(about it)*
LYN COLLINS

PE 5602 Stereo
2391 044

LYN COLLINS

title **THINK (ABOUT IT)** / *year* **1972** / *label* People /
art direction Lee Lebowitz

Lyn Collins was the featured female singer for the James
Brown Revue from 1971–1976. *Think*, her first solo LP,
would produce one of James Brown's most heavily sampled
hits ever, a fiercely funky ode to women's lib. Lee Lebowitz's
gospel-influenced art direction was probably influenced by
Brown's nickname for Collins – the "Female Preacher". **○**
Lyn Collins war von 1971 bis 1976 *die* Sängerin der James
Brown Revue. Auf ihrer ersten Solo-LP *Think* produzierte
sie einen der am häufigsten gesampelten Hits von James

Brown – eine heftige Funk-Ode an Women's Liberation.
Lee Lebowitz' vom Gospel beeinflusste Covergestaltung
wurde wahrscheinlich von James Browns Spitznamen für
Lyn Collins inspiriert: »Female Preacher«. **○**
Lyn Collins a été la chanteuse vedette de la James Brown
Revue de 1971 à 1976. *Think*, son premier album en solo,
allait produire l'un des tubes de James Brown les plus samplés de l'histoire, une ode férocement funky à la libération
de la femme. Les réminiscences de gospel de la direction
artistique de Lee Lebowitz ont probablement été influen-
cées par le surnom que Brown avait donné à Collins,
« la Prédicatrice ».

TMC 5269

COMMODORES

title **MACHINE GUN** / *year* **1974** / *label* Motown /
photography Jim Britt

Absent from the Commodores' funky debut are the gentle
ballads that would later define the Alabama ensemble.
Photographer Jim Britt did lots of work with a post-Hitsville
Motown, snaring promotional photos for the legendary
label's entire roster, plus bringing out the best of an exuberant Marvin Gaye for *Let's Get It On* and the multiple-
exposure montage featured on *Live!* **O**

Auf dem funkigen Debüt der Commodores fehlen noch
die sanften Balladen, für die das Alabama-Ensemble später
so berühmt werden sollte. Der Fotograf Jim Britt arbeitete

in der Post-Hitsville-Ära viel für Motown und produzierte
Promo-Fotos für die gesamte Truppe dieses legendären
Labels. Außerdem holte er aus einem überschäumenden
Marvin Gaye für *Let's Get It On* und für *Live!* in einer
Montage mit Mehrfachbelichtung das Beste heraus. **O**

Les ballades mélodieuses qui allaient par la suite définir
le style des Commodores étaient absentes du premier
album de ce groupe de l'Alabama. Le photographe Jim Britt
a beaucoup travaillé pour Motown après l'époque
« Hitsville » du label et a pris des clichés promotionnels
de tous les artistes de cette maison légendaire. Il a en outre
révélé le meilleur d'un Marvin Gaye exubérant pour *Let's
Get It On* et sur le montage à expositions multiples de son
Live!

HONEY CONE

title **SOULFUL TAPESTRY** /
year **1971** / *label* Hot Wax /
photography Jimmy Mack

CON FUNK SHUN

title **CON FUNK SHUN** /
year **1976** / *label* Mercury /
photography Frederick Toma /
cover concept Linda Lou McCall

NORMAN CONNORS

title **YOU ARE MY STARSHIP** / *year* **1976** / *label* Buddah / *design* Ed Caraeff / *photography* Ed Caraeff

© 1979 James Davis

CORDIAL
title **THEIR FIRST** / *year* **1979** / *label* Tolimar

Audrey Revell has owned San Francisco's Doré Studios since 1955. In the late '80s, Revell produced a series of religious pictures, which found their way to grateful inmates at nearby San Quentin State Prison. Her popularity among prisoners led to the genesis of *Doing Time With Jesus*, a quarterly featuring the art and poetry of young men on Death Row. ◐

Audrey Revell war seit 1955 Inhaber der Doré Studios in San Francisco. Ende der 80er Jahre produzierte Revell eine Serie religiöser Bilder, die ihren Weg zu den dankbaren In-

sassen des nahegelegenen Staatsgefängnisses San Quentin fanden. Revells Beliebtheit unter den Gefangenen führte zum Entstehen von *Doing Time With Jesus*. In dieser Quartalszeitschrift wurden Kunst und Poesie junger Männer im Todestrakt vorgestellt. ◐

Audrey Revell est propriétaire des Doré Studios de San Francisco depuis 1955. À la fin des années 1980, elle a produit une série d'images religieuses qui sont arrivées entre les mains des pensionnaires de la prison voisine de San Quentin. Sa popularité chez les prisonniers a conduit à la création de *Doing Time With Jesus*, une revue trimestrielle qui publie les œuvres artistiques et la poésie des jeunes condamnés à la peine de mort.

CORNELIUS BROTHERS AND SISTER ROSE

title **CORNELIUS BROTHERS AND SISTER ROSE** / *year* **1972** / *label* United Artists

DON CORNELIUS & THE SOUL TRAIN GANG

title **SOUL TRAIN '75** / *year* **1975** / *label* Soul Train / *design* Gribbitt! / *photography* Antonin Kratochvil / *art direction* Acy Lehman

THE COUNTS

title **LOVE SIGN** / *year* **1973** / *label* Aware / *art direction* Wonder Graphics / *illustration* Overton Lloyd

After brief stints at the Cotillion & Westbound labels, this gifted group moved to the small Aware label and created their most out-there record. This time out the band took a break from its usual "sound of the moment" composing to style a jazzy funk odyssey worthy of the great cover by master illustrator of funky space freaks, Overton Lloyd. ❍ Nach kurzen Abstechern zu den Musikverlagen Cotillion und Westbound sattelte diese begnadete Gruppe auf das kleine Label Aware um und kreierte dort ihr abgefahrenstes

Album. Diesmal nahm sich die Band eine Auszeit von ihrer Kompositionsweise im Stil eines »sound of the moment«, um sich auf eine jazzige Funk-Odyssee zu begeben, die des großartigen Covers vom Meisterillustratoren der funkigen Space-Freaks, Overton Lloyd, würdig war. ❍ Après de brefs passages chez les labels Cotillion et Westbound, ce groupe talentueux a signé chez le petit label Aware et a créé son disque le plus avant-gardiste. Cette fois, ils ont délaissé leur formule de composition « son du moment » pour créer une odyssée funk jazzy qui fait honneur à la superbe pochette du maestro illustrateur des fanas funky de l'espace, Overton Lloyd.

DON COVAY
title **SEE-SAW** / *year* **1966** / *label*
Atlantic / *design* Loring Eutemey /
photography Jerry Czember

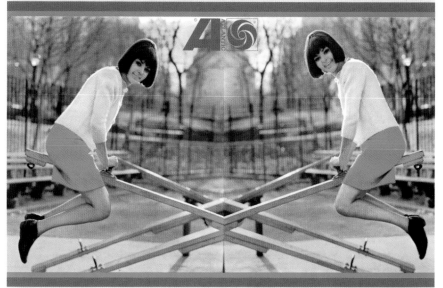

CREATION

title **CREATION** / *year* **1974** / *label* Atco / *design* Pacific Eye & Ear / *illustration* Drew Struzan & Bill Garland

California design agency Pacific Eye and Ear enlisted two of the heaviest illustrators in the business for this relatively unnoticed full-length recording by Creation. It is hard to determine a clear division of labor between cartoonist Bill Garland and photorealist Drew Struzan, both credited for this colorful and imaginative album cover. **O**

Die kalifornische Designagentur Pacific Eye und Ear beauf-tragte für diese relativ wenig beachtete Langspielplatte von Creation zwei Schwergewichte der Illustratorenbranche. Man kann nur schwerlich eine Grenze zwischen der Arbeit des Cartoonisten Bill Garland und der des Fotorealisten Drew Struzan ziehen, die beide dieses farbenprächtige und einfallsreiche Cover gestalteten. **O**

Pour cet enregistrement longue durée de Creation, passé relativement inaperçu, l'agence de graphisme californienne Pacific Eye and Ear a engagé deux des illustrateurs les plus galonnés du milieu. Il est difficile de déterminer clairement la division du travail entre le dessinateur Bill Garland et la peintre photoréaliste Drew Struzan, qui ont créé cette po-chette d'album colorée et pleine d'imagination.

title MIGRATION / *year* **1974** / *label* Sussex /
design Mick Haggerty / *photography* Suzanne Ayres /
art direction Carl Overr

Designer Mick Haggerty worked in several media, from
printmaking, to illustration, to duct-taping stuffed animals
together by their arms. Here he deconstructs and recon-
structs a series of Creative Source headshots, some rendering three-dimensional composites of the vocal quintet's
faces. **O**
Der Designer Mick Haggerty arbeitet mit unterschiedlichs-
ten Medien: von Druckgrafiken über Illustrationen bis hin

zu mit Klebeband am Arm verbundenen Stofftieren. Hier
zerschnitt er eine Serie von Porträtaufnahmen der Band
und setzte sie wieder zusammen, was bei einigen Köpfen
des Vokalquintetts zu einer dreidimensionalen Wirkung der
Gesichter führte. **O**
Le graphiste Mick Haggerty a travaillé sur de nombreux
supports, de la gravure à l'illustration, en passant par les
animaux en peluche attachés les uns aux autres par du
ruban adhésif. Ici, il déconstruit et reconstruit une série de
portraits de Creative Source, dont certains composent des
représentations tridimensionnelles des visages du quintette.

CROWN HEIGHTS AFFAIR

title **DO IT YOUR WAY** / *year* **1976** / *label* De-Lite /
photography Mickey Mathis / *art direction* Stanley
Hochstadt

Hailing from the district of the same name in Brooklyn,
New York, the Crown Heights Affair generated a wealth
of organic dance music during their industrious tenure.
De-Lite's acquisition of the band in the mid '70s found the
expansive ensemble following the lead of label-mates Kool
& the Gang in their transition to disco. ◐

Das Ensemble Crown Heights Affair stammt aus dem
gleichnamigen Distrikt von Brooklyn und produzierte eine
Fülle organischer Tanzmusik. Als De-Lite Mitte der 70er
Jahre die Band akquirierte, befand sich das expansive Ensemble wie die Label-Kollegen Kool and the Gang gerade
im Übergang zur Disco-Musik. ◐
Ce groupe originaire du district de Brooklyn du même nom
a généré une abondante production de musique de danse.
Lorsque le label De-Lite s'est assuré ses services au milieu
des années 1970, le groupe conquérant suivait le chemin
de ses collègues de label Kool and the Gang dans leur transition vers le disco.

CRYSTAL WINDS

title **FIRST FLIGHT** / *year* **1982** /
label Crystal Winds / *art direction*
Album Arts & Paul Gibson /
illustration Marvin Young/Album
Arts

KING CURTIS

title **GET READY** / *year* **1970** /
label Atco / *design* Stanisław
Zagorski / *photography* Lee
Friedlander

CYMANDE

title **PROMISED HEIGHTS** / *year* **1974** / *label* Janus / *art direction* Neil Terk / *illustration* Barbara Bergman

This group of Guyanese and Jamaican ex-pats derived their ensemble's name from the patois word for dove. Appropriately, Art Director Neil Terk used this painting by Barbara Bergman to incorporate the band's name into a context that represented the group's Caribbean connections and mystical motifs. **O**

Diese Gruppe mit Auswanderern aus Guyana und Jamaika leitet den Namen ihres Ensembles vom Patois-Wort für

Taube ab. Entsprechend verwendete der Art Director Neil Terk dieses Gemälde von Barbara Bergman, um den Namen der Band in einen Zusammenhang mit den karibischen Wurzeln und den mystischen Motiven der Gruppe zu stellen. **O**

Ce groupe d'expatriés guyanais et jamaïcains tient son nom d'un mot de patois qui signifie colombe. Le directeur artistique Neil Terk a donc utilisé cette peinture de Barbara Bergman pour donner au nom du groupe un contexte qui représentait ses racines caribéennes et ses penchants mystiques.

DAMN SAM THE MIRACLE MAN AND THE SOUL CONGREGATION

title **DAMN SAM THE MIRACLE MAN AND THE SOUL CONGREGATION** / *year* **1970** / *label* Tay-Ster / *design* A.J. Branham & Jahim Jones

This album cover and the frantic funk gem it encases leave more questions than answers for befuddled listeners. It is quite possible that the crude rendering of this space pharaoh is the Miracle Man himself, as no one in the band is named Sam. Vocalist A.J. Branham takes partial credit for this mystical rendering, the only fitting façade for a record of this ilk. **O**

Das Albumcover und das wilde Funk-Juwel dahinter lassen den verdatterten Hörer mit mehr Fragen als Antworten

zurück. Es ist recht gut möglich, dass die krude Darstellung dieses Weltall-Pharaos der Miracle Man selber ist, weil keiner aus der Band Sam heißt. Der Sänger A.J. Branham heimste für diese mystische Darstellung – die einzig passende Hülle für eine Aufnahme dieser Provenienz – zum Teil die Lorbeeren ein. **O**

Cette pochette d'album et la perle de funk effréné qu'elle renferme soulèvent plus de questions qu'elles ne donnent de réponses aux auditeurs perplexes. Il est tout à fait possible que la représentation simpliste de ce pharaon de l'espace soit le Miracle Man lui-même, car aucun membre du groupe ne se prénomme Sam. Le chanteur A.J. Branham a participé à cette illustration mystique, la seule façade appropriée pour un disque de cet acabit.

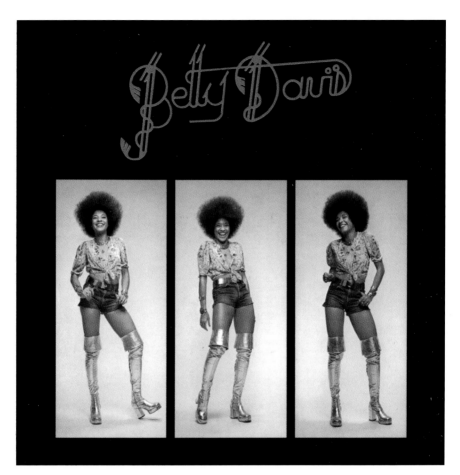

BETTY DAVIS

title **BETTY DAVIS** / *year* **1973** / *label* Just Sunshine /
design Ron Levine / *photography* Mel Dixon

Considering Davis' modeling background, fashion photographer Mel Dixon was a natural fit for this playful shoot.
One of the first African-Americans to break into the
industry, his work appeared frequently in *Jet* and *Ebony*,
where he was even the subject of a Coca-Cola campaign
that urged readers to write to the pioneering photographer
regarding his loyalty to the beverage. ◔

Wenn man Betty Davis' Erfahrungen als Model berücksich-
tigt, war der Modefotograf Mel Dixon eine ganz natürliche
Wahl für dieses verspielte Shooting. Er war einer der ersten
Afroamerikaner, die in der Branche Fuß fassen konnten,

und seine Arbeiten erschienen regelmäßig in *Jet* und *Ebony*,
wo er sogar das Thema einer Coca-Cola-Kampagne war,
in der die Leser eingeladen wurden, dem Fotografenpionier
etwas bezüglich seiner Loyalität zu diesem Getränk zu
schreiben. ◔

Étant donné l'expérience de Davis dans le mannequinat,
le photographe de mode Mel Dixon était un choix logique
pour cette séance de photos pleine de bonne humeur.
Il fut l'un des premiers Afro-Américains à percer dans le
secteur, et son travail est apparu fréquemment dans *Jet* et
Ebony, où il a même été le sujet d'une campagne de Coca-
Cola, qui demandait aux lecteurs d'écrire à ce photographe
d'avant-garde à propos de sa loyauté envers la boisson
pétillante.

BETTY DAVIS

title **NASTY-GAL** / *year* **1975** / *label* Island /
design Antonio Lopez / *photography* Lorrie Sullivan

During her brief marriage to Miles Davis, North Carolina native Betty Davis made a lasting impact on the jazz trumpeter, introducing him to the electrified sounds of Jimi Hendrix, and Sly and the Family Stone. As a performer, Betty's own musical output was rife with rebellion and raw sexuality, as illustrated by the evocative cover and content of 1975's *Nasty-Gal*. ⊙

Während ihrer kurzen Ehe mit Miles Davis hinterließ die aus North Carolina stammende Betty Davis einen bleibenden Eindruck bei dem Jazztrompeter und machte ihn mit

den elektrifizierten Klängen von Jimi Hendrix und Sly and the Family Stone vertraut. Auf der Bühne war Betty Davis' eigene musikalische Leistung voller Rebellion und roher Sexualität, wie es auch das sinnträchtige Cover und der Inhalt von *Nasty-Gal* von 1975 veranschaulichen. ⊙

Pendant son bref mariage avec Miles Davis, Betty Davis, originaire de la Caroline du Nord, avait marqué durablement le trompettiste de jazz en l'initiant aux sons électrisants de Jimi Hendrix et de Sly and the Family Stone. En tant qu'interprète, la production musicale de Betty regorgeait de rébellion et de sensualité à l'état brut, comme l'illustrent la pochette et le contenu évocateurs de son album de 1975, *Nasty-Gal*.

DAYTON

title **FEEL THE MUSIC** / *year* **1983** / *label* Capitol /
art direction Roy Kohara & Peter Shea

This progressive entourage from the Buckeye State has a lot
in common – sound and personnel – with Dayton, Ohio's
boogie pioneers, Zapp. Album designer Roy Kohara, a Capitol Records mainstay in the '80s, received a Grammy in 1980
for his package design of Bob Seger's *Against the Wind.* **◐**
Dayton, diese progressive Entourage aus Ohio, hat mit
Zapp, den Boogie-Pionieren aus Ohio, eine Menge gemeinsam, nämlich den Sound und die Besetzung. Der Album-
gestalter Roy Kohara, eine wesentliche Säule von Capitol
Records in den 80er Jahren, erhielt 1980 einen Grammy für
seinen Entwurf für *Against the Wind* von Bob Seger. **◐**
Cet entourage progressiste de l'Ohio a beaucoup en commun (son et personnel) avec les pionniers du boogie de la
ville de Dayton, Zapp. Le graphiste de la pochette, Roy
Kohara, un pilier de Capitol Records dans les années 1980,
a reçu un prix Grammy en 1980 pour la conception de la
pochette de l'album *Against the Wind* de Bob Seger.

DEE DEE, BARRY
& THE MOVEMENTS

title **SOUL HOUR** / *year* **1968** / *label* MPS / *design* Heinz Bähr / *photography* P. G. Deker & Sammy R. Nuesch

German jazz imprint MPS (Musik Produktion Schwarzwald, or Black Forest Music Production) was heralded by the music community for providing superior fidelity, engaging cover art, and distinctive content. Detroit native Dee Dee McNeil, who would go on to join the Watts Prophets, trades vocal duties with Barry Window while the Movements execute a mixed bag of standards in funky fashion. ○
Den deutschen Jazzverlag MPS (Musik Produktion Schwarzwald) feierte man in der Musikgemeinde für seine

überdurchschnittliche Klangtreue, seine faszinierenden Cover und charakteristischen Inhalte. Dee Dee McNeil aus Detroit, der später zu den Watts Prophets wechseln sollte, kam mit Barry Window seinen gesanglichen Pflichten nach, während die Movements eine funkige und bunte Mischung an Standards ablieferten. ○
Dans la communauté de la musique, le label de jazz allemand MPS (Musik Produktion Schwarzwald, ou Production de musique de la Forêt-Noire) était considéré comme une source de haute fidélité, avec des pochettes intéressantes et un contenu original. Dee Dee McNeil, originaire de Detroit, qui allait bientôt rejoindre les Watts Prophets, donne de la voix avec Barry Window tandis que les Movements exécutent un florilège de standards à la sauce funky.

DEE FELICE TRIO
title **IN HEAT** / *year* **1969** / *label* Bethlehem /
art direction W. Hughes

Solarized and polarized to capacity, this Cincinnati trio
crafted poppy piano jazz in the vein of Ramsey Lewis.
Although Bethlehem Records had no shortage of inventive
album covers, thanks largely to legendary designer Burt
Goldblatt, little can be gleaned about the W. Hughes credited for designing this eccentric image. **O**
Solarisiert und polarisiert bis zum Anschlag, produziert
dieses Trio aus Cincinnati farbenprächtigen Piano-Jazz nach

Art von Ramsey Lewis. Obwohl es bei Bethlehem Records
dank des legendären Gestalters Burt Goldblatt keinen
Mangel an einfallsreichen Plattenhüllen gab, ist über
W. Hughes, der dieses exzentrische Bild gestaltet hat, wenig
herauszubekommen. **O**
Solarisé et polarisé à n'en plus pouvoir, ce trio de Cincinnati
concoctait du jazz piano pop dans la veine de Ramsey
Lewis. Bethlehem Records n'était pas à court de pochettes
d'album inventives, grâce au légendaire graphiste Burt
Goldblatt, mais l'on ne sait pas grand-chose de W. Hughes,
crédité pour la conception de cette image excentrique.

DELEGATION
title **EAU DE VIE** / *year* **1980** /
label Ariola / *design* Chuck Loyola
Hutton / *photography* Bruce
Hemming

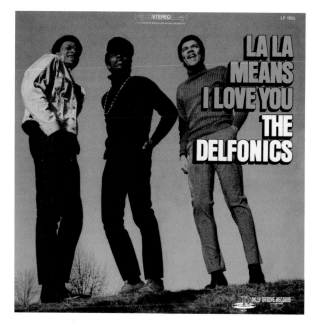

THE DELFONICS
title **LA LA MEANS I LOVE
YOU** / *year* **1968** / *label* Philly
Groove / *design* Forlenza Venosa
Assoc.

THE DELLS
title **THE MIGHTY MIGHTY DELLS** / *year* **1974** / *label* Chess / *art direction* Davis Fried Krieger & Ted Amber / *illustration* Alex Ebel

THE DELLS
title **THE DELLS** / *year* **1974** / *label* Cadet / *design* Hiroshi Yamashita / *art direction* Neil Terk

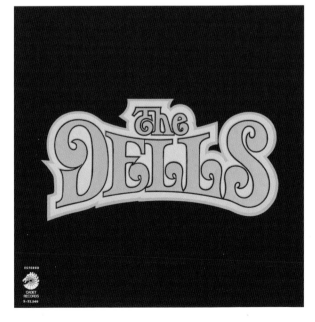

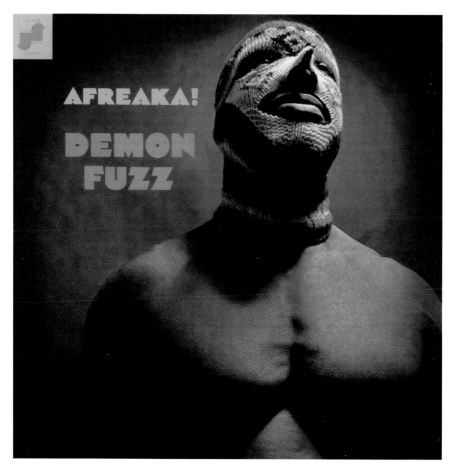

AFREAKA!
DEMON
FUZZ

DEMON FUZZ

title **AFREAKA!** / *year* **1970** / *label* Janus

Demon Fuzz helped pioneer London's burgeoning Afro Rock scene in the late '60s, giving momentum to a movement immortalized by the Equals, Cymande, and Osibisa. Although Demon Fuzz founder Paddy Corea couldn't recall the gentleman's name, the cover model was an actual wrestler, of Guyanese descent, living in Manchester at the time of the record's conception. **O**

Demon Fuzz leistete Pionierarbeit in der Ende der 60er Jahre in London aufkeimenden Afrorock-Szene und verlieh einer Bewegung Schwung, die von den Equals, Cymande und Osibisa unsterblich gemacht wurde. Paddy Corea, der Gründer von Demon Fuzz, konnte sich nicht an den Namen des Gentlemans auf dem Cover erinnern, es handelte sich jedenfalls um einen echten Wrestler, der aus Guyana stammte und damals in Manchester lebte. **O**

Demon Fuzz a contribué à l'émergence de la scène afro-rock à Londres à la fin des années 1960, en donnant de l'élan à un mouvement immortalisé par les Equals, Cymande et Osibisa. Paddy Corea, le fondateur de Demon Fuzz, n'est pas arrivé à se rappeler le nom de l'homme photographié pour la pochette, mais il s'agissait d'un véritable lutteur, d'origine guyanaise, qui vivait à Manchester à l'époque où le disque à été conçu.

GINO DENTIE AND THE FAMILY

title **DIRECT DISCO** / *year* **1976** / *label* Crystal Clear / *photography* Jon Kolesar

DEODATO

title **DEODATO 2** / *year* **1973** / *label* CTI / *design* Bob Ciano / *photography* Alen MacWeeney

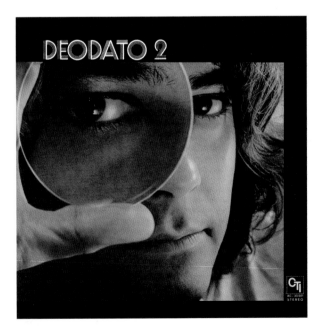

DETROIT EMERALDS

title **FEEL THE NEED** / *year* **1977** / *label* Westbound /
photography Joel Brodsky / *art direction* Bob Defrin

Another definitive Joel Brodsky creation, the female body is
used here creatively and to great effect, giving the album's
title literal meaning. It is perhaps no coincidence that the
hand pictured here has three rings, one for each member
of the Motor City trio. This album, particularly the title
track, introduced the Detroit Emeralds, and Westbound
Records as a whole, to the budding disco community. **O**
Eine andere unverkennbare Schöpfung von Joel Brodsky:
Hier werden die weiblichen Rundungen kreativ und höchst
wirkungsvoll eingesetzt, was dem Albumtitel eine buch-

stäbliche Bedeutung verleiht. Es ist wahrscheinlich kein
Zufall, dass die hier dargestellte Hand drei Ringe trägt: einen
für jedes Mitglied des Trios aus Motor City. Dieses Album
und vor allem sein Titelstück führten die Detroit Emeralds
und Westbound Records bei der gerade aufblühenden
Discogemeinde ein. **O**
Voici une autre création essentielle de Joel Brodsky. Ici, l'utilisation créative du corps féminin fonctionne à merveille
pour donner au titre de l'album son interprétation littérale.
Les trois bagues ne sont peut-être pas là par hasard, elles
pourraient représenter les trois membres du trio. Cet album, et particulièrement le morceau-titre, a présenté les
Detroit Emeralds et Westbound Records à la communauté
naissante du disco.

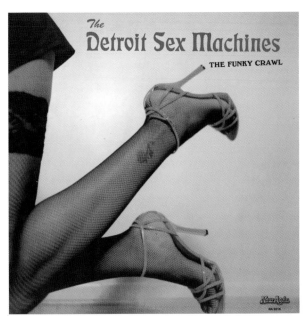

**THE DETROIT
SEX MACHINES**
title **THE FUNKY CRAWL** /
label Now-Again

**THE DETROIT
SPINNERS**
title **MIGHTY LOVE** / *year* **1974** /
label Atlantic / *design* Stanislaw
Zagorski / *illustration* Stanislaw
Zagorski

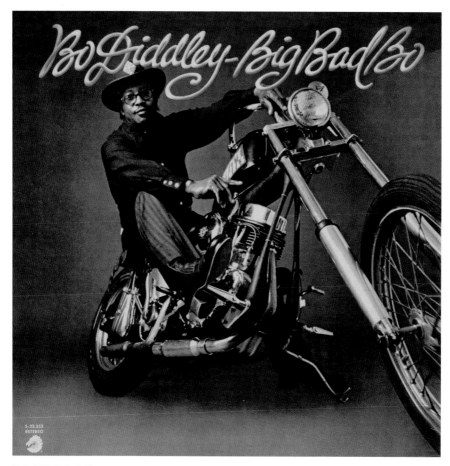

BO DIDDLEY

title **BIG BAD BO** / *year* **1974** / *label* Chess /
photography Hank Dunning / *art direction* Neil Terk

A graduate of the Philadelphia College of Art's industrial
design program, Neil Terk made his start with album cover
design. Although his client base quickly shifted from record
labels to international corporations, he maintained an
interest in industrial design. In 1985 he founded Terk
Technologies Corporation and began manufacturing
more powerful and attractive consumer antennas – the
first alternatives to rabbit ears. **O**
Neil Terk machte seinen Abschluss in Industriedesign am
Philadelphia College of Art, doch am Anfang seiner berufli-
chen Laufbahn stand die Gestaltung von Plattenhüllen.
Obwohl seine Kundenbasis bald von Musikverlagen zu

international tätigen Firmen wechselte, bewahrte er sein
Interesse an Industriedesign. 1985 gründete er die Terk
Technologies Corporation und begann mit der Produktion
von leistungsfähigeren und attraktiven Antennen (der
ersten Alternative zu den als »Rabbit Ears« bezeichneten
Dipol-Fernsehantennen). **O**
Diplômé du programme de design industriel du College of
Art de Philadelphie, Neil Terk a commencé sa carrière dans
la création de pochettes d'album. Son portefeuille de
clients a vite compté plus de multinationales que de labels
de disques, mais il a conservé un intérêt dans le design industriel. Il a fondé Terk Technologies Corporation en 1985
et a commencé à fabriquer des antennes tv plus puissantes
et plus esthétiques pour le grand public, les premières alternatives aux vieilles antennes à deux branches.

DISC·O·TECH

title **THE MAGIC DISCO MACHINE** / *year* **1975** / *label* Motown / *design* Brian Hagiwara/ Rod Dyer, Inc. / *photography* David Alexander / *art direction* Katarina Pettersson

BILL DOGGETT

title **HONKY TONK POPCORN** / *year* **1969** /
label Polydor/King / *design* Dan Quest Art Studio

Organist Bill Doggett was already an accomplished recording artist when he teamed up with James Brown's backing
band for this funky outing. The name "Honky Tonk Popcorn" is a composite of two popular songs by Doggett and
Brown, respectively, and is indicated subtly on the cover
by the color variation between the two individual titles
"Honky Tonk" and "Popcorn". **O**
Der Organist Bill Doggett war bereits ein vollendeter Stu-
diomusiker, als er sich für diese funkige Produktion mit der

Backing-Band von James Brown zusammentat. Im Namen
»Honky Tonk Popcorn« werden zwei populäre Songtitel
von Doggett bzw. Brown zusammengezogen. Darauf verweist auch ganz dezent die Farbvariation des Covers zwischen den beiden individuellen Titeln »Honky Tonk« und
»Popcorn«. **O**
L'organiste Bill Doggett était déjà un artiste de label accompli lorsqu'il fit équipe avec le groupe qui accompagnait
James Brown pour cette promenade funky. Le nom
« Honky Tonk Popcorn » est composé des titres de deux
morceaux populaires de Doggett et Brown respectivement,
ce qui est subtilement indiqué sur la pochette par la diffé-
rence de couleur entre « Honky Tonk » et « Popcorn ».

LOU DONALDSON

title **HOT DOG** / *year* **1969** / *label* Blue Note /
photography Frank Gauna / *art direction* Frank Gauna

Lou Donaldson took to the swinging Sixties sound like few
of his bop-era contemporaries. His alto sax seemed to
move from jazz to soul effortlessly, and *Hot Dog* is certainly
a high point for Lou and his funky sidemen. Frank Gauna, a
close friend of Andy Warhol, supplied the suggestively mod
art and design to lay the mustard on this tasty snack. **O**
Lou Donaldson fand Gefallen an den Swinging Sixties wie
nur wenige seiner Zeitgenossen der Bop-Ära. Sein Altsaxophon scheint mühelos vom Jazz zum Soul zu wechseln,

und *Hot Dog* war sicher ein Höhepunkt für Lou und seine
funkigen Mitstreiter. Frank Gauna, ein enger Freund von
Andy Warhol, lieferte die anregende Mod-Art und die
Gestaltung, damit dieser leckere Snack auch seinen Senf
bekam. **O**
Lou Donaldson aimait le son swing des années 1960
comme peu de ses contemporains de l'ère du bop. Son
saxo alto semblait passer du jazz à la soul sans le moindre
effort, et *Hot Dog* est sans aucun doute un sommet pour
Lou et ses comparses. C'est Frank Gauna, un ami intime
d'Andy Warhol, qui a fourni cette pochette mod suggestive
pour assaisonner cet en-cas savoureux avec un peu de
moutarde piquante.

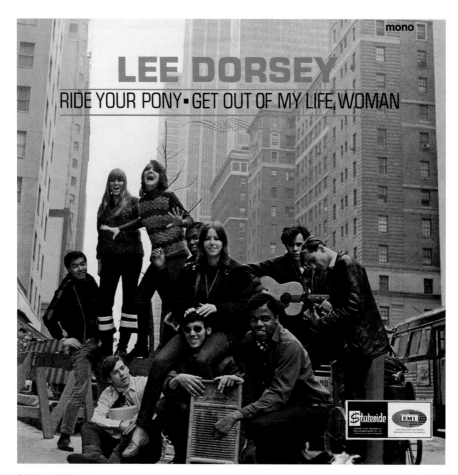

LEE DORSEY

title **RIDE YOUR PONY – GET OUT OF MY LIFE, WOMAN** / *year* **1966** / *label* Stateside / *design* Steven Craig / *photography* Steven Craig

Lee Dorsey's first album for the Amy label was loaded with soul. Bolstered by Allen Toussaint's writing and production and an unfaltering groove laid down by backing band The Meters, this is a perfect snapshot of early New Orleans funk. Steven Craig's cover shot of a multi-cultural gaggle of fresh-faced kids perfectly captured the energy of young America on the cusp of seeing civil rights laws enacted. **O**
Lee Dorseys erstes Album für das Label Amy war von Soul gesättigt. Es war ein perfekter Schnappschuss des frühen Funk aus New Orleans, verstärkt durch Songwriting und

Produktion von Allen Toussaint und einen unerschütter-lichen Groove, den die Backingband The Meters darunter-gelegt hat. Das Coverfoto von Steven Craig zeigt eine multikulturelle Schar milchbärtiger Kids und fängt das dynamische junge Amerika an der Schwelle zur Einlösung der Civil Rights perfekt ein. **O**
Le premier album de Lee Dorsey pour le label Amy était débordant de soul. Soutenu par l'écriture et la production d'Allen Toussaint, et par le groove assuré des Meters qui l'accompagnent, cet album est un polaroïd parfait de la première époque du funk de la Nouvelle-Orléans. Sur la pochette, la troupe multiculturelle de jeunes aux joues fraîches photographiée par Steven Craig traduisait parfaite-ment l'énergie d'une jeune Amérique sur le point de voir les droits civils devenir réalité.

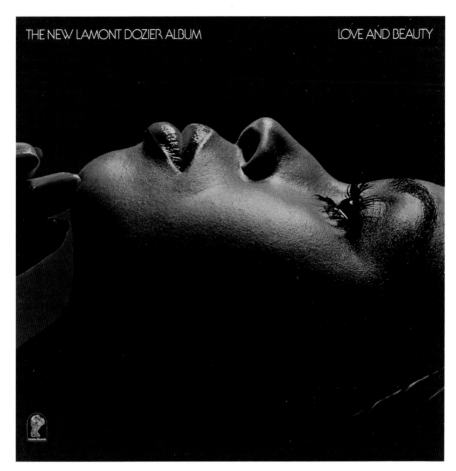

THE NEW LAMONT DOZIER ALBUM   LOVE AND BEAUTY

LAMONT DOZIER

title **LOVE AND BEAUTY** / *year* **1974** / *label* Invictus /
design Ed Lee & Gerard Huerta / *photography* Don
Hunstein

For Dozier's first solo album on his own label, designer Ed
Lee turned to veteran Don Hunstein to capture the strong,
regal beauty of the soulful Holland-Dozier-Holland sound.
Hunstein had been a house photographer for Columbia
Records since the late '50s, shooting iconic images of Miles
Davis, Johnny Cash, and Bob Dylan. **O**
Für Doziers erstes Soloalbum bei seinem eigenen Label
wandte sich der Designer Ed Lee an den Veteranen Don

Hunstein, um die kraftvolle, königliche Schönheit des souligen Sounds von Holland-Dozier-Holland einzufangen.
Hunstein war seit Ende der 50er Jahre Hausfotograf bei
Columbia Records und schuf symbolträchtige Bilder von
Miles Davis, Johnny Cash und Bob Dylan. **O**
Pour le premier album en solo de Dozier sur son propre
label, le graphiste Ed Lee s'est adressé au vétéran Don
Hunstein pour capturer la beauté puissante et noble de
la soul de Holland-Dozier-Holland. Hunstein avait été
photographe chez Columbia Records depuis la fin des
années 1950 et avait pris des clichés emblématiques de
Miles Davis, Johnny Cash et Bob Dylan.

DR. BUZZARD'S ORIGINAL
SAVANNAH BAND

title **DR. BUZZARD'S ORIGINAL SAVANNAH BAND
MEETS KING PENETT** / *year* **1978** / *label* RCA Victor /
design Franz Krauns / *illustration* Brian Zick

Formed in the Bronx, Dr. Buzzard's Original Savannah
Band's founder August Darnell romanticized the sophisticated sounds and styles of the '30s and '40s, incorporating
antique motifs into his group's modern blend of disco and
island rhythms. Cover artist Brian Zick entertained several
revisions of this final composition whilst accommodating
the uncompromising Darnell and his distinct vision. **O**
Obwohl Dr. Buzzard's Original Savannah Band in der Bronx
entstand, schwärmte deren Gründer August Darnell für die

ausgefeilten Sounds und Styles der 30er und 40er Jahre und
nahm auch antike Motive in seine moderne Mischung aus
Disco und Inselrhythmen auf. Der Coverkünstler Brian Zick
fertigte mehrere Überarbeitungen seiner finalen Komposition an, um dem kompromisslosen Darnell und seiner ganz
eigenen Vision Rechnung zu tragen. **O**
Bien que Dr. Buzzard's Original Savannah Band se soit
formé dans le Bronx, son leader, August Darnell, a donné
un caractère romantique aux sons et styles des années
1930 et 1940 en incorporant des motifs anciens au mélange
moderne de disco et de rythmes des îles de ce groupe.
L'auteur de la pochette, Brian Zick, a accepté de revoir
plusieurs fois sa copie jusqu'à arriver à cette composition
finale pour satisfaire la vision très personnelle et exigeante
de Darnell.

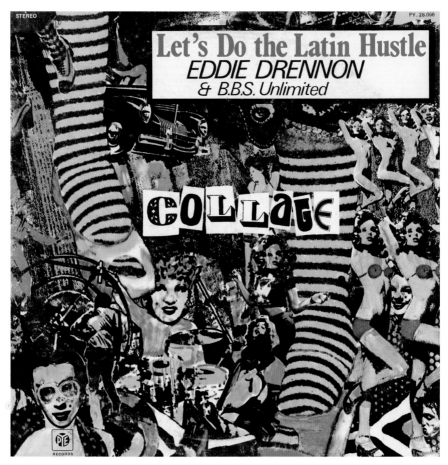

STEREO

PY. 28.066

Let's Do the Latin Hustle
EDDIE DRENNON
& B.B.S. Unlimited

COLLAGE

PYE RECORDS

EDDIE DRENNON
& B.B.S. UNLIMITED
title **LET'S DO THE LATIN HUSTLE** / *year* **1976** /
label Pye / *design* Larry Brill

A classically trained violinist, Eddie Drennon has recorded
and performed extensively within the realms of Latin, soul,
pop, and jazz. His natural knack for string arrangement is
illustrated on his own disco productions, including "Let's
Do the Latin Hustle", "Do What You Gotta Do", and Esther
Williams' often-sampled "Last Night Changed it All". ◗
Eddie Drennon war ein klassisch ausgebildeter Geigenspie-
ler und leistete innerhalb der Bereiche Latin, Soul, Pop und

Jazz eine Vielzahl an Aufnahmen und Auftritten ab. Seine
natürliche Gabe für Streicherarrangements wird auf seinen
eigenen Discoproduktionen deutlich, zu denen »Let's Do
the Latin Hustle«, »Do What You Gotta Do« und das
oft gesampelte »Last Night Changed it All« von Esther
Williams gehören. ◗
Violoniste de formation classique, Eddie Drennon a beaucoup enregistré et joué dans les domaines de la musique
latine, de la soul, de la pop et du jazz. Son talent naturel
pour les arrangements de cordes est illustré sur ses propres
productions de disco, notamment *Let's Do the Latin
Hustle*, *Do What You Gotta Do*, et *Last Night Changed it
All* d'Esther Williams, souvent samplé.

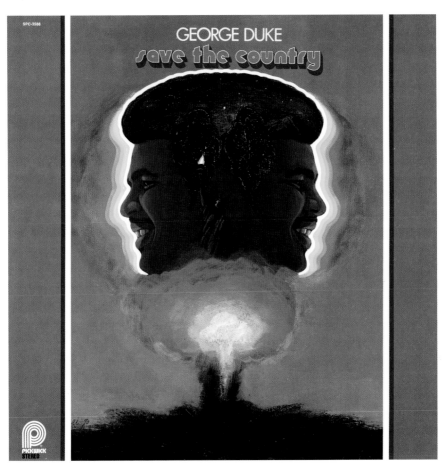

GEORGE DUKE

title **SAVE THE COUNTRY** / *year* **1978** / *label* Pickwick /
design Woody Woodward / *illustration* Mike Nakai

At the time of *Save The Country*'s conception, George
Duke was performing frequently with Frank Zappa, whose
adventurous influence saturates many of these funky
originals and pop interpolations. Soon after this record's
release, Duke would sign with German jazz foundry MPS,
leading to the most outrageous records of the accomplished keyboardist's career. **O**

Als das Konzept für *Save The Country* entwickelt wurde,
trat George Duke häufig mit Frank Zappa auf, dessen aben-

teuerlicher Einfluss viele dieser funkigen Originale und
Interpolierungen des Pop durchdringt. Bald nachdem diese
Platte herauskam, sollte Duke bei der deutschen MPS un-
terschreiben, was zu den abscheulichsten LPs in der ganzen
Karriere des versierten Keyboarders führte. **O**

À l'époque de la conception de *Save the Country*, George
Duke jouait souvent avec Frank Zappa, dont l'influence
audacieuse imprègne beaucoup des originaux funk et interpolations pop contenus dans ce disque. Peu après la sortie
de cet album, Duke allait signer avec le creuset du jazz
allemand MPS, ce qui allait mener à la création des disques
les plus extravagants de la carrière de ce claviériste
accompli.

GEORGE DUKE

title **MASTER OF THE GAME** / *year* **1979** /
label Epic / *design* David Fisher

This album found Duke assuming the role of producer in a greater capacity. As his band expanded, Duke began forfeiting vocal duties to a rising roster of new singers. *Master of the Game* was a pseudo-sequel to *Follow the Rainbow*; it featured the same musicians and yielded the same successful blend of danceable rhythms and jazz fundamentals. **○**

Dieses Album legt Zeugnis darüber ab, dass George Duke mehr und mehr die Produzentenrolle übernahm. Als sich seine Band vergrößerte, überließ Duke seine Sangespflichten einem emporkommenden Ensemble neuer Sänger. *Master of the Game* war ein Pseudo-Nachfolger von *Follow the Rainbow*: An diesem Album waren die gleichen Musiker beteiligt, und es bot den gleichen erfolgreichen Mix aus tanzbaren Rhythmen und Jazz-Grundlagen. **○**

Pour cet album, le rôle de producteur de Duke s'est étendu. Au fur et à mesure que son groupe grandissait, il a commencé à abandonner la partie vocale à une équipe montante de nouveaux chanteurs. *Master of the Game* était une sorte de suite donnée à *Follow the Rainbow*; on y retrouve les mêmes musiciens, ainsi que le même mélange très réussi de rythmes dansants et d'ingrédients essentiels du jazz.

GENE DUNLAP

title **PARTY IN ME** / *year* **1981** / *label* Capitol / *art direction* Roy Kohara & Peter Shea / *illustration* Robert Rodriguez

New Orleans native Robert Rodriguez honed his distinctive brand of whimsical realism for *Party In Me*, crafting a very literal interpretation of the album title. As a drummer, Gene Dunlap's sophisticated brand of modern R&B combined the songwriting of Kashif with the production prowess of Quincy Jones, rendering an ageless artifact in the genre of grown-folks music. **O**
Der aus New Orleans stammende Robert Rodriguez gab seiner charakteristischen Marke eines skurrilen Realismus

mit *Party In Me* den Feinschliff, wobei er eine sehr wörtliche Interpretation des Albumtitels schuf. Als Drummer kombinierte Gene Dunlap mit seiner ausgefeilten Spielart eines modernen R&B das Songwriting von Kashif mit dem Können von Quincy Jones als Produzent und erbrachte so ein zeitloses Artefakt von »Grown Folks Music«. **O**
Robert Rodriguez, natif de la Nouvelle-Orléans, a peaufiné son style très personnel de réalisme farfelu pour *Party In Me*, en donnant une interprétation très littérale du titre de l'album. Le style sophistiqué de R&B moderne du batteur Gene Dunlap combinait la composition de Kashif à la production surdouée de Quincy Jones, avec pour résultat un artefact intemporel dans les standards de la musique moderne.

DYNAMIC SUPERIORS

title **GIVE** & **TAKE** / *year* **1977** /
label Motown / *design* Snyder
Butler Company / *photography*
Howard Deshong / *art direction*
Carl Overr

DYSON'S FACES

title DYSON'S FACES /
year **1975** / *label* Dimitri
Music Company /
design Bobby Thornton

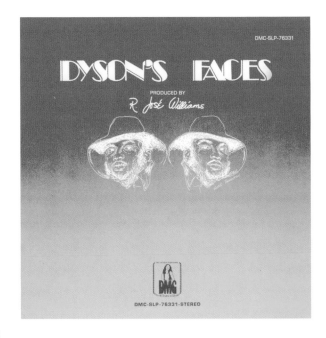

EARTH, WIND & FIRE

title **EARTH, WIND AND FIRE** / *year* **1971** /
label Warner Bros. / *art direction* Ed Thrasher /
illustration Russ Smith

During his industrious tenure at Warner Bros., Ed Thrasher pushed the boundaries of cover art, earning more than a dozen Grammy nominations for his impressive packaging. Here batik, an ancient art form in which ink-resistant wax is used to create colorful patterns and pictures, is utilized to make this organic rendering of the Chicago ensemble. ○

Während seiner sehr produktiven Zeit bei Warner Bros. trieb Ed Thrasher die Kunst der Covergestaltung zu neuen Höhen und wurde für seine beeindruckenden Plattenhül-

len mit über einem Dutzend Grammy-Nominierungen gewürdigt. Hier wird das Chicagoer Ensemble sehr organisch in Batik dargestellt. Bei dieser uralten Technik wird farbbeständiges Wachs verwendet, um farbenfrohe Muster und Bilder zu schaffen. ○

Ed Thrasher a bien employé son temps lorsqu'il était en fonction chez Warner Bros. Il a repoussé les limites artistiques des pochettes de disque et a récolté plus d'une douzaine de nominations aux prix Grammy pour ses réalisations remarquables. Ici, il utilise le batik, un art ancien qui consiste à créer des motifs et des images colorées à l'aide de cire résistante à l'encre, pour obtenir ce portrait organique du groupe de Chicago.

EARTH, WIND & FIRE

title **HEAD TO THE SKY** / *year* **1973** / *label* CBS

Earth, Wind & Fire was poised for commercial success
and this album foreshadowed the group's approaching
mainstream appeal. "Evil" and "Keep Your Head to the
Sky" struck perfect balances between the band's musical
mysticism and precise penchant for the funk. **O**
Earth, Wind & Fire standen an der Schwelle des kommer-
ziellen Erfolgs, und dieses Album ließ schon den nahenden
Mainstream-Erfolg der Gruppe erkennen. »Evil« und »Keep
Your Head to the Sky« schafften die perfekte Balance zwischen dem musikalischen Mystizismus der Band und ihrer
präzisen Vorliebe für Funk. **O**
Earth, Wind & Fire était en route pour le succès commercial, et cet album présageait de l'attrait que le groupe allait
exercer sur le grand public. *Evil* et *Keep Your Head to the Sky*
atteignent un équilibre parfait entre le mysticisme musical
du groupe et son penchant précis pour le funk.

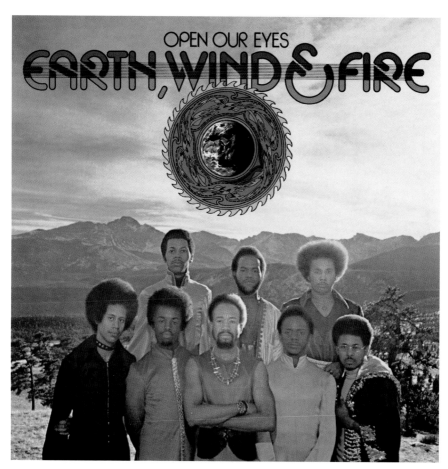

EARTH, WIND & FIRE

title **OPEN OUR EYES** / *year* **1974** / *label* CBS / *photography* Lee Lawrence

Recorded at Caribou Ranch in Nederland, Colorado, this record was given a cover by photographer Lee Lawrence, who chose the surrounding Rockies to provide a natural backdrop for what would become Earth, Wind & Fire's first gold record. Costume designer Martine Colette used much of the money she earned designing the group's lavish garments to construct a refuge for wild and exotic animals just outside of Los Angeles. **O**

Diese Aufnahme wurde auf der Caribou Ranch in Nederland, Colorado, aufgezeichnet. Sie erhielt ein Cover des Fotografen Lee Lawrence, der die umliegenden Rockies als natürliche Umgebung für das Coverfoto wählte. Diese LP

sollte später als erste der Platten von Earth, Wind & Fire vergoldet werden. Die Kostümdesignerin Martine Colette setzte viel von dem Geld ein, das sie durch die Gestaltung der verschwenderischen Kleidungsstücke der Gruppe verdiente, um direkt vor den Toren von Los Angeles ein Schutzgebiet für wild lebende und exotische Tiere aufzubauen. **O**

Enregistré dans les studios de Caribou Ranch à Nederland, dans le Colorado, ce disque a été illustré par le photographe Lee Lawrence, qui a choisi le paysage des montagnes Rocheuses pour donner une toile de fond naturelle à ce qui allait devenir le premier disque d'or d'Earth, Wind & Fire. La costumière Martine Colette a employé une bonne partie de l'argent qu'elle a gagné en créant les splendides tenues du groupe pour construire un refuge pour les animaux sauvages et exotiques en bordure de Los Angeles.

EARTH, WIND & FIRE

title **SPIRIT** / *year* **1976** / *label* CBS /
design Tom Steele / *photography* Ethan
Russell

EAST HARLEM BUS STOP

title **GET ON DOWN!** / *year* **1976** / *label* D&M Sound /
art direction Mick Wells / *illustration* C. Ellis

D&M Sound was one of the first labels to wholeheartedly
embrace disco music. Founders Dave Miller and Marty
Wilson committed their time and talents to bolster the
burgeoning movement, issuing innovative dance records in
an effort to change the unfavorable reputation that disco
earned from music critics. **O**
D&M Sound war eine der ersten Plattenfirmen, die sich
ernsthaft mit Disco-Musik befassten. Die Firmengründer

Dave Miller und Marty Wilson widmeten der aufkeimenden Bewegung Zeit und Talent. Sie veröffentlichten innovative Dance-Platten, um dem unvorteilhaften Ruf
entgegenzuwirken, in dem die Disco-Mucke bei Musik-
kritikern stand. **O**
D&M Sound a été l'un des premiers labels à s'ouvrir sans
réserve à la musique disco. Ses fondateurs Dave Miller et
Marty Wilson ont consacré leur temps et leur talent à sou-
tenir ce mouvement naissant, en faisant sortir des disques
de danse innovants pour contrer la réputation négative
que les critiques avaient donnée à ce genre.

CLEVELAND EATON & THE GARDEN OF EATON

title **KEEP LOVE ALIVE** / *year* **1979** /
label Ovation / *design* Jim Schubert/
AGI / *photography* John Alderson

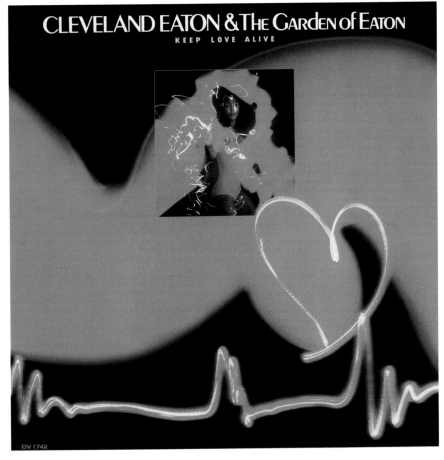

THE EMOTIONS

title **FLOWERS** / *year* **1976** / *label* Columbia / *design* Ron Coro & Tom Steele / *photography* Norman Seeff

Chicago's Hutchinson sisters started out recording soul records for Stax in the late '60s. With *Flowers* the group had moved to Columbia Records and began a successful transformation. Ron Coro and Tom Steele's graphic exuberance shines on this cover. They posterized Norman Seeff's shot of the singers and used an expressionistic splash of colors to emphasize the funky new direction the group was taking. **O**
Die Hutchinson-Schwestern aus Chicago starteten Ende der 60er Jahre ihre Soul-Aufnahmen für Stax. Für *Flowers* wechselte die Gruppe zu Columbia und begann ihre erfolgreiche Transformation. Die grafische Verspieltheit von Ron

Coro und Tom Steele bringt dieses Cover regelrecht zum Leuchten. Sie unterzogen Norman Seeffs Foto der Sängerinnen einer Tontrennung und arbeiteten mit expressionistischen Farbtupfern, um die neue Ausrichtung der Gruppe zum Funk zu betonen. **O**
Les sœurs Hutchinson, originaires de Chicago, ont commencé à enregistrer des disques de soul pour Stax à la fin des années 1960. Avec *Flowers*, le groupe était passé dans les rangs de Columbia et commençait une transformation très réussie. L'exubérance visuelle de Ron Coro et Tom Steele brille de tous ses feux sur cette pochette. Ils ont postérisé le cliché que Norman Seeff avait pris des chanteuses et l'ont agrémenté de grandes éclaboussures de couleurs pour souligner la nouvelle direction funk que le groupe était en train de prendre.

ENCHANTMENT

title **ENCHANTMENT** / *year* **1976** /
label United Artists / *photography*
Frank Kelleogy / *art direction* Michael
Mendel/Maurer Productions /
illustration Teresa Fasolino

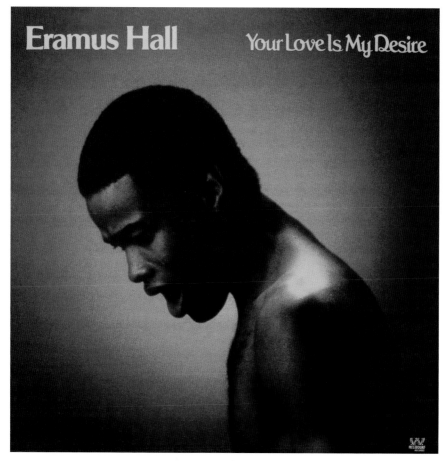

ERAMUS HALL

title **YOUR LOVE IS MY DESIRE** / *year* **1980** /
label Westbound

The masculine-sounding name and solitary male subject
on the cover might give listeners the impression that
Eramus Hall was a solo artist. Eramus Hall was, in fact, a
funk group from Chicago, signed to Westbound Records.
Although they could not replace former label-mates Funkadelic, who left the Detroit label in the mid-'70s, they did
bring a sophisticated, if more moderate brand of funk to
the legendary imprint. **O**

Der maskulin klingende Name und das vereinzelte männ-
liche Motiv auf dem Cover könnten den Hörern den Eindruck vermitteln, dass Erasmus Hall ein Solokünstler sei.
Weit gefehlt: Erasmus Hall war in Wirklichkeit eine Funk-

Truppe aus Chicago, bei Westbound Records unter Vertrag.
Obwohl sie Funkadelic als ehemalige Kollegen auf diesem
Label nicht ersetzen konnten, weil diese Mitte der 70er die
Detroiter Plattenfirma verlassen hatten, brachten sie eine
raffinierte, wenn nicht gar eher moderate Spielart von Funk
in diesen legendären Musikverlag. **O**

Le nom à consonance masculine et l'homme photographié
seul sur la pochette peuvent donner l'impression qu'Eramus Hall était un soliste. Mais en fait, Eramus Hall était
un groupe de funk originaire de Chicago, travaillant chez
Westbound Records. Bien qu'ils n'aient pas pu remplacer
leurs anciens collègues de Funkadelic, qui avaient quitté le
label de Detroit au milieu des années 1970, ils apportèrent
à cette marque légendaire un style de funk sophistiqué,
bien que plus modéré.

COKE ESCOVEDO

title **COMIN' AT YA!** / *year* **1976** / *label* Mercury /
design Desmond Strobel / *photography* David Alexander /
art direction John Kosh/AGI

As creative director for Apple Records, London native John
Kosh had a hand in several high-visibility designs, most
notably The Beatles' often-imitated *Abbey Road*. Despite
pioneering work in British and American rock markets, it
would be his design work with Linda Ronstadt that would
earn him each of his three Grammys. **○**
Als Kreativdirektor für Apple Records nahm der aus London stammende John Kosh auf zahlreiche Coverentwürfe

Einfluss, die praktisch zum visuellen Allgemeingut wurden,
darunter auch das oft imitierte Albumcover für *Abbey
Road* von den Beatles. Trotz seiner Pionierarbeit auf dem
britischen und amerikanischen Rockmarkt sollten es die
Coverentwürfe für Linda Ronstadt sein, die ihm seine drei
Grammys einbrachten. **○**
Le Londonien John Kosh a participé à plusieurs pochettes
très célèbres lorsqu'il était directeur de la création chez
Apple Records, notamment pour *Abbey Road* des Beatles,
qui a souvent été imitée. Malgré son travail pionnier sur
les marchés britannique et américain du rock, ce sont ses
graphismes réalisés avec Linda Ronstadt qui allaient lui va-
loir chacun de ses trois prix Grammy.

RICHARD EVANS

title **RICHARD EVANS** / *year* **1979** / *label* Horizon /
design Junie Osaki & Lynn Robb / *photography* Dean
Tokuno / *art direction* Roland Young

From the smeared lipstick-looking signature by designers
Junie Osaki and Lynn Robb to the abstract figurative photo
by Dean Tokuno this cover screams New Wave Funk. Bassist Richard Evans was often busy helping further the creative
output of others as a producer and arranger. This was his
second LP as leader and it is full of hard jazz-tinged funk. **O**
Von der verschmierten Signatur mit Lippenstiftästhetik der
Gestalter Junie Osaki und Lynn Robb bis hin zum abstrakt-

figurativen Foto von Dean Tokuno trieft dieses Cover förm-
lich vor New Wave Funk. Der Bassist Richard Evans hat sich
viel damit beschäftigt, als Produzent und Arrangeur den
kreativen Output anderer Musiker voranzutreiben. Für ihn
als Bandleader war dies die zweite LP voll mit hartem, jazz-
gefärbtem Funk. **O**
De la signature des graphistes Junie Osaki et Lynn Robb, qui
semble écrite au rouge à lèvres, à la photo figurative abstraite
de Dean Tokuno, cette pochette sent le funk new wave à
plein nez. Le bassiste Richard Evans aidait souvent d'autres
musiciens à peaufiner leur travail en officiant comme producteur ou arrangeur. Cet album était son deuxième en tant
que leader, et il regorge de funk brut teinté de jazz.

BRC 77006

STRAIGHT UP
EXIT 9

EXIT 9

title **STRAIGHT UP** / *year* **1975** / *label* Brunswick

In the mid-'70s, Brunswick Records' Alonzo Tucker was scouring the country, searching tirelessly for new, untapped talent. His efforts resulted in a geographically and stylistically scattered assortment of funky recordings. This singular release by Exit 9 is no exception. Like early offerings from Crown Heights Affair and Bohannon, Exit 9 was able to concoct danceable music without incorporating the constricting elements of disco. **O**

Mitte der 70er Jahre streifte Alonzo Tucker von Brunswick Records auf der unermüdlichen Suche nach neuen, unerschlossenen Talenten durchs Land. Diese Mühen führten zu einer geografisch und stilistisch sehr zerstreuten An-

sammlung von Funk-Aufnahmen. Die einzelne Veröffentlichung von Exit 9 bildet da keine Ausnahme. Wie Crown Heights Affair und Bohannon mit ihren frühen Werken konnte auch Exit 9 tanzbare Musik ohne die einschränkenden Elemente von Disco ausbrüten. **O**

Au milieu des années 1970, Alonzo Tucker, de Brunswick Records, battait le pays dans une recherche inlassable de nouveaux talents inexploités. Ses efforts ont produit un assortiment d'enregistrements de funk très hétéroclites en termes géographiques et stylistiques.. Cet album singulier d'Exit 9 en est un bon exemple. À l'instar des premières productions de Crown Heights Affair et Bohannon, Exit 9 savait concocter de la musique de danse sans avoir recours aux éléments contraignants du disco.

EXPERIENCE UNLIMITED

title **EXPERIENCE UNLIMITED** / *year* **1977** /
label Black Fire / *illustration* Malik Edward

Artist Malik Edward received the bulk of his formal training in the Marine Corps where he illustrated manuals, posters, and assorted materials for the Armed Forces. He spent the '70s and '80s freelancing in Washington, D.C., where he no doubt met up with go-go luminaries Experience Unlimited, contributing this mystical composition to E.U.'s self-titled debut. **O**

Der Künstler Malik Edward erhielt den Großteil seiner formalen Ausbildung im Marine Corps, wo er Handbücher, Plakate und verschiedene andere Arbeitsunterlagen des Militärs illustrierte. Er verbrachte die 70er und 80er Jahre als Freiberufler in Washington, D.C., wo er zweifellos die Go-go-Gestirne Experience Unlimited traf und dann für das Debüt gleichen Namens diese mystische Komposition beisteuerte. **O**

La majeure partie de la formation officielle de l'artiste Malik Edward s'est déroulée chez les marines, où il illustrait des manuels, des affiches et toutes sortes de documents pour l'armée. Il a passé les années 1970 et 1980 à travailler en freelance à Washington, D.C., où il a sans aucun doute rencontré les as du go-go, Experience Unlimited, et leur a donné cette composition mystique pour leur premier album éponyme.

F.B.I.

title **F.B.I.** / *year* **1976** / *label* Good Earth / *design* Roger Lowe / *photography* Josef Cross & Masakazu Sakomizu

Perhaps a British response to Earth, Wind & Fire, F.B.I. recorded their lone album for Good Earth Records in 1976. Whether it was photographer Masakazu Sakomizu or designer Roger Lowe who coordinated this ocular portrait, they were certainly making the most of the existing design technology available in the late '70s. **O**
Vielleicht als Reaktion auf Earth, Wind & Fire nahmen F.B.I. ihr einziges Album 1976 für Good Earth Records auf. Es ist

nicht bekannt, ob der Fotograf Masakazu Sakomizu oder der Designer Roger Lowe dieses okulare Porträt koordinierte, aber sicherlich haben sie die existierende Technologie ausgereizt, die Ende der 70er Jahre verfügbar war. **O**
F.B.I., qui était peut-être la réponse britannique à Earth, Wind & Fire, a enregistré son unique album chez Good Earth Records en 1976. Que ce soit le photographe Masakazu Sakomizu ou le graphiste Roger Lowe qui s'est chargé de concevoir ce portrait oculaire, il a sans aucun doute tiré le meilleur parti des technologies disponibles en matière de graphisme à la fin des années 1970.

THE FABULOUS COUNTS

title **JAN JAN** / *year* **1969** / *label* Cotillion /
design Haig Adishian / *photography* Ted Robinson

From the marquee-lights style typography to the uniform green suits this cover screams typical session band, which couldn't have been further from the truth. And placing them in wooded surroundings comes in direct contrast with the gritty Detroit funk sound that these cats were laying down. Although they began with this record as primarily an instrumental group, they would soon transform to a full-on funk machine when they dropped the "Fabulous" and signed to the Westbound label. ◗

Wegen dieses Covers springt einen der Gedanke »typische Sessionband« geradezu an, was aber trotz der Typografie im Markisenstil und der uniformen grünen Anzüge nicht weiter von der Wahrheit entfernt sein könnte. Dass sie auch noch vor eine waldige Umgebung gestellt werden, setzt den direkten Kontrast zum grobkörnigen Detroiter Funksound dieser Grafen. Schon bald begann die Transformation zur kompletten Funk-Maschine, als sie das »Fabulous« kippten und bei Westbound ihren Vertrag unterschrieben. ◗

Depuis la typographie qui imite les enseignes de music-hall jusqu'aux uniformes verts, cette pochette indique clairement qu'il s'agit d'une session d'enregistrement en groupe typique, et pourtant il n'en est rien. Elle les place plus dans un décor boisé, ce qui est en opposition directe avec le funk abrasif de ces gars de Detroit. Ils se sont vite transformés en machine à funk pleine puissance lorsqu'ils ont enlevé « Fabulous » de leur nom et ont signé avec le label Westbound.

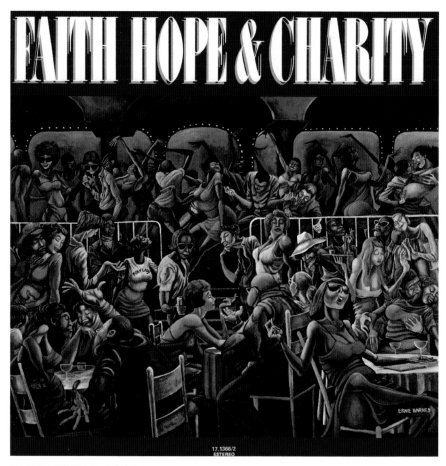

FAITH HOPE & CHARITY

title **FAITH HOPE** & **CHARITY** / *year* **1978** / *label* 20th
Century Fox / *design* J. Daniel Chapman / *art direction* Joey
Reynolds / *illustration* Ernie Barnes

Cover artist, and former football player, Ernie Barnes is best
known for his painting *Sugar Shack*, featured prominently
on the cover of Marvin Gaye's 1976 album *I Want You*. The
painting also graced the set of the American sitcom *Good
Times*, in which it, along with several other Barnes pieces,
was attributed to aspiring artist James Evans, Jr., famously
portrayed by actor Jimmie Walker. ○
Der Coverkünstler und ehemalige Footballspieler Ernie
Barnes wurde in erster Linie für sein Gemälde *Sugar Shack*

bekannt, das das Cover von Marvin Gayes Album *I Want
You* von 1976 ziert. Das Gemälde schmückte auch den Set
der amerikanischen Fernsehkomödie *Good Times*, in der
es neben anderen Werken von Barnes dem aufstrebenden
Künstler James Evans Jr. zugeschrieben wurde, hervorragend
porträtiert durch den Schauspieler Jimmie Walker. ○
L'illustrateur de pochette et ancien joueur de football Ernie
Barnes est plus connu pour son tableau *Sugar Shack* qui
orne l'album *I Want You* de Marvin Gaye. Le même tableau
a également décoré le plateau de la sitcom américaine
Good Times, dans laquelle plusieurs autres œuvres de
Barnes étaient attribuées à l'artiste en herbe James Evans Jr.,
joué par Jimmie Walker.

FANTASTIC FOUR

GOT TO HAVE YOUR LOVE

FANTASTIC FOUR

title **GOT TO HAVE YOUR LOVE** / *year* **1977** / *label* Atlantic / *photography* Jim Houghton / *art direction* Abie Sussman & Bob Defrin

Bob Defrin held several positions within Atlantic's creative department, executing or orchestrating design for a broad range of acts. Although Detroit's Fantastic Four were signed to hometown funk foundry Westbound Records, a distribution deal with Atlantic granted the talented quartet access to major-label resources without having to sacrifice creative freedom. **O**

Bob Defrin hatte in der Kreativabteilung von Atlantic verschiedene Positionen inne und gestaltete selbst oder koordinierte die Gestaltung für eine große Bandbreite von

Künstlern. Obwohl die Detroiter Fantastic Four bei der Funk-Schmiede Westbound Records in der gleichen Stadt unter Vertrag standen, wurde dem talentierten Quartett durch einen Deal des Vertriebs mit Atlantic der Zugang zu den Ressourcen des großen Plattenverlags möglich, ohne dass die vier kreative Freiheiten hätten opfern müssen. **O**

Bob Defrin a occupé plusieurs postes au sein du service de la création chez Atlantic, réalisant ou orchestrant le graphisme pour de nombreux artistes très différents. Les Fantastic Four, originaires de Detroit, avaient un contrat avec le creuset du funk de leur ville, Westbound Records, mais un accord de distribution passé avec Atlantic a donné à ce quartette talentueux l'accès à des ressources dignes d'une grande maison de disques, sans pour autant sacrifier leur liberté créative.

THE FATBACK BAND

title **HOT BOX** / *year* **1980** / *label* Spring /
design Dan Sneberger / *art direction* Bob Helmall

Possessing a range of meanings, from a way of ingesting drugs to sexual innuendo, the ambiguous colloquialism in the title is given a more favorable meaning by illustrator Dan Sneberger, by airbrushing this luminous portable radio. No stranger to double entendre, Fatback's successful single "Backstrokin'" is a suggestive charade that remains barely presentable to this day. **O**
In dem Titel stecken mehrere mögliche Bedeutungsebenen (von einer Variante des Drogenkonsums bis zu sexuellen

Anzüglichkeiten), doch die umgangssprachliche Mehrdeutigkeit interpretiert der Illustrator Dan Sneberger gefälliger, indem er ein leuchtend rotes Kofferradio in Airbrush-Technik abbildet. Zweideutigkeiten waren Fatback nicht fremd, und ihre erfolgreiche Single »Backstrokin'« ist eine suggestive Charade, die bis zum heutigen Tage kaum präsentabel ist. **O**
Le titre de cet album peut signifier plusieurs choses très différentes, par exemple une façon de se droguer, ou une insinuation sexuelle. L'illustrateur Dan Sneberger lui donne ici un sens plus innocent en peignant à l'aérographe cette radio portable éclatante. Fatback est un habitué des doubles sens, et son tube *Backstrokin'* est une devinette suggestive qui reste à peine présentable aujourd'hui.

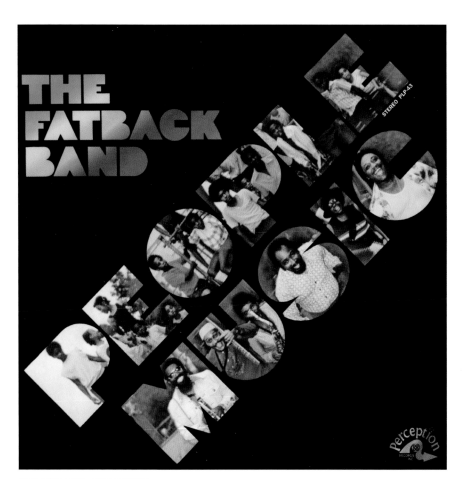

THE FATBACK BAND

title **PEOPLE MUSIC** / *year* **1973** / *label* Perception /
photography Reginald Wickham / *art direction* Fred Stark

A step up from their debut, this sophomore disc seized on
leader/drummer Bill Curtis and the band's party sound
perfectly. Fred Stark's playful use of type, placing the group's
portraits by photographer Reginald Wickham within the
album title, effectively captures their street music vibe. **O**
Bei seiner zweiten Scheibe legte der Bandleader und Drummer Bill Curtis mit seiner Band beim Partysound – verglichen mit dem Debüt – noch ordentlich nach. Fred Stark

fing durch seinen verspielten Umgang mit der Schrift die
Street-Music-Stimmung sehr gut ein: Er verwendete die
vom Fotografen Reginald Wickham aufgenommenen Porträts und integrierte sie in den Schriftzug des Albumtitels. **O**
Un degré au-dessus de leur premier album, ce deuxième
disque saisit parfaitement le son festif du leader / batteur
Bill Curtis et de son groupe. Fred Stark joue avec la typographie en plaçant les portraits de groupe réalisés par le
photographe Reginald Wickham dans les lettres du titre de
l'album et réussit à transmettre l'atmosphère urbaine de sa
musique.

FAZE-O

title **GOOD THANG** / *year* **1978** / *label* She / *photography* Joel Brodsky

This photograph is only slightly sensual when compared to the unabashed eroticism of the seven-part series that photographer Joel Brodsky conceptualized for the Ohio Players. All selections on *Good Thang* were arranged by the Players, so it's not unlikely that the Ohio ensemble played a part in enlisting Brodsky's services for this album from Faze-O. ○ Dieses Foto ist nur entfernt sinnlich, wenn man es mit der ungenierten Erotik der siebenteiligen Serie des Fotografen

Joel Brodsky vergleicht, die er für die Ohio Players entwarf. Alle Stücke auf *Good Thang* wurden von den Players arrangiert. Von daher ist es nicht unwahrscheinlich, dass das Ohio-Ensemble seinen Teil dazu beitrug, dass Brodsky den Auftrag für dieses Album von Faze-O bekam. ○ La sensualité de cette photographie est bien pâle comparée à l'érotisme sans voile de la série de sept pochettes que le photographe Joel Brodsky a conçue pour les Ohio Players. Ces derniers ont arrangé toutes les sélections sur *Good Thang*, on peut donc supposer qu'ils ont eu quelque chose à voir dans le choix de Brodsky pour réaliser la pochette de cet album de Faze-O.

FAZE-O
title **BREAKIN' THE FUNK** /
year **1979** / *label* She

RICHARD "DIMPLES" FIELDS
title **DIMPLES** / *year* **1981** / *label*
Boardwalk / *design* Jeffery Fey/
Art Hotel / *photography* Norman
Seeff / *cover concept* Joyce Bogart

FIRST CHOICE

title **HOLD YOUR HORSES** / *year* **1979** /
label Gold Mind / *photography* Michael Tighe

It's hard to tell that a Michael Tighe photograph lies beneath the abundant airbrushing and retouching featured on First Choice's *Hold Your Horses*. Tighe, who is best known for his sharp and shadowy celebrity portraits, rarely even shoots in color, making the exaggerated hues of this group portrait seem all the more unusual. **○**
Es ist dem Cover von First Choice für *Hold Your Horses* kaum anzumerken, dass ihm ein Foto von Michael Tighe

zugrunde liegt, das mehrfach mit Airbrushing und Retusche überarbeitet wurde. Tighe ist bekannt für seine spitzen und schattenhaften Porträts von Prominenten und hat nur selten in Farbe fotografiert. Insofern erscheinen die aufgebauschten Farbnuancen dieses Gruppenporträts noch ungewöhnlicher. **○**
Sur la pochette de cet album de First Choice, on a du mal à reconnaître la photographie de Michael Tighe sous les abondantes retouches. Tighe, qui est plus connu pour ses portraits de célébrités nets et remplis d'ombre, travaille rarement en couleur, ce qui rend les coloris exagérés de ce portrait de groupe encore plus inhabituels.

FIRST CHOICE

title **DELUSIONS** / *year* **1977** / *label*
Gold Mind / *design* Lori L. Lambert /
photography William Douglas King /
art direction Stanley Hochstadt

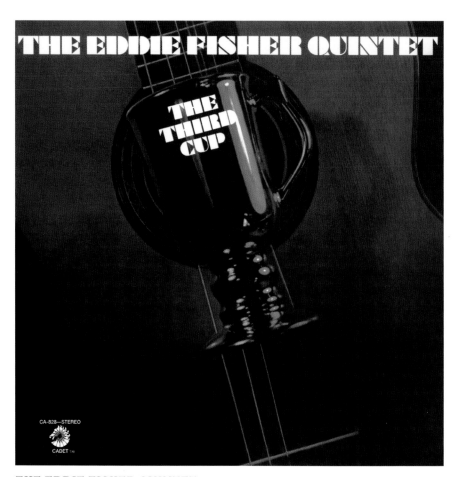

THE EDDIE FISHER QUINTET

title **THE THIRD CUP** / *year* **1969** / *label* Cadet / *design* Jerry Griffith / *photography* Jerry Griffith

The debut from Eddie Fisher, a jazz guitarist out of St Louis, was a sophisticated workout that prefigured the kind of smooth jazz funk that would come out on the CTI label a few years later. Chicago designer/photographer Jerry Griffith would often use the artists' chosen instrument as a design element for their covers. ⚫

Das Debüt des aus St. Louis stammenden Jazzgitarristen Eddie Fisher war eine raffinierte Arbeit, die schon jene Art von sanftem Jazz-Funk andeutete, die ein paar Jahre später auf dem Label CTI erscheinen sollte. Der Designer und Fotograf Jerry Griffith (Chicago) nutzte oft das Instrument des Musikers als Gestaltungselement für seine Coverentwürfe. ⚫

Les débuts d'Eddie Fisher, un guitariste de jazz de Saint-Louis, étaient un exercice sophistiqué qui préfigurait le style de smooth jazz que l'on allait trouver chez le label CTI quelques années plus tard. Le graphiste / photographe de Chicago Jerry Griffith a souvent utilisé les instruments de prédilection des artistes dans la composition visuelle de leurs pochettes.

FOUR TOPS NOW!

THE KEY
WHAT IS A MAN
MY PAST JUST CROSSED MY FUTURE
DON'T LET HIM TAKE YOUR LOVE FROM ME
ELEANOR RIGBY
LITTLE GREEN APPLES
DO WHAT YOU GOTTA DO
MAC ARTHUR PARK
DON'T BRING BACK MEMORIES
WISH I DIDN'T LOVE YOU SO
OPPORTUNITY KNOCK (FOR ME)
THE FOOL ON THE HILL

FOUR TOPS

title **FOUR TOPS NOW!** / *year* **1969** /
label Tamla Motown

Shown here just five years into their Motown career, the
Four Tops' dependable roster would remain unchanged for
decades to come. Not until tenor Lawrence Payton's 1997
passing would the combo have to seek new talent. Perhaps
equally as impressive, lead vocalist Levi Stubbs would never
pursue a solo career, defying another paradigm of vocal-
quartet culture. ◐

Als dieses Bild entstand, bewegten sich die Four Tops bei
Motown schon fünf Jahre auf der Karriereleiter, und auch
in den folgenden Jahrzehnten sollte sich ihre verlässliche

Gruppierung nicht ändern. Erst als 1997 der Tenor Lawrence Payton starb, musste sich die Combo auf die Suche
nach neuen Talenten machen. Vielleicht ist es ebenso ein-
drucksvoll, dass der Leadsänger Levi Stubbs nie eine Solokarriere einschlagen sollte, was einem weiteren Paradigma
der Kultur der Vokalquartette widerspricht. ◐

Représentés ici cinq ans après le début de leur carrière chez
Motown, la composition des membres des Four Tops allait
rester inchangée pendant des décennies. Ce n'est qu'après
le décès du ténor Lawrence Payton en 1997 que la formation allait chercher de nouveaux talents. Le chanteur principal Levi Stubbs n'a jamais cherché à faire carrière en solo,
autre exception remarquable à la règle que l'on peut obser-
ver dans les quartettes de chant.

ARETHA FRANKLIN
title **YOUNG, GIFTED AND BLACK** / *year* **1972** /
label Atlantic / *design* Stanislaw Zagorski & Alyse Koylan /
photography Ken Cunningham

Just months shy of her 30th birthday, Aretha Franklin released *Young, Gifted and Black*, perhaps her most highly
acclaimed studio effort of the '70s. The photograph was
taken by former flame Ken Cunningham, with whom the
singer had one son, Kecalf, whose name is a product of his
parents' sequential initials. ○
Nur wenige Monate vor Aretha Franklins 30. Geburtstag
erschien *Young, Gifted and Black*, vielleicht ihre beliebteste

Studioaufnahme aus den 70er Jahren. Das Foto wurde
von ihrer früheren Flamme Ken Cunningham geschossen,
mit dem die Sängerin einen Sohn namens Kecalf hat.
Dieser Name setzt sich aus den Initialen seiner Eltern
zusammen. ○
Quelques mois avant son trentième anniversaire, Aretha
Franklin a sorti *Young, Gifted and Black*, qui est sans doute
son album en studio le plus acclamé des années 1970.
La photographie a été prise par son ancien petit ami Ken
Cunningham, avec qui la chanteuse avait eu un enfant,
Kecalf, dont le nom est une combinaison des initiales de
ses parents.

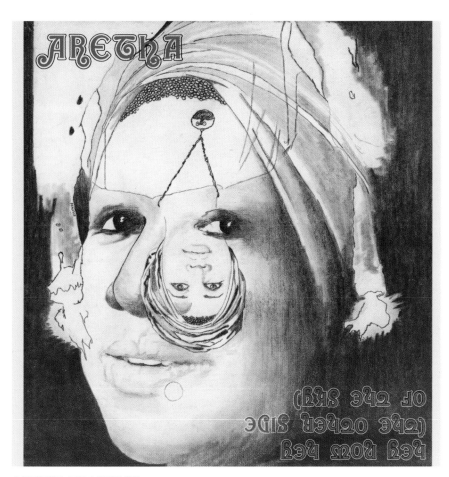

ARETHA FRANKLIN
title **HEY NOW HEY (THE OTHER SIDE OF THE SKY)** / *year* **1973** / *label* Atlantic / *design* Aretha Franklin, Ken Cunningham & Jim Dunn

Heralded for showcasing Franklin's versatility, *Hey Now Hey*'s cover art is ironically one aspect of this album that did not receive rave reviews. Aretha's biographer, Mark Bego, declared that Jim Dunn's superimposed pencil sketches "looked like an entry in a junior high school art contest". The gatefold features caricatures of Aretha, with wings, and producer Quincy Jones sleeping in a set of passing clouds. **O**
Hey Now Hey wurde als Beispiel für Aretha Franklins Vielseitigkeit gepriesen, doch das Cover ist ironischerweise ein Aspekt dieses Albums, der keinen sonderlichen Anklang

fand. Arethas Biograf Mark Bego erklärte, dass die einander überlagernden Bleistiftzeichnungen »aussehen wie etwas, das man bei einem Kunstwettbewerb in der Schule einreicht«. Auf der Innenhülle sind Karikaturen von Aretha mit Flügeln zu sehen – und wie der Produzent Quincy Jones in einem Wolkenbett schläft. **O**
Censé annoncer la polyvalence des talents de Franklin, le dessin qui orne la pochette de *Hey Now Hey* est malheureusement, et c'est bien l'ironie de la chose, le seul aspect de cet album qui n'ait pas reçu de critiques dithyrambiques. Selon le biographe d'Aretha, Mark Bego, les esquisses au crayon superposées de Jim Dunn « ressemblaient à ce qu'un lycéen aurait pu envoyer au concours de dessin de son école ». À l'intérieur de la pochette, on trouve des caricatures d'Aretha, avec des ailes, et le producteur Quincy Jones dormant sur des nuages.

CAROLYN FRANKLIN
title **BABY DYNAMITE!** / *year* **1969** / *label* RCA Victor

As the youngest sister of singing sensation Aretha Franklin, Carolyn was poised for greatness. Accompanied by eldest sister Erma, the Franklin sisters would provide perfect harmony for Aretha on a number of releases, with Carolyn even writing a number of hits for the middle sister, including "Ain't No Way", and "Angel". ⊙

Als jüngste Schwester der Gesangssensation Aretha Franklin war Carolyn schon darauf vorbereitet, berühmt zu werden.

Begleitet von der ältesten Schwester Erma sollten die Franklin-Schwestern für Aretha auf einer Reihe von Alben ihre perfekten Harmonien liefern, und Carolyn schrieb sogar ein paar Hits für die mittlere Schwester, darunter »Ain't No Way« und »Angel«. ⊙

Carolyn, la petite sœur du phénomène de la chanson, Aretha Franklin, était destinée à la grandeur. Avec sa sœur aînée Erma, elle allait assurer un accompagnement parfait pour Aretha sur plusieurs albums et allait même lui écrire plusieurs succès, notamment *Ain't No Way* et *Angel*.

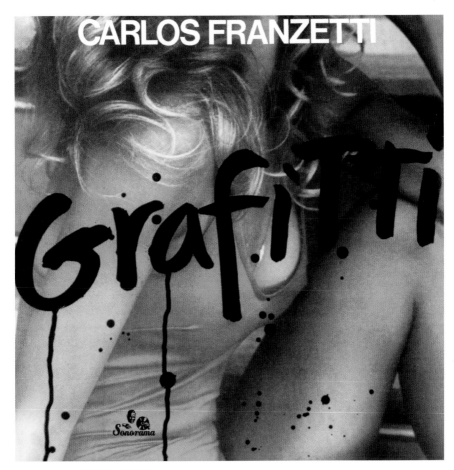

CARLOS FRANZETTI

title **GRAFITTI** / *year* **1977** / *label* Sonorama

Argentinean pianist Carlos Franzetti began his musical education at the age of six, receiving instruction at the National Conservatory in his native Buenos Aires. After briefly studying piano and composition in Mexico, he relocated to New York City, where his formal education would be polished at the prestigious Juilliard School. ❍
Der argentinische Pianist Carlos Franzetti begann mit seiner musikalischen Ausbildung im Alter von sechs Jahren und

besuchte dafür das Staatliche Konservatorium seiner Heimatstadt Buenos Aires. Nachdem er kurze Zeit Klavier und Komposition in Mexiko studiert hatte, zog er nach New York City um, wo er seine formelle Ausbildung an der renommierten Juilliard School vollendete. ❍
Le pianiste argentin Carlos Franzetti a commencé à étudier la musique à l'âge de six ans, au conservatoire national de sa ville natale, Buenos Aires. Après avoir brièvement étudié le piano et la composition à Mexico, il a déménagé à New York, où son éducation formelle allait être parfaite à la prestigieuse Juilliard School.

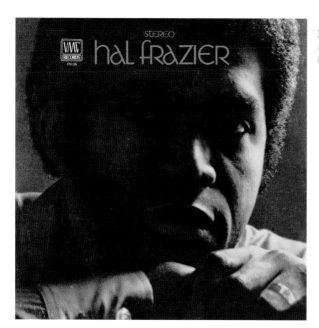

HAL FRAZIER
title **HAL FRAZIER** / *year* **1968** /
label Vance Music Corp.

GEORGE FREEMAN
title **MAN** & **WOMAN** / *year*
1974 / *label* Groove Merchant /
design David Lartaud / *photography*
Manuel Gonzales / *art direction*
Frank Daniel

THE FRIENDS OF DISTINCTION

title **REAL FRIENDS** / *year* **1970** / *label* RCA Victor /
design Frank Mulvey / *illustration* Dave Wilcox

Although the bulk of his work was done with Motown,
widely varied cover concepts by Frank Mulvey can be
found on albums by artists ranging from Jimmy Castor to
Jimmy Buffett. Here, an imaginative, if not exaggerated
portrait by Dave Wilcox graces the cover of this RCA
release, one of the last successful records for this feel-good
quartet. **O**
Frank Mulvey hat zwar größtenteils für Motown gearbeitet,
es finden sich unter seinen Arbeiten aber auch sehr vielsei-

tige Coverkonzepte für Alben von Künstlern, die von
Jimmy Castor bis Jimmy Buffett reichen. Hier ziert ein fan-
tasievolles, wenn nicht gar übertriebenes Porträt von Dave
Wilcox das Cover dieses RCA-Albums, eine der letzten
erfolgreichen Scheiben dieses Wohlfühlquartetts. **O**
Bien que Frank Mulvey ait principalement travaillé avec
Motown, on peut aussi trouver ses concepts de pochette
très variés sur les albums d'artistes allant de Jimmy Castor à
Jimmy Buffett. Ici, Dave Wilcox signe un portrait imaginatif
mais assez réaliste pour la pochette de cet album sorti chez
RCA, l'un des derniers disques à succès de ce quartette
ennemi de la mauvaise humeur.

FUNK, INC.

title **HANGIN' OUT** / *year* **1973** /
label Prestige / *design* Phil Carroll /
photography Tony Lane / *art direction*
Tony Lane

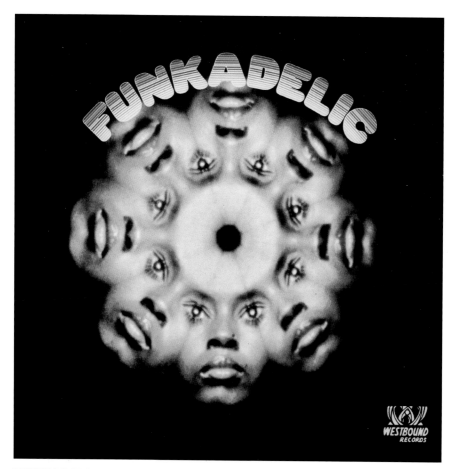

WESTBOUND
RECORDS

FUNKADELIC

title **FUNKADELIC** / *year* **1970** / *label* Westbound /
design The Graffiteria

Whether placing John Lee Hooker inside an eyeball or
Muddy Waters inside *Yellow Submarine*, the Graffiteria was
instrumental in adding a psychedelic sheen to black cover
art in the mid-'70s. Here, a solitary woman (potentially the
same subject as in Funkadelic's follow-up, *Maggot Brain*) is
given a kaleidoscopic makeover to achieve this simple, yet
engaging image. ❍
Egal ob John Lee Hooker in einer Iris platziert oder Muddy
Waters ins *Yellow Submarine* gesteckt wurde, die Graffiteria
war maßgeblich daran beteiligt, dass die schwarze Cover-

kunst Mitte der 70er Jahre einen psychedelischen Glanz
bekam. Hier wird eine einzelne Frau (wahrscheinlich die
gleiche wie auf dem Nachfolgeralbum *Maggot Brain*
von Funkadelic) kaleidoskopisch überarbeitet, um dieses
einfache und doch spannende Bild zu schaffen. ❍
Que ce soit en plaçant John Lee Hooker dans un œil, ou
Muddy Waters dans *Yellow Submarine*, un sous-marin
jaune, la Graffiteria a joué un rôle essentiel dans le style
psychédélique des pochettes de disque des artistes noirs
au milieu des années 1970. Ici, une femme (peut-être la
même que sur l'album suivant de Funkadelic, *Maggot
Brain*) subit un traitement kaléidoscopique pour obtenir
cette image simple mais captivante.

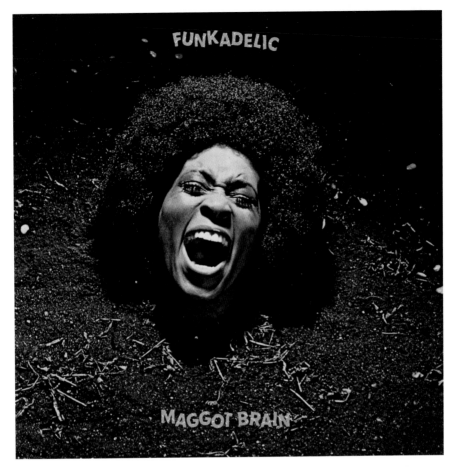

FUNKADELIC

MAGGOT BRAIN

FUNKADELIC

title **MAGGOT BRAIN** / *year* **1971** / *label* Westbound / *design* Paula Bisacca/The Graffiteria / *photography* Joel Brodsky / *art direction* David Krieger

Although the Graffiteria is credited for this controversial cover, it is likely that pervasive producer George Clinton is lurking behind the eccentric scenes of this grisly concept. The back cover features a clean skull in place of the model's horrified head, with liner notes citing the Process Church of the Final Judgement, a bygone religious movement often condemned for their satanic rituals. ○

Die Graffiteria zeichnet für dieses kontroverse Cover verantwortlich, doch wahrscheinlich lauerte der allgegenwärtige Produzent George Clinton hinter den exzentrischen Szenen dieses grausigen Konzepts. Die Plattenrückseite zeigt anstelle des entsetzten Gesichts einen sauberen Schädel, und in den Liner Notes wird die »Process-Church of the Final Judgement« zitiert, eine mittlerweile aufgelöste religiöse Bewegung, die wegen ihrer satanischen Grundsätze oft verurteilt wurde. ○

Bien que cette pochette polémique soit attribuée à la Graffiteria, on peut deviner l'influence du producteur omniprésent George Clinton dans les coulisses excentriques de ce concept macabre. Le verso de la pochette présente un crâne au lieu de la tête horrifiée du mannequin, avec des notes d'accompagnement qui citent Process-Church of the Final Judgement, un ancien mouvement religieux souvent condamné pour ses fondements sataniques.

FUNKADELIC

title **UNCLE JAM WANTS YOU** / *year* **1979** / *label*
Warner Bros. / *design* George Clinton, April Wildflower &
Pedro Bell/Funk Committee / *photography* Diem M. Jones

Diem M. Jones was an integral member of the Funk Mob,
serving as both art director of Uncle Jam Records and the
official photographer aboard the Mothership. Funkadelic's
increasingly militant attitude towards the funk is reflected
in this depiction of George Clinton, fashioned after the
portrait most often associated with Black Panther founder
Huey Newton. **O**
Diem M. Jones war ein wesentliches Mitglied des Funk
Mob, er diente als Art Director von Uncle Jam Records

und war gleichzeitig der offizielle Fotograf an Bord des
Mothership. Funkadelics immer militanterer Einstellung
dem Funk gegenüber entspricht die Darstellung von
George Clinton auf dem Cover. Hier wurde das Porträt
von Huey Newton, dem Begründer der Black-Panther-
Bewegung, nachgestellt. **O**
Diem M. Jones était un membre à part entière de Parliament-Funkadelic et officiait à bord du vaisseau mère en
tant que directeur artistique d'Uncle Jam Records et photographe officiel. L'attitude de plus en plus militante de
Funkadelic envers le funk se reflète dans cette représentation de George Clinton, inspirée du portrait que l'on
associe le plus souvent avec Huey Newton, le fondateur
des Black Panthers.

FUSE ONE
title **SILK** / *year* **1981** / *label* CTI /
design Jonathan Andrews

GALAXY
title **HOT, WET AND STICKY** /
year **1978** / *label* Arista

STEREO

what's going on
MARVIN GAYE

T5310
TAMLA

ORCHESTRA CONDUCTED
AND ARRANGED BY
DAVID VAN DePITT

MARVIN GAYE

title **WHAT'S GOING ON** / *year* **1971** / *label* Tamla
Motown / *photography* James Hendin / *art direction* Curtis
McNair

A truly monumental achievement, Marvin Gaye's *What's
Going On* almost never saw the light of day. Berry Gordy,
the head of Motown, hated the single so much that he
refused to release it. Gaye threatened to walk and was
vindicated when the single stayed at #1 on the R&B charts
for five weeks. The passion and pain of a tumultuous world
is channeled through every groove of this album and James
Hendin's somewhat gothic portrait of Marvin in the rain
captures the mood perfectly. **O**
Eine wahrhaft monumentale Leistung ist *What's Going On*
von Marvin Gaye, aber beinahe hätte diese Platte nicht das

Licht der Welt erblickt. Berry Gordy, der Kopf von Motown,
hasste die Single so sehr, dass er sich weigerte, sie zu veröf-
fentlichen. Gaye drohte zu gehen und behielt Recht, als
die Single fünf Wochen lang die Nummer eins der R&B-
Charts blieb. Aus jedem Groove strömen Leidenschaft und
Schmerz einer wirren Welt, und James Hendins Porträt von
Marvin im Regen fängt diese Stimmung perfekt ein. **O**
Ce succès véritablement monumental de Marvin Gaye a
failli ne jamais voir le jour. Berry Gordy, le directeur de
Motown, détestait tellement le single qu'il refusait de l'édi-
ter. Gaye menaça de partir, et il devint clair qu'il avait eu
raison lorsque le single resta numéro un des classements
R&B pendant cinq semaines. Chacun des rythmes charrie
la passion et la douleur d'un monde tumultueux, et le portrait un brin gothique que James Hendin a réalisé de Marvin Gaye sous la pluie saisit parfaitement cette atmosphère.

MARVIN GAYE

title **TROUBLE MAN** / *year* **1972** /
label Tamla Motown / *photography* Jim Britt

After the massive success of *What's Going On*, Marvin Gaye became the highest-paid black artist of the day, but more importantly he won a level of creative control that would open the doors to a deeper, more soulful studio sound. When asked to score the 1972 blaxploitation movie *Trouble Man*, he took the opportunity and moved, as did Motown, to Los Angeles. **O**

Nach dem durchschlagenden Erfolg von *What's Going On* wurde Marvin Gaye der höchstdotierte schwarze Künstler seiner Zeit. Vor allem aber erreichte er einen Grad der künstlerischen Kontrolle, der ihm die Türen zu einem tieferen und souligeren Studiosound öffnete. Als ihm angetragen wurde, die Filmmusik für den Blaxploitation-Film *Trouble Man* von 1972 zu komponieren, ergriff er die Gelegenheit und zog – wie Motown – nach Los Angeles um. **O**

Après l'énorme succès de *What's Going On*, Marvin Gaye devint l'artiste noir le mieux payé de l'époque mais, surtout, il obtint un niveau de contrôle créatif qui allait ouvrir la voie vers un son de studio plus profond et plus expressif. Lorsqu'on lui demanda de composer la musique du film de blaxploitation de 1972 *Trouble Man*, il saisit l'occasion et déménagea à Los Angeles, comme Motown.

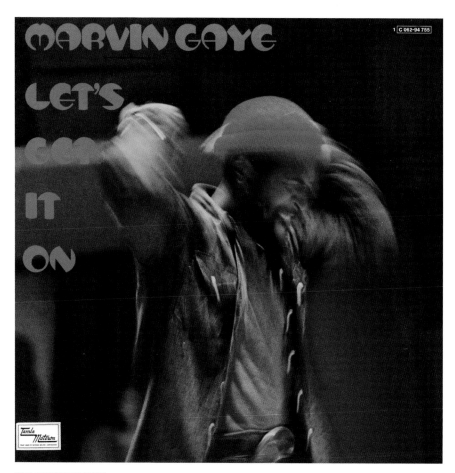

MARVIN GAYE
title **LET'S GET IT ON** / *year* **1973** /
label Tamla Motown / *photography* Jim Britt

Oozing with sex, Marvin Gaye's follow-up to his master-piece *What's Going On* moves away from social outcry to the sensual. Jim Britt was Motown's Art Director and head photographer when the label relocated to the west coast in the early '70s. A former jazz singer, Britt's ability to catch intimate moments comes through in all of his work, as it does in this intense shot of Gaye in the studio. **O**
Bei dem Nachfolger für sein Meisterstück *What's Going On* bewegt sich Marvin Gaye weg von der sozialen Anklage und wechselt zu sinnlichen Klängen, dabei trieft seine Stim-

me vor Sex-Appeal. Jim Britt war Art Director bei Motown und leitender Fotograf, als das Label Anfang der 70er Jahre an die Westküste umzog. Der ehemalige Jazzsänger Britt offenbart in seinen Arbeiten eine besondere Fähigkeit, intime Momente einzufangen – das gilt auch für dieses eindrucksvolle Foto von Marvin Gaye im Studio. **O**
Débordant d'érotisme, l'album qui suit le chef-d'œuvre de Marvin Gaye, *What's Going On*, s'éloigne du cri social pour se rapprocher de la sensualité. Jim Britt était le directeur artistique et le photographe en chef de Motown lorsque le label déménagea sur la côte ouest au début des années 1970. Britt était un ancien chanteur de jazz, et sa capacité à capturer des moments intimes est évidente dans tout son travail, comme dans ce cliché intense de Gaye en studio.

MARVIN GAYE

title **IN OUR LIFETIME** / *year* **1981** / *label* Motown /
design Ginny Livingstone / *art direction* Johnny Lee /
illustration Neil Breeden

Released in 1981, this would be Marvin Gaye's last record
for Motown after his anger over the label remixing the
original sessions and rushing the release. Gaye's original
vision for the record finally saw the light of day over
25 years later and holds up against his earlier masterpieces
as the work of an equally funky if not wiser artist. Neil
Breeden's cover art mirrors the singer's world-weary
outlook at a dark time in his life. **O**
Dies sollte die letzte Platte von Marvin Gaye für Motown
sein, nachdem er sich mit dem Label wegen der Neuabmi-
schung der Originalsessions und der übereilten Veröffentli-

chung zerstritten hatte. Gayes ursprüngliche Vision für diese Platte erschien erst über 25 Jahre später und kann neben
seinen früheren Meisterwerken als Arbeit eines ebenso
funkigen, aber gereifteren Künstlers bestehen. Neil Breedens
Coverkunst bildet die lebensüberdrüssigen Anschauungen
des Sängers in einer dunklen Zeit seines Lebens ab. **O**
Ce disque sorti en 1981 allait être le dernier de Marvin
Gaye chez Motown. Il n'avait pas apprécié le moins du
monde que le label remixe les sessions originales et préci-
pite la sortie de l'album. La vision originale de Gaye a finalement vu le jour plus de 25 ans plus tard et soutient la
comparaison avec ses chefs-d'œuvre antérieurs comme le
fruit d'un artiste toujours aussi funky, mais pas forcément
plus sage. L'illustration de Neil Breeden pour la pochette
reflète le regard désabusé que le chanteur portait sur le
monde à cette époque tourmentée de sa vie.

GOODY GOODY

title **GOODY GOODY** / *year* **1978** / *label* Atlantic /
design Sandi Young / *photography* Jim Houghton

Written, produced, and arranged by disco vibraphonist
Vince Montana Jr., this record is the lone product of Goody
Goody, fronted by Montana's daughter Denise. The tattoo
is presumably fake, and the bosom belongs to no member
of this Philly ensemble. Commercial photographer
Jim Houghton captured this busty image in the same
New York studio he used for AC/DC's *Highway to Hell*. ○
Diese Platte wurde vom Disco-Vibraphonisten Vince
Montana Jr. komponiert, produziert und arrangiert. Sie ist
das einzige Produkt von Goody Goody mit der Frontfrau

Denise, Montanas Tochter. Die Tätowierung ist wahrscheinlich nicht echt, und mit einem solchen Busen kann kein
Mitglied dieses Philly-Ensembles protzen. Der Werbefoto-
graf Jim Houghton nahm dieses vollbusige Bild im gleichen
New Yorker Studio auf, in dem er an *Highway to Hell* von
AC/DC arbeitete. ○
Écrit, produit et arrangé par le vibraphoniste disco Vince
Montana Jr., ce disque est le seul produit de Goody Goody,
mené par la fille de Montana, Denise. Le tatouage est sans
doute factice, et la poitrine n'appartient à aucun membre
de ce groupe de Philadelphie. Le photographe commercial
Jim Houghton a pris cette photo pigeonnante dans le studio new-yorkais qu'il avait déjà utilisé pour l'album *Highway
to Hell* d'AC / DC.

GRAHAM CENTRAL STATION
title **AIN'T NO 'BOUT-A-DOUBT IT** / *year* **1975** /
label Warner Bros. / *illustration* Rob Springett

Formerly of Sly and the Family Stone, Larry Graham is
often credited for inventing the slapping technique now
ubiquitous in modern bass-playing. Prior to this whimsical
portrait of Graham's camp, artist Rob Springett composed
the funky fantasies illustrated on Herbie Hancock's
competitively perplexing albums *Thrust* and *Sextant*. ⊙
Früher war Larry Graham bei Sly and the Family Stone. Ihm
wird die Erfindung der Slaptechnik zugesprochen, die zum

modernen Bassspiel heutzutage dazugehört. Bevor er
dieses schräge Porträt von Grahams Camp schuf, hatte der
Künstler Rob Springett die funkigen Fantasie-Illustrationen
für Herbie Hancocks verblüffende Alben *Thrust* und *Sextant* komponiert. ⊙
Ancien membre de Sly and the Family Stone, Larry Graham
est souvent cité comme l'inventeur de la technique du
slapping, aujourd'hui très répandue chez les bassistes modernes. Avant ce portrait farfelu de la bande de Graham,
l'artiste Rob Springett avait composé les délires funky illus-
trés sur les albums *Thrust* et *Sextant* de Herbie Hancock,
plus déconcertants l'un que l'autre.

LONDON

AL GREEN
GETS NEXT
TO YOU

AL GREEN
title **AL GREEN GETS NEXT TO YOU** /
year **1971** / *label* London

The chemistry between producer Willie Mitchell and singer
Al Green was starting to reach a fever pitch with 1971's
Al Green Gets Next to You. Green's inventive remake of the
Temptations' "I Can't Get Next To You" and his own "Tired
of Being Alone" stand out against the cohesive collection
of sturdy Memphis soul. ⬤
Die Zusammenarbeit zwischen dem Produzenten Willie
Mitchell und dem Sänger Al Green erreichte mit der Platte

Al Green Gets Next to You von 1971 ihren Siedepunkt.
Al Greens originelles Remake des Songs »I Can't Get Next
To You« von den Temptations und sein eigenes »Tired of
Being Alone« stechen aus dieser in sich geschlossenen
Sammlung mit handfestem Memphis-Soul hervor. ⬤
Le courant qui passait entre le producteur Willie Mitchell
et le chanteur Al Green commençait à faire des étincelles
avec cet album de 1971. L'interprétation inventive que
Green a donnée à *I Can't Get Next To You* des Temptations
et à son propre *Tired of Being Alone* se démarque de cette
collection bien ficelée de soul vigoureuse de Memphis.

AL GREEN
title **I'M STILL IN LOVE WITH YOU** /
year **1972** / *label* London

Considered one of the most widely-seen images of Al
Green, this cover for *I'm Still In Love With You* encapsulates
some of the Memphis artist's most extraordinary recordings. From "Love and Happiness" to the country-tinged,
Kristofferson-penned "For the Good Times", Green's
sophomore outing with producer Willie Mitchell rivals the
preceding *Let's Stay Together* as the present-day preacher's
magnum opus. **O**
Das Cover für *I'm Still In Love With You* gilt als eines der am
weitesten verbreiteten Bilder von Al Green. Dahinter verbirgt sich eine der außergewöhnlichsten Aufnahmen des

Musikers aus Memphis. Von »Love and Happiness« bis
zum Country-gefärbten und von Kristofferson verfassten
»For the Good Times« sticht diese zweite Aufnahme von
Green mit dem Produzenten Willie Mitchell den Vorgänger
Let's Stay Together als Magnum Opus des heutigen Predi-
gers aus. **O**
Considérée comme l'une des images les plus célèbres d'Al
Green, la pochette de *I'm Still In Love With You* renferme
quelques-uns des enregistrements les plus extraordinaires
de cet artiste de Memphis. De *Love and Happiness* à *For
the Good Times*, teinté de nuances country et écrit par
Kristofferson, le deuxième album de Green avec le producteur Willie Mitchell fait concurrence à son album précédent *Let's Stay Together*, et l'on n'arrive pas à décider lequel
est son œuvre maîtresse.

GREY & HANKS

title **YOU FOOLED ME** /
year **1978** / *label* RCA / *design*
George Corsillo/Gribbitt! /
photography Ron Slenzak /
art direction Tim Bryant/Gribbitt!

HAMBONE

title **BIG FAT JUICY FUN** /
year **1981** / *label* Salsoul /
design Roy Mendl / *photography*
Len Kaltman / *art direction* Stan
Hochstadt

HERBIE HANCOCK

title **THE SPOOK WHO SAT BY THE DOOR** / *year*
1973 / *label* United Artists / *art direction* Leslie Thomas

Based on the Sam Greenlee novel, *The Spook Who Sat By The Door* is about Dan Freeman, the CIA's first African-American agent, who, after serving five years as the agency's token black employee, uses his training to organize young black men, creating urban guerillas to fight for social justice. Leslie Thomas had drawn posters for odd Westerns and horror films before composing this dynamic scene. **O**

Der nach dem Roman von Sam Greenlee *The Spook Who Sat By The Door* gedrehte Film handelt von Dan Freeman, dem ersten afroamerikanischen Agenten des CIA. Er diente fünf Jahre lang der Agentur als schwarzer Quotenmann und nutzte dann seine Ausbildung, um junge Schwarze zu Stadtguerrilleros auszubilden, die für soziale Gerechtigkeit kämpfen. Leslie Thomas hatte bereits Plakate für skurrile Western- und Horrorfilme gemalt, bevor er diese dynamische Szene komponierte. **O**

Adapté du roman de Sam Greenlee, *The Spook Who Sat By The Door* est l'histoire de Dan Freeman, le premier agent afro-américain de la CIA, qui, après avoir servi d'alibi politiquement correct à l'agence gouvernementale pendant cinq ans, utilise sa formation pour organiser des jeunes Noirs et créer des guérillas urbaines luttant pour la justice sociale. Leslie Thomas avait dessiné des affiches pour des westerns et des films d'horreur de série B avant de composer cette scène dynamique.

HERBIE HANCOCK

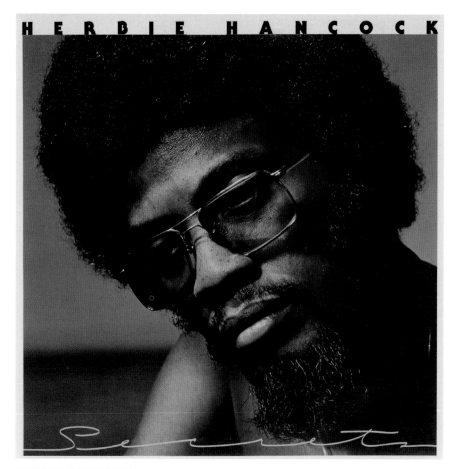

HERBIE HANCOCK

title **SECRETS** / *year* **1976** / *label* CBS /
photography Herb Greene / *art direction* Ron Coro

Herb Greene worked in and around the San Francisco area, collecting some of the most intimate portraits to date of talented locals Jerry Garcia, Sly Stone, and others. Outside of Haight-Ashbury, Greene also captured memorable moments with Rod Stewart, John Bonham, and this seaside portrait of Herbie Hancock. **O**
Herb Greene arbeitete im Großraum San Francisco und konnte in der Gegend einige der bisher intimsten Porträts von talentierten Persönlichkeiten wie Jerry Garcia, Sly Stone und anderen sammeln. Außerhalb von Haight-Ashbury gelang es Greene, mit Rod Stewart oder John Bonham denkwürdige Momente einzufangen und vor der Kulisse des Ozeans dieses Porträt von Herbie Hancock festzuhalten. **O**
Herb Greene travaillait dans la région de San Francisco et est l'auteur des portraits les plus intimistes jamais réalisés des talents locaux tels que Jerry Garcia ou Sly Stone, entre autres. Près du quartier de Haight-Ashbury, Greene a également immortalisé des moments mémorables avec Rod Stewart et John Bonham, ainsi que ce portrait de Herbie Hancock pris en bord de mer.

HARLEM RIVER DRIVE

title **HARLEM RIVER DRIVE** / *year* **1971** / *label* Roulette / *design* Ruby Mazur's Art Department

Brooklyn-born Ruby Mazur got his start in album design at age twenty-one, when Paramount Records hired him as art director. Since then, he has generated over 3,000 album covers, including the ubiquitous mouth and tongue, intrinsically associated with The Rolling Stones, for their "Tumbling Dice" single. **O**
Der in Brooklyn geborene Ruby Mazur war 21 Jahre alt, als er seine Karriere als Covergestalter begann und Paramount

Records ihn als Art Director einstellte. Seither hat er über 3.000 Plattenhüllen hervorgebracht, u. a. schuf er für die Single »Tumbling Dice« die allgegenwärtige ausgestreckte Zunge, die ein Synonym für die Rolling Stones geworden ist. **O**
Ruby Mazur, né a Brooklyn, a fait ses débuts dans la création de pochettes de disque à 21 ans, lorsque Paramount Records l'a engagé comme directeur artistique. Depuis, il a créé plus de 3000 pochettes, notamment la fameuse bouche tirant la langue si étroitement associée aux Rolling Stones pour leur single *Tumbling Dice*.

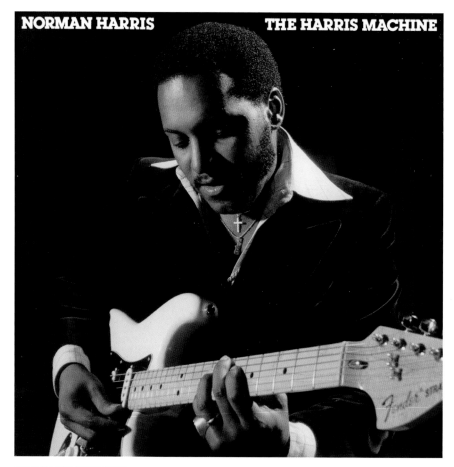

NORMAN HARRIS THE HARRIS MACHINE

NORMAN HARRIS

title **THE HARRIS MACHINE** / *year* **1980** / *label*
Philadelphia International / *photography* Ronald G. Harris

Norman Harris was a founding member of MFSB and one
third of the production trio of Baker-Harris-Young. This, his
only solo LP, is a great showcase for his fluid guitar-playing
that can be heard on countless Philly soul hits from the '60s
through the '80s. His virtuosic style made it possible for him
to compose string and horn arrangements on his guitar. **O**
Norman Harris war Gründungsmitglied von MFSB und
bildet ein Drittel des Produktionstrios Baker-Harris-Young.

Dies ist seine einzige Solo-LP, auf der er sein flüssiges Gitarrenspiel vorstellt. Das ist auf zahllosen Philly-Soul-Hits der
60er bis hin zu den 80er Jahren zu hören. Sein virtuoser Stil
ermöglichte es ihm, auf seiner Gitarre Streicher- und Bläser-
arrangements zusammenzustellen. **O**
Norman Harris était un membre fondateur de MFSB et
faisait partie du trio de production Baker-Harris-Young.
Cet album est le seul qu'il ait sorti en solo, et c'est une
vitrine magnifique pour son jeu fluide à la guitare, que l'on
peut entendre sur une multitude de tubes de Philadelphie
des années 1960, 1970 et 1980. Ce virtuose composait les
arrangements de cordes et de cuivres sur sa guitare.

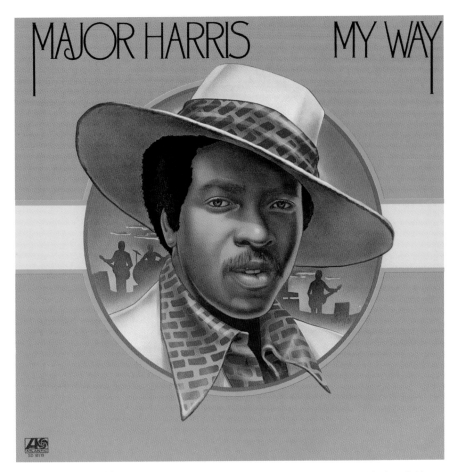

MAJOR HARRIS

title **MY WAY** / *year* **1974** / *label* Atlantic

Cousin to producer Norman Harris, Major had shuffled between singing groups including the Delfonics since the mid-'60s. His solo debut, written, produced, and arranged for the most part by Bobby Eli, is a high point for Philly soul. It contains the stirring ballad and Top Ten hit "Love Won't Let Me Wait". **O**

Major Harris, Cousin des Produzenten Norman Harris, wechselte seit Mitte der 60er Jahre zwischen verschiedenen Gesangsgruppen und war z. B. auch bei den Delfonics. Sein Solodebüt wurde größtenteils von Bobby Eli geschrieben, produziert und arrangiert und ist ein Höhepunkt des Philly Souls. Es enthält die rührende Ballade »Love Won't Let Me Wait«, die auch unter die Top Ten gelangte. **O**

Cousin du producteur Norman Harris, Major avait chanté dans différents groupes vocaux, notamment les Delfonics, depuis le milieu des années 1960. Son premier album en solo, dont la plus grande partie a été écrite, produite et arrangée par Bobby Eli, est un grand moment de la soul de Philadelphie. Il contient *Love Won't Let Me Wait*, une ballade émouvante qui a atteint le Top 10 dans les classements.

DONNY HATHAWAY
title **EXTENSION OF A MAN** /
year **1973** / *label* Atlantic / *design*
Jeffrey Blue / *art direction* Jeffrey Blue

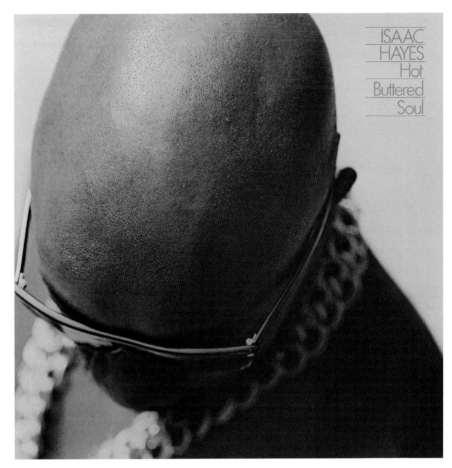

ISAAC HAYES

title **HOT BUTTERED SOUL** / *year* **1969** / *label* Stax /
design Christopher Whorf / *photography* Bob Smith /
art direction Honeya Thompson

After his debut album's lackluster performance, Isaac Hayes
resigned from his role as producer and arranger at Stax.
However, when Atlantic acquired the Memphis label's back
catalog, Stax executive Al Bell issued a call to arms, request-
ing all able-bodied staffers to cut new material at once.
Hayes was granted complete creative control of *Hot Buttered
Soul*, yielding an album whose expansive arrangements and
imaginative covers helped forge Hayes' musical legacy. **O**
Nachdem seinem Debütalbum nur wenig Erfolg beschieden
war, fand sich Isaac Hayes mit seiner Rolle als Produzent
und Arrangeur bei Stax ab. Als dann allerdings Atlantic die

Rechte am Backkatalog des Labels aus Memphis erwarb,
rief der Stax-Manager Al Bell zur Mobilmachung und forderte alle einsatztauglichen Kräfte auf, neues Material zu
mischen. Hayes wurde die künstlerische Kontrolle über *Hot
Buttered Soul* zugesichert, was zu einem Album führte, dessen ausgedehnte Arrangements und Coverversionen dazu
beitrugen, seinen musikalischen Ruhm zu untermauern. **O**
Après sa performance peu brillante sur son premier album,
Isaac Hayes rendit son tablier de producteur et arrangeur
chez Stax. Mais lorsqu'Atlantic acheta le catalogue perma-
nent du label de Memphis, Al Bell, un directeur de Stax,
lança un appel aux armes et demanda à tout le personnel
apte à servir de graver du neuf, Hayes compris. Hayes avait
un contrôle créatif total sur *Hot Buttered Soul*, ce qui a donné un album dont les arrangements coûteux et les versions
imaginatives ont contribué à forger son héritage musical.

ISAAC HAYES

title **BLACK MOSES** / *year* **1972** / *label* Stax / *photography*
Joel Brodsky / *art direction* David Krieger/The Graffiteria /
packaging AGI

This picture reveals only a fraction of this cover-art landmark. When unfolded completely, the hooded portrait
becomes a cross-shaped rendering of a messianic Hayes,
bedecked in sandals and robe. Although Hayes, at the time
a devout Christian, later considered his personification
of Black Moses to be sacrilegious, many in the black community found the image to be an uplifting and enduring
depiction of the legendary performer. **O**
Dieses Bild zeigt nur einen Bruchteil dieses Meilensteins der
Coverkunst. Vollständig entfaltet, entsteht aus dem verhüll-
ten Albumporträt die kreuzförmige Darstellung eines mes-

sianischen Hayes, der mit Robe und Sandalen geschmückt
ist. Obwohl Hayes zu jener Zeit strenggläubiger Christ war
und seine Personifizierung eines schwarzen Moses später
frevlerisch fand, betrachteten viele aus der schwarzen Ge-
meinschaft dieses Bild als eine moralisch erhebende und
bleibende Darstellung des legendären Performers. **O**
Cette image ne révèle qu'une partie d'un monument des
pochettes de disque. Lorsqu'on le déplie complètement, ce
portrait en capuche devient une représentation en forme
de croix d'un Isaac Hayes en messie à sandales et à tunique.
À l'époque, Hayes était un membre fervent de l'Église
chrétienne, et il allait par la suite considérer que son portrait en Moïse noir était un sacrilège. Mais au sein de la
communauté noire, beaucoup furent marqués et inspirés
par cette représentation du légendaire artiste.

HEATWAVE

title **CENTRAL HEATING** / *year* **1978** / *label* Epic / *design* Michael Ross

Michael Ross had created colorful compositions for Elton John and the Beach Boys, before generating this conservative, yet searing design for Heatwave. Best known for sparking the songwriting career of Rod Temperton (see Michael Jackson's "Rock With You" or "Thriller"), Heatwave would begin to be plagued by line-up changes and tragedy following this release, resulting in their eventual disbandment in the early '80s. **O**

Michael Ross hat farbenfrohe Kompositionen für Elton John und die Beach Boys geschaffen, bevor er dieses eher konservative und doch hitzige Design für Heatwave entwickelte. Die Gruppe wurde vor allem bekannt, weil Bandmitglied Rod Temperton hier seine Karriere als Songwriter begann (er schrieb für Michael Jackson »Rock With You« und »Thriller«), aber nach dieser Veröffentlichung wurde Heatwave von dauernd wechselnden Besetzungen und anderen Tragödien geplagt, was Anfang der 80er Jahre schließlich zur Auflösung führte. **O**

Michael Ross a créé des compositions hautes en couleur pour Elton John et les Beach Boys avant de produire ce graphisme plus sobre, mais néanmoins brûlant, pour Heatwave. Ce groupe est surtout célèbre pour avoir suscité la carrière d'auteur-compositeur de Rod Temperton (*Rock With You* ou *Thriller* de Michael Jackson). Après cet album, Heatwave allait souffrir d'une série de défections et de tragédies qui s'est soldée par la dissolution du groupe au début des années 1980.

HI-TENSION

title **HI-TENSION** / *year* **1978** / *label* Island

Because of their members' relative ages and evenly distributed singing duties, Hi-Tension is often categorized as a boy
band in the annals of British music history. None the less,
North London's Hi-Tension created an innovative brand of
Brit-funk, indigenous to a portion of the world where, prior
to groups like The Real Thing, Gonzales, and Hi-Tension
themselves, disco music had only been an import. **O**
Wegen des relativ jungen Alters ihrer Mitglieder und der
gleichmäßig verteilten Sangespflichten wird Hi-Tension in
den Annalen der britischen Musikgeschichte oft als Boy-

band kategorisiert. Nichtsdestotrotz schufen Hi-Tension
aus dem Norden von London ihre innovative Marke des
Brit-Funk, der in einem Teil der Welt heimisch wurde, wo
Discomusik vor Gruppen wie The Real Thing, Gonzales
und Hi-Tension selbst nur ein Import gewesen war. **O**
Dans les annales de l'histoire de la musique britannique,
Hi-Tension est souvent classé dans la rubrique des boys
bands, à cause de l'âge de ses membres et du fait qu'ils
se répartissaient le chant à parts égales. Ce groupe du nord
de Londres a pourtant créé un style de funk britannique
innovant, dans une région où, avant les groupes tels que
The Real Thing, Gonzales ou Hi-Tension, la musique disco
ne pouvait être qu'importée.

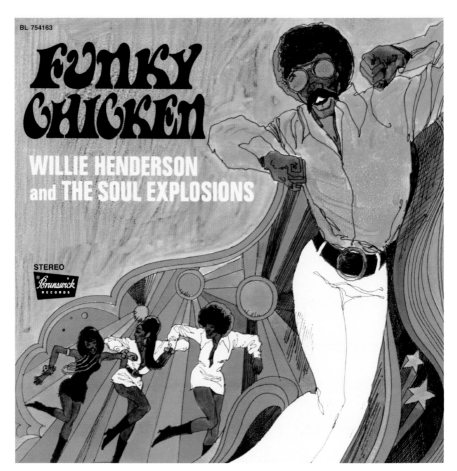

BL 754163

FUNKY CHICKEN

WILLIE HENDERSON and THE SOUL EXPLOSIONS

STEREO

Brunswick
RECORDS

WILLIE HENDERSON
AND THE SOUL EXPLOSIONS

title **FUNKY CHICKEN** / *year* **1970** / *label* Brunswick

Willie Henderson started out as a sax for hire backing Chicago heavyweights like Syl Johnson, and Alvin Cash. He soon got a gig working at Brunswick and teamed up with producer Carl Davis. He arranged, produced, and played on records by the Chi-Lites, Jackie Wilson, and Tyrone Davis. This was his debut as a leader and as the cover graphic illustrates this was a seriously silly funk affair. ⦿
Willie Henderson begann seine Laufbahn als Saxophonist auf Abruf und spielte für Chicagoer Schwergewichte wie Syl Johnson und Alvin Cash. Er bekam bald einen Gig bei Brunswick und tat sich mit dem Produzenten Carl Davis

zusammen. Als Arrangeur, Produzent und Musiker drückte er verschiedenen Platten von Jackie Wilson, Tyrone Davis und den Chi-Lites seinen Stempel auf. Dies war sein Debüt als Bandleader, und die Covergrafik verdeutlicht, um welch ernsthaft-affige Funk-Affäre es sich hier handelt. ⦿
Willie Henderson a commencé sa carrière en louant ses services de saxophoniste à des poids lourds de Chicago tels que Syl Johnson et Alvin Cash. Il n'a pas tardé à décrocher un travail chez Brunswick et a fait équipe avec le producteur Carl Davis. Il a arrangé, produit et joué sur des disques des Chi-Lites, de Jackie Wilson et de Tyrone Davis. Cet album était son premier en tant que leader et, comme le montre l'illustration de la pochette, c'était du funk qui ne se prenait pas vraiment au sérieux.

EDDIE HOLMAN

title **A NIGHT TO REMEMBER** /
year **1977** / *label* Salsoul / *design*
Ted Amber & Ron Canagata /
photography Joel Brodsky / *art direction*
David Krieger/DFK

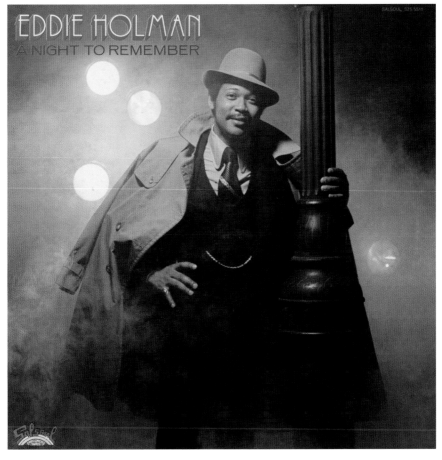

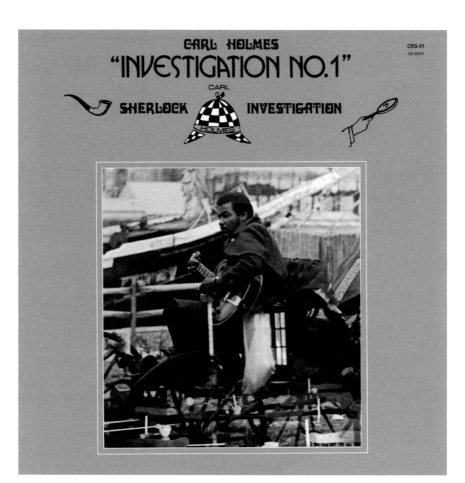

CARL HOLMES
title **INVESTIGATION NO.1** / *year* **1974** / *label* CRS

The first full-length release on Curtis R. Staten's self-named label, *Investigation No. 1* is packed full of high-intensity Philly funk, including the musical travel brochure "Get Down Philly Town", which compares the city of Brotherly Love favorably to the Big Apple and the Windy City. Carl "Sherlock" Holmes' acrobatic guitar-playing is rivaled only by his smooth, yet sturdy singing. **O**

Diese erste Langspielaufnahme auf dem nach ihm selbst benannten Label von Curtis R. Staten ist *Investigation No. 1.* Es erscheint vollgepackt mit intensivem Philly Funk, u. a. mit dem musikalischen Reiseprospekt »Get Down Philly Town«, in dem die Stadt der brüderlichen Liebe (die Wortbedeutung von Philadelphia) beim Vergleich mit dem Big Apple und der Windy City positiv abschneidet. Das akrobatische Gitarrenspiel von Carl »Sherlock« Holmes wird nur von seinem sanften, aber kraftvollen Gesang übertroffen. **O**

Premier album longue durée chez le label éponyme de Curtis R. Staten, *Investigation No. 1* est rempli de funk de Philadelphie à haute intensité, notamment la brochure touristique musicale *Get Down Philly Town*, qui vante les mérites de la ville en la comparant à New York et à Chicago. Le jeu acrobatique de Carl « Sherlock » Holmes à la guitare n'est concurrencé que par son chant mélodieux et énergique à la fois.

The Black Motion Picture Experience

SUPER FLY ★ SHAFT
TROUBLE MAN ★ ACROSS 110TH ST
SLAUGHTER
FREDDIE'S
DEAD
LADY SINGS
THE BLUES
BEN ★ 2001

The Cecil Holmes Soulful Sounds

THE CECIL HOLMES SOULFUL SOUNDS

title **THE BLACK MOTION PICTURE EXPERIENCE** /
year **1973** / *label* Buddah / *art direction* Glen Christensen

To capitalize on the soundtrack craze of the '70s, band-leader Cecil Holmes took a crack at some of the decade's most powerful themes. To send the point home, Art Director Glen Christensen arranged these protagonist impersonators and supporting-cast facsimiles amidst a sea of uniform, drop-shadowed font. Although not a block-buster, *The Black Motion Picture Experience* is a certified classic among record collectors. **O**

Der Bandleader Cecil Holmes wollte aus der Soundtrack-welle der 70er Jahre noch Kapital schlagen und wagte sich an einige der stärksten Melodien des Jahrzehnts. Um dies

noch mehr zu unterstreichen, arrangierte der Art Director Glen Christensen die Darsteller der Protagonisten und Nebenfiguren unter einem Meer uniformer Schlagschat-tenschriften. Es hat zwar nicht zum Blockbuster gereicht, aber *The Black Motion Picture Experience* ist unter Platten-sammlern ein amtlicher Klassiker. **O**

Espérant tirer parti de l'engouement pour les bandes originales dans les années 1970, le leader de groupe Cecil Holmes s'est essayé à faire des versions de certains des mor-ceaux les plus marquants de la décennie. Pour faire passer cette idée, le directeur artistique Glen Christensen a disposé des imitations de héros et de personnages secondaires de ces films au milieu d'une mer de lettres ombrées. Bien que l'album n'ait pas été un grand succès, *The Black Motion Picture Experience* est un classique certifié chez les collec-tionneurs de disques.

STEREO · STEREO · STEREO · STEREO · STEREO · STEREO · STEREO · STEREO · ST

PR 7435

SOUL MESSAGE
RICHARD "GROOVE" HOLMES

RICHARD "GROOVE" HOLMES

title **SOUL MESSAGE** / *year* **1965** / *label* Prestige /
design Don Schlitten / *photography* Don Schlitten

Don Schlitten's free-spirited design and photo for Richard
"Groove" Holmes' first release on the Prestige label
embodies the soaring spirit of the organist's soul jazz
styling. Holmes had the impressive ability to play uplifting
leads while keeping the rhythm going with his infectious
bass-lines. **O**
Don Schlittens unkonventionelles Design und sein Foto für
das erste Album von Richard »Groove« Holmes beim Label

Prestige verkörpern den sich aufschwingenden Geist des
Soul-Jazz-Stils dieses Organisten. Holmes besaß die beein-
druckende Fähigkeit, mitreißende Melodien zu spielen,
während er den Rhythmus mit seinen infektiösen Basslinien
vorantrieb. **O**
Le graphisme et la photo désinvoltes de Don Schlitten
pour le premier album de Richard « Groove » Holmes chez
le label Prestige incarnent l'énergie débordante de la soul-
jazz de cet organiste. Holmes avait l'impressionnante capacité de jouer des mélodies entraînantes tout en maintenant
le rythme grâce à ses lignes de basse contagieuses.

HOT CHOCOLATE

title **HOT CHOCOLATE** /
year **1971** / *label* Co-Co Cleveland /
illustration Dick Dugan

REDD HOTT

title **#1** / *year* **1982** / *label* Venture /
design Ken Brown

THELMA HOUSTON
title **ANY WAY YOU LIKE IT** /
year **1976** / *label* Motown / *design*
Ron Dyer, Inc. / *photography* Harry
Langdon / *art direction* Frank
Mulvey

HUMMINGBIRD
title **WE CAN'T GO ON
MEETING LIKE THIS** / *year*
1976 / *label* A&M / *design* John
Pasche / *photography* John
Thornton / *art direction* Fasio
Nicoli

"Fancy Dancer"–Bobbi Humphrey

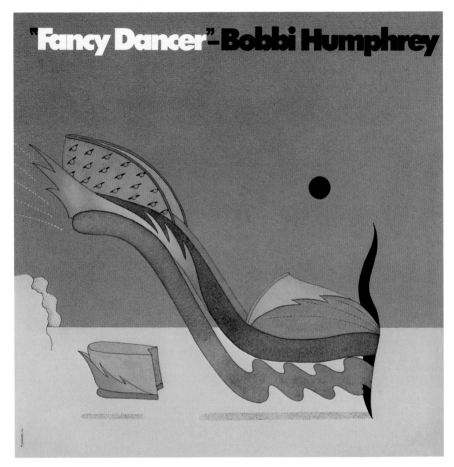

BOBBI HUMPHREY

title **FANCY DANCER** / *year* **1975** / *label* Blue Note /
design Ria Lewerke / *art direction* Bob Cato & Lloyd Ziff /
illustration Barbara Nessim

The cover of this funky flautist's fifth and final recording
for Blue Note features a then contemporary illustration by
Barbara Nessim. Although not made explicit here, this form
most closely resembles Nessim's avant-garde-meets-fashion
illustrations of high-heeled shoes from her own Imelda
Marcos Collection. ✪
Auf dem Cover der fünften und letzten Platte dieses funkigen Flötisten für Blue Note ist eine damals aktuelle Illus-

tration von Barbara Nessim zu sehen. Obwohl es hier
nicht explizit angegeben wurde, erinnert diese Form noch
am ehesten an die Avantgarde-trifft-Mode-Illustrationen
von Stöckelschuhen aus ihrer eigenen Imelda Marcos
Collection. ✪
La pochette du cinquième et dernier album que ce flûtiste
funky a enregistré pour Blue Note est décorée d'une illustration contemporaine de Barbara Nessim. Bien que cela
ne soit pas explicite ici, cette forme ressemble beaucoup
aux illustrations de chaussures à talons de la collection
Imelda Marcos de l'artiste, à la croisée de l'avant-garde et
de la mode.

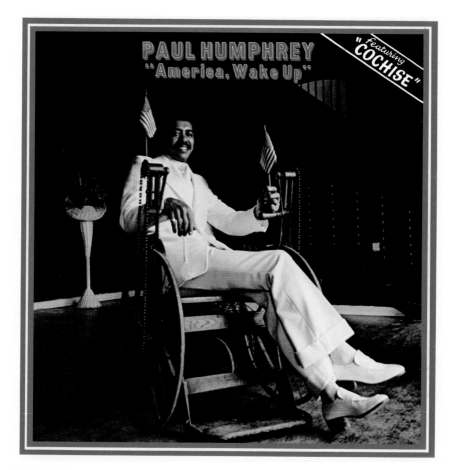

PAUL HUMPHREY

title **AMERICA, WAKE UP** / *year* **1974** / *label* Blue Thumb / *design* Barry Feinstein / *photography* Barry Feinstein

Barry Feinstein was a top magazine and record cover photographer shooting artists like Bob Dylan and Steve McQueen. His free-wheeling cover shot for this record captured one of the funkiest drummers ever. Paul Humphrey was the heart of many soul hits for others and he made the most of his second record as a leader. ◗
Barry Feinstein arbeitete als Top-Fotograf für Magazine und Plattenfirmen. Er lichtete Künstler wie Bob Dylan und Steve

McQueen ab. Sein lockeres Coverfoto für dieses Album zeigt einen der funkigsten Drummer überhaupt: Paul Humphrey war die Quelle für viele andere Soul-Hits und holte aus seiner zweiten Aufnahme als Bandleader das Optimum heraus. . ◗
Barry Feinstein était un grand photographe de magazine et de pochettes de disques, et il avait travaillé avec des artistes comme Bob Dylan ou Steve McQueen. Sur cette pochette, il fait un portrait original de l'un des batteurs les plus funky de l'histoire. Paul Humphrey avait été l'épine dorsale de nombreux succès d'autres musiciens de soul, et il a su tirer le meilleur parti de son deuxième disque en tant que leader.

WILLIE HUTCH

title **ODE TO MY LADY** / *year* **1975** / *label* Motown / *photography* Jim Britt / *art direction* Katarina Pettersson

Willie Hutch began singing with doo-wop group The Ambassadors when he was a teenager in Texas. He went on to highly successful collaborations including work with The Jackson 5, Marvin Gaye, and Smokey Robinson, before he stepped into the spotlight as a solo artist in the late '60s. This insistently funky soul album was his best-selling solo record and included the hit "Love Power". **O**
Als Teenager in Texas sang Willie Hutch zuerst bei der Doo-Wop-Gruppe The Ambassadors. Weiter ging's für ihn mit

sehr erfolgreichen Gemeinschaftsproduktionen, z. B. mit den Jackson 5, Marvin Gaye und Smokey Robinson, bevor er sich Ende der 60er Jahre um seine Solokarriere kümmerte. Dieses ausgesprochen funkige Soulalbum war seine meistverkaufte Soloplatte und enthält den Hit »Love Power«. **O**
Willie Hutch a commencé à chanter avec le groupe de doo-wop The Ambassadors au Texas, alors qu'il était adolescent. Il a par la suite décroché des collaborations très réussies avec notamment les Jackson 5, Marvin Gaye et Smokey Robinson, avant de prendre le devant de la scène en solo à la fin des années 1960. Cet album de soul au funk insistant est son disque en solo qui s'est le mieux vendu. Il contient le tube *Love Power*.

ORIGINAL SOUNDTRACK FROM THE MOTION PICTURE
COMPOSED, ARRANGED, PRODUCED AND PERFORMED BY

THE MACK   WILLIE HUTCH

M766L

WILLIE HUTCH

title **THE MACK** / *year* **1973** / *label* Motown /
photography Jim Britt

The blaxploitation craze was in full swing and Motown spared no expense on this lavish recording. Jim Britt's sharp-focus portrait of Hutch became the outline for the die-cut gatefold cover. From the cautionary lyrics to the gritty funk, this classic score would be the soundtrack for generations of pimps to come. ○

Die Blaxploitation-Welle war in vollem Schwange, und Motown scheute bei dieser verschwenderischen Aufnahme weder Kosten noch Mühen. Jim Britts pointiertes Porträt von Hutch wurde zum Blickfang für das Ausklappalbum. Mit seinen mahnenden Texten und dem schmutzigen Funk sollte diese Filmmusik der klassische Soundtrack für Generationen angehender Zuhälter werden. ○

L'engouement pour le cinéma de blaxploitation battait son plein, et Motown n'a reculé devant aucune dépense pour cet enregistrement luxueux. Le portrait acéré que Jim Britt a réalisé de Hutch forme le contour découpé de la couverture dépliante de cette pochette. Depuis ses paroles à ne pas mettre entre toutes les oreilles jusqu'à son funk graveleux, cette bande originale allait devenir un classique pour les générations de maquereaux à venir.

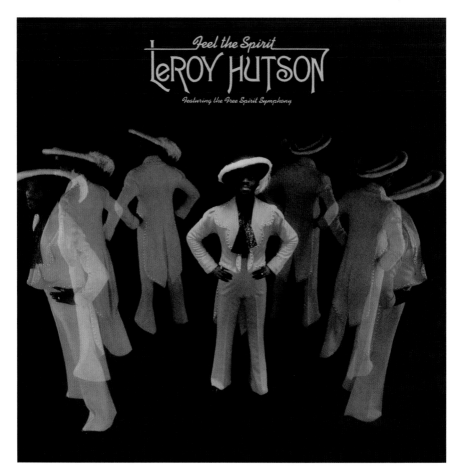

LEROY HUTSON

title **FEEL THE SPIRIT** / *year* **1976** / *label* Curtom /
photography Richard Fegley / *art direction* Jim Schubert

Leroy Hutson had taken over the reins from Curtis
Mayfield as lead singer of the Impressions for a two-album
stint in the early '70s. This, his fourth solo LP, shows him at
the height of his powers. As a writer, arranger, and producer
everything seems to have clicked for this session, which is
full of sweeping symphonic arrangements and discofied
funk. Veteran *Playboy* photographer Richard Fegley captured the multi-faceted artist with a playfully flamboyant
multiple-exposure cover shot. **O**
Leroy Hutson hatte Anfang der 70er für zwei Alben als
Leadsänger der Impressions die Zügel von Curtis Mayfield
übernommen. Dies ist seine vierte Solo-LP und zeigt ihn

auf dem Höhepunkt seines künstlerischen Schaffens. Die
Session ist voller mitreißender sinfonischer Arrangements
und discofiziertem Funk. Der *Playboy*-Hausfotograf Richard
Fegley fing den vielseitigen Künstler für dieses Cover in
einer verspielt-großspurigen Mehrfachbelichtung ein. **O**
Leroy Hutson avait repris le leadership de Curtis Mayfield
en tant que chanteur principal des Impressions, le temps
de deux albums au début des années 1970. Cet album, le
quatrième en solo, le montre au sommet de son art. En
tant qu'auteur, arrangeur et producteur, il semble que tout
ait trouvé sa place pour cette session d'enregistrement, qui
regorge d'arrangements symphoniques généreux et de
funk à la mode disco. Le photographe vétéran de *Playboy*,
Richard Fegley, a représenté cet artiste à multiples facettes
avec un cliché à expositions multiples pour cette pochette
au panache facétieux.

LEROY HUTSON

title **HUTSON** / *year* **1975** / *label* Curtom / *design* Joe Kotleba / *photography* Richard Fegley / *art direction* Jim Schubert/AGI

Jim Schubert's sense of design is always clean. He tends to lean toward a centralized image of the artist with a strong choice of type, which contributes to his covers' evocative nature without being in-your-face artsy. Much like the warm soul productions of Leroy Hutson, Schubert's magic lies in the small details that build to the overall effect. **○** Jim Schubert hat stets ein sehr klares Gespür für gute Gestaltung. Er arbeitet gern mit einem in die Mitte gerückten Bild des Musikers, das er dann mit kräftigen Schrifttypen ausstattet. Das trägt zur bewegenden Natur seiner Cover bei, ohne dass sie einen auf Kunst machen und den Betrachter gleich anspringen. Ähnlich wie bei den warmen Soul-Produktionen von Leroy Hutson zaubert Schubert kleine Details, die die Gesamtwirkung schaffen. **○** Jim Schubert a toujours aimé les graphismes nets. Il a tendance à choisir une image centrée de l'artiste et à l'agrémenter d'une police de caractères typée, qui contribue au caractère évocateur de ses pochettes sans pour autant les rendre trop esthétisantes. À l'instar de la musique soul chaleureuse de Leroy Hutson, la magie de Schubert réside dans les petits détails qui contribuent à l'effet d'ensemble.

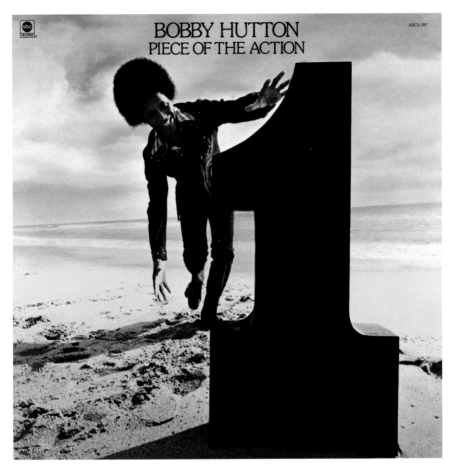

BOBBY HUTTON

title **PIECE OF THE ACTION** / *year* **1973** / *label* ABC / *design* Alan Sekuler / *photography* Al Kramer / *art direction* Ruby Boyd Mazur

The California coastline is a short drive from downtown Los Angeles, making it a convenient resource for industry folks in need of a dependable backdrop. From his native Oklahoma, Hutton would segue through an apprentice-ship at Motown and recording contracts at Chess and Phillips before releasing this bundle of Northern Soul on ABC-Dunhill. **O**

Die kalifornische Küste ist nur eine kurze Autofahrt von Downtown Los Angeles entfernt und wird so zu einer be-

quem erreichbaren Ressource für Leute aus der Branche, die eine attraktive Kulisse brauchen. Hutton kam aus Okla-homa und war in eine Ausbildung bei Motown eingestie-gen. Er hatte Plattenverträge mit Chess und Phillips, bevor er dann auf ABC-Dunhill dieses Bündel mit Northern Soul herausbrachte. **O**

La côte californienne est suffisamment proche du centre-ville de Los Angeles pour que le monde de la musique y ait régulièrement recours comme toile de fond efficace. Parti de son Oklahoma natal, Hutton allait enchaîner sur un apprentissage chez Motown puis des contrats chez Chess et Phillips, avant de sortir ce bouquet de northern soul chez ABC-Dunhill.

PHYLLIS HYMAN
title **YOU KNOW HOW TO LOVE
ME** / *year* **1979** / *label* Arista /
photography John Ford / *art direction*
Donn Davenport

IMPACT

title **IMPACT** / *year* **1976** / *label*
Atco / *photography* Paul Wilson /
art direction Arnie Roberts / *illustration*
Charles Santore

THE IMPRESSIONS
title **BIG SIXTEEN VOL. 2** /
year **1968** / *label* EMI/Stateside

THE IMPRESSIONS
title **THREE THE HARD WAY** /
year **1974** / *label* Get Back

THE IMPRESSIONS

title **TIMES HAVE CHANGED** / *year* **1972** / *label* Curtom / *design* Glen Christensen / *photography* Hal Wilson / *packaging* Milton Sincoff

Although Curtis Mayfield had stepped down as lead singer for The Impressions, he continued writing and producing for the Chicago group, who would remain productive members of his Curtom roster. Mayfield's vocal replacement would come in the form of Leroy Hutson, who joined the group merely three months after graduating from Washington, D.C.'s Howard University. ❍
Obwohl Curtis Mayfield sich als Leadsänger für die Impressions zurückgezogen hatte, komponierte und produzierte

er weiterhin für die Chicagoer Gruppe, die als produktive Mitglieder weiterhin bei seinem Label Curtom blieben. Mayfield wurde stimmlich durch Leroy Hutson ersetzt, der kaum drei Monate nach seinem Abschluss an der Howard University in Washington, D.C., zu der Gruppe stieß. ❍
Curtis Mayfield avait quitté son rôle de chanteur principal pour les Impressions, mais il continuait d'écrire et de produire pour ce groupe de Chicago, qui allait rester un membre productif de son label Curtom. C'est Leroy Hutson qui allait remplacer Mayfield au chant. Il a rejoint le groupe trois mois seulement après avoir obtenu son diplôme à l'université Howard de Washington, D.C.

THE IMPRESSIONS

title **FINALLY GOT MYSELF TOGETHER** / *year* **1973** / *label* Curtom / *photography* Joel Brodsky / *art direction* Olga Romero

Excello 8031

'THE FUNK IS... IN OUR MUSIC'

THE INGRAM KINGDOM

title **THE INGRAM KINGDOM** / *year* **1976** /
label Excello / *design* Dan Quest & Associates /
photography Estrada Bros.

This was the debut from Norman "Butch" Ingram and his
funky family. Butch started the band after an accident
forced him to give up a career in professional basketball. He
taught himself how to play the bass, bought some recording equipment, and got the family together. They came up
with this great soul LP from NJ that features sister Barbara
on vocals. Her gospel inflections help steer the set between
hard-edged funk and sweeter soul moments. **O**
Dies war das Debüt von Norman »Butch« Ingram und seiner Funk-Family. Butch rief die Band ins Leben, nachdem
ein Unfall ihn dazu gezwungen hatte, seine Karriere als

Basketball-Profi aufzugeben. Er brachte sich das Bassspielen
bei, kaufte Aufnahmegeräte und trommelte die Familie
zusammen. Sie brauten diese großartige LP mit Indepen-
dent-Soul aus New Jersey, auf der seine Schwester Barbara
als Sängerin zu hören ist. Deren Gospel-Einsprengsel helfen,
den Kurs zwischen knallhartem Funk und harmonischeren
Soul-Momenten zu halten. **O**
Ce disque était le premier album de Norman « Butch »
Ingram et de sa famille funky. Butch a mis le groupe sur
pied après un accident qui l'a forcé à abandonner sa carrière dans le basket-ball professionnel. Il a appris la basse en
autodidacte, acheté du matériel d'enregistrement et rassemblé la famille. Le résultat est ce superbe album de soul du
New Jersey, avec sa sœur Barbara au chant. Ses inflexions de
gospel font naviguer le disque entre des moments de funk
pur et dur et des moments de soul plus doux.

Weldon Irvine...Sinbad

WELDON IRVINE

title **SINBAD** / *year* **1976** / *label* RCA /
art direction Acy Lehman / *illustration* Ted Coconis

Inspired by the intensely personal work that both Marvin Gaye and Stevie Wonder were putting out, Weldon Irvine created a well-balanced set of heavy funk and deep soul that rivals anything he had done before. Ted Coconis, whose work had appeared everywhere from *Playboy* to *Ladies' Home Journal*, supplied the intricate, fantastical cover painting, which portrays Irvine as the mythical Persian sailor. **◑**

Inspiriert von Marvin Gaye und Stevie Wonder schuf Weldon Irvine eine gut ausgewogene Mischung aus mächtigem Funk und Deep Soul, die es mit allem aufnehmen konnte, was er vorher gemacht hatte. Ted Coconis, dessen Arbeiten überall vom *Playboy* bis zum *Ladies' Home Journal* erschienen waren, lieferte das komplexe, fantastische Gemälde für das Cover, auf dem Irvine als der persische Seefahrer aus der Legende porträtiert ist. **◑**

Inspiré par le travail très intime que Marvin Gaye et Stevie Wonder faisaient à l'époque, Weldon Irvine a créé un album équilibré de soul profonde et de funk intense qui vaut largement tout ce qu'il avait fait auparavant. Les illustrations de Ted Coconis ont été publiées dans de nombreux magazines, de *Playboy* à *Ladies' Home Journal*. C'est lui qui a fourni l'image complexe et fantasmagorique de la pochette, qui représente Irvine sous les traits du légendaire marin perse.

THE ISLEY BROTHERS

title **IT'S OUR THING** / *year* **1969** / *label* Polydor /
photography James Kriegsman / *art direction* Acy R.
Lehman

James Kriegsman's strong portrait of the brothers in hip
street garb signaled that they were making a clear break
from their earlier R&B style with this release. The look and
sound were right on point with the new funk sound that
was starting to come into its own. The heavy rhythms and
funky guitar sound took them to the next level. The cut
"It's Your Thing" – a sly reference to the album's title –
would prove to be their first #1 single. ⭕
James Kriegsmans kraftvolles Porträt der Brothers in
hipper Straßenkleidung signalisiert, dass sie mit diesem
Release einen klaren Schnitt zu ihrem früheren R&B-Stil

vornehmen. Look und Sound trafen genau mit dem neu-
en Funk-Sound zusammen, der gerade voll zur Geltung
kam. Mit diesen schweren Rhythmen und dem funkigen
Gitarrensound erreichten sie die nächste Stufe. Das Stück
»It's Your Thing« – eine listige Anspielung auf den
Albumtitel – sollte sich als ihre erste Nummer-eins-Single
erweisen. ⭕
Le portrait intense que James Kriegsman a réalisé des frères
Isley en costumes urbains branchés indiquait qu'avec cet
album ils se démarquaient franchement de leur ancien style
R&B. Leur look et leur son étaient parfaitement synchro
avec l'apparition du funk, qui commençait à se faire une
place. Leurs rythmes prégnants et leur guitare funky les ont
fait monter de catégorie. Le morceau *It's Your Thing* – une
allusion au titre de l'album – allait être leur premier single.

THE ISLEY BROTHERS

title **GIVIN' IT BACK** / *year*
1971 / *label* T-Neck / *photography*
Michael Ochs / *art direction* Cozbi
Sanchez-Cabrera

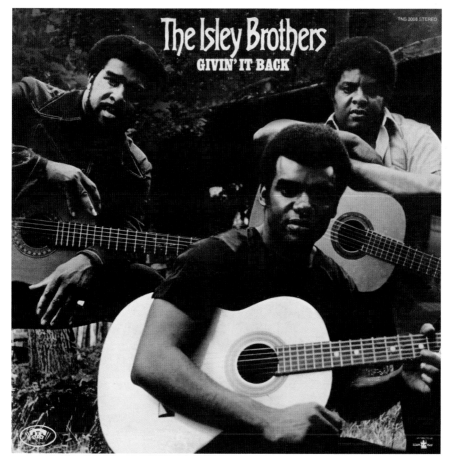

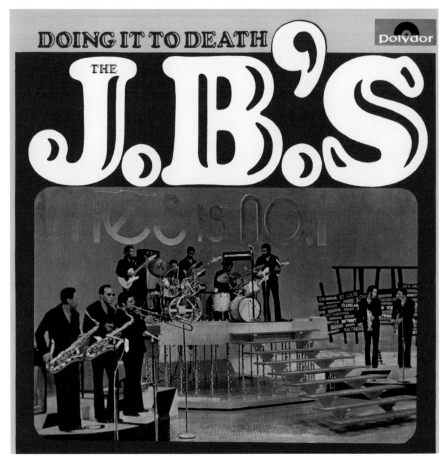

THE J.B.'S

title **DOING IT TO DEATH** / *year* **1973** / *label* Polydor

This same photograph was used a few months before to identify James Brown's versatile backing band on the jacket for the *Black Caesar* soundtrack. The photo implies that Brown may have only stepped out of frame momentarily, as the band is arranged in backing formation and a large banner, boasting James' relative ranking, suggests that the Godfather of Soul is not far away. **O**

Genau das gleiche Foto wurde wenige Monate früher benutzt, um die vielseitige Backingband von James Brown auf der Hülle für den Soundtrack von *Black Caesar* abzubilden.

Das Foto lässt darauf schließen, dass Brown nur mal eben von der Bühne gegangen ist, denn die Band ist als Backgroundband aufgestellt und ein großer Schriftzug, der großspurig den relativen Rang von James Brown angibt, legt nahe, dass der Godfather of Soul gleich wieder zurück ist. **O**

Cette photographie avait déjà été utilisée quelques mois plus tôt pour identifier le groupe aux talents multiples qui accompagnait James Brown sur la jaquette de la bande originale de *Black Cesar, le parrain de Harlem*. On peut penser que Brown s'est absenté un moment du cadre : le groupe est en place, prêt à jouer, et une grande bannière vantant la place de numéro 1 de James suggère que le Parrain de la soul n'est pas bien loin.

THE J.B.'S

title **HUSTLE WITH SPEED** / *year* **1975** / *label* People / *art direction* Bill Levy / *illustration* Fred Marcellino

James Brown's band of renowned musicians was pulling into the station for one final stop. This would be their final release with the classic line-up including Fred Wesley & Maceo Parker. Fred Marcellino's highly polished work often had a surrealistic bent to it. The design for this seminal funk record closely resembles the music by being futuristic, while at the same time nodding back to classic imagery of the past. **O**

James Browns Band mit bekannten Musikern fährt hier zu einem endgültigen Stopp in den Bahnhof ein. Dies sollte ihr finales Album in der klassischen Besetzung mit Fred Wesley und Maceo Parker sein. Die Hochglanzarbeiten von Fred Marcellino hatten oft eine surrealistische Anmutung. Die Covergestaltung für diese bahnbrechende Funk-Aufnahme ähnelt der Musik, weil sie futuristisch ist und sich gleichzeitig vor der klassischen Bildgebung der Vergangenheit verneigt. **O**

Le groupe de célèbres musiciens de James Brown faisait ici un dernier arrêt sur la route. Cet album allait être le dernier avec tous ses membres légendaires, notamment Fred Wesley et Maceo Parker. Le travail très peaufiné de Fred Marcellino était souvent surréaliste. La pochette de ce monument du funk ressemble beaucoup à la musique futuriste qu'elle illustre, tout en faisant un clin d'œil aux images classiques du passé.

THE JACKSON 5

title **ABC** / *year* **1970** / *label* Tamla
Motown

THE JACKSON 5

title **GET IT TOGETHER** / *year* **1973** / *label* Tamla
Motown / *design* Desmond Strobel/AGI / *illustration*
John Cabalka

Desmond Strobel's inventive die-cut cover design uncovers the playful energy of the band's new sound. Michael's voice had fully matured by this point and that coupled with the proto-disco of some of the heavier funk cuts make this the best record the brothers put out on Motown during the '70s. **⊙**

Desmond Strobels einfallsreiche Gestaltung mit gestanztem Cover offenbart die verspielte Energie des neuen Sounds der Band. Michaels Stimme war zu diesem Zeitpunkt vollkommen ausgereift, und gekoppelt mit dem Disco-Vorläufer einiger mächtiger Funk-Stücke wird dies zur besten Platte, die die Gebrüder während der 70er Jahre bei Motown herausbrachten. **⊙**

La pochette inventive de Desmond Strobel révèle l'énergie du nouveau son du groupe. La voix de Michael avait atteint sa maturité. Si l'on y ajoute l'ébauche de disco que l'on peut entendre sur quelques-uns des morceaux les plus funky de l'album, on obtient l'un des meilleurs disques que les frères aient sortis dans les années 1970 chez Motown.

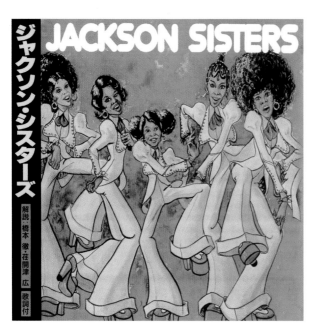

ジャクソン・シスターズ

解説：橋本 徹・荏開津 広 歌詞付

JACKSON SISTERS
title **JACKSON SISTERS** /
year **1976** / *label* Tiger Lily

MELVIN JACKSON
title **FUNKY SKULL** / *year*
1969 / *label* Limelight / *design*
Tom Staebler / *photography* Alan
Levine / *art direction* Desmond
Strobel

MICHAEL JACKSON

title **OFF THE WALL** / *year* **1979** / *label* Epic /
design Mike Salisbury / *photography* Steve Harvey

After the success of *The Wiz* Mike Salisbury contacted
Michael Jackson's agent and said he wanted to help create
an image for the superstar during his transition from kid
to adult. By combining the ideas of Frank Sinatra in *Vegas*
and Gene Kelly in *An American in Paris*, Salisbury brought
out the sophisticated, yet laid-back cool branding that the
future king of pop needed. ⦾
Nach dem Erfolg von *The Wiz* kontaktierte Mike Salisbury
Michael Jacksons Agenten und meinte, er wolle dabei hel-

fen, das Image für den Superstar im Übergang vom Kind
zum Erwachsenen zu schaffen. Indem er die Ideen von
Frank Sinatra in *Vegas* und Gene Kelly in *An American in
Paris* kombinierte, brachte Salisbury das anspruchsvolle
und gleichzeitig lässig-coole Branding hervor, das der King
of Pop brauchte. ⦾
Après le succès de *The Wiz,* Mike Salisbury a contacté
l'agent de Michael Jackson et lui a déclaré vouloir contri-
buer à créer une image pour la transition de la superstar
vers l'âge adulte. En combinant les idées de Frank Sinatra à
Vegas et de Gene Kelly dans *Un Américain à Paris*, Salisbury
a créé l'image de marque sophistiquée mais décontractée
dont le Roi de la pop avait besoin.

MICHAEL GREGORY JACKSON

title **GIFTS** / *year* **1979** / *label* Arista /
design Michael Gregory Jackson
& Katrinka Blickle / *photography*
Anthony Barboza / *art direction*
Katrinka Blickle

MILLIE JACKSON

title **CAUGHT UP** / *year* **1974** / *label* Spring /
design David Wiseltier

David Wiseltier brought an appropriately dark design concept for the cover to Millie Jackson's soulful opera about
being caught in the web of love. Brad Shapiro's lush production, full of sweeping strings and the swamp-filled funk
of the Muscle Shoals Rhythm Section, gives Millie's husky
delivery and gritty rap the space it needs to wallow in her
pain and let loose her fury. ⊙

David Wiseltier brachte für das Cover von Millie Jacksons
souliger Oper ein angemessen düsteres Gestaltungskon-
zept mit. Auf ihrer Platte geht es darum, wie man sich im

Netz der Liebe verheddern kann. Brad Shapiros üppige
Produktion mit mitreißenden Streicherklängen und dem
sumpfigen Funk der Muscle Shoals Rhythm Section verleiht Millies heiserer Darbietung und dem schmutzigen Rap
den Raum, den es braucht, damit sie sich ihrem Schmerz
hingeben und ihre Wut entfesseln kann. ⊙

David Wiseltier a choisi un concept graphique sombre
pour cette pochette, qui convient bien à l'opéra soul de
Millie Jackson sur les pièges de l'amour. La production
luxueuse de Brad Shapiro, pleine de cordes amples et du
funk marécageux du groupe Muscle Shoals Rhythm Section, donne à la voix rauque de Millie l'espace dont elle a
besoin pour explorer sa douleur et déchaîner sa fureur.

THE JACKSONS

title **LIVE** / *year* **1981** / *label* CBS /
design Tony Lane & Nancy Donald /
photography Lynn Goldsmith &
Todd Gray

RICK JAMES

title **STREET SONGS** / *year* **1981** / *label* Motown /
design Ginny Livingstone / *photography* Ron Slenzak /
art direction Johnny Lee

Buffalo, New York native Rick James breathed new life into
the Motown label, accruing several plaques with his unique
brand of punk funk. Although not immediately apparent
from the cover, the back implies that the ladies in the background are being led away by a police officer for soliciting
their services, presumably with James as their proprietor. ◗
Der aus Buffalo, New York, stammende Rick James hauchte
dem Motown-Label neues Leben ein und sammelte mit

seinem unnachahmlichen Punk Funk verschiedene Orden
ein. Auf dem Cover wird es zwar nicht gleich ersichtlich,
doch die Plattenrückseite zeigt, dass die Damen im Hintergrund von einem Polizisten abgeführt werden, weil sie ihre
Dienste angeboten haben, wahrscheinlich mit James als
ihrem Zuhälter. ◗
Rick James, natif de la ville de Buffalo, dans l'État de New
York, a insufflé une nouvelle vie au label Motown en accu-
mulant plusieurs récompenses grâce à son style unique de
punk funk. Bien que la pochette ne soit pas très explicite,
le verso indique que les femmes du second plan sont
emmenées par un policier pour lui avoir proposé leurs services, sans doute avec James comme souteneur.

AL JOHNSON

title **PEACEFUL** / *year* **1978** / *label* Marina / *design*
Debra Martinez Franqui / *photography* John Dentato

Al Johnson formed his first singing ensemble while attend-
ing Washington, D.C.'s Howard University. *Peaceful* was his
first of three solo albums, after which he would rejoin the
ranks of the Unifics, with whom he still performs. New
York photographer John Dentato has shot several album
covers, but now specializes in weddings and portraiture. **O**
Al Johnson gründete sein erstes Gesangsensemble, während er die Howard University in Washington D.C. besuchte. *Peaceful* war das erste von drei Soloalben, nach denen

er in die Riege der Unifics zurückkehrte, mit denen er noch
immer auftritt. Der New Yorker Fotograf John Dentato hat
mehrere Fotos für Plattencover geschossen, verlegte sich
aber später auf Hochzeiten und Porträts. **O**
Al Johnson a monté son premier ensemble vocal alors qu'il
étudiait à l'université Howard de Washington, D.C. *Peaceful*
a été le premier de trois albums en solo, après quoi Johnson
allait rejoindre les rangs des Unifics, avec qui il se produit
toujours aujourd'hui. Le photographe new-yorkais John
Dentato a réalisé les photographies de plusieurs pochettes
d'album, mais se spécialise aujourd'hui dans les mariages et
les portraits.

LORRAINE JOHNSON

title **LEARNING TO DANCE ALL OVER AGAIN** /
year **1978** / *label* Prelude / *design* Ancona Design Atelier /
photography Bernard Vidal

This is the kind of wrong-headed cover design that has given disco a bad name to so many of the casual passers-by. The white, gilded model who is so overtly "Learning to Dance All Over Again" is not Lorraine Johnson. It's unfortunate that the label decided to hide this amazing disco diva, but her earthy voice rings true throughout the album, which includes the early House anthem "Feed the Flame". **O**

Wegen dieser Art von starrköpfigem Coverdesign bekam Disco für viele, die eher beiläufig draufschauten, seinen schlechten Namen. Das weiße, vergoldete Model, das so offen »mit dem Tanzen ganz von vorne anfängt«, ist nicht Lorraine Johnson. Sehr bedauerlich, dass die Plattenfirma beschloss, diese erstaunliche Disco-Diva nicht aufs Cover zu lassen, doch ihre erdige Stimme ertönt mit Macht auf diesem Album, das auch die frühe House-Hymne »Feed the Flame« beherbergt. **O**

Voici le genre de pochette inepte qui a donné une mauvaise réputation au disco auprès du public. Le mannequin blanc et or qui s'évertue à « réapprendre à danser » n'est pas Lorraine Johnson. Il est regrettable que le label ait décidé de cacher cette merveilleuse diva du disco, mais sa voix terrienne résonne tout au long de l'album, qui contient l'un des premiers hymnes de la house, *Feed the Flame.*

SYL JOHNSON

title **IS IT BECAUSE I'M BLACK** / *year* **2002** / *label* Twinight / *design* Jerry Griffith / *photography* Jerry Griffith

Syl Johnson had been making his way up the R&B ladder for over a decade as a bluesman who had moved to more of a straight soul sound; by the time of his sophomore record he was ready to explore the deeper issues of race and pride. His blend of hard-hitting funk and heart-rending soul makes for one of the best records of its kind to ever come out of Chicago. Jerry Griffith often used non-traditional imagery and playful type in his cover designs. **○**
Syl Johnson hat sich als Bluesmann, der sich in Richtung eines unverwandten Soul-Sounds bewegte, über ein Jahrzehnt lang die R&B-Leiter hochgearbeitet. Als seine zweite

Scheibe erschien, war er bereit, grundlegende Themen wie Rasse und Stolz zu erforschen. Seine Mischung aus knallhartem Funk und herzergreifendem Soul sorgt für eine der besten Aufnahmen ihrer Art, die man je aus Chicago gehört hat. Jerry Griffith gestaltete seine Cover oft mit einer nicht-traditionellen Bildsprache und spielerischen Schriften. **○**
Syl Johnson avait entrepris de grimper les échelons du R&B depuis plus de dix ans. Ce bluesman s'était reconverti dans la soul, et pour son deuxième album il était prêt à explorer les thèmes de la race et de la fierté. Son mélange de funk percutant et de soul poignante fait de ce disque l'un des meilleurs de son genre à avoir vu le jour à Chicago. Jerry Griffith utilisait souvent des images et des lettres originales pour ses pochettes.

THE JONES GIRLS

title **GET AS MUCH LOVE AS YOU CAN** / *year* **1981** /
label Philadelphia International / *design* Allen Weinberg /
photography Bobby Holland

Throughout the '70s, Shirley, Brenda, and Valorie Jones
employed the familial congruency of their agreeable voices
as backing singers on recordings by Teddy Pendergrass,
Aretha Franklin, and Diana Ross, among others. With a
spectrum of Philadelphia songwriters pooling their best
disco output, The Jones Girls' gentle harmonies added an
element of elegance to the dance-floor gems featured
herein. **O**
Während der 70er Jahre setzten Shirley, Brenda und Valorie
Jones die familiäre Übereinstimmung ihrer angenehmen

Stimmen als Backgroundsängerinnen für Aufnahmen z. B.
von Teddy Pendergrass, Aretha Franklin und Diana Ross ein.
Ein ganzes Spektrum von Philadelphia-Songwritern legt
hier seinen besten Disco-Output zusammen, und die sanf-
ten Harmonien der Jones Girls ergänzen die auf dieser
Scheibe versammelten Dancefloor-Juwelen mit eleganten
Elementen. **O**
Tout au long des années 1970, Shirley, Brenda et Valorie
Jones ont utilisé l'affinité génétique de leurs voix mélodieuses comme choristes sur des enregistrements de Teddy
Pendergrass, Aretha Franklin et Diana Ross, entre autres.
Toute une équipe de compositeurs de chez Philadelphia a
mis en commun ses meilleures productions de disco, et les
harmonies délicates des Jones Girls ont ajouté leur élégance
aux perles des pistes de danse que renferme cet album.

THE JONES GIRLS

title **AT PEACE WITH WOMAN** /
year **1980** / *label* Philadelphia
International / *design* Ed Lee & Phyllis
H.B. / *photography* McGowan/Coder

SIDE ONE
VIBE-ING THEME...
PRELUDE TA HELL...
NEEDLE 'N SPOON...
COLD TURKEY...

SIDE TWO
SOUL OF BLACK FOLKS...
COURT IS CLOSED...
INSIDE BLACK AMERICA...
TIMES ARE HARD,
FRIENDS ARE FEW...

DEL JONES

title **POSITIVE VIBES** / *year* **1972** / *label* Hikeka /
design Tim Sanders & Deborah Simpson

On Del Jones' *Positive Vibes,* funky drum-breaks give way
to atmospheric flute solos, stanzas of political poetry, and
cosmic accompaniment of the highest order. The simple
iconic imagery featured on the cover makes a concise visual
statement, while the back discloses the abundant knowledge encapsulated in this Philadelphia-recorded rarity. **O**
Auf *Positive Vibes* von Del Jones gehen funkige Drum-
Breaks in atmosphärische Flötensoli über, begleitet von
Strophen mit politischer Poesie und einer kosmischen

Begleitung allerhöchster Ordnung. Die einfache, symbolträchtige Bildgebung des Covers trifft prägnante visuelle
Aussagen, während auf der Rückseite die geballte Kompe-
tenz aufgeführt wird, die auf dieser Rarität aus Philadelphia
versammelt ist. **O**
Sur cet album de Del Jones, les improvisations funky à la
batterie cèdent la place à des solos de flûte évocateurs, à
des couplets de poésie politique et à des accompagne-
ments cosmiques de premier ordre. L'image simple et
symbolique de la pochette fait preuve de concision visuelle
dans son message, tandis que le verso dévoile les abondantes connaissances que renferme cette rareté enregistrée
à Philadelphie.

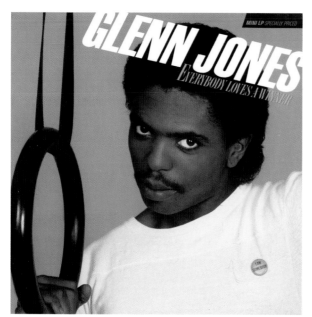

GLENN JONES
title **EVERYBODY LOVES
A WINNER** / *year* **1982** /
label RCA / *photography* Beverly
Parker / *art direction* Ron Kellum

QUINCY JONES
title **"IN THE HEAT OF
THE NIGHT"** / *year* **1967** /
label United Artists

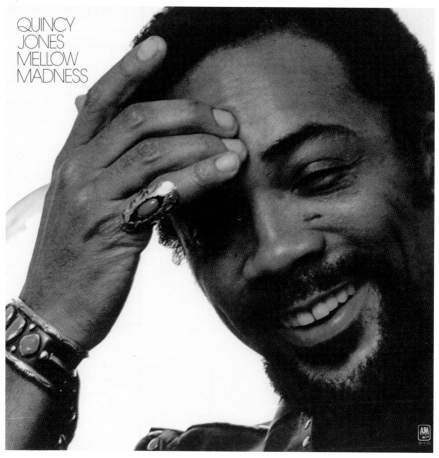

QUINCY
JONES
MELLOW
MADNESS

QUINCY JONES

title **MELLOW MADNESS** / *year* **1975** / *label* A&M /
design Chuck Beeson / *photography* Norman Seeff /
art direction Roland Young

Because of all his accomplishments as a writer, producer
(Michael Jackson's *Thriller*), conductor, and arranger it is
sometimes hard to remember what a great band-leader
Quincy Jones was in his own right. This 1975 release is a
lesser-known, but outstanding-quality testament to this
great trumpeter's contribution to funk. **O**
Wegen seiner besonderen Fähigkeiten als Texter, Produzent
(*Thriller* von Michael Jackson), Dirigent und Arrangeur ver-
gisst man leicht, was für ein ausgezeichneter Bandleader
Quincy Jones selber gewesen ist. Diese Platte von 1975 ist
ein weniger bekanntes, doch qualitativ hervorragendes
Testament des ausgezeichneten Trompeters und seines
Beitrags zum Funk. **O**
Au milieu de tous ses succès d'auteur, producteur (*Thriller*,
de Michael Jackson), directeur et arrangeur, on a parfois
tendance à oublier que Quincy Jones était aussi un grand
leader de groupe. Cet album de 1975 est peu connu, mais
c'est un excellent témoignage de la contribution de ce
grand trompettiste au funk.

STEREO UAS 5214

ORIGINAL MOTION PICTURE SCORE
THEY CALL ME MISTER TIBBS
MUSIC COMPOSED AND CONDUCTED BY
QUINCY JONES

QUINCY JONES

title **THEY CALL ME MISTER TIBBS** / *year* **1970** /
label United Artists / *art direction* Frank Gauna

This was the sequel to *In the Heat of the Night*, which also boasted a score by Quincy Jones, although this soundtrack is quite a different animal from its predecessor. Where the first film had a bluesy countrified swagger, the second was all city and the title track sets the tone with a hard, organ-driven funk blast that cements the album at the top of the blaxploitation pantheon along with *Shaft* and *Super Fly*. ◐
Dieser Nachfolger von *In the Heat of the Night* konnte sich ebenfalls einer Filmmusik von Quincy Jones rühmen, obwohl dieser Soundtrack zu einer ganz anderen Liga gehört

als sein Vorgänger. Wo der erste Film bluesartig-ländlich daherkommt, war der zweite komplett urban. Das Titelstück stimmt einen mit seiner harten, von der Orgel dominierten Funk-Rakete schon gut ein und lässt dieses Album neben *Shaft* und *Super Fly* im Blaxploitation-Pantheon ganz nach oben schnellen. ◐
Ce film était la suite de *Dans la chaleur de la Nuit*, dont la bande originale était également de Quincy Jones, bien que celle-ci soit d'une tout autre espèce. Alors que le premier film avait une atmosphère blues country décontractée, le deuxième était 100 % urbain et le morceau-titre donne le ton avec une explosion de funk et d'orgue qui cimente la position de l'album au sommet du panthéon de la blaxploitation aux côtés de *Shaft* et de *Super Fly*.

MARGIE JOSEPH

title **MARGIE JOSEPH** / *year* **1973** / *label* Atlantic /
design Loring Eutemey / *photography* Joel Brodsky

Joel Brodsky was one of the greatest photographers of the
rock and soul scene from the mid-'60s through the late
'70s. His sexy and confident image of Margie Joseph for her
first LP on the Atlantic label captures her beauty, but the
way she confronts the viewer leaves no question as to her
position as a woman who demands respect. **O**

Von Mitte der 60er bis Ende der 70er Jahre war Joel Brodsky
einer der besten Fotografen der Rock- und Soul-Szene. Sein

Bild von Margie Joseph für ihre erste LP auf dem Atlantic-
Label ist sexy und souverän. Es fängt ihre Schönheit ein,
doch die Art, wie sie sich dem Betrachter zumutet, lässt
keinen Zweifel daran, dass sie sich als Frau sieht, die Respekt
verlangt. **O**

Joel Brodsky fut l'un des plus grands photographes de la
scène du rock et de la soul, du milieu des années 1960 à
la fin des années 1970. Le portrait sexy et plein d'assurance
qu'il a réalisé de Margie Joseph pour son premier album
chez le label Atlantic met en valeur sa beauté, mais son
attitude face au spectateur ne laisse aucun doute : c'est
une femme qui exige le respect.

STEREO

JP-1001

MOODS & GROOVES
Ju-Par Universal Orchestra

JU-PAR UNIVERSAL ORCHESTRA
title **MOODS** & **GROOVES** / *year* **1976** / *label* Ju-Par

The Ju-Par Universal Orchestra was a versatile ensemble, based along Detroit's infamous 8-Mile Road. Thanks are due largely to producer/arranger/pianist Dick Boyell as well as guitarist Phil Upchurch for the grounded, yet sophisticated grooves featured herein. The cover photograph was most likely purchased from a stock agency as experts have confirmed that no such waterfalls exist in the Motor City. **O**
Das Ju-Par Universal Orchestra war ein vielseitiges Ensemble und hatte seinen Standort in der berüchtigten 8-Mile Road von Detroit. Dank gebührt hauptsächlich dem Pro-

duzenten, Arrangeur und Pianisten Dick Boyell sowie dem Gitarristen Phil Upchurch für ihre erdigen und doch ausgefeilten Grooves auf dieser Scheibe. Das Cover wurde wahrscheinlich mit einem Agentur-Foto bestückt, denn Experten bestätigen, dass es in der Motor City keinen solchen Wasserfall gibt. **O**
Le Ju-Par Universal Orchestra était un ensemble polyvalent, qui avait sa base le long de la tristement célèbre « 8-Mile Road » de Detroit. Il faut remercier le producteur / arrangeur / pianiste Dick Boyell ainsi que le guitariste Phil Upchurch pour les grooves solides mais sophistiqués de cet album. La photo de la pochette a sans doute été achetée à une banque d'images, car des experts ont confirmé que cette chute d'eau est introuvable à Detroit.

KAY-GEES

title HUSTLE WIT EVERY MUSCLE / *year* **1975** /
label Polydor / *design* Frank Daniel / *photography* Howard
Winters

American funk fans should recognize this album by its alternative title, *Keep on Bumpin' & Masterplan*, named after
its two most notorious and routinely sampled tracks. Kool
& the Gang founder Robert Bell worked closely with his
younger brother Kevin to ensure that Kevin's Kay-Gees
exhibited all the funkiness of his own revered combo. **O**
Die amerikanischen Funk-Fans sollten dieses Album von
seinem alternativen Titel her kennen: *Keep on Bumpin' &*

Masterplan, benannt nach den beiden berühmtesten und
am häufigsten gesampelten Tracks. Robert Bell, der Gründer von Kool and the Gang, arbeitete eng mit seinem
jüngeren Bruder Kevin zusammen und stellte sicher, dass
Kevins Kay-Gees all die Funkiness seiner eigenen verehrten
Combo besaß. **O**
Les fans de funk américains devraient connaître cet album
sous son autre titre *Keep on Bumpin' & Masterplan*, tiré de
ses deux morceaux les plus célèbres et les plus samplés.
Robert Bell, le fondateur de Kool and the Gang, a travaillé
en étroite collaboration avec son petit frère Kevin pour
s'assurer que les Kay-Gees, le groupe de Kevin, fasse autant
honneur au funk que son propre groupe légendaire.

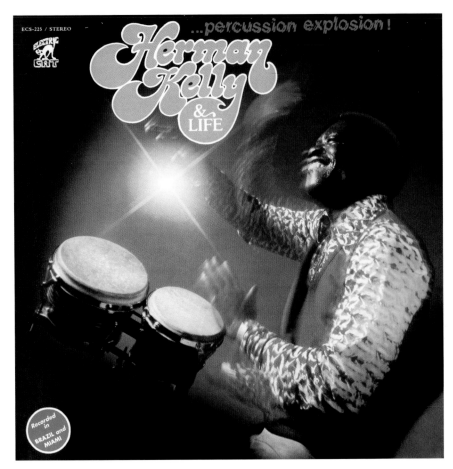

ECS-225 / STEREO

...percussion explosion!

HERMAN Kelly & LIFE

Recorded in BRAZIL and MIAMI

HERMAN KELLY & LIFE

title **PERCUSSION EXPLOSION!** / *year* **1978** /
label Electric Cat / *design* Drago Fernandez /
photography Al Freddy

Al Freddy has been working the Miami music scene for
over thirty years, photographing album covers for indigenous artists from the Floridian worlds of bass, rap, and
Latin. Recorded in both Miami and Brazil, Herman Kelly's
Percussion Explosion! is just that, thanks largely to the
break-beat classic, "Dance to the Drummer's Beat". ✪
Al Freddy arbeitete mehr als 30 Jahre in der Musikszene
von Miami und schuf Fotos für Albumcover einheimischer

Künstler, die sich in der Bass-, Rap- und Latinszene Floridas
tummelten. Die *Percussion Explosion!* von Herman Kelly
wurde in Miami und Brasilien aufgezeichnet und ist dank
des Breakbeat-Klassikers »Dance to the Drummer's Beat«
auch genau so eine Explosion geworden. ✪
Al Freddy travaille sur le monde de la musique à Miami
depuis plus de trente ans et prend des clichés pour les
pochettes d'album d'artistes floridiens des mondes de la
Miami bass, du rap et de la musique latine. Enregistré à
Miami et au Brésil, cet album de Herman Kelly est effective-
ment une explosion de percussions, surtout grâce au
classique du breakbeat *Dance to the Drummer's Beat.*

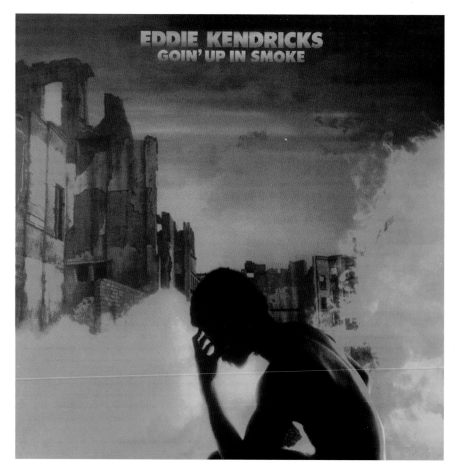

EDDIE KENDRICKS

title **GOIN' UP IN SMOKE** / *year* **1976** / *label* Tamla /
design Glen Christensen / *photography* Tom Kelley /
art direction Wriston Jones

Photographer Tom Kelley Sr. is best known for his Red
Velvet Collection, a series of sexy stills that featured an unknown Marilyn Monroe posing nude across vast expanses
of red velvet. However, it was Tom Kelley Jr. who posed
singer Eddie Kendricks before this bombed-out European
backdrop, employing dry ice and colored gels to achieve
this dramatic cover. **O**
Der Fotograf Tom Kelley Sr. wurde bekannt für seine Red
Velvet Collection. Bei dieser Serie erotischer Bilder posierte

die damals noch unbekannte Marilyn Monroe nackt auf
Unmengen von rotem Samt. Tom Kelley Jr. war es, der den
Sänger Eddie Kendricks vor diesen ausgebombten Hinter-
grund in Europa stellte und mit Trockeneis und farbigen
Gels dieses dramatische Cover schuf. **O**
Le photographe Tom Kelley Sr. est connu pour sa collec-
tion *Red Velvet,* une série de clichés où une inconnue du
nom de Marilyn Monroe posait nue sur du velours rouge.
C'est cependant Tom Kelley Sr. qui a fait poser le chanteur
Eddie Kendricks devant ce fond d'Europe bombardée et a
employé de la glace carbonique et des gels colorés pour
obtenir cette pochette spectaculaire.

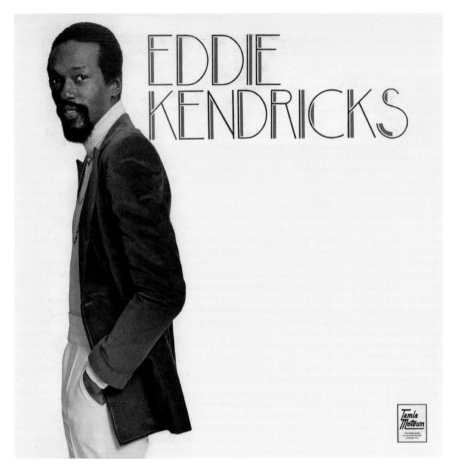

EDDIE KENDRICKS

title **EDDIE KENDRICKS** / *year* **1973** /
label Tamla Motown / *photography* Jim Britt

Motown photographer Jim Britt captured this casual,
yet confident portrait of Eddie Kendricks for his self-titled
release on Motown subsidiary, Tamla. Britt and Kendricks
were far from strangers, as the photographer would take
many lasting images of the famous tenor, both as a solo
artist and as a component of The Temptations' most
famous incarnation. **O**
Der Motown-Fotograf Jim Britt schoss dieses lässige und
doch selbstbewusste Porträt von Eddie Kendricks für
dessen Album gleichen Namens, erschienen beim Label

Tamla, der Tochterfirma von Motown. Britt und Kendricks
waren einander beileibe keine Unbekannten mehr, hatte
der Fotograf den berühmten Tenor als Solokünstler wie
auch als Mitglied der berühmten Temptations doch schon
auf vielen unvergesslichen Bildern festgehalten. **O**
C'est le photographe de Motown Jim Britt qui a pris ce
portrait décontracté mais plein d'assurance d'Eddie
Kendricks pour son album éponyme chez Tamla, une filiale
de Motown. Britt et Kendricks n'étaient pas des étrangers
l'un pour l'autre, car le photographe allait être l'auteur de
nombreuses images marquantes du célèbre ténor, en tant
qu'artiste soliste et membre de l'incarnation la plus célèbre
des Temptations.

back to soul
ANNA KING

MAKE UP YOUR MIND / IF SOMEBODY TOLD YOU

COME ON HOME · SITTING IN THE DARK · THAT'S WHEN I CRY · I FOUND YOU · I DON'T WANT TO CRY · NIGHT TIME IS THE RIGHT TIME
TENNESSEE WALTZ · BABY, BABY, BABY · COME AND GET THESE MEMORIES · IF YOU DON'T THINK

STEREO SRS 67059

ANNA KING

title **BACK TO SOUL** / *year* **1964** / *label* Smash /
design Wayne Printing Corp.

Philadelphia native Anna King joins the ranks of soul sisters
Tammi Terrell and Lyn Collins as female alumni of the James
Brown Revue. Although King's tenure with the Godfather
of Soul lasted only one year, the partnership yielded several
singles and one precious full-length for Smash Records. **O**
Die in Philadelphia geborene Anna King reiht sich ein in die
Riege der Soul Sisters Tammi Terrell und Lyn Collins als Kol-
leginnen der James Brown Revue. Obwohl ihre Anstellung
beim Godfather of Soul nur ein Jahr währte, ergab die
Partnerschaft mehrere Singles und eine kostbare Langspielplatte für Smash Records. **O**
Anna King, originaire de Philadelphie, rejoint les rangs des
soul sisters Tammi Terrell et Lyn Collins comme ancienne
élève de la James Brown Revue. Bien qu'elle ne soit restée
qu'un an aux côtés du Parrain de la soul, ce partenariat
a donné lieu à plusieurs singles et à un magnifique disque
longue durée chez Smash Records.

**EVELYN
"CHAMPAGNE"
KING**
title **SMOOTH TALK** /
year **1977** / *label* RCA Victor

**MIKE JAMES
KIRKLAND**
title **DOIN' IT RIGHT** /
year **1973** / *label* Bryan

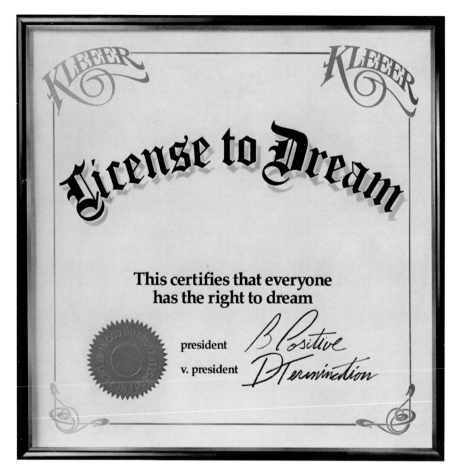

KLEEER

title **LICENSE TO DREAM** / *year* **1981** / *label* Atlantic

After serving a term as disco progenitor Patrick Adams' notorious Universal Robot Band, the New York quartet decided to chart their own course as the newly renamed Kleeer. Authorized by the cleverly conceived B. Positive and D. Termination, Kleeer's *License to Dream* set a competitive pace for futuristic funk outfits like Slave and Cameo. ○ Nachdem die Musiker dieses New Yorker Quartetts eine Zeit lang als Disco-Urahnen gedient hatten, beschloss die berühmt-berüchtigte Universal Robot Band von Patrick Adams, eigene Wege zu gehen, und benannte sich in Kleeer

um. Mit der Autorisierung auf dem Cover durch das schlau ausgedachte Wortspiel *B. Positive* (sei positiv) und *D. Termination* (Entschlossenheit) setzten Kleeer auf ihrem Album *License to Dream* einen konkurrenzfähigen Standard für futuristische Funk-Formationen wie Slave und Cameo. ○ Après avoir officié un temps dans le célèbre groupe Universal Robot Band du maître du disco Patrick Adams, le quartette a décidé de suivre son propre chemin sous le nouveau nom de Kleeer. Certifié par messieurs B. Positive et D. Termination, l'album *License to Dream* de Kleeer donnait un exemple ambitieux pour les groupes de funk futuristes tels que Slave ou Cameo.

BOOBIE KNIGHT
& THE SOULCIETY

title **SOUL AIN'T NO NEW THING** /
year **1972** / *label* RCA

No, that's not a typographical error – that's just Boobie
Knight and the Soulciety posing for their recorded debut.
This band of session musicians was assembled by RCA's
recent acquisition, producer Harvey Fuqua, who was instrumental in the development of Motown, distributing the
budding label's earliest releases, and giving Marvin Gaye his
start. **O**
Nein, das ist kein typografischer Fehler, sondern einfach nur
Boobie Knight and the Soulciety, die für ihr Debütalbum

posieren. Diese Band aus Sessionmusikern wurde vom
Produzenten Harvey Fuqua zusammengestellt, einem
Neuzugang bei RCA. Fuqua war bei der Entwicklung von
Motown behilflich und sorgte für den Vertrieb der frühes-
ten Veröffentlichungen dieses sich gerade entfaltenden
Labels. Er verhalf auch Marvin Gaye an den Start. **O**
Non, ce n'est pas un accident typographique, c'est simplement Boobie Knight and the Soulciety posant pour
l'enregistrement de leurs débuts. Ce groupe de musiciens
de studio a été réuni par le producteur Harvey Fuqua
peu après son arrivée chez RCA. Il a joué un rôle essentiel
dans le développement de Motown en distribuant les
premiers albums du label naissant et en donnant sa chance
à Marvin Gaye.

**GLADYS KNIGHT
& THE PIPS**
title **CLAUDINE** / *year* **1974** / *label*
Buddah / *design* Marlene Bergman

**JAMES KNIGHT
AND THE BUTLERS**
title **BLACK KNIGHT** / *label* Cat /
photography Peter Nashick

KONGAS

title **AFRICANISM** / *year* **1977** / *label* Polydor /
photography Patrick Perroquin

Photographer Patrick Perroquin shot several covers for
French producer Cerrone, whose numerous productions
integrated elements of electronica and erotica, yielding a
sexy brand of distinctly European dance music. Despite
Cerrone's frequent use of alligators to honor his Malligator
imprint, this baby reptile's V-shaped snout indicates that it
is most likely a crocodile. ❍
Der Fotograf Patrick Perroquin schoss verschiedene Cover
für den französischen Produzenten Cerrone, bei dessen
zahlreichen Produktionen Elemente von Electronica und

Erotika integriert sind, was diese unvergleichlich europäi-
sche Tanzmusik sehr sexy macht. Cerrone arbeitete zu
Ehren seines Labels Malligator oft mit Alligatoren, doch in
diesem Fall lässt die V-förmige Schnauze dieses Babyreptils
darauf schließen, dass hier höchstwahrscheinlich ein Kro-
kodil am Schwanz hängt. ❍
Le photographe Patrick Perroquin a travaillé sur plusieurs
pochettes pour le producteur français Cerrone, dont
l'œuvre prolifique combinait musique électronique et érotisme, et affichait un style de musique de danse sensuel et
très européen. Cerrone utilisait souvent des alligators en
référence à son label Malligator, mais le museau triangulaire
de ce jeune reptile indique qu'il s'agit plutôt d'un crocodile.

KOOL & THE GANG

title **WILD AND PEACEFUL** / *year* **1973** / *label* De-Lite /
design Richard Askew / *illustration* Joseph Askew

New Jersey native Joseph Askew performed in early incarnations of the Gang, before following his love of drawing and painting to the Art Students League of New York. For this landscape he enlisted the old master technique, combining egg tempera with oil paint, an effective procedure he gleaned from colleague and fellow cover artist Mati Klarwein. ❍

Der aus New Jersey stammende Joseph Askew trat in früheren Gruppierungen der Gang auf, bevor er in der Art Students League of New York seiner Liebe für das Zeichnen und Malen nachgab. Für diese Landschaft setzte er eine Technik der alten Meister ein und kombinierte Eitempera mit Ölfarbe. Diese wirksame Prozedur hatte er bei seinem Kollegen und Covergestalter Mati Klarwein ausfindig gemacht. ❍

Joseph Askew, originaire du New Jersey, a joué avec les premières formations du Gang, avant de suivre sa passion pour le dessin et la peinture qui l'a mené à la Ligue des étudiants d'art de New York. Pour ce paysage, il a utilisé une vieille technique de maître, qui combine une détrempe à l'œuf avec de la peinture à l'huile, un procédé efficace qu'il tenait de son collègue également créateur de pochettes de disque, Mati Klarwein.

KOOL AND THE GANG

title **OPEN SESAME** / *year* **1976** / *label* De-Lite /
illustration Arthur Thompson

Between the early-career funk of "Jungle Boogie" and later-career disco of "Ladies' Night", the Jersey City ensemble endured a mild metamorphosis, encapsulated on the mid-career oddity, *Open Sesame*. Despite being panned by critics for funk depravity, the intricate horns and perfect pacing of the title track earned "Open Sesame" an honorable spot on the *Saturday Night Fever* soundtrack. **O**

Zwischen dem frühen Funk vom Anfang ihrer Karriere wie »Jungle Boogie« und dem späteren Disco-Kracher »Ladies Night« durchlief das Ensemble aus Jersey City eine milde Metamorphose, die sich auf *Open Sesame*, dieser Kuriosität aus der mittleren Phase ihrer Karriere, ganz ausgeprägt zeigt. Obwohl diese Platte von der Kritik wegen ihres verkommenen Funks verrissen wurde, verdiente sich das Titelstück »Open Sesame« wegen seiner komplexen Bläser-sätze und des perfekten Tempos einen Ehrenplatz im Soundtrack von *Saturday Night Fever*. **O**

Entre le funk du début de sa carrière (*Jungle Boogie*) et le disco qui a suivi (*Ladies Night*), ce groupe de Jersey City est passé par une petite métamorphose illustrée dans cette curiosité de milieu de carrière, *Open Sesame*. Cet album a été éreinté par la critique pour crime de dépravation du funk, mais la complexité des cuivres et la perfection du rythme du morceau-titre ont valu à *Open Sesame* une place honorable sur la bande originale de *Saturday Night Fever*.

FELA ATI AFRIKA 70

title **AUTHORITY STEALING** / *year* **1980** /
label Kalakuta / *illustration* Frances Kuboye

Despite losing his mother, his master tapes, and large portions of his home during several unsanctioned police raids on his Lagos compound, Fela Kuti lashed out against all offending parties on *Authority Stealing*. Fela's niece Frances Kuboye, also a well-known singer and television hostess, created this controversial cover, taking shots at the CIA, the oil industry, and several powerful African politicians. **O**

Obwohl er durch verschiedene eigenmächtige Polizeirazzien auf seinem Gelände in Lagos seine Mutter und seine Mastertapes verlor und große Teile seines Zuhauses zerstört wurden, teilte Fela Kuti auf *Authority Stealing* kräftig gegen alle seine Angreifer aus. Felas Nichte Frances Kuboye, ebenfalls eine bekannte Sängerin und Fernsehmoderatorin, schuf dieses kontroverse Cover und rückte dabei die CIA, die Ölindustrie und verschiedene mächtige afrikanische Politiker ins Fadenkreuz. **O**

Bien qu'il ait perdu sa mère, les masters de ses enregistrements et de larges portions de sa maison au cours de plusieurs raids policiers arbitraires dans son quartier de Lagos, avec *Authority Stealing* Fela Kuti s'en est pris violemment à ses agresseurs. C'est la nièce de Fela, Frances Kuboye, chanteuse connue et animatrice de télévision, qui a créé cette pochette polémique critiquant la CIA, l'industrie pétrolière et plusieurs poids lourds de la politique africaine.

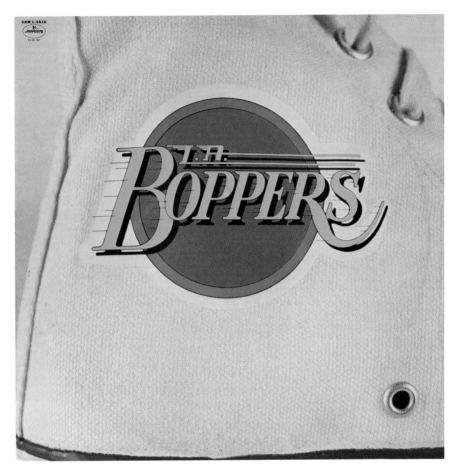

L.A. BOPPERS
title **L.A. BOPPERS** / *year* **1980** /
label Mercury / *photography* Elliot
Gilbert / *art direction* Art Sims

LABELLE
title **CHAMELEON** / *year* **1976** / *label* CBS / *design* Ed Lee & Andy Engel / *illustration* Guy Fery

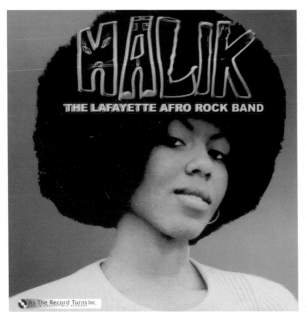

THE LAFAYETTE AFRO ROCK BAND
title **MALIK** / *year* **1976** / *label* As The Record Turns

LAKESIDE

title **FANTASTIC VOYAGE** / *year* **1980** / *label* Solar

The funkiest pirates since P-Funk donned feathered caps, these Ohio transplants hit the L.A. vibe just right on their 4th LP. An infectious bass line and spirited vocals took the band from rocky waters to smooth sailing up the charts all the way to #1 with the classic title cut. **O**

Die funkigsten Piraten, seit man sich im P-Funk federgeschmückte Hütchen aufgesetzt hat. Diese aus Ohio angespülte Band traf mit ihrer vierten LP haargenau die L.A.-Stimmung. Ansteckende Basslinien und ihr beseelter Gesang brachten die Band aus stürmischer See in ruhigeres Gewässer, wo sie mit dem Titelklassiker direkt auf Platz 1 der Charts segeln konnten. **O**

Les pirates les plus funky depuis P-Funk portaient des chapeaux à plumes. Sur leur quatrième album, ces transfuges de l'Ohio ont mis le doigt sur l'atmosphère de L.A. Une ligne de basse contagieuse et des voix fougueuses ont soufflé dans les voiles du groupe et l'ont fait voguer en première place des classements avec le morceau-titre, devenu un classique.

LAKESIDE

title **SHOT OF LOVE** / *year* **1978** / *label* Solar / *design* Tim Bryant/Gribbitt! / *illustration* Drew Struzan

Drew Struzan was in high demand when Lakeside's Solar Records debut came out. His decidedly stylized, yet uncannily representational style of airbrush-painting had kept him working steadily as a cover artist since the early '70s. He had just finished his first movie poster for the Star Wars franchise, which would be the start of a lifelong relationship with George Lucas and Steven Spielberg. He would go on to be one of the most recognized illustrators in the world. ⭘ Drew Struzan war schwer gefragt, als das Debüt von Lakeside bei Solar Records erschien. Seinem entschlossen stilisierenden und doch frappierend gegenständlichen

Airbrush-Stil verdankte er seit den frühen 70er Jahren kontinuierlich Aufträge als Coverkünstler. Er hatte gerade sein erstes Filmplakat für die *Star Wars*-Reihe fertiggestellt, was den Beginn einer lebenslangen Beziehung zu George Lucas und Steven Spielberg markierte. Er wurde zu einem der bekanntesten Illustratoren der Welt. ⭘ Drew Struzan était très demandé lorsque le premier album de Lakeside est sorti chez Solar Records. Son style de peinture à l'aérographe très stylisée mais extrêmement réaliste lui avait fourni du travail régulier en tant qu'illustrateur de pochettes depuis le début des années 1970. Il venait juste de terminer sa première affiche pour la trilogie de *Star Wars*, ce qui allait être le début d'une longue relation avec George Lucas et Steven Spielberg. Il allait devenir l'un des illustrateurs les plus célèbres du monde.

BILLY LARKIN
& THE DELEGATES

title **HOLD ON!** / *year* **1966** / *label* Fontana

Designed in a time when a pretty face could help propel
an unknown artist, Billy Larkin's organ-jazz bombshell easily
rivals the arbitrary brunette chosen to market it. In addition
to the Isaac Hayes/David Porter-penned title track, the
quartet crafts clever adaptations of several unlikely compositions, including the garage rock standard "Dirty Water",
and Bob Dylan's "Blowin' in the Wind". ⊙

Das Cover wurde in einer Zeit gestaltet, als ein hübsches
Gesicht einem unbekannten Musiker zu einem guten Start
verhelfen konnte, aber Billy Larkins orgelgetränkte Jazz-
bombe konnte mit Leichtigkeit mit jener willkürlich zur

Vermarktung gewählten brünetten Dame mithalten. Ne-
ben dem von Isaac Hayes und David Porter komponierten
Titelstück schuf das Quartett außerdem gewitzte Adaptio-
nen mehrerer ungleichartiger Kompositionen, darunter der
Garagenrock-Standard »Dirty Water« und Bob Dylans
»Blowin' in the Wind«. ⊙

Sur cette pochette conçue à une époque où un joli minois
pouvait aider à lancer la carrière d'un artiste inconnu, la
bombe de jazz propulsée à l'orgue de Billy Larkin concurrence sans peine l'inconnue brune choisie pour en faire
la publicité. Outre le morceau-titre écrit par Isaac Hayes
et David Porter, le quartette réalise des adaptations intelli-
gentes de plusieurs compositions improbables, notamment
le standard du garage rock *Dirty Water* et *Blowin' in the
Wind* de Bob Dylan.

DENISE LASALLE
title **TRAPPED BY A THING
CALLED LOVE** / *year* **1972** /
label Westbound / *photography* Joel
Brodsky / *art direction* David Krieger

THE LAST POETS

Douglas **3**

THE LAST POETS

title **THE LAST POETS** / *year* **1971** / *label* Douglas 3 /
photography Doug Harris

A template for rap, the debut from The Last Poets is a
spare affair full of syncopated patter and hand percussion.
Members Abiodun Oyewole, Alafia Pudim, and Umar
Bin Hassan, plus the percussionist Nilaja, make their way
through an urban jungle of revolutionary words that
are as fresh and vibrant today as they were when this was
recorded. **O**
Dieses Debüt der Last Poets ist eine Matrize für Rap, eine
karge Angelegenheit voller Synkopen und Hand-Percus-
sions. Zu den letzten Poeten gehören Abiodun Oyewole,

Alafia Pudim und Umar Bin Hassan plus der Percussionist
Nilaja. Sie bahnen sich ihren Weg durch einen urbanen
Dschungel revolutionärer Worte, die heute so frisch
und pulsierend sind wie damals, als sie aufgenommen
wurden. **O**
Le premier album des Last Poets est une œuvre dépouillée
qui préfigurait le rap, remplie de prose syncopée et de
percussions à main. Les membres du groupe, Abiodun
Oyewole, Alafia Pudim et Umar Bin Hassan, plus le percussionniste Nilaja, se fraient un chemin à travers une jungle
urbaine de mots révolutionnaires qui sont tout aussi
actuels et significatifs aujourd'hui que lorsqu'ils ont été
enregistrés.

RONNIE LAWS
title **PRESSURE SENSITIVE** /
year **1975** / *label* Blue Note / *design*
Bob Cato / *art direction* Bob Cato /
illustration Peter Lloyd

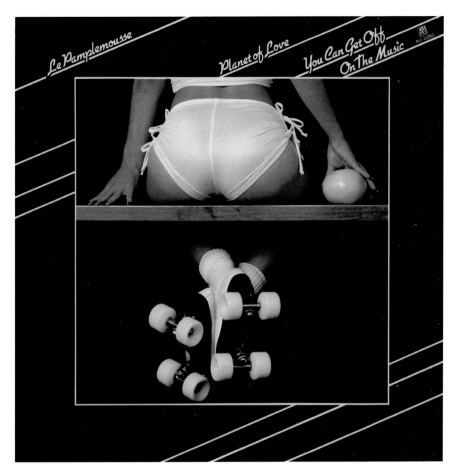

LE PAMPLEMOUSSE
title **PLANET OF LOVE – YOU CAN GET OFF ON THE MUSIC** / *year* **1979** / *label* AVI / *design* The Committee / *photography* James Mares

Whether the band was called Le Pamplemousse, El Coco, or Saint Tropez, the two men behind the music were Laurin Rinder & W. Michael Lewis. Between them they had played on everything from jazz to 1950s rock 'n' roll to Motown soul to acid rock. They got in on the ground floor of the disco movement as just another gig, but these multi-instrumentalists' contributions to disco would be immeasurable. ◗

Egal ob die Band Le Pamplemousse, El Coco oder Saint Tropez hieß – hinter der Musik steckten Laurin Rinder

und W. Michael Lewis. Sie hatten einfach alles gespielt – von Jazz über Rock'n'Roll der 50er Jahre und Motown Soul bis zu Acid Rock. Bei Disco stiegen sie wie zu einem weiteren Gig im Erdgeschoss ein, doch der Beitrag dieser Multiinstrumentalisten zur Disco-Bewegung war unermesslich. ◗

Que le groupe se soit appelé Le Pamplemousse, El Coco ou Saint Tropez, les deux hommes derrière la musique étaient Laurin Rinder et W. Michael Lewis. À eux deux, ils avaient tout joué, du jazz, du rock'n'roll des années 1950, de la soul de Motown, et même de l'acid rock. Ils ont fait leur entrée dans le disco à travers un petit job qui n'avait rien de particulier, mais ces multi-instrumentistes allaient apporter à ce genre musical une contribution incommensurable.

women's love rights ♥ laura lee

LAURA LEE

title **WOMEN'S LOVE RIGHTS** / *year* **1971** /
label Hot Wax / *design* Craig Braun, Inc. /
photography Armen Khachaturian

With her sleepy eyes and raspy voice, Laura Lee helped lead the way for the strong soul sister in the late '60s and early '70s. The power of her bluesy funk stems from her early days as a gospel singer, and much like the cover to this album she is positioned as a no-nonsense woman emerging from the trappings of an old-school man's world. ❍
Mit ihren Schlafzimmeraugen und der kratzigen Stimme hatte Laura Lee Ende der 60er und Anfang der 70er Jahre den Weg für die starke Soul Sister geebnet. Die Power ihres bluesigen Funk stammt aus ihren frühen Tagen als Gospelsängerin, und ähnlich wie auf dem Cover dieses Albums positioniert sie sich als geradlinige Frau, die aus den Fallstricken einer altmodischen Männerwelt hervortritt. ❍
Avec ses paupières lourdes et sa voix rauque, Laura Lee était la chef de file des femmes fortes de la soul à la fin des années 1960 et au début des années 1970. La puissance de son funk teinté de blues est issue de ses débuts de chanteuse de gospel et, tout comme elle est représentée sur la pochette, c'est une femme qui a les pieds sur terre et qui a su faire son chemin dans un monde traditionnellement masculin.

LEMURIA

title **LEMURIA** / *year* **1978** / *label* Heaven

Kirk Thompson, a veteran of local Hawaiian group Kalapana, founded the spiritual funk ensemble Lemuria. He said, "We named the group and the album after the legendary Pacific continent." There were 16 members culled from the best players Hawaii had to offer, including percussionist "Master" Henry Gibson, who had performed with the likes of Curtis Mayfield, Rotary Connection, and Donny Hathaway. The modern soul sound was built around four female vocalists called The Ladies Of Lemuria. ●
Kirk Thompson, ein Veteran der Gruppe Kalapana aus Hawaii, gründete das spirituelle Funk-Ensemble Lemuria. Er sagt: »Wir tauften Gruppe und Album auf den Namen des legendären pazifischen Kontinents.« Die 16 Mitglieder wurden aus den besten auf Hawaii zu findenden Musikern ausgewählt, z. B. der Perkussionist »Master« Henry Gibson, der mit Größen wie Curtis Mayfield, Donny Hathaway und Rotary Connection aufgetreten war. Ihr moderner Soulsound rankte sich um vier Sängerinnen, die sich »The Ladies Of Lemuria« nannten. ●
C'est Kirk Thompson, un vétéran du groupe hawaïen Kalapana, qui a créé la formation de funk spirituel Lemuria. D'après lui, « le groupe et l'album ont été baptisés d'après le légendaire continent du Pacifique du même nom ». Le groupe comptait 16 membres, sélectionnés parmi les meilleurs musiciens qu'Hawaï avait à offrir, notamment le percussionniste « Master » Henry Gibson, qui avait joué, entre autres, avec Curtis Mayfield, Rotary Connection et Donny Hathaway. Leur son de modern soul était construit autour de quatre chanteuses appelées « Ladies of Lemuria ».

O'DONEL LEVY
title EVERYTHING I DO GONNA
BE FUNKY / *year* 1974 / *label*
Groove Merchant / *design* David
Lartaud / *photography* Manny
Gonzales / *art direction* Frank Daniel

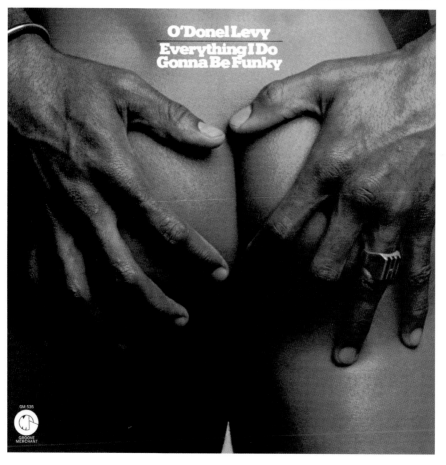

RAMSEY LEWIS ♦ SUN GODDESS

RAMSEY LEWIS

title **SUN GODDESS** / *year* **1974** / *label* Columbia /
design John Berg / *photography* Herb Breuer

Herb Breuer's electrifying cover photo sets the mood for
Ramsey Lewis' ode to sun-kissed funk. Lewis' former
drummer, Maurice White, matches the great keyboardist's
gospel-inflected playing with intensity, while White's group
Earth, Wind & Fire lend their mighty groove-oriented funk
to great effect. ❍
Das elektrisierende Coverfoto von Herb Breuer stimmt
auf den sonnenverwöhnten Funk von Ramsey Lewis ein.

Maurice White, der frühere Schlagzeuger von Lewis, nimmt
es in seiner Spielweise mit der Intensität des vom Gospel
beeinflussten großen Keyboarders auf, während Whites
Gruppe Earth, Wind & Fire ihren kraftvollen, Groove-orien-
tierten Funk sehr wirkungsvoll einsetzt. ❍
La photo électrisante de Herb Breuer pour la pochette
donne le ton pour l'ode au funk ensoleillé de Ramsey Lewis.
L'ancien batteur de Lewis, Maurice White, répond avec
intensité au jeu teinté de gospel du claviériste, tandis que
le groupe Earth, Wind & Fire de White prête son puissant
funk groovy.

Ramsey Lewis

Love Notes

RAMSEY LEWIS

title **LOVE NOTES** / *year* **1978** / *label* CBS

The cover shot captures Lewis' hands in mid-action, ready to caress the keys, yet held in perpetually delicious tension over them. Utilizing a plethora of funky keyboards and getting an assist from Stevie Wonder, this is the jumping-off point for the soul jazz sound that is still popular today. **O**
Das Cover zeigt die Finger von Lewis mitten im Spiel und bereit, die Klaviertasten zu liebkosen, aber sie verharren noch in einer delikaten Spannung über den Tasten. Dies war, unterstützt von einer Fülle funkiger Keyboards und mit dem Beistand von Stevie Wonder, der zündende Funke für den auch heute noch populären Souljazz-Sound. **O**
La photo de la pochette saisit les mains de Lewis en pleine action, prêtes à caresser les touches mais suspendues dans une délicieuse tension perpétuelle au-dessus d'elles. L'album emploie une pléthore de claviers funky et a bénéficié de l'aide de Stevie Wonder. C'est la rampe de lancement du son soul-jazz qui est toujours populaire aujourd'hui.

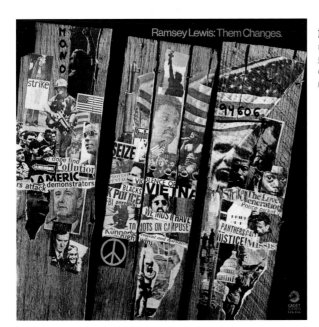

RAMSEY LEWIS
title **THEM CHANGES** /
year **1970** / *label* Cadet /
design Dick Fowler /
photography Alan Levine

**LIGHT OF
THE WORLD**
title **CHECK US OUT** /
year **1982** / *label* EMI / *design*
Cream / *photography* Gered
Mankowitz / *art direction* Cream

The LIGHTMEN plus ONE

ENERGY CONTROL CENTER

LIGHTIN' RECORDS

STEREO

THE LIGHTMEN PLUS ONE
title **ENERGY CONTROL CENTER** / *year* **1972** /
label Lightin' / *illustration* Anthony X Haynes

Anthony X Haynes provided the ominous, afrocentric image of cosmic chaos that leads the way into the musical universe of Bubbha Thomas & The Lightmen. With an arsenal of John Coltrane licks and Sun Ra space jazz, this surprising Texas outfit churn out a heavy set of funky cuts. ⭘
Anthony X Haynes lieferte das ominöse, afrikanisch inspirierte Bild eines kosmischen Chaos, das den Weg ins musi-

kalische Universum von Bubbha Thomas & The Lightmen ebnet. Mit einem Arsenal an John-Coltrane-Licks und Space Jazz im Stil von Sun Ra rührt dieser erstaunliche Texas-Trupp eine mächtige Mischung funkiger Stücke zusammen. ⭘
C'est Anthony X Haynes qui a fourni l'image sinistre de chaos cosmique qui sert de porte d'entrée à l'univers musical de Bubbha Thomas & The Lightmen. Avec un arsenal de riffs à la Coltrane et un jazz cosmique à la Sun Ra, ce surprenant groupe texan a composé un album solidement funky.

**LONNIE LISTON
SMITH & THE
COSMIC ECHOES**
title **REFLECTIONS OF A
GOLDEN DREAM** / *year* **1976** /
label Flying Dutchman /
art direction Acy Lehman /
illustration Jack Martin

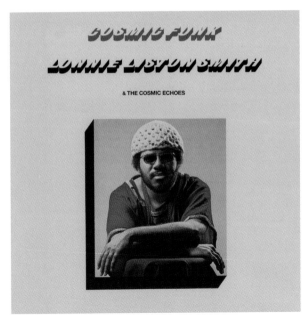

**LONNIE LISTON
SMITH & THE
COSMIC ECHOES**
title **COSMIC FUNK** / *year* **1974** /
label Flying Dutchman / *design*
Haig Adishian / *photography*
Charles Stewart

STEREO

cat
1601

LITTLE BEAVER
title **LITTLE BEAVER** / *year* **1972** / *label* Cat / *design* Drago / *photography* Pogo

Willie Hale was a hugely influential part of the Miami funk scene. His syncopated guitar style could be heard on most of Henry Stone's TK label offerings as featured prominently on the intro to Betty Wright's "Clean Up Woman". His debut, for the TK offshoot Joey, has a deeper blues roots funk sound than the more disco-friendly records of the parent label. **O**

Willie Hale spielte in der Funk-Szene von Miami eine äußerst einflussreiche Rolle. Sein synkopierter Gitarrenstil findet sich auf den meisten Aufnahmen, die auf Henry Stones Label TK gemacht wurden – besonders prominent bei dem Intro von Betty Wrights »Clean Up Woman«. Sein Debüt bei dem TK-Ableger Joey wurzelt mit seinen Funk-Sounds tiefer im Blues als die disco-freundlicheren Scheiben der Mutterfirma. **O**

Willie Hale a eu une influence énorme sur la scène du funk à Miami. On pouvait entendre sa guitare syncopée sur la plupart des disques du label TK de Henry Stone, par exemple dans l'intro de *Clean Up Woman* de Betty Wright. Son premier album, sorti chez Cat label, une filiale de TK, affiche un son funk enraciné dans le blues qui se démarque des disques plus disco de la maison mère.

STEREO BL754164

THE LOST GENERATION
title **THE SLY, SLICK AND THE WICKED** /
year **1970** / *label* Brunswick

This Chicago vocal quartet came out of the box swinging. Their debut is a dazzling blend of sweet harmonies and soft psychedelic overtones that are easily the equal to label-mates the Chi-Lites, whose leader, Eugene Record, produced the LP. The same-titled first single had been such a massive hit it allowed Brunswick to buy itself out and become independent from its parent label, Decca Records. ◗

Dieses Vokalquartett aus Chicago trat von Anfang an schwungvoll auf. Das Debüt ist eine glänzende Mischung angenehmer Harmonien und sanfter, psychedelischer Obertöne, die mit Leichtigkeit neben den Label-Kollegen von den Chi-Lites bestehen können, deren Leadsänger Eugene Record die LP produzierte. Die erste Single gleichen Namens war ein so durchschlagender Erfolg, dass Brunswick sich von seiner Muttergesellschaft Decca Records freikaufen und unabhängig weiter bestehen konnte. ◗

Le premier album de ce quartette vocal de Chicago est un mélange éblouissant d'harmonies mélodieuses et d'inflexions psychédéliques qui le mettent sur un pied d'égalité avec ses collègues du même label, les Chi-Lites, dont le leader Eugene Record a produit ce disque. Le premier single, qui porte le même titre, a été un tel succès qu'il a permis au label Brunswick de se racheter et de couper le cordon avec sa maison mère, Decca Records.

LOVE COMMITTEE
title **LAW** & **ORDER** / *year* **1978** /
label Salsoul / *design* Lori L. Lambert /
photography Robert Belott / *art
direction* Stanley Hochstadt

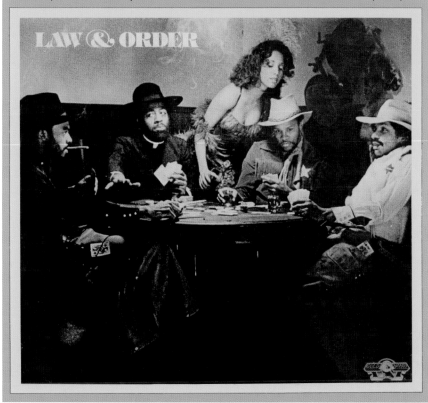

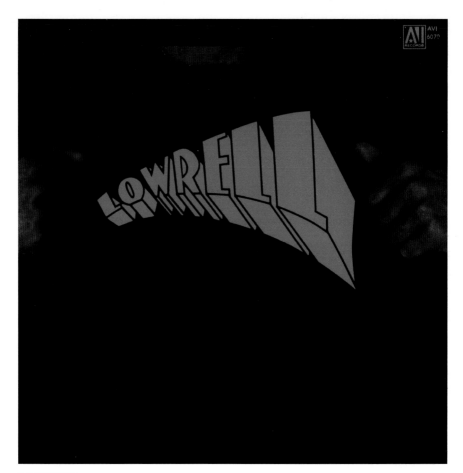

LOWRELL

title **LOWRELL** / *year* **1979** / *label* AVI /
art direction Jacket Art

As Lowrell Simon's name stretched across the cover of his
solo debut like Superman's logo busting out of his civilian
garb, this Chicago native was busting out on his own. He
had been involved in singing groups since the mid-'60s,
with his last one being The Lost Generation from 1969–
1974. His solo debut was a highly polished funk production
with a laid-back groove and big sound and contained the
often-sampled cut "Mellow Mellow Right On". **○**

So wie Lowrell Simons Name sich über das Cover seines
Solodebüts erstreckt, als platze das Logo von Superman aus
seinen Zivilklamotten heraus, so startete dieser gebürtige
Chicagoer auch durch wie eine Rakete. Er mischte seit

Mitte der 60er Jahre in verschiedenen Gesangsgruppen
mit, zuletzt von 1969 bis 1974 bei The Lost Generation.
Sein Solodebüt war eine höchst ausgefeilte Funk-Produkti-
on mit relaxtem Groove sowie einem großformatigen
Sound, die das oft gesampelte Stück »Mellow Mellow
Right On« enthielt. **○**

Pendant que son nom s'étirait en travers de la pochette de
son premier album en solo, comme le logo de Superman
s'échappant de son costume civil, Lowrell Simon faisait sa
propre échappée. Ce natif de Chicago avait fait partie de
groupes de chant depuis le milieu des années 1960, le plus
récent étant The Lost Generation, de 1969 à 1974. Cet
album était une production funky très soignée avec un
groove décontracté et un son ample, et contenait *Mellow
Mellow Right On*, un morceau fréquemment samplé.

CARRIE LUCAS
title **STREET CORNER
SYMPHONY** / *year* **1978** / *label*
Solar / *design* Tim Bryant/Gribbitt! /
illustration Vince Topizo

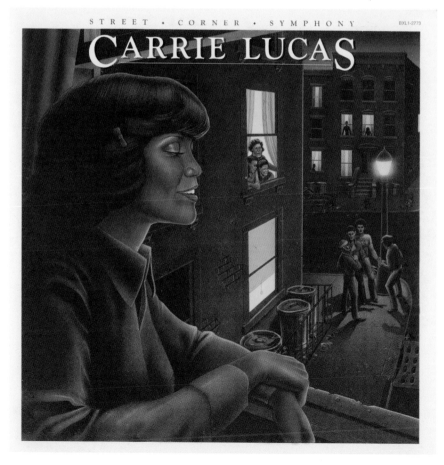

JON LUCIEN

title **MIND'S EYE** / *year* **1974** / *label* RCA /
art direction Acy Lehman

Billed by RCA as "the Black Sinatra", Jon Lucien had a gentle baritone which did not quite earn him a reputation on a par with Ol' Blue Eyes, but validated his talents in the '70s soul-jazz community. With this often being an inhospitable climate for vocalists, Lucien's powerful pipes, paired with his bossa-Caribbean guitar-work, made up for any stigma he may have endured as a jazz singer in the finicky field. **O** Von RCA als »Black Sinatra« angekündigt, hatte Jon Lucien einen sanften Bariton. Das führte nicht zu einer Reputation auf Augenhöhe mit Ol' Blue Eyes, untermauerte aber seinen

Ruf in der Soul-Jazz-Community der 70er Jahre, die Sängern nicht immer ein eben gastliches Klima bot, doch mit seiner kräftige Stimme und seinem bossa-karibischen Gitarren-spiel glich er jedes Stigma aus, das er als Jazzsänger vielleicht in dieser peniblen Branche hätte erdulden müssen. **O** Qualifié de « Sinatra noir » par RCA, Jon Lucien avait un baryton doux qui ne lui a pas vraiment valu une réputation comparable à celle du crooner aux yeux bleus, mais qui a validé ses talents dans la communauté soul-jazz des années 1970. Ce climat était souvent inhospitalier pour les chan-teurs, mais l'organe puissant de Lucien, combiné à sa gui-tare bossa caribéenne, a compensé tous les stigmates de chanteur de jazz dont il a pu souffrir dans ce domaine pointilleux.

PAT LUNDY

title **LOVING YOU – THE FUNKIEST FEELING** /
year **1977** / *label* Pyramid / *design* Ely Besalel /
photography Jim Collier

Pat Lundy had been floating around the music business for many years, first as a member of the Symbols and then as a solo artist with records spanning 20 years on labels such as Deluxe, Columbia, and RCA. Unfortunately she never hit it big during her lifetime and this would be her final release, although this record did contain the track "Work Song" which would go on to be one of her most sought after and sampled cuts. **O**
Pat Lundy hatte sich schon viele Jahre in der Musikbranche herumgetrieben, zuerst als Mitglied der Symbols und dann

als Solosängerin. Labels wie Deluxe, Columbia und RCA dokumentierten ihre über zwanzigjährige Aufnahmetätigkeit. Leider schaffte sie nie einen echten Durchbruch, und dies sollte ihre letzte Veröffentlichung sein, dabei enthielt diese Scheibe das Stück »Work Song«, bekannt als einer ihrer begehrtesten und am häufigsten gesampelten Titel. **O**
Pat Lundy a arpenté le monde de la musique pendant de nombreuses années, tout d'abord comme membre des Symbols, puis en tant qu'artiste en solo avec des disques qui sont sortis sur une période de plus de 20 ans chez des labels tels que Deluxe, Columbia et RCA. Elle n'a malheureusement jamais eu de grand succès de son vivant, et cet album allait être le dernier. Il contient *Work Song*, qui est devenu l'un de ses morceaux les plus recherchés et les plus samplés.

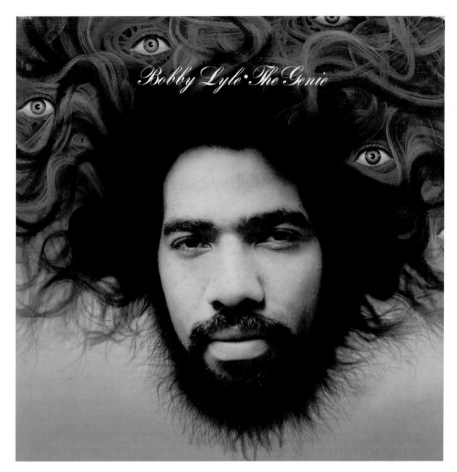

BOBBY LYLE

title **THE GENIE** / *year* **1977** / *label* Capitol /
design Art Sims / *photography* Norman Seeff /
art direction Roy Kohara / *illustration* Shusei Nagaoka

Photographer Norman Seeff seemed most comfortable in the studio, where, free from environmental distractions, the personalities of subjects like Ray Charles, Bill Withers, and Frank Zappa were best illustrated. Here, Seeff's simple portrait of pianist Bobby Lyle is exaggerated by Japanese illustrator Shusei Nagaoka, whose psychedelic mysticism famously suited several Earth, Wind & Fire records, visually accentuating the band's musical ascension into increasingly progressive territory. **O**
Der Fotograf Norman Seeff fühlte sich scheinbar im Studio am wohlsten, wo er frei von Ablenkungen Persönlichkeiten

wie Ray Charles, Bill Withers und Frank Zappa ablichten konnte. Hier wird Seeffs einfaches Porträt des Pianisten Bobby Lyle durch den japanischen Illustrator Shusei Nagaoka aufgebauscht, dessen berühmter psychedelischer Mystizismus mehrere Alben von Earth, Wind & Fire zierte und so auch visuell akzentuierte, wie die Band musikalisch in immer progressiveres Territorium aufstieg. **O**
Le photographe Norman Seeff semblait plus à l'aise en studio où, à l'abri des distractions de leur environnement, les personnalités de sujets comme Ray Charles, Bill Withers ou Frank Zappa étaient mieux mises en lumière. Ici, le portrait tout simple que Seeff a réalisé de Bobby Lyle est retravaillé par l'illustrateur japonais Shusei Nagaoka, dont le mysticisme psychédélique a orné plusieurs disques d'Earth, Wind & Fire et a illustré l'ascension musicale du groupe vers un territoire de plus en plus progressiste.

DLP 12001 - STEREO

SOUL FEVER marie queenie lyons

DE LUXE

MARIE QUEENIE LYONS

title **SOUL FEVER** / *year* **1970** / *label* Deluxe /
design Dan Quest Art Studio

As the story goes, Marie Queenie Lyons was born in the
south and grew up in Ohio, before she moved to New York
in 1963 and began working with King Curtis. She soon met
James Brown and it was his influence that opened up the
arena for her powerful voice to shine. But she is a true soul
enigma, and much like the cover to her only release she
seems to have disappeared into the R&B ether. **O**

Der Legende nach wurde Marie Queenie Lyons im Süden
der USA geboren und wuchs in Ohio auf, bevor sie 1963
nach New York zog und ihre Zusammenarbeit mit King

Curtis begann. Bald traf sie James Brown, der ihr den Weg
auf die Bühne ebnete, wo ihre kraftvolle Stimme so richtig
leuchten konnte. Doch sie ist ein echtes Soul-Mysterium,
und wie auf dem Cover für ihre einzige Veröffentlichung
angedeutet, scheint sie im R&B-Äther verschwunden zu
sein. **O**

D'après ce qu'on dit, Marie Queenie Lyons est née dans le
Sud et a grandi dans l'Ohio avant de partir à New York en
1963 et de travailler avec King Curtis. Elle a vite rencontré
James Brown, et c'est son influence qui a ouvert le passage
pour laisser éclater sa voix puissante. Mais elle est une véritable énigme de la soul et, comme sur la pochette de son
seul album, elle semble avoir disparu dans l'éther du R&B.

MACEO
title **US** / *year* **1974** / *label* Polydor

The muted earth tones and the slice-of-life portraits on the cover of *Us* give a sense of the down home grooves that sax man Maceo and The J.B.'s laid down. Parker's return to the James Brown fold after a three-year absence is a hodge-podge of original tunes and re-workings of J.B. classics all executed by this well-oiled machine. **O**

Die gedeckten Erdtöne und die aus dem Leben gegriffenen Porträts auf dem Cover von *Us* kündigen schon die boden-ständigen Grooves an, die der Saxmann Maceo und die

J.B.'s hier servieren. Parkers Rückkehr zu James Browns Mannschaft nach dreijähriger Abwesenheit führte zu einem Sammelsurium aus Originalstücken und Überar-beitungen von JB-Klassikern, die von dieser gut geölten Maschinerie aufgeführt wurden. **O**

Les couleurs sourdes et les portraits « pris sur le vif » de la pochette de *Us* représentent le ton traditionnel des grooves que l'homme au saxo Maceo et les J.B.'s ont gravés sur ce disque. Le retour de Parker dans le groupe de James Brown après une absence de trois ans est un pot-pourri de morceaux originaux et de classiques de JB retravaillés, tous exécutés par cette machine bien huilée. **O**

MAGNUM

title **FULLY LOADED** / *year* **1974** / *label* The Phoenix

This is the sole recording by this obscure group from San Pedro, CA. They had a penchant for mixing Latin, soul, and psychedelic rock into their funk, producing an explosive sound. While the album states that it is a "Cal Wade Production", keyboardist Michael Greene appears to have been the group's leader and chief songwriter. His arrangements are jazzy in the best sense of the word and intensely percussive. **O**

Dies ist die einzige Aufnahme dieser obskuren Gruppe aus San Pedro (Kalifornien). Sie mischte mit Vorliebe Latin, Soul und psychedelischen Rock in ihren Funk und produzierte damit einen explosiven Sound. Auf dem Album steht zwar,

dass es sich um eine »Cal Wade Production« handelt, doch der Keyboarder Michael Greene scheint der Leader und wichtigste Songwriter der Gruppe gewesen zu sein. Seine Arrangements sind im besten Sinne des Wortes jazzig und sehr percussionlastig. **O**

Ceci est le seul enregistrement réalisé par ce groupe obscur de la ville californienne de San Pedro. Ils aimaient mélanger de la musique latine, de la soul et du rock psychédélique à leur son funk, et en obtenaient un résultat explosif. La mention « Cal Wade Production » que porte l'album ne change rien au fait qu'il semble que le claviériste Michael Greene ait été le leader du groupe et l'auteur principal. Ses arrangements sont jazzy, dans le meilleur sens du terme, et intensément percutants.

TIM MAIA

title **RACIONAL VOL. 1** / *year* **1974** / *label* Seroma

Released on his own label Seroma, Tim Maia's *Racional Vol. 1* (and later *Vol. 2*) was an outgrowth of his involvement with the religious/philosophical sect Universo em Desencanto (Universe in Disenchantment). With spokenword interludes between the soft psychedelic cuts, this LP put Maia in a class all by himself by seamlessly blending a laid-back Brazilian vibe with American funk in a Curtis Mayfield mode. **O**

Tim Maia brachte *Racional Vol. 1* (und später *Vol. 2*) auf seinem eigenen Label Seroma heraus. Es ist ein Nebenprodukt seines Engagements in der religiös-philosophischen Sekte *Universo em Desencanto* (Universum in Entzaube-

rung). Mit Intermezzi aus gesprochenen Worten zwischen den sanften psychedelischen Cuts war diese LP von Maia eine Klasse für sich. Hier wird eine relaxte brasilianische Stimmung übergangslos mit amerikanischem Funk im Stil von Curtis Mayfield verwoben. **O**

Sorti sous le propre label de Tim Maia, Seroma, le premier volume de *Racional* (et plus tard le deuxième volume) était une conséquence de son engagement dans la secte religieuse / philosophique Universo em Desencanto (Univers en désenchantement). Avec des interludes parlés entre les morceaux de soft psychedelic, cet album range Maia dans une catégorie à part en mélangeant une atmosphère brésilienne décontractée avec du funk américain dans le style de Curtis Mayfield.

THE MAIN INGREDIENT
title **EUPHRATES RIVER** / *year* **1974** / *label* RCA /
art direction Acy Lehman / *illustration* Walter Rogers

Bert De Coteaux's lush production fit perfectly with The Main Ingredient's trio of singers: Tony Silvester, Luther Simmons, Jr., and Cuba Gooding. While this record didn't yield any major hits for the group it sits firmly in the middle of their output as a solid testament to sweet soul. Art director Acy Lehman commissioned painter Walter Rogers to produce the afrocentric cover that mirrors the sensual sounds of the group. **O**
Die prachtvolle Produktion von Bert De Coteaux passte perfekt zum Sängertrio von Main Ingredient: Tony Silvester, Luther Simmons Jr. und Cuba Gooding. Zwar brachte diese

Aufnahme der Gruppe keine großen Hits ein, doch sie fügt sich als solides Beispiel für melodischen Soul ausgezeichnet in ihr Portfolio ein. Der Art Director Acy Lehman beauftragte den Maler Walter Rogers damit, ein erkennbar afrikanisch inspiriertes Cover zu schaffen, das die sinnlichen Klänge der Gruppe spiegelt. **O**
La production opulente de Bert De Coteaux s'ajuste à la perfection aux trois chanteurs de Main Ingredient : Tony Silvester, Luther Simmons Jr. et Cuba Gooding. Ce disque n'a pas rapporté de grand tube au groupe, mais il occupe une place centrale dans leur travail comme témoin solide de la sweet soul. Le directeur artistique Acy Lehman a chargé le peintre Walter Rogers de créer la pochette africanisante qui reflète les sons sensuels du groupe.

THE MAIN INGREDIENT

title **SHAME ON THE WORLD** / *year* **1975** / *label* RCA /
design Aristovulos / *photography* Nick Sangiamo /
art direction Acy Lehman

Nick Sangiamo's work always had a sobering quality to it.
He liked to work in muted tones, often with some sort
of trick photography. The gold death masks of The Main
Ingredient on the cover to their second release of 1975
signal a more somber outing than that year's earlier intensity of *Rolling Down a Mountainside.* **O**
Den Arbeiten von Nick Sangiamo ist stets eine ernüch-
ternde Qualität eigen. Er setzte gern gedeckte Farben ein,

oft mit irgendeinem Fototrick. Die goldenen Totenmasken
der Musiker von The Main Ingredient auf dem Cover ihres
zweiten Albums von 1975 signalisieren, dass diese Scheibe
düsterer geriet als das eindringliche Album *Rolling Down a
Mountainside,* das früher im Jahr erschienen war. **O**
Le travail de Nick Sangiamo a toujours cherché à faire
réfléchir. Il aimait travailler dans des couleurs sourdes,
souvent avec des effets spéciaux de photographie.
Les masques mortuaires dorés de The Main Ingredient
sur la pochette de leur deuxième album sorti en 1975
indiquent une atmosphère plus sombre par rapport à
l'intensité de *Rolling Down a Mountainside,* un an plus tôt.

MIRIAM MAKEBA
title **THE WORLD OF MIRIAM MAKEBA** / year **1963** / label RCA

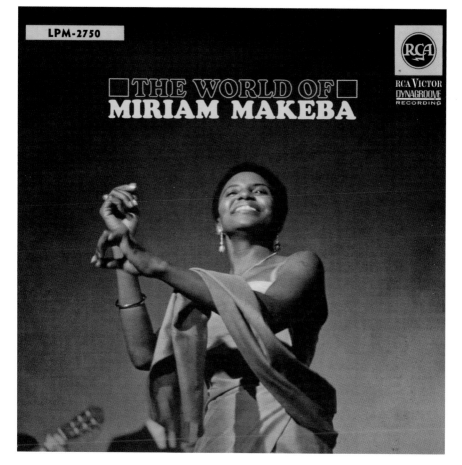

LPM-2750

THE WORLD OF
MIRIAM MAKEBA

RCA

RCA VICTOR
DYNAGROOVE
RECORDING

MALO

title **MALO** / *year* **1972** / *label* Warner Bros. / *design*
John & Barbara Casado / *art direction* Chris Whorf /
illustration Jesus Helguera

This is the debut from this San Francisco Latin rock group
led by Jorge Santana, the brother of Carlos. Jesus Helguera's
illustrations were ubiquitous in Mexican American homes
for generations. He produced popular calendar artwork
that was full of powerful Aztec warrior kings and their
beautiful brides. The inclusion of his work on this cover
helped build a strong Latino identity and sense of pride
with the fans. **O**
Dies ist das Debütalbum der Latin-Rock-Gruppe aus San
Francisco, angeführt von Jorge Santana, dem Bruder von
Carlos. Seit Generationen waren die Illustrationen von Jesus

Helguera in mexikanisch-amerikanischen Häusern allgegenwärtig. Er schuf sehr populäre Kunstkalender mit kraftvollen aztekischen Kriegerkönigen und ihren wunderschönen Bräuten. Dass seine Arbeit auf diesem Cover
landete, erfüllte Latino-Fans mit einem Gefühl des Stolzes
und half dabei, eine starke Identität aufzubauen. **O**
Cet album marque les débuts de ce groupe de rock latin
de San Francisco mené par Jorge Santana, le frère de Carlos.
Les illustrations de Jesus Helguera ont été omniprésentes
dans les foyers des Mexicains américains pendant plusieurs
générations. Il est connu du public pour ses calendriers
remplis de puissants guerriers aztèques accompagnés de
leurs superbes épouses. L'utilisation de cette image a contribué à construire une identité et un sentiment de fierté
latino auprès des fans.

MANCHILD
title **POWER AND LOVE** /
year **1977** / *label* United Artists /
photography Pamoja Photos

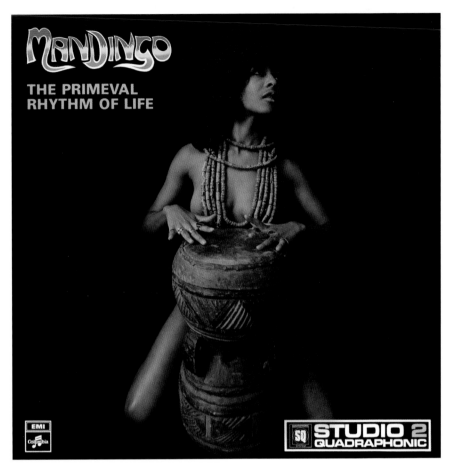

MANDINGO

title **THE PRIMEVAL RHYTHM OF LIFE** / *year* **1973** / *label* EMI Columbia / *design* T. Wymark / *photography* Volkert

British easy-listening orchestra leader Geoff Love got an incredible line-up of studio musicians to produce this percussion-heavy monster of Afro funk in 1973. It is a fierce, primal set that uses fuzz guitars and odd early electronic sounds to augment the jungle rhythms to a dizzying effect. Volkert's provocative cover photo is tame compared to the wild party going on within. **O**

Geoff Love, der Leiter eines britischen Easy-Listening-Orchesters, bekam eine unglaubliche Studiomusiker-besetzung, um dieses schwer schlagzeuglastige Afrofunk-Monster von 1973 zu produzieren. Eine wilde, urtümliche Platte, die von Fuzz-Gitarren und eigenartigen frühen Elektrosounds nur so strotzt, um die Dschungelrhythmen mit schwindelerregender Wirkung zu pushen. Volkerts provokatives Coverfoto wirkt verglichen mit der dahinter verborgenen wilden Party eher zahm. **O**

Le chef d'orchestre easy-listening britannique Geoff Love a réuni une équipe incroyable de musiciens de studio pour créer ce monstre nourri aux percussions d'afro-funk en 1973. C'est un album féroce et primaire qui utilise des pédales fuzz sur les guitares et d'étranges sons électroniques pour amplifier les rythmes jungle jusqu'à provoquer le tournis. La photo provocante de Volkert sur la pochette est presque insipide comparée à la débauche sauvage gravée sur le disque.

MANDRÉ
title **MANDRÉ** / *year* **1977** / *label*
Motown / *art direction* Carl Overr /
illustration Bob Hickson

2391 030

MANDRILL

title **MANDRILL IS** / *year* **1972** / *label* Polydor /
design Joseph Westerfield & Mandrill / *art direction*
Ron Nackman / *illustration* Joseph Westerfield

The Wilson brothers, Carlos, Lou, and Ric, were Panama-
nian by birth, but their sound was pure New York. Bedford-
Stuyvesant, Brooklyn, to be more precise. The neighborhood was the proverbial melting-pot in the late '60s, with
its West Indian, Latin salsa, and rock vibes all living on top
of each other. The group's tight harmonies and swirling
psychedelic funk was in full effect on this, their second
album. **O**
Die Wilson-Brüder Carlos, Lou und Ric stammen gebürtig
aus Panama, aber ihr Sound ist New York pur: Bedford-

Stuyvesant und Brooklyn – um es genauer zu sagen. Ihr
Viertel war der sprichwörtliche Schmelztiegel Ende der 60er
Jahre, mit Klängen aus Westindien, Latin, Salsa und Rock.
Ihre dichten Harmonien und ihr wirbelnder psychedelischer Funk kommen auf ihrem zweiten Album so richtig
zur Geltung. **O**
Les frères Wilson, Carlos, Lou et Ric, était panaméens de
naissance, mais leur son était 100 % new-yorkais. Du quartier de Bedford-Stuyvesant, à Brooklyn, pour être plus
précis. Ce quartier était la quintessence du melting-pot à
la fin des années 1960, avec ses influences antillaises, salsa
et rock cohabitant dans un mille-feuille serré. Les harmonies impeccables et le funk psychédélique du groupe
avaient pris toute leur ampleur sur ce second album.

AB 4144

We Are One ✦✦ Mandrill

MANDRILL

title **WE ARE ONE** / *year* **1977** / *label* Arista

By 1977, disco had taken over the R&B charts. Most funk bands were vying for a piece of the disco pie, but the Wilson brothers chose to continue on the path they had been traveling for the better part of a decade. The sound here is a little smoother than their earliest releases, but the intensity and craftsmanship is still in the forefront of their music. **O**

1977 waren die R&B-Charts von Disco durchtränkt. Die meisten Funk-Bands wollten auch ein Stück vom Disco-Kuchen, aber die Wilson-Brüder entschieden sich dafür, weiter auf dem Pfad zu gehen, auf dem sie schon fast ein ganzes Jahrzehnt lang gewandelt waren. Der Sound auf diesem Album ist ein wenig eingängiger als bei ihren ersten Veröffentlichungen, doch im Vordergrund stehen weiterhin Intensität und handwerkliches Können. **O**

En 1977, le disco avait pris d'assaut les classements R&B. La plupart des groupes de funk rivalisaient pour leur part du gâteau disco, mais les frères Wilson ont choisi de poursuivre le chemin qu'ils avaient emprunté depuis le début de la décennie. Ici, le son est un peu plus lisse que dans leurs opus précédents, mais l'intensité et le savoir-faire sont toujours au premier plan de leur musique.

THE MANHATTANS

title **THE MANHATTANS** / *year*
1976 / *label* CBS / *design* Marie De
Oro & John Berg / *photography* Shig
Ikeda

MCA-2250

MAN'S THEORY

title **JUST BEFORE DAWN** / year **1977** /
label MCA / photography Frank Laffitte

Frank Laffitte often liked to shoot the intimate portraits for his covers with a soft focus or some sort of blurring effect, as he had done with Teddy Pendergrass, Lou Rawls, and Phoebe Snow, among others. This approach also worked well for the soothing jazz-tinged soul of Man's Theory. While there are a few up-tempo funk cuts on the group's sole release they seem to be most at home when they slow things down and lay it all in the groove. **O**
Frank Laffitte arbeite bei seinen intimen Cover-Porträts oft und gerne mit einem Weichzeichner und einer Art Unschärfefilter, wie z. B. bei den Porträts von Teddy Pender-

grass, Lou Rawls und Phoebe Snow. Das funktionierte auch bei dem beruhigenden, jazzgefärbten Soul von Man's Theory. Zwar gibt es auch ein paar Uptempo-Funk-Stücke auf der einzigen Veröffentlichung der Gruppe, doch offensichtlich fühlten sie sich am ehesten heimisch, wenn sie es ruhig angehen ließen und sich auf den Groove konzentrierten. **O**
Frank Laffitte aimait souvent donner un effet de flou aux portraits intimistes qu'il photographiait pour ses pochettes, comme il l'a fait, entre autres, pour Teddy Pendergrass, Lou Rawls et Phoebe Snow. Cette approche fonctionnait aussi pour la soul apaisante teintée de jazz de Man's Theory. Bien que l'unique album du groupe compte quelques morceaux rythmés, on les sent plus à l'aise quand ils ralentissent et font confiance au groove.

A TASTE
Ricardo Marrero
& The Group

RICARDO MARRERO
& THE GROUP

title **A TASTE** / *year* **1976** / *label* TSG

Truly a holy grail among collectors, this fabled NYC salsa funk LP was originally released on a label that had allegedly stolen the master tapes and had no intention of distributing it once pressed up. Many copies were destroyed as part of a tax scam, with only a handful ever making their way to the public. Fortunately it was saved from obscurity and given a proper re-release on the Jazzman label in 2009. **⊙** Diese sagenhafte NYC-Salsa-Funk-LP ist für Sammler wirklich ein Heiliger Gral. Sie wurde ursprünglich auf einem Label veröffentlicht, das angeblich die Master-Bänder gestohlen haben soll und nicht die Absicht hatte, sie auszu-

liefern, nachdem sie gepresst worden war. Viele der Platten wurden als Teil eines Steuerbetrugs vernichtet, nur eine Handvoll erreichte überhaupt die Öffentlichkeit. Zum Glück bewahrte man die Scheibe davor, in die Dunkelheit des Vergessens zu versinken, und verschaffte ihr 2009 auf dem Label Jazzman ein angemessenes Revival. **⊙** Cet album légendaire de funk salsa new-yorkais est le Graal des collectionneurs. À l'origine, il est sorti chez un label qui aurait volé les bandes master et n'aurait eu aucunement l'intention de le distribuer après l'avoir gravé. De nombreuses copies ont été détruites dans une affaire de fraude fiscale, et une poignée seulement est arrivée jusqu'au public. Heureusement, l'album a été sauvé de l'oubli, et le label Jazzman l'a réédité en bonne et due forme en 2009.

ESTHER MARROW

title **SISTER WOMAN** / *year* **1972** /
label Fantasy / *design* Tony Lane /
photography Nima Yakubo

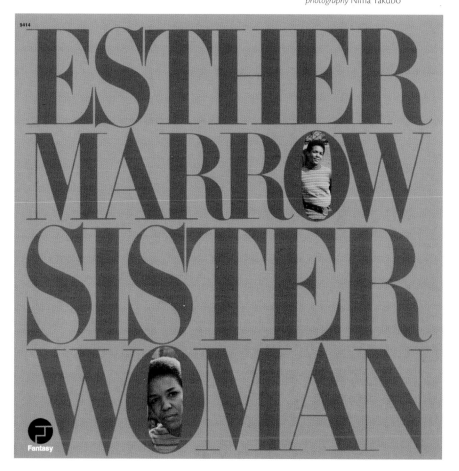

SABU MARTINEZ
title **AFRO TEMPLE** / *year* **1973** /
label Grammofon Verket

This native New Yorker was the Conga King. He performed
with many jazz luminaries such as Art Blakey and Dizzy
Gillespie, as he spread the sounds of his Afro-Cuban roots.
He moved to Sweden with his wife in 1967 and there
would create his deepest funk offering. *Afro Temple* is an
explosive record. Martinez never saw himself as just a time-
keeper; he always breathed life into his conga-playing. **O**
Dieser gebürtige New Yorker war der King der Congas. Er
trat mit vielen Jazz-Größen wie Art Blakey und Dizzy Gillespie auf und verbreitete die Sounds seiner afrokubanischen
Wurzeln. Er zog 1967 mit seiner Frau nach Schweden um,
wo er dann sein tiefgründigstes Funk-Werk schaffen sollte.
Afro Temple ist eine explosive Platte. Martinez betrachtete
sich nie einfach nur als Taktgeber, sondern hauchte seinem
Congaspiel Leben ein. **O**
Ce New-Yorkais était le roi des congas. Il a répandu le son
de ses racines afro-cubaines en jouant avec de nombreux
génies du jazz tels qu'Art Blakey ou Dizzy Gillespie. Il a déménagé en Suède avec sa femme en 1967, et c'est là-bas
qu'il allait créer son œuvre la plus funky. *Afro Temple* est un
disque explosif. Martinez ne s'est jamais contenté de suivre
le rythme, il insufflait toujours de la vie dans ses congas.

THE MARVELETTES
title **THE MARVELLOUS MARVELETTES** / *year* **1964** / *label* Tamla Motown / *design* Barni Wright / *art direction* Rudy Calvo

HARVEY MASON
title **MARCHING IN THE STREET** / *year* **1975** / *label* Arista / *design* Nancy Greenberg / *art direction* Bob Heimall / *illustration* Janet Mager

JAMES MASON   RHYTHM OF LIFE

JAMES MASON

title **RHYTHM OF LIFE** / *year* **1977** / *label* Chiaroscuro /
design James Mason / *photography* Rollo Phlecks /
art direction Ron Warwell / *illustration* Karl Blickenderfer

Chiaroscuro Records sought to issue releases they felt paralleled their name. Normally used in art history, chiaroscuro refers to the contrasting properties of light and dark without regard to color. At the label's inception, their meager budget only permitted monochromatic record sleeves, making their name all the more relevant. Here, former Roy Ayers guitarist James Mason enjoys his radiant debut. **O**
Bei Chiaroscuro Records wollte man Platten herausbringen, die dem Namen des Musikverlags entsprechen. Dieser Begriff stammt aus der Kunstgeschichte und bezieht sich auf die kontrastierenden Eigenschaften von Hell und Dunkel ohne Berücksichtigung von Farbe. In den Anfangstagen des Labels erlaubte das dürftige Budget nur einfarbige Plattenhüllen, wodurch dessen Name noch deutlicher unterstrichen wurde. Hier genießt James Mason, der ehemalige Gitarrist von Roy Ayers, freudestrahlend sein Debüt. **O**
Chiaroscuro Records voulait produire de la musique qui entrait en résonnance avec son nom. Utilisé dans le domaine de la critique d'art, le terme *chiaroscuro* (clair-obscur) fait allusion à l'effet de contraste entre les parties sombres et éclairées, sans tenir compte de la couleur. Au début, le maigre budget du label n'autorisait que des pochettes d'album monochromatiques, ce qui donnait encore plus de poids à ce nom. Ici, l'ancien guitariste de Roy Ayers, James Mason, savoure ses débuts rayonnants.

SD 5205

MASS PRODUCTION

title **THREE MILES HIGH** / *year* **1978** / *label* Cotillion / *photography* Steinbicker/Houghton / *art direction* Bob Defrin

Earl Steinbicker and James Houghton were sought-after fashion and commercial photographers from the mid '60s to the late '70s. Their inventive approach to record covers often included studio manipulation of an advanced nature (long before Photoshop made such things more readily available), as with the visual pun of having Mass Production's fly outfits replaced with the photo of clouds here. ❂
Earl Steinbicker und James Houghton waren seit Mitte der 60er bis Ende der 70er Jahre begehrte Mode- und Werbe-

fotografen. Zur ihrem einfallsreichen Vorgehen bei Platten-covern gehörten anspruchsvolle Bildmanipulationen im Fotostudio (lange bevor so etwas durch Photoshop erleichtert wurde) wie z. B. hier mit dem visuellen Gag, die Kostüme von Mass Production durch Wolken zu ersetzen. ❂
Earl Steinbicker et James Houghton ont été des photo-graphes de mode très recherchés de la moitié des années 1960 à la fin des années 1970. Leur approche inventive des pochettes de disque impliquait souvent une manipulation sophistiquée en studio (bien avant que Photoshop ne mette ce genre d'effet à la portée de tous), comme ici avec ce clin d'œil visuel qui remplace les tenues de vol de Mass Production par une photo de nuages.

MAXAYN

title **BAIL OUT FOR FUN!** / *year* **1974** / *label* WEA /
design Designed Communications / *photography* Ginny
Winn

Ginny Winn's effervescent portrait of singer/pianist Maxayn
Lewis framed by the cloud of her blonde wig captures the
fun-loving spirit of this forgotten band named for their lead
singer. This collection of bubbling funk and gospel-tinged
soul would be the group's third and final outing before
changing directions and leaders to become Maxayn's hus-
band André's space-funk band Mandré. **○**
Ginny Winns übersprudelndes Porträt der Sängerin und
Pianistin Maxayn Lewis, umwölkt von ihrer blonden Perü-
cke, fängt den lebenslustigen Geist dieser vergessenen Band
ein, die sich nach ihrer Leadsängerin nannte. Die Sammlung
von sprudelndem Funk und gospelgefärbtem Soul sollte
die dritte und letzte Platte der Gruppe sein, bevor sie Richtung und Leitung wechselte und zur Space-Funk-Band
Mandré wurde, geleitet von Maxayns Ehemann André. **○**
Le portrait effervescent que Ginny Winn a réalisé de la
chanteuse / pianiste Maxayn Lewis, encadrée par le nuage
de sa perruque blonde, saisit la bonne humeur de ce
groupe oublié, baptisé du nom de sa chanteuse. Cet album
de funk pétillant et de soul teintée de gospel allait être le
troisième et le dernier du groupe avant de changer de
direction et que Maxayn et son mari André ne forment le
groupe de space-funk Mandré.

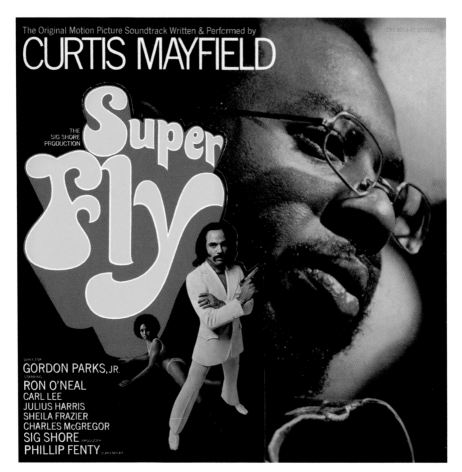

The Original Motion Picture Soundtrack Written & Performed by

CURTIS MAYFIELD

THE
SIG SHORE
PRODUCTION

Super Fly

DIRECTED BY
GORDON PARKS, JR.
STARRING
RON O'NEAL
CARL LEE
JULIUS HARRIS
SHEILA FRAZIER
CHARLES McGREGOR
SIG SHORE PRODUCER
PHILLIP FENTY SCREENPLAY

CURTIS MAYFIELD

title **SUPER FLY** / *year* **1972** / *label* Curtom /
art direction Glen Christensen / *packaging* Milton Sincoff

Curtis Mayfield was arguably the brightest star in the *Super Fly* universe, minting this unforgettable masterpiece in conjunction with the 1972 blaxploitation film. Ron O'Neal, featured on the die-cut overlay, is dwarfed in comparison to the stoic Mayfield, who makes a brief cameo in the film to perform his own "Pusherman". **O**
Curtis Mayfield war zweifellos der leuchtendste Stern im *Super Fly*-Universum und prägte dieses unvergessliche Meisterstück zusammen mit dem Blaxploitation-Film von 1972. Ron O'Neal erscheint auf dem ausgestanzten Overlay zwergenhaft im Vergleich zu dem stoischen Gesicht von Mayfield, der im Film einen kurzen Cameo-Auftritt als »Pusherman« hat. **O**
Curtis Mayfield était peut-être l'étoile la plus brillante de l'univers de *Super Fly*, avec ce chef-d'œuvre inoubliable qui accompagne le film de blaxploitation de 1972. Ron O'Neal, représenté sur la manchette découpée, est minuscule comparé au stoïque Mayfield, qui fait une brève apparition dans le film pour jouer son morceau *Pusherman*.

CURTIS MAYFIELD

title **BACK TO THE WORLD** / *year* **1973** /
label Curtom / *art direction* Glen Christensen /
illustration Gary Wolkowitz / *packaging* Milton Sincoff

The title track to Curtis Mayfield's 1973 release was an ode to American soldiers fighting in Vietnam, and their often emotional and difficult return home. Illustrator Gary Wolkowitz constructed this colorful montage, juxtaposing various members of African-American society – students, children, and hustlers – against paradoxical images of patriotism, including tattered flags, fighter jets, and the United States Capitol Building. **O**

Das Titelstück dieses Albums von Curtis Mayfield aus dem Jahr 1973 war eine Ode an die amerikanischen Soldaten, die in Vietnam kämpften und unter großen emotionalen Schwierigkeiten heimkehrten. Der Illustrator Gary Wolkowitz montierte auf diesem farbenprächtigen Bild verschiedene Mitglieder der afroamerikanischen Gesellschaft – Studenten, Kinder und Gauner – neben widersprüchlichen Bildern des Patriotismus wie zerrissenen Flaggen, Kampfjets und dem Capitol. **O**

Le morceau-titre de l'album de 1973 de Curtis Mayfield était un hommage aux soldats américains qui se battaient au Vietnam, dont le retour à la maison était souvent difficile et chargé d'émotions. L'illustrateur Gary Wolkowitz a composé ce montage coloré en juxtaposant différents membres de la société afro-américaine (étudiants, enfants et voyous) et des images paradoxales de patriotisme, drapeaux déchirés, avions de combat et le Capitole des États-Unis d'Amérique.

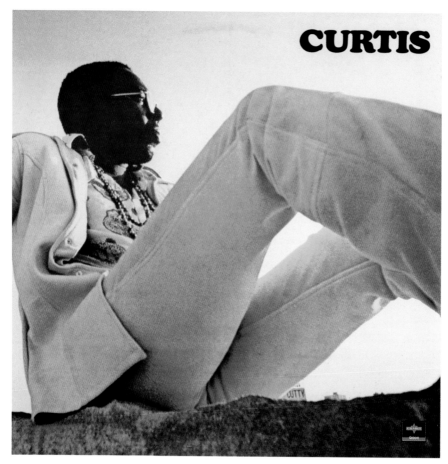

CURTIS

CURTIS MAYFIELD

title **CURTIS** / *year* **1970** / *label* Curtom / *photography* Bob Cato

Bob Cato was integral in transforming the medium of album design from a packaging necessity to a valuable platform for cultural expression. After successful stints at *Harper's Bazaar* and *Glamour*, Cato gained employment at Columbia Records where, beginning in 1960, he spent an entire decade revolutionizing the visual aspect of record production. **O**

Bob Cato hat wesentlich dazu beigetragen, dass das Plattencover als Medium den Schritt von der notwendigen Verpackung zu einem wertvollen Träger künstlerischen Ausdrucks vollziehen konnte. Nach seiner erfolgreichen Tätigkeit für *Harper's Bazaar* und *Glamour* wurde Cato bei Columbia Records angestellt, wo er 1960 begann und ein ganzes Jahrzehnt damit verbrachte, den visuellen Aspekt der Plattenproduktion zu revolutionieren. **O**

Bob Cato a joué un rôle fondamental dans la transformation de la pochette d'album, de simple emballage nécessaire à précieuse plateforme d'expression culturelle. Après quelques incursions fort réussies chez *Harper's Bazaar* et *Glamour*, Cato a décroché un poste chez Columbia Records où, à partir de 1960, il a passé toute une décennie à révolutionner l'aspect visuel de l'industrie du disque.

MAZE

title MAZE FEATURING FRANKIE BEVERLY /
year **1977** / *label* Capitol / *art direction* Roy Kohara /
illustration Shusei Nagaoka

Shusei Nagaoka's paintings graced many classic album covers of the late '70s and early '80s. His work always has a sense of the futuristic even though he often uses ancient, spiritual imagery. The image of the overlapping Healing Hands with the maze running through them would become a symbol of the band's smooth California soul. The warm light radiating from the palms mirrors the warm tone of Frankie Beverly's voice. **O**
Die Gemälde von Shusei Nagaoka zierten von Ende der 70er bis Anfang der 80er Jahre viele LP-Klassiker. Seine Arbeiten haben stets einen futuristischen Touch, obwohl er

oft mit einer altertümlichen und spirituellen Metaphorik arbeitet. Das Bild der einander überlappenden heilenden Hände mit dem Labyrinth, das sie verknüpft, wurde zum Symbol des weichen kalifornischen Souls der Band. Das den Handflächen entströmende warme Licht entspricht dem warmen Klang von Frankie Beverlys Stimme. **O**
Les tableaux de Shusei Nagaoka ont orné les pochettes de nombreux grands albums de la fin des années 1970 et du début des années 1980. Son œuvre a toujours eu une sensibilité futuriste, bien qu'il utilise souvent des images spirituelles et anciennes. Cette image de deux « mains qui guérissent » superposées, parcourues d'un labyrinthe, allait devenir le symbole de la soul californienne lisse du groupe. La lumière chaude qui irradie des paumes évoque le timbre chaleureux de la voix de Frankie Beverly.

GEORGE & GWEN McCRAE

title **TOGETHER** / *year* **1975** / *label* Cat / *design* Drago / *photography* Mario Algaze

GWEN McCRAE

title **ON MY WAY** / *year* **1982** / *label* Atlantic / *photography* Herbert Schulz / *art direction* Sandi Young

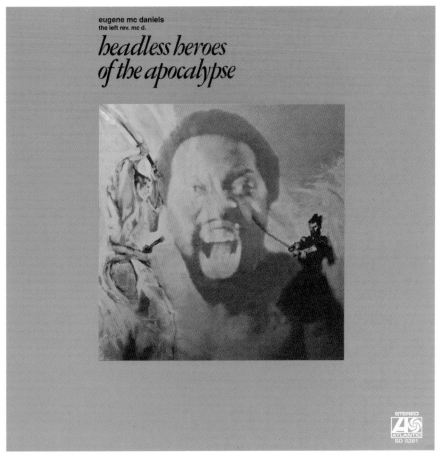

eugene mc daniels
the left rev. mc d.

*headless heroes
of the apocalypse*

STEREO
ATLANTIC
SD 8281

EUGENE McDANIELS
title HEADLESS HEROES OF THE APOCALYPSE /
year **1971** / *label* Atlantic / *design* Tomas Nittner /
photography Bill Del Conte / *illustration* Harvey Konigsberg

The Left Reverend screams between two warring samurai on the cover of his left-field funk opus. This record caught the attention of Nixon's White House because of its incendiary political content, possibly accounting for its present-day rarity. McDaniels' similarly dissenting single "Compared to What" was a hit for both Les McCann and Roberta Flack, who each recorded their own renditions of the timeless tune in 1969. **O**

Der Left Reverend brüllt auf dem Cover seines abseitigen Funk-Opus zwischen zwei kämpfenden Samurais hindurch. Diese Aufnahme zog wegen ihres aufrührerischen politi-schen Inhaltes zu Nixons Zeit die Aufmerksamkeit des Weißen Hauses auf sich, was wahrscheinlich dazu führte, dass dieses Album heute zur Rarität geworden ist. Die auf ähnliche Weise nonkonformistische Single »Compared to What« war sowohl für Les McCann als auch für Roberta Flack ein Hit; beide nahmen 1969 eine eigene Interpretation dieses zeitlosen Stücks auf. **O**

Sur la pochette de cet ovni du funk, le « Révérend de gauche » hurle entre deux samouraïs en plein duel. Ce disque a attiré l'attention du gouvernement de Nixon à cause de son contenu politique incendiaire, ce qui explique peut-être qu'il soit devenu rare. Le single également dissi-dent de McDaniels, *Compared to What*, a été un succès pour Les McCann et Roberta Flack, qui ont chacun enregis-tré leur propre version de ce morceau intemporel en 1969.

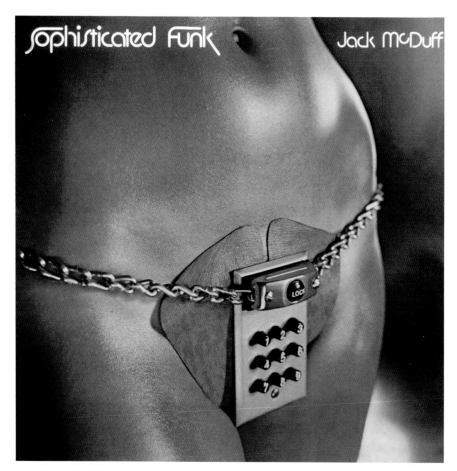

JACK McDUFF

title **SOPHISTICATED FUNK** / *year* **1976** / *label* Chess / *design* Kay Ritta / *photography* Kay Ritta / *art direction* Dudley Thomas

A cast of newcomers from funk outfit Brother to Brother helps the elder McDuff manage a mélange of glossy compositions for 1976's *Sophisticated Funk*. Although the modern-day chastity belt appears firmly affixed to this somewhat picturesque mid-section, the back cover reveals that someone amongst this intergenerational combo was able to resolve the constrictive predicament, to the presumed delight of all parties involved. **O**

Eine Newcomer-Besetzung der Funk-Truppe Brother to Brother verhalf dem älteren McDuff dazu, für das Album *Sophisticated Funk* von 1976 diese Melange aus Hochglanz-kompositionen abzumischen. Obwohl der hochmoderne Keuschheitsgürtel auf dem sehr anschaulichen Schoß wie fest fixiert wirkt, enthüllt die Plattenrückseite, dass irgend-wer aus dieser generationsübergreifenden Combo in der Lage war, wohl zur Freude aller Beteiligten, diese hinderliche Vorrichtung zu beseitigen. **O**

Une équipe de nouveaux venus issus du groupe de funk Brother to Brother aide le vétéran McDuff sur un mélange de compositions luxueuses pour cet album de 1976. Au recto de la pochette, la ceinture de chasteté moderne semble solidement verrouillée sur ces hanches sculpturales, mais le verso montre que quelqu'un parmi les membres de ce groupe intergénérationnel a réussi à résoudre cette situa-tion fâcheuse, à la grande joie des intéressés.

McFADDEN & WHITEHEAD

title **MCFADDEN &
WHITEHEAD** / *year* **1979** / *label*
Philadelphia International / *design*
Phyllis H.B. / *photography* Ronald
G. Harris / *art direction* Ed Lee

WAYNE McGHIE & THE SOUNDS OF JOY

title **WAYNE MCGHIE** & **THE
SOUNDS OF JOY** / *year* **1970** /
label Birchmount / *design* Michael
Clasby / *photography* Neil Evans

JIMMY McGRIFF

title **BLACK PEARL** / *year* **1971** / *label* Blue Note /
art direction Norman Seeff / *illustration* John Van
Hamersveld

At age 22, Baltimore native John Van Hamersveld created
the iconic artwork for the historical surf documentary,
Endless Summer. He was soon creating widely varied album
covers and concert posters for The Beatles, The Rolling
Stones, and Jimi Hendrix. The face on Jimmy McGriff's
Black Pearl bears a striking resemblance to Hamersveld's
Johnny face character, which Shepard Fairey has stated
served as inspiration for his Giant series. ❍

Mit 22 schuf der aus Baltimore stammende John Van
Hamersveld die Poster-Ikone für die historische Surfer-
Dokumentation *Endless Summer*. Bald schon gestaltete

er vielfältigste Plattenhüllen und Konzertplakate für die
Beatles, die Rolling Stones und Jimi Hendrix. Das Gesicht
auf Jimmy McGriffs *Black Pearl* hat eine bestechende
Ähnlichkeit mit dem Johnny-Gesicht von Hamersveld, das
ihm nach Aussage von Shepard Fairey als Inspiration für
seine Giant-Serie diente. ❍

C'est à l'âge de 22 ans que John Van Hamersveld, originaire
de Baltimore, a créé la célèbre illustration du documentaire
mythique sur le surf, *Endless Summer*. Il a continué sur sa
lancée et a créé des pochettes d'album et des affiches
de concert dans des styles très variés pour les Beatles, les
Rolling Stones et Jimi Hendrix. Sur la pochette de *Black
Pearl*, de Jimmy McGriff, le visage présente une ressem-
blance frappante avec Johnny, le personnage du logo de
Hamersveld, que Shepard Fairey a cité plusieurs fois comme
étant l'inspiration de sa série *Giant*.

JIMMY McGRIFF

title **SOUL SUGAR** / year **1971** / label Capitol

Soul Sugar is an integral chapter in the funk odyssey pre-
cipitated by Philadelphia funk legend Jimmy McGriff. With
Sonny Lester and Horace Ott producing and arranging
several consecutive bombshells for the versatile organist,
McGriff would follow the prolific pair to their newly minted Groove Merchant label following this Capitol release. ✪
Soul Sugar ist ein integrales Kapitel in der Funk-Odyssee,
die von der Philadelphia-Funklegende Jimmy McGriff be-
schleunigt wurde. Nachdem Sonny Lester und Horace Ott

für den vielseitigen Organisten mehrere aufeinanderfolgen-
de Knaller produziert und arrangiert hatten, sollte McGriff,
nachdem er diese Platte bei Capitol herausgebracht hatte,
dem überaus produktiven Paar zu seinem neu gegründeten
Label Groove Merchant folgen. ✪
Soul Sugar constitue tout un chapitre de l'odyssée du funk,
condensé par la légende du funk de Philadelphie Jimmy
McGriff. Sonny Lester et Horace Ott ayant produit et arrangé plusieurs engins explosifs de suite pour cet organiste aux
talents multiples, McGriff allait les suivre à l'ouverture de
leur tout nouveau label Groove Merchant après cet album
sorti chez Capitol.

HAROLD MELVIN & THE BLUE NOTES

title **TO BE TRUE** / *year* **1975** / *label* Philadelphia International / *design* Ed Lee & Gerard Huerta / *photography* Don Hunstein

Don Hunstein's love for photography began in the Air Force, where constant European travel yielded an endless supply of engaging subjects. Upon his return to the States, Hunstein started a slow and steady ascent through New York's commercial and advertising worlds, parlaying apprenticeships into assistantships, eventually becoming head photographer for Columbia Records. **O**
Don Hunsteins Liebe zur Fotografie begann bei der Air Force, wo er auf seinen vielen Reisen in Europa mit span-

nenden Motiven versorgt war. Zurück in den Staaten begann Hunstein seinen langsamen und kontinuierlichen Aufstieg in der New Yorker Welt des Kommerz und der Werbung, baute Praktikantenstellen zu Assistentenstellen aus und wurde schließlich Cheffotograf für Columbia Records. **O**
Don Hunstein est tombé amoureux de la photographie lorsqu'il était dans l'armée de l'air, et ses voyages incessants en Europe lui ont donné une source inépuisable de sujets captivants. À son retour aux États-Unis, Hunstein a commencé une ascension lente mais régulière dans le monde new-yorkais du commerce et de la publicité. Stagiaire, puis assistant, il a fini par devenir photographe en chef pour Columbia Records.

THE METERS

title **STRUTTIN'** / *year* **1970** / *label* Josie / *design*
The Graffiteria / *photography* The Graffiteria /
art direction Janie Gans

Janie Gans served as both the production manager and art
director for Jubilee Records (parent company to Josie) for
thirteen years. Strut advocates the Meters mimic their
landmark instrumental "Cissy Strut" with the enclosed
adaptation, "Chicken Strut". The Graffiteria marks the funky
occasion by kindly providing this repetitive rooster. **O**
Janie Gans diente der Plattenfirma Jubilee Records (unter
deren Dach auch das Label Josie angesiedelt war) dreizehn

Jahre lang gleichzeitig als Produktionsleiterin und Art Director. Die Meters parodieren hier als Propagandisten von
Struttin' ihr denkwürdiges Instrumentalstück »Cissy Strut«
mit der Adaption »Chicken Strut«. Die Graffiteria legte zu
diesem funkigen Anlass einen Hahn mehrfach übereinan-
der (denn nichts anderes bedeutet »Struttin'« wörtlich:
Herumstolzieren wie ein Gockel). **O**
Janie Gans a été à la fois chargée de production et direc-
trice artistique pour Jubilee Records (société mère de Josie)
pendant treize ans. Ces partisans de la frime que sont les
Meters font un clin d'œil à leur morceau instrumental historique *Cissy Strut* avec l'adaptation *Chicken Strut*. La Graffiteria a marqué cette occasion funky avec ce coq multiplié.

METROPOLIS

title **THE GREATEST SHOW ON EARTH** / *year* **1978** /
label Salsoul / *design* Paula Bisacca / *photography* Robert
Belott

Tom Moulton and Thor Baldursson were the masterminds
behind Metropolis. With their combined disco pedigree it
was inevitable that they would create some classic dance-
floor hits. They tapped Philadelphia's premier backing singers the Sigma Sweethearts (Carla Benson, Evette Benton,
and Barbara Ingram) to provide the celestial choir to their
soaring disco odes to New York City. **O**
Tom Moulton und Thor Baldursson waren die Draht-
zieher bei Metropolis. Aufgrund ihrer gemeinsamen Disco-

Herkunft war es unausweichlich, dass sie ein paar klassische
Dancefloor-Hits schaffen würden. Dafür griffen sie auf die
besten Backgroundsängerinnen der Plattenfirma Philadel-
phia zurück: die Sigma Sweethearts mit Carla Benson,
Evette Benton und Barbara Ingram. So bekamen sie diesen
überirdischen Chor für ihre himmelstürmenden Disco-
Oden an New York City. **O**
Tom Moulton et Thor Baldursson étaient les cerveaux de
Metropolis. Avec leur expérience du disco, il était inévitable
qu'ils créent quelques classiques des pistes de danse. Ils ont
eu recours aux meilleures choristes de Philadelphie, les
Sigma Sweethearts (Carla Benson, Evette Benton et Barbara
Ingram), pour les chœurs célestes de leurs odes disco ly-
riques à la ville de New York.

MFSB

title **PHILADELPHIA FREEDOM** / *year* **1975** /
label Philadelphia International / *design* Ed Lee /
illustration Alex Edel

This group of diverse jazz, funk, and soul musicians was the backbone of the "Philly Sound" pioneered by Gamble & Huff for the Philadelphia International Records label. This was their third release and included such hits as "Morning Tears" and "Get Down with the Philly Sound". Ed Lee was the designer of choice for the majority of the group's output. His work for them went from the depths of the ghetto to the fantastical, but always had a romantic edge to it. ○ Diese Gruppe von unterschiedlichen Jazz-, Funk- und Soulmusikern war das Rückgrat des »Philly Sound«, als dessen Pioniere Gamble & Huff für das Label Philadelphia Interna-

tional Records gelten. Es war ihr drittes Album, zu dem Hits wie »Morning Tears« und »Get Down with the Philly Sound« gehörten. Ed Lee war der Wunschgestalter für die Mehrzahl der Veröffentlichungen dieser Gruppe. Seine Arbeiten für sie reichten vom tiefsten Ghetto bis zu fantastischen Welten, hatten aber stets einen romantischen Unterton. ○ Ce groupe hétéroclite de musiciens de jazz, de funk et de soul était la colonne vertébrale du « son de Philadelphia » dont Gamble & Huff avaient été les pionniers pour le label Philadelphia International Records. Il s'agissait de leur troisième opus et il comprenait des tubes comme *Morning Tears* et *Get Down with the Philly Sound*. C'est le graphiste Ed Lee qui s'est chargé d'illustrer la majorité des productions du groupe. Le travail qu'il a réalisé pour eux va de la profondeur du ghetto au fantastique, mais a toujours eu une touche de romantisme.

MFSB TSOP
The Sound Of Philadelphia

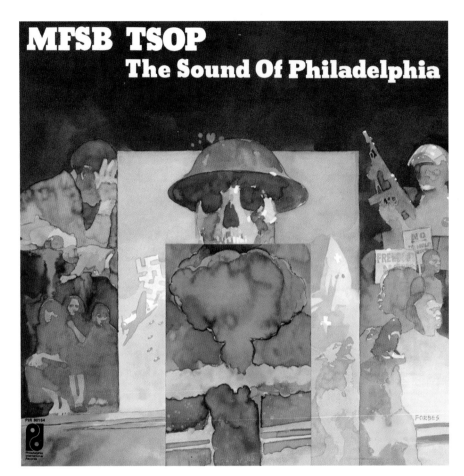

MFSB
title **TSOP – THE SOUND OF PHILADELPHIA** /
year **1973** / *label* Philadelphia International /
art direction Ed Lee / *illustration* Bart Forbes

This collection, the UK release of *Love is the Message*, is comprised mostly of covers of popular R&B tunes and would yield the template for disco to come with the track "TSOP". Bart Forbes supplied the ominous cover illustration. It is slightly out of character for the talented artist, who is better known for his action-oriented *Sports Illustrated* work. **○**

Diese Sammlung, die UK-Ausgabe von *Love is the Message*, besteht hauptsächlich aus Coverversionen beliebter R&B-

Melodien und sollte mit dem Stück »TSOP« die Vorlage für die aufkommende Disco-Musik liefern. Bart Forbes steuerte die bedrohliche Coverillustration bei. Sie ist für den talentierten Künstler eher untypisch, der bekannt ist für seine actionorientierten Arbeiten bei *Sports Illustrated*. **○**

Cette compilation, l'édition britannique de *Love is the Message*, est constituée principalement de reprises de morceaux de R&B populaires et allait servir de modèle au disco naissant avec le titre *TSOP*. Bart Forbes est l'auteur de l'illustration lugubre de la pochette. Elle est un peu inhabituelle pour cet artiste talentueux, qui est plus connu pour les images remplies d'action qu'il a réalisées pour *Sports Illustrated*.

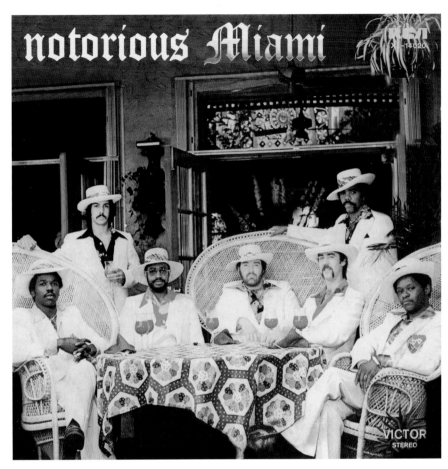

![notorious Miami album cover]

MIAMI

title **NOTORIOUS MIAMI** / *year* **1976** / *label* RCA Victor / *photography* Joe Elbert / *art direction* Howard Smiley & Richard Roth

This was the second album from Willie Clarke and the TK Records family of labels' house-band. Because of the popularity of their first record, label head Henry Stone gave them a bigger budget for this album, which incorporated more strings and horns. Joe Elbert got a music degree from Indiana University, but soon moved over to photography with a gig at *The Courier-Tribune*. Later he moved to *The Miami Herald* where he was eventually promoted to picture editor and then Director of Photography. **○**

Dies war das zweite Album von Willie Clarke und seiner Hausband für die Labels von TK Records. Weil das erste Album so populär wurde, stockte der Labelchef Henry Stone den Etat auf, und man konnte sich mehr Streicher und Bläser leisten. Joe Elbert studierte Musik an der Indiana University, wechselte aber bald zur Fotografie und bekam einen Job beim *Courier-Tribune*. Später wechselte er zum *Miami Herald*, wo er Leiter des Fotoressorts wurde. **○**

Cet album était le deuxième de Willie Clarke et du groupe résident de la famille de labels de TK Records. Grâce au succès de leur premier album, le directeur du label, Henry Stone, leur avait accordé un budget plus important pour cet album, où l'on entend plus de cordes et de cuivres. Joe Elbert a obtenu un diplôme de musique à l'université de l'Indiana, mais s'est vite tourné vers la photographie avec un job temporaire au journal *The Courier-Tribune*. Par la suite, il a travaillé au *Miami Herald*, où il a été promu éditeur photographique puis directeur de la photographie.

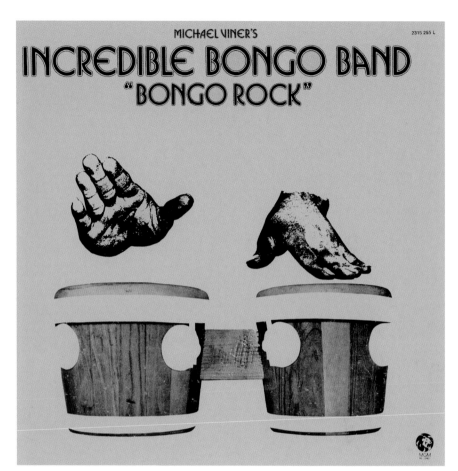

MICHAEL VINER'S
INCREDIBLE BONGO BAND

title **"BONGO ROCK"** / *year* **1973** / *label* MGM

Bongo Rock encased several catchy instrumentals, most notably "Apache", once cited by DJ Kool Herc as "the national anthem of hip-hop." On the kit, *Bongo Rock* featured Jim Gordon, who laid down legendary back-beats for Traffic, Steely Dan, and John Lennon. Providing memorable hand percussion was Bahamian conguero King Errisson, who played with Miles and recorded at Motown, but has since settled into a nice touring gig with Neil Diamond, which has endured several decades. **O**

Auf *Bongo Rock* finden sich mehrere eingängige Instrumentalstücke, vor allem »Apache«, das DJ Kool Herc einmal als »Nationalhymne des Hiphop« bezeichnete. Auf dem namensgebenden Instrument brilliert Jim Gordon, der bei Traffic, Steely Dan und John Lennon für legendäre Backbeats gesorgt hat. Bemerkenswerte Hand-Perkussion lieferte auch der Conguero King Errisson von den Bahamas, der mit Miles musiziert und bei Motown aufgenommen hat, dann aber für mehrere Jahrzehnte mit Neil Diamond auf schöne Tourneen ging. **O**

Bongo Rock contient plusieurs morceaux instrumentaux accrocheurs, notamment *Apache*, que DJ Kool Herc a qualifié de « hymne national du hip-hop ». Jim Gordon était à la batterie. Il a fourni des backbeats légendaires pour Traffic, Steely Dan et John Lennon. Aux percussions à main, on trouvait le joueur de congas bahamien King Errisson, qui a joué avec Miles et a enregistré chez Motown, mais s'est depuis installé dans un job temporaire en tournée avec Neil Diamond, qui a fini par s'étirer sur plusieurs décennies.

THE MIGHTY
CLOUDS OF JOY
title **TRUTH IS THE POWER** /
year **1977** / *label* ABC /
design Kathy Mashburn /
photography Norman Seeff /
art direction Frank Mulvey

MIGHTY FIRE
title **MIGHTY FIRE** / *year* **1982** /
label Elektra / *design* John Barr /
art direction Ron Coro & Norm
Ung / *illustration* Joo Chung

MIGHTY RYEDERS

title **HELP US SPREAD THE MESSAGE** / *year* **1978** /
label Sun Glo / *photography* Johnson Of Miami /
art direction Armand Leighton

Armand Leighton's far-out design for this obscure outfit's
sole LP has helped keep it feverishly sought after by
collectors since its 1978 release on the small Florida label
Sun Glo Records Inc. The seven-piece group had a deep
understanding of how to balance the sophisticated
arrangements, tight vocal styling, and funky jazz instrumentation to create a timeless sound. **O**
Die abgefahrene Gestaltung von Armand Leighton für die
einzige LP dieser obskuren Truppe hat dazu geführt, dass
sie nun fieberhaft von Sammlern gesucht wird, nachdem
sie 1978 auf dem kleinen Florida-Label Sun Glo Records Inc.
erschien. Die siebenköpfige Gruppe verstand viel davon,
wie man ausgefeilte Arrangements, dichte Gesangseinlagen
und funkige Jazz-Instrumentierung ausgewogen balanciert,
um einen zeitlosen Sound zu kreieren. **O**
La pochette originale d'Armand Leighton pour l'unique
album de ce petit groupe obscur a contribué à entretenir
l'intérêt fiévreux des collectionneurs depuis sa sortie en
1978 chez le petit label de Floride Sun Glo Records Inc. Les
sept membres du groupe savent parfaitement équilibrer
des arrangements sophistiqués, des voix bien placées et une
instrumentation funk-jazz pour créer un son intemporel.

THE MODULATIONS

title **IT'S ROUGH OUT HERE** /
year **1975** / *label* Buddah /
photography Joel Brodsky / *packaging*
Milton Sincoff

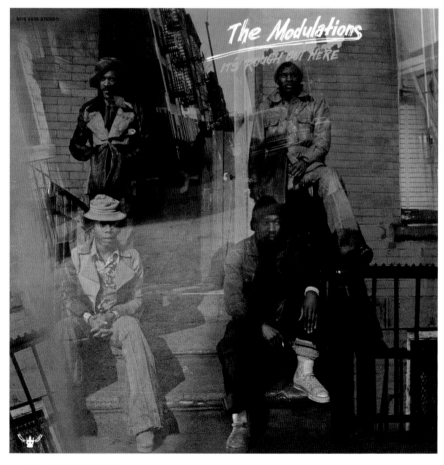

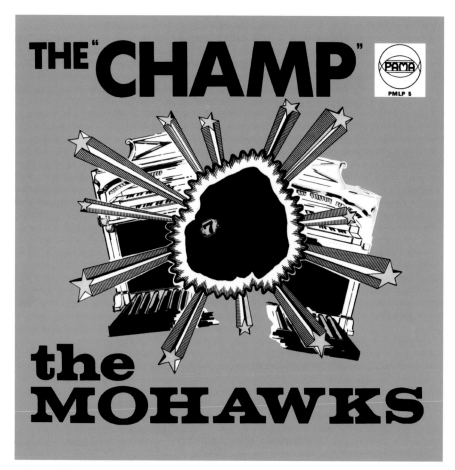

THE MOHAWKS

title **THE "CHAMP"** / *year* **1968** / *label* Pama

Original copies of this all-time classic workout have a red fist smashing its way through a Hammond organ. Alan Hawkshaw's gut-punch funk did much the same. The Mohawks was a studio project by mastermind Hawkshaw, whose organ-driven funk had produced some of the most heavy-hitting library productions (records used for TV shows and commercials) during the '60s & '70s. **○**
Im Original ist auf diesem klassischen Evergreen eine rote Faust abgebildet, die eine Hammondorgel zerschlägt. Der Funk von Alan Hawkshaw wirkte ähnlich wie ein Schlag in die Magengrube. The Mohawks waren ein Studioprojekt des genialen Hawkshaws, der mit seinem orgellastigen Funk während der 60er und 70er Jahre einige der erfolgreichsten Library Productions (Platten für Fernsehshows und Werbung) geschaffen hatte. **○**
Sur les copies originales de ce grand classique, c'était un poing rouge qui passait à travers un orgue Hammond, à l'image du funk viscéral et contondant d'Alan Hawkshaw. The Mohawks était un projet de studio dont le cerveau était Hawkshaw. Son funk gonflé à l'orgue avait produit quelques-uns des morceaux les plus utilisés pour les génériques de télévision et les publicités des années 1960 et 1970.

T.S. MONK
title **HOUSE OF MUSIC** /
year **1980** / *label* Mirage /
photography Jim Houghton /
art direction Bob Defrin

MONTANA
title **I LOVE MUSIC** / *year* **1978** /
label Atlantic / *art direction* Sandi
Young / *illustration* Roger Huyssen

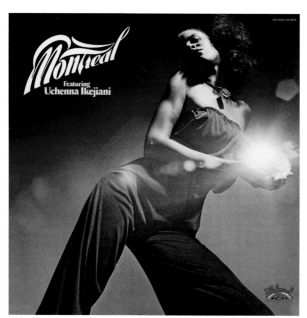

MONTREAL FEATURING UCHENNA IKEJIANI

title **MONTREAL FEATURING UCHENNA IKEJIANI** /
year **1978** / *label* Salsoul / *design*
Paula Swauger / *photography*
Belott/Wolfson Photography /
art direction Stanley Hochstadt

MELBA MOORE

title **PEACH MELBA** / *year* **1975** /
label Buddah / *photography* Mario
Casilli / *packaging* Milton Sincoff

MORNING, NOON &
NIGHT

title **MORNING, NOON** & **NIGHT** /
year **1977** / *label* United Artists /
art direction Sid Maurer / *illustration*
Jeannie Welch

RAMON MORRIS

title **SWEET SISTER FUNK** / *year* **1974** / *label* Groove Merchant / *photography* Chuck Stewart / *art direction* Sam Alexander

Perhaps the rarest album released on the Groove Merchant label, Ramon Morris' sweet tenor sax holds court on this soulful session of jazz funk at its best. Chuck Stewart had been photographing jazz greats from Louis Armstrong to Billie Holiday for a couple of decades already when he snapped this intimate cover portrait. **O**

Dies ist vielleicht das exzeptionellste Album, das beim Label Groove Merchant erschienen ist. Bei dieser souligen Jazz-funk-Session läuft Ramon Morris mit seinem fantastischen Tenorsaxophon zur Höchstform auf. Chuck Stewart hatte bereits seit ein paar Jahrzehnten Jazzikonen von Louis Armstrong bis zu Billie Holiday fotografiert, als ihm dieses intime Porträt für das Cover gelang. **O**

C'est peut-être l'album le plus rare sorti chez le label Groove Merchant. Le saxo ténor moelleux de Ramon Morris est entouré de sa cour dans cette session de jazz funk expressif au meilleur de sa forme. Lorsqu'il a pris ce portrait intime pour la pochette, Chuck Stewart photographiait déjà les grands du jazz depuis une vingtaine d'années, de Louis Armstrong à Billie Holiday.

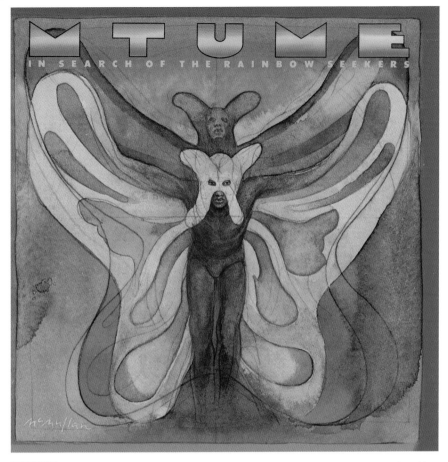

MTUME

title **IN SEARCH OF THE RAINBOW SEEKERS** /
year **1980** / *label* Epic / *illustration* James McMullan

James Mtume, percussionist, and Reggie Lucas, guitarist,
were former sidemen of Miles Davis before founding this
afrocentric funk band. This 1980 release was their second
for Epic Records and met with a modicum of success, but
the follow-up would produce the all-time classic in its
title-song, "Juicy Fruit". James McMullan illustrated the
New York magazine story about a Brooklyn discotheque
that inspired the movie *Saturday Night Fever*. **◐**
Der Perkussionist James Mtume und der Gitarrist Reggie
Lucas waren früher Mitstreiter von Miles Davis, bevor sie
ihre Funkband gründeten. Diese Platte von 1980 war ihre

zweite für Epic Records und erzielte nur minimalen Erfolg,
doch das Nachfolgealbum enthielt mit dem Titelsong
»Juicy Fruit« einen echten Klassiker. James McMullan illustrierte eine Story im *New York*-Magazin über eine Diskothek
in Brooklyn – was wiederum Inspirationsquelle für den
Film *Saturday Night Fever* wurde. **◐**
James Mtume, percussionniste, et Reggie Lucas, guitariste,
ont accompagné Miles Davis avant de créer ce groupe de
funk africanisant. Cet opus de 1980 était le deuxième qu'ils
réalisaient chez Epic Records et n'a rencontré qu'un succès
très relatif, mais le suivant allait amener un classique des
classiques avec son morceau-titre, *Juicy Fruit*. James
McMullan a illustré l'article paru dans le *New York Magazine* sur une discothèque de Brooklyn qui allait inspirer le
film *La Fièvre du samedi soir*.

JUGGY MURRAY JONES DPL

Inside America

DISCO

JUPITER
JAZZ

JUGGY MURRAY JONES
title **INSIDE AMERICA – DISCO** / *year* **1976** /
label Jupiter

Henry "Juggy" Murray, Jr. had clocked over twenty years in
the music industry before cutting this collection of
straightforward funk and disco psychedelia. In 1957, Murray
established Sue Records, one of the first black-owned record labels in the country. After moving to Los Angeles in
the early '70s, he began recording dance records as Juggy
Murray Jones, developing disco gems well into his fifties.

Henry »Juggy« Murray Jr. war schon mehr als zwanzig Jahre
in der Musikbranche tätig, als er diese Sammlung schnör-
kelloser Funk- und Disco-Psychedelika abmischte. 1957
gründete Murray Sue Records, eine der ersten Plattenfirmen des Landes, die Schwarzen gehörte. Nach seinem Um-
zug Anfang der 70er Jahre nach Los Angeles begann er als
Juggy Murray Jones mit der Aufnahme von Tanzmusik und
entwickelte bis weit in seine Fünfziger hinein verschiedene
Discoperlen.

Henry « Juggy » Murray Jr. comptait déjà plus de vingt ans
dans le secteur de la musique lorsqu'il a gravé cette collection de morceaux psychédéliques dans la plus pure veine
du funk et du disco. Murray a créé Sue Records en 1957.
C'était l'un des premiers labels du pays dirigé par un Noir.
Au début des années 1970, il partit à Los Angeles, où il
commença à enregistrer des disques de musique de danse
sous le nom de Juggy Murray Jones, et continua de
produire des perles du disco jusqu'à la cinquantaine bien
sonnée.

MYSTIQUE

title **MYSTIQUE** / *year* **1977** /
label Curtom / *design* Tom Nikosey /
photography Richard Fegley /
art direction Jim Ladwig/AGI

F-9440

Natural Essence
In Search
of Happiness

Fantasy

NATURAL ESSENCE

title **IN SEARCH OF HAPPINESS** / *year* **1973** / *label*
Fantasy / *photography* Tony Lane / *art direction* Tony Lane

Rasheed Ali started this spiritual jazz/funk band at Music
& Art High School in NYC. As he said, "We wanted to
represent Black Music in the school's annual Semi-Annual
concert because the Black Student Union was tired of a
classical music-only format." Later, pianist Nat Adderley Jr.
joined the band, which led to the involvement of family
members Julian "Cannonball" Adderley and Nat Adderley
coming in as producers for the group's sole release. **○**
Rasheed Ali gründete diese spirituelle Jazz/Funk-Band an
der Music & Art High School in New York City. Er sagte:
»Wir wollten, dass Black Music beim halbjährlich stattfindenden Schulkonzert ihren Platz bekommt, weil die Black

Student Union von einem rein klassischen Musikformat
genug hatte«. Später trat der Pianist Nat Adderley Jr. der
Band bei. Das führte dazu, dass weitere Mitglieder dieser
Familie wie Julian »Cannonball« Adderley und Nat Adderley als Produzenten für die einzige Veröffentlichung zu der
Gruppe hinzustießen. **○**
Rasheed Ali a créé ce groupe de spiritual jazz / funk à la
Music & Art High School de New York. Comme il l'a dit,
« nous voulions représenter la musique noire au concert
semestriel de l'école, parce que l'association des étudiants
noirs en avait assez du format exclusivement classique ».
Plus tard, le pianiste Nat Adderley Jr. a rejoint le groupe,
ce qui a conduit à la participation de son oncle et de son
père, Julian « Cannonball » Adderley et Nat Adderley, qui
ont produit le seul album du groupe.

NATURAL FOUR

title **NATURAL FOUR** / *year* **1974** / *label* Curtom /
photography Joel Brodsky / *art direction* Olga Romero

This sweet soul outfit started out in Oakland, CA in 1967.
They moved to Chicago and eventually signed to Curtis
Mayfield's Curtom label in 1972. With the transition only
lead singer Chris James stayed in the group. Leroy Hutson's
gorgeous production laid the bed for their smooth
harmonies. **O**

Diese tolle Soulformation begann 1967 im kalifornischen
Oakland. Sie zogen nach Chicago und kamen schließlich

1972 bei Curtis Mayfields Label Curtom unter. Bei diesem
Übergang blieb nur der Leadsänger Chris James in der
Truppe. Leroy Hutsons hinreißende Produktion legte die
Grundlage für ihre weichen Harmonien. **O**

Cet ensemble de sweet soul a vu le jour à Oakland, en
Californie, en 1967. Ses membres partirent à Chicago et
finirent par signer chez le label Curtom de Curtis Mayfield
en 1972. Avec la transition, seul le chanteur principal Chris
James est resté dans le groupe. La magnifique production
de Leroy Hutson forme un lit moelleux pour y coucher
leurs harmonies veloutées.

LOVE POTION

THE NEW BIRTH

title **LOVE POTION** / *year* **1976** / *label* Warner Bros. /
design Norman Seeff & Melvin Wilson / *photography*
Norman Seeff / *art direction* Bob Lockart

Photographer Norman Seeff, a former emergency medical
doctor from Soweto, South Africa, packed his bags in 1969
and left to pursue an artistic career in New York. After a
brief, yet successful stint working with famed designer
Bob Cato, he moved out west and never looked back. His
dynamic, playful portraits are often shot in black & white,
giving the contemporary images a classic look. ⊙
Der Fotograf Norman Seeff war früher Notarzt im südafri-
kanischen Soweto. Er packte 1969 seine Sachen und verließ
das Land, um in New York seine Karriere als Künstler voran-

zutreiben. Nach einer kurzen, aber erfolgreichen Phase der
Zusammenarbeit mit dem berühmten Designer Bob Cato
machte er sich nach Westen auf und schaute nie mehr
zurück. Seine dynamischen, verspielten Porträts nahm er
oft in Schwarzweiß auf, was den zeitgenössischen Bildern
ihren klassischen Look verlieh. ⊙
Le photographe Norman Seeff, un ancien médecin urgen-
tiste de Soweto, en Afrique du Sud, a fait ses bagages en
1969 et est parti poursuivre une carrière artistique à New
York. Il a passé une période brève mais productive à travailler avec le célèbre graphiste Bob Cato, puis est parti dans
l'Ouest sans regarder en arrière. Ses portraits dynamiques et
ludiques sont souvent en noir et blanc, ce qui donne un
style classique à ces images modernes.

THE NEW BIRTH

title **IT'S BEEN A LONG TIME** / *year* **1973** / *label* RCA /
photography David B. Hecht / *art direction* Acy Lehman

Long-time RCA go-to photographer David B. Hecht's most
famous subject was probably Elvis Presley, for whom he
shot the cover to the King's second RCA release. Otherwise
one of his recurring themes was the female form in fantastical settings. He had shot many such covers for Latin lounge
records since the 1950s, and it's nice to see him revisit the
theme for the way-out soul of The New Birth's 5th LP. **O**
Das berühmteste Individuum, das der langjährige und zu-
verlässige Fotograf von RCA, David B. Hecht, vor die Linse
bekam, war wahrscheinlich Elvis Presley. Hecht schoss das
Foto für die zweite RCA-Veröffentlichung des »Kings«. An-

sonsten war eines seiner Lieblingssujets weibliche Formen
in fantastischer Umgebung. Er hat seit den 50er Jahren viele
solcher Cover für Latin Lounge Records geschossen, und es
ist schön, dass er für den abgefahrenen Soul der fünften LP
von The New Birth dieses Motiv erneut aufgriff. **O**
David B. Hecht a longtemps été le photographe de référence chez RCA. Il a réalisé la photo du deuxième album
sorti chez RCA d'Elvis Presley, sans doute son modèle le
plus célèbre. L'un de ses sujets de prédilection était la
plastique féminine dans des décors extravagants. Il avait
fait de nombreuses couvertures de ce style pour les disques
de musique latine lounge des années 1950, et l'on apprécie
de le voir revisiter ce thème pour la soul excentrique du
cinquième album des New Birth.

**THE NEW ROTARY
CONNECTION**

title **"HEY, LOVE"** / *year* **1971** / *label*
Cadet / *design* Michael Mendel/
Maurer Productions / *photography*
Peter Amft/Daily Planet

NEWBAN

title **NEWBAN** / *year* **1977** / *label* Guinness

Newban first got together in White Plains, NY before moving to California. They recorded two boogie-filled funk records in 1977 before changing their name to Atlantic Starr. Their debut is full of the tight group-style funk that would make their future incarnation a popular R&B act through the 1990s. ●
Newban fanden sich in White Plains, New York, zusammen, bevor sie nach Kalifornien umzogen. Sie nahmen 1977 zwei Funk-Platten voller Boogie auf, bevor sie ihren Namen in Atlantic Starr änderten. Ihr Debüt ist vollgepackt mit dem dichten Funk im Gruppenstil, der ihre zukünftige Inkarnation in den 90er Jahren zu einem beliebten R&B-Act machen sollte. ●
Le groupe Newban s'est formé à White Plains, dans l'État de New York, avant de partir en Californie. Il a enregistré deux disques de funk saturé de boogie en 1977 avant de prendre le nom d'Atlantic Starr. Le style de funk en groupe de ce premier album allait rendre la future formation de R&B populaire tout au long des années 1990.

DAVID NEWMAN
title **NEWMANISM** / *year* **1974** /
label Atlantic / *design* Bob Defrin &
Basil Pao / *illustration* Peter Lloyd

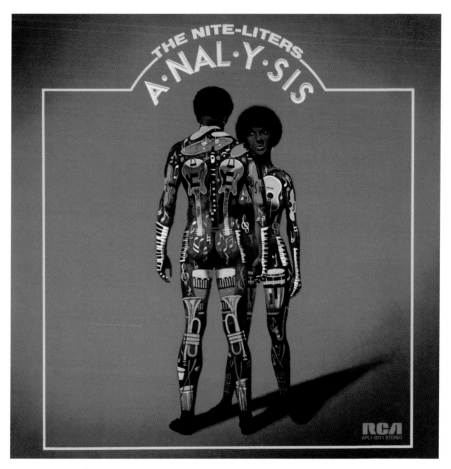

THE NITE-LITERS

title **A.NAL.Y.SIS** / *year* **1973** / *label* RCA /
design Dean Ellis / *art direction* Acy Lehman

The back cover of this inventive album contains an informative key, extrapolating the musical significance of this anatomical diagram. Although a thorough account is provided, the central positioning of the flute causes "thrills and chills to run up and down the spine", while the couple's piano hands causes "fingers [to] become alive, wiggle and wave with sound". **O**

Auf der Rückseite dieses originellen Albums wird in einer informativen Legende die musikalische Bedeutung dieses anatomischen Diagramms herausgearbeitet. Trotz dieser gründlichen Aufstellung wirkt die zentrale Positionierung der Flöte so, dass »Nervenkitzel und Schauer den Rücken rauf und runter laufen«, während die Pianohände des Paares dafür sorgen, dass »die Finger lebendig werden und zu den Klängen schlängeln und flattern«. **O**

Au dos de la pochette de cet album inventif, une légende informative explique la signification musicale de ce diagramme anatomique. Un compte-rendu détaillé est fourni : la position centrale de la flûte provoque des « frissons tout le long de la colonne vertébrale » et, avec les touches de piano sur les mains, « les doigts prennent vie, s'agitent et ondulent en rythme ».

STEREO

RCΛ
LSP-4430

THE NITE-LITERS

title **THE NITE-LITERS** / *year* **1970** / *label* RCA

Harvey Fuqua had a long and storied career from doo-wop singer in the 1950s to being an instrumental part of the growing Motown label in the 1960s. After he left Motown, Fuqua signed to RCA and was producer and Svengali to groups like The Nite-Liters, New Birth, and Love, Peace and Happiness. The Nite-Liters' debut had a great influence on the burgeoning instrumental funk scene, and the band could hold their own against contemporaries The J.B.'s or The Meters. **O**

Harvey Fuqua betrieb eine lange und geschichtsträchtige Karriere, beginnend als Doo-Wop-Sänger in den 50er Jahren bis hin zu seiner zentralen Funktion beim wachsenden Motown-Label in den 60ern. Nachdem er Motown verlassen

hatte, unterschrieb Fuqua bei RCA und war Produzent sowie Svengali für Gruppen wie The Nite-Liters, The New Birth und Love, Peace and Happiness. Das Debüt der Nite-Liters hatte großen Einfluss auf die aufkeimende Instrumental-Funk-Szene, und die Band konnte gut mit Zeitgenossen wie den J.B.'s oder den Meters mithalten. **O**

Harvey Fuqua a mené une carrière longue et historique. Chanteur de doo-wop dans les années 1950, il a joué un rôle capital dans la croissance de Motown dans les années 1960. Après avoir quitté le label, Fuqua a signé chez RCA et est devenu le producteur et le gourou de groupes tels que les Nite-Liters, New Birth et Love, Peace and Happiness. Le premier album des Nite-Liters a eu une grande influence sur la scène balbutiante du funk instrumental, et le groupe pouvait se mesurer sans peine à ses contemporains les J.B.'s ou les Meters.

Ntu
with
Gary Bartz
SINGERELLA
A Ghetto Fairy Tale

Prestige

NTU WITH GARY BARTZ

title **SINGERELLA A GHETTO FAIRY TALE** /
year **1974** / *label* Prestige / *photography* Gary Bartz /
art direction Tony Lane

One of Gary Bartz's later albums for Prestige, this sounds like a ghetto-funk operetta that never got produced for the stage: he even went so far in his concept as to take the cover photos himself. Bartz's alto sax and matter-of-fact singing style lead the group through an urban jungle with the assistance of Larry Mizell's cosmically inflected mix-down. ●

Dies ist eines der späteren Alben von Gary Bartz für Prestige und klingt wie eine Ghetto-Funk-Operette, die es nie auf die Bühne geschafft hat. Bei seinem Konzept ging er sogar soweit, dass er die Coverfotos selbst schoss. Bartz' Altsaxophonspiel und sein nüchterner Gesangsstil geleitete die Gruppe durch einen urbanen Dschungel, unterstützt von Larry Mizell und seiner kosmisch durchdrungenen Abmischung. ●

Cet album est l'un des derniers de Gary Bartz pour Prestige, et il fait penser à une opérette ghetto-funk qui n'aurait jamais été mise en scène : il a même poussé son concept jusqu'à prendre les photos de la pochette lui-même. Son saxo alto et sa voix prosaïque conduisent le groupe à travers une jungle urbaine avec l'aide du mixage aux inflexions cosmiques de Larry Mizell.

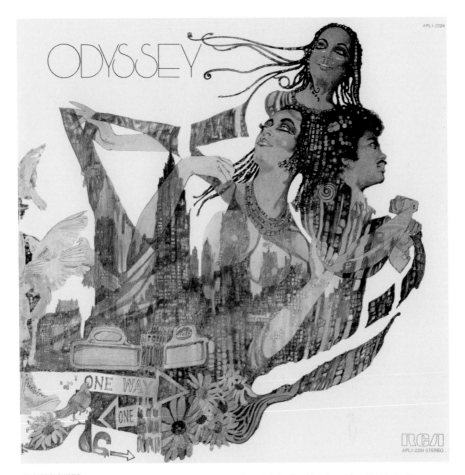

APL1-2204

APL1-2204 STEREO

ODYSSEY

title **ODYSSEY** / *year* **1977** / *label* RCA Victor /
illustration Ted Coconis

This New York City act was originally known as the Lopez
Sisters. The Caribbean-born group added Filipino singer
Tony Reynolds and changed their name to Odyssey for
their debut LP, which contained their biggest hit, "Native
New Yorker". With his distinct mix of cartooning and detailed painting, cover artist Ted Coconis supplied the visual
ode to the group's adopted home, which lends an airy
quality that jives perfectly with the music. **O**
Diese Gruppe aus New York City trat ursprünglich unter
dem Namen Lopez Sisters auf. Der Filipino-Sänger Tony
Reynolds trat der in der Karibik geborenen Gruppe bei, und
sie benannte sich für ihre Debüt-LP in Odyssey um. Auf

dieser Scheibe fand sich ihr größter Hit »Native New
Yorker«. Mit seiner speziellen Mischung aus detailreicher
Malerei und Cartoonstil lieferte der Covergestalter Ted
Coconis zur neuen Heimat der Gruppe eine visuelle Ode
und verlieh ihr eine lässig-luftige Qualität, die perfekt mit
der Musik swingt. **O**
Ce groupe new-yorkais d'origine caribéenne avait débuté
sous le nom des Lopez Sisters. Avec l'arrivée du chanteur
philippin Tony Reynolds, la formation prit le nom
d'Odyssey pour son premier album, qui renferme leur plus
grand succès, *Native New Yorker*. Avec son mélange caractéristique de bande dessinée et de peinture, le créateur
de la pochette, Ted Coconis, compose une ode à la ville
d'adoption du groupe et y insuffle une légèreté qui s'harmonise parfaitement avec leur musique.

OHIO PLAYERS

title **SKIN TIGHT** / *year* **1974** / *label* Mercury / *design*
Len Willis, Gnu World / *photography* Richard Fegley /
art direction Jim Ladwig/AGI

This horn-driven funk group was as well known for their
bouncy exuberant playing as for their sensual record
covers. This was their first release for Mercury and Art
Director Jim Ladwig chose a more subtle approach to the
S&M-inspired, sexed-up cover concept that designer David
Krieger and photographer Joel Brodsky had served up on
the band's earlier Westbound output. **O**
Diese bläserlastige Funktruppe war ebenso bekannt für ihr
lebhaftes und überschwängliches Spiel wie für ihre sinnli-

chen Plattencover. Dies war ihre erste Veröffentlichung für
Mercury, und der Art Director Jim Ladwig wählte einen
subtileren Ansatz für das von S&M inspirierte, erotisch auf-
geheizte Coverkonzept, das der Designer David Krieger und
der Fotograf Joel Brodsky den ehemaligen Westbound-
Veteranen aufgedrückt hatten. **O**
Ce groupe de funk qui fait la part belle à la trompette était
connu pour son jeu exubérant et dynamique, ainsi que
pour ses pochettes de disque sensuelles. Ceci est leur premier album pour Mercury, et le directeur artistique Jim
Ladwig a choisi une approche plus subtile du concept
sexualisé et inspiré du SM que le graphiste David Krieger et
le photographe Joel Brodsky avaient concocté pour l'album
précédent du groupe chez Westbound.

OHIO PLAYERS

title **ANGEL** / *year* **1977** / *label* Mercury / *photography*
Victor Skrebneski / *art direction* Jim Ladwig/AGI & Ohio
Players

After a few highly racy and controversial covers, Art Director Jim Ladwig scaled things back for this 1977 release.
Victor Skrebneski's stunning black & white photo has all of
the grace and beauty of a chiaroscuro charcoal drawing. As
with all the Ohio Players covers, this one is a gatefold and
the front image, with the woman's arms and legs truncated,
brings to mind a classical sculpture. ❂

Nach ein paar höchst gewagten und kontroversen Covern
kochte Art Director Jim Ladwig die Emotionen für diese
Platte aus dem Jahr 1977 etwas herunter. Das verblüffende

Schwarzweißfoto von Victor Skrebneski besitzt den voll-
kommenen Liebreiz und die Schönheit einer Chiaroscuro-
Kohlezeichnung. Wie bei allen Covern der Ohio Players
konnte man auch dieses ausklappen. Das Bild auf der Vor-
derseite, bei dem Arme und Beine der Frau abgeschnitten
sind, erinnert an eine klassische Skulptur. ❂

Après quelques pochettes salées et controversées, le directeur artistique Jim Ladwig a arrondi les angles pour cet album de 1977. La superbe photo en noir et blanc de Victor
Skrebneski a toute la grâce et la beauté d'un clair-obscur au
fusain. Comme pour toutes les pochettes des Ohio Players,
il s'agit d'un dépliant, et l'image de la couverture, avec les
bras et les jambes du sujet coupés par le cadre, évoque une
sculpture classique.

The O'Jays · Family Reunion

THE O'JAYS

title **FAMILY REUNION** / *year* **1975** / *label* Philadelphia
International / *design* Ed Lee / *illustration* David A. Leffel

David A. Leffel's classical approach to painting lends an air
of familiarity and warmth to the O'Jays' fourth Philadelphia
International release. The incomparable Gamble & Huff
production always gave this tight vocal group a sublime
bed of blessed-out soul to lie in. This would be founding
member William Powell's final recording and it is a beautiful send-off. **O**
David A. Leffels Anleihe bei der klassischen Malerei gab der
vierten Veröffentlichung der O'Jays auf Philadelphia International ihren Beiklang von Ungezwungenheit und Wärme.

Mit ihrer unvergleichlichen Produktion schenkten Gamble
& Huff dieser Vokalgruppe stets ein edles Bett aus gesegne-
tem Soul, auf dem sie ruhen konnte. Dies sollte die letzte
Aufnahme mit dem Gründungsmitglied William Powell
sein – ein wunderschönes Abschiedsgeschenk. **O**
Avec son approche classique de la peinture, David A. Leffel
confère familiarité et chaleur au quatrième album des
O'Jays chez Philadelphia International. La production incomparable de Gamble & Huff a toujours donné à ce
groupe vocal très uni une sublime base de soul spirituelle
sur laquelle se reposer. Ce disque allait être le dernier enregistrement du membre fondateur William Powell, et c'est
un adieu magnifique.

THE O'JAYS

title **SHIP AHOY** / *year* **1973** /
label Philadelphia International /
art direction Ed Lee / *illustration*
James Barkley

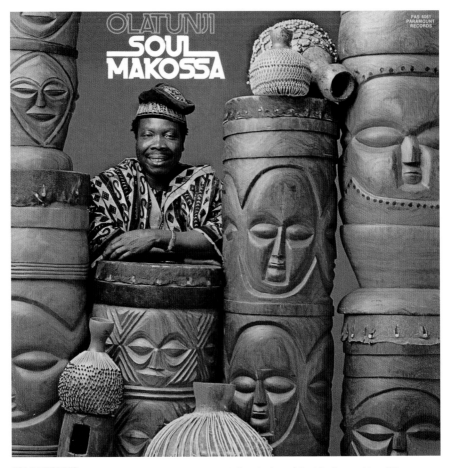

OLATUNJI

title **SOUL MAKOSSA** / *year* **1973** / *label* Paramount /
design Ron Canagata / *photography* Joel Brodsky /
art direction David Krieger

Babatunde Olatunji had been putting out records of
traditional Nigerian drumming and chanting since 1959.
This early '70s release is based around the Manu Dibango
classic that gives the album its title. David Krieger was the
creative director of the NYC ad agency Davis-Fried-Krieger
and designed many record covers. He favored hiring photographers, like Joel Brodsky, from outside of the music
world to get a new perspective on the musicians they were
working with. **O**
Babatunde Olatunji brachte seit 1959 Platten mit traditionellen nigerianischen Trommeln und Gesang heraus. Dieser

Release basiert auf dem Klassiker von Manu Dibango, von
dem das Album auch seinen Titel bekam. David Krieger
war Kreativdirektor bei der New Yorker Werbeagentur
Davis-Fried-Krieger und gestaltete viele Plattenhüllen. Er
engagierte gerne Fotografen, die außerhalb der Musikszene
tätig waren, wie z. B. Joel Brodsky, um einen neuen Blick auf
die Musiker zu bekommen, mit denen sie arbeiteten. **O**
Babatunde Olatunji faisait des disques de percussions et de
chants nigériens traditionnels depuis 1959. Cet album du
début des années 1970 est basé sur le classique de Manu
Dibango qui lui a donné son titre. David Krieger était le
directeur de la création de l'agence de publicité new-yorkaise Davis-Fried-Krieger et avait créé de nombreuses pochettes de disque. Il aimait embaucher des photographes
extérieurs au monde de la musique, comme Joel Brodsky,
afin d'obtenir une perspective neuve sur les musiciens.

OLYMPIC RUNNERS
title PUT THE MUSIC WHERE
YOUR MOUTH IS / *year* 1974 /
label London

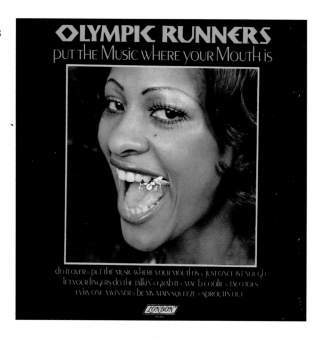

**ONE WAY
FEATURING
AL HUDSON**
title ONE WAY FEATURING
AL HUDSON / *year* 1980 /
label MCA / *art direction* Vartan /
illustration Michael Bryan

ONENESS OF JUJU
title **AFRICAN RHYTHMS** / *year* **1975** / *label* Black Fire / *design* Janet Brown / *illustration* Muzi Branch

THE ORIGINALS
title **ANOTHER TIME ANOTHER PLACE** / *year* **1978** / *label* Fantasy / *art direction* Phill Carroll / *illustration* Gary Ruddell / *cover concept* Glenn "Cookie" Price & Tyrone "Tiny" Sanders

MICHAEL ORR

title **SPREAD LOVE** / *year* **2000** / *label* Counterpoint /
design Kenneth & Dorothy Orr / *illustration* M. Orr

From the outsider artwork to the earthy production, this
lost classic has long been desired by in-the-know collectors.
Originally released in Detroit on the private Sunstar label in
1976, it aspires to the heights of Stevie Wonder, Gil Scott-
Heron, and Quincy Jones. Orr's rich voice digs deep into
the soulful jazz that he and Carey Harris crafted and comes
up with the pot of gold at the end of the rainbow. **O**
Von seiner nonkonformistischen Covergestaltung bis zu
seiner erdigen Produktion wurde dieser verlorene Klassiker
zu einem heiß begehrten Sammlerstück. Ursprünglich kam

das Album 1976 in Detroit auf dem privaten Label Sunstar
heraus und strebte nach den unerreichten Höhen eines
Stevie Wonder, Gil Scott-Heron oder Quincy Jones. Orrs
facettenreiche Stimme ist tief in dem souligen Jazz verwur-
zelt, den er gemeinsam mit Carey Harris schuf, und erreichte am Ende des Regenbogens den Topf mit Gold. **O**
Depuis son illustration faite par un outsider jusqu'à sa
production terrienne, ce classique perdu a longtemps été
l'objet du désir pour les collectionneurs avertis. Il est sorti
en 1976 à Detroit, chez le label Sunstar, et aspire à atteindre
les altitudes de Stevie Wonder, Gil Scott-Heron et Quincy
Jones. La voix riche d'Orr creuse profondément le jazz soul
que lui et Carey Harris ont concocté, et en exhume le chau-
dron d'or proverbial caché au pied de l'arc-en-ciel.

Thomas Warkentin

LEE OSKAR

title **LEE OSKAR** / *year* **1976** / *label* United Artists /
illustration Thomas Warkentin

Lee Oskar had been War's secret weapon. A harmonica
virtuoso, his solo debut draws from his former band's funky
multi-cultural sound with a touch of eastern-European folk
music in the mix. Thomas Warkentin's work as a technical
illustrator can be seen in his attention to detail. His fantastical, imaginative painting for this cover foreshadows his
work on the *Star Trek* comic strip. ●
Lee Oskar war die Geheimwaffe von War. Das Solodebüt
dieses Harmonikavirtuosen speist sich aus den funkigen
multikulturellen Klängen seiner ehemaligen Band mit ei-

nem Touch osteuropäischer Folkmusik. Thomas Warken-
tins Ausbildung als technischer Zeichner erkennt man an
seiner Beachtung von Details. Sein fantastisches und ein-
fallsreiches Bild für dieses Cover lässt schon seine Arbeit an
den *Star Trek*-Comics erahnen. ●
Lee Oskar avait été l'arme secrète de War. Les débuts en
solo de ce virtuose de l'harmonica continuent dans la ligne
du son multiculturel de son ancien groupe, avec en plus un
soupçon de musique traditionnelle d'Europe de l'Est. On
peut déceler l'expérience de Thomas Warkentin comme
illustrateur technique dans son attention aux détails. Le
tableau plein d'imagination qu'il a réalisé pour cette pochette est un avant-goût de son travail sur la bande dessinée *Star Trek*.

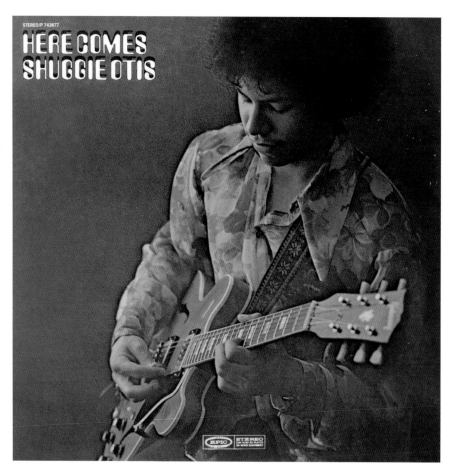

STEREO/P 743877

HERE COMES SHUGGIE OTIS

SHUGGIE OTIS
title **HERE COMES SHUGGIE OTIS** / *year* **1970** /
label Epic / *photography* Ergo

Sitting on the fuzzy, psychedelic side of folksy blues, Shuggie, the son of R&B big-band leader Johnny Otis, was still a teenager when his debut was recorded. The elder Otis produced and co-wrote the album with his son. While Shuggie's vocals would mature over his next couple of albums, his guitar-playing here is breathtaking. **O** Shuggie, der Sohn des R&B-Bigband-Leaders Johnny Otis, weilt auf der verschwommenen, psychedelischen Seite des

volkstümlichen Blues. Er war noch ein Teenager, als sein Debüt aufgenommen wurde. Vater Otis produzierte und schrieb dieses Album gemeinsam mit seinem Sohn. Der Gesang von Shuggie sollte auf den nächsten Alben weiter reifen, doch sein Gitarrenspiel hier ist atemberaubend. **O** Shuggie, le fils du leader de big band R&B Johnny Otis, était encore un adolescent lorsqu'il a enregistré son premier album, que l'on peut situer sur le versant psychédélique-fuzz du blues rustique. Il a coécrit l'album avec son père, qui l'a produit. La voix de Shuggie devait encore prendre de la maturité sur ses albums suivants, mais ici, son jeu à la guitare est à couper le souffle.

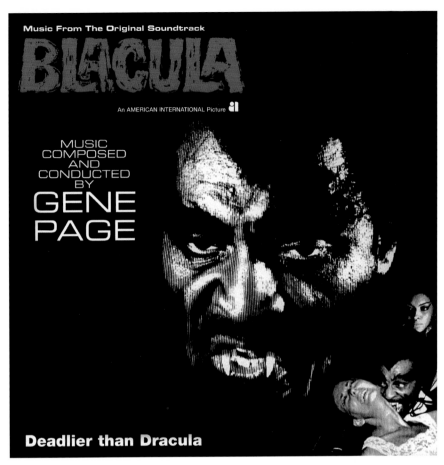

Music From The Original Soundtrack

BLACULA

An AMERICAN INTERNATIONAL Picture

MUSIC
COMPOSED
AND
CONDUCTED
BY
GENE
PAGE

Deadlier than Dracula

GENE PAGE
title **BLACULA** / *year* **1972** / *label* RCA Victor

Using an array of traditional and non-traditional instruments, Gene Page's rich and nuanced score accentuated the variations in suspense and surprise, illustrating *Blacula*'s dichotomy of love and horror, all the while keeping up with the engaging performance delivered by Shakespearian actor and lead William Marshall. **O**

Gene Page setzte für seinen nuancierten Soundtrack eine Vielzahl traditioneller und nicht-traditioneller Instrumente ein, um den Wechsel zwischen Spannung und Überra-schung zu akzentuieren. Damit wird in *Blacula* die Gegensätzlichkeit von Liebe und Horror illustriert, und außerdem ist der Soundtrack auch der faszinierenden Schauspielkunst des Shakespeare-Mimen William Marshall in der Hauptrolle gewachsen. **O**

Grâce à un arsenal d'instruments traditionnels et moins traditionnels, la bande originale riche et nuancée de Gene Page accentuait les variations entre suspense et surprise pour illustrer la dichotomie amour / horreur de *Blacula, le vampire noir*, tout en suivant le jeu captivant de l'acteur shakespearien qui tenait le rôle principal, William Marshall.

PARLIAMENT

title **MOTHERSHIP CONNECTION** / *year* **1975** /
label Casablanca / *design* Gribbitt! / *art direction* Gribbitt!

From the space bass of Bootsy Collins to the squiggling Minimoog of Bernie Worrell, George Clinton's band of merry funkateers took funk where no band had been before. The interstellar mythology of the Mothership and all its freaky inhabitants (which at this point included ex-James Brown horn-men Maceo Parker and Fred Wesley) would start here. **O**

Die fröhlichen Funkateers von George Clintons Band brachten mit dem spacigen Bass von Bootsy Collins und dem verschnörkelten Minimoog von Bernie Worrell den Funk dorthin, wo vorher noch keine Band gewesen war. Die interstellare Mythologie vom Mothership und all seinen freakigen Bewohnern (zu denen zu diesem Zeitpunkt auch die vormals bei James Brown spielenden Bläser Maceo Parker und Fred Wesley gehörten) sollte auf diesem Album ihren Anfang nehmen. **O**

Depuis la guitare cosmique de Bootsy Collins jusqu'aux gigotements du minimoog de Bernie Worrell, le groupe de joyeux drilles de George Clinton a emmené le funk là où aucun groupe n'était jamais allé. La mythologie interstellaire du vaisseau mère et de tous ses occupants excentriques (qui comprenaient à ce moment-là les anciens trompettistes de James Brown, Maceo Parker et Fred Wesley) était née.

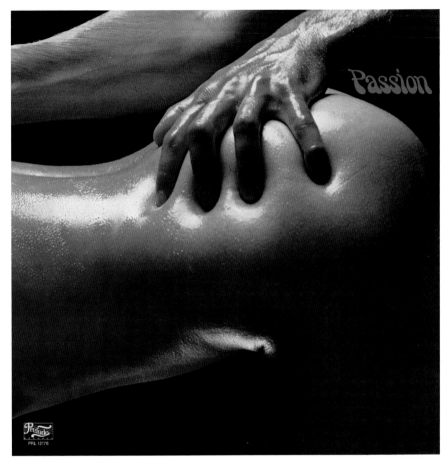

PASSION

title **PASSION** / *year* **1979** / *label* Prelude / *design* Ancona Design Atelier / *photography* Trudy Schlachter

Trudy Schlachter's cover shot for this Paradise Garage classic exudes the hot and greasy disco heat as much as the slinky tracks within do. According to leader Ray Martinez, this group was the same as Amant, but because of contractual issues with TK Records they had to change names for the new Prelude project. **O**

Trudy Schlachters Coverfoto für die Hülle dieses Klassikers aus der Paradise Garage verströmt ebenso wie die aufrei- zenden Klänge darin eine heiße und schlüpfrige Disco-Hitze. Dem Bandleader Ray Martinez zufolge war diese Gruppe die gleiche wie Amant, doch wegen vertraglicher Probleme mit TK Records mussten sie für das neue Prelude-Projekt ihren Namen ändern. **O**

La photo que Trudy Schlachter a réalisée pour la pochette de ce classique du Paradise Garage exsude la chaleur étouffante et poisseuse du disco tout autant que la musique qu'elle illustre. Selon son leader Ray Martinez, ce groupe était le même qu'Amant, mais des problèmes liés à leur contrat avec TK Records les a poussés à changer de nom pour le nouveau projet de Prelude.

ORIGINAL MUSIC FROM THE METRO-GOLDWYN-MAYER FILM

SHAFT in Africa

ABCX-793

Main title song by the
Four Tops
"Are You Man Enough"

Written by
Dennis Lambert & Brian Potter

Original score composed,
arranged and conducted by
Johnny Pate

COPYRIGHT © 1973 METRO-GOLDWYN-MAYER, INC.

JOHNNY PATE
title **SHAFT IN AFRICA** / *year* **1973** / *label* ABC

For special agent John Shaft's tenure in Africa, Chicago arranger Johnny Pate was enlisted to create perhaps the most compelling soundtrack in the original *Shaft* trilogy, rivaling that of Isaac Hayes' original. Pate achieved his most enduring successes arranging for Curtis Mayfield-era Impressions, achieving expansive sounds from his modest ensembles. **O**
Für die Dienstzeit von Special Agent John Shaft in Afrika wurde der Arrangeur Johnny Pate aus Chicago beauftragt, den vielleicht überwältigendsten Soundtrack der originalen

Shaft-Trilogie zu schaffen und so mit dem Original von Isaac Hayes die Klingen zu kreuzen. Pate erlangte seine dauerhaftesten Erfolge, als er für die Impressions in ihrer Curtis-Mayfield-Ära die Arrangements machte und aus seinen mäßigen Ensembles weitläufige Klänge herausholte. **O**
Pour la mission de l'agent spécial John Shaft en Afrique, Johnny Pate, arrangeur de Chicago, a été chargé de créer l'une des bandes originales les plus captivantes de la trilogie de *Shaft*, qui fait concurrence à l'original d'Isaac Hayes. Pate a obtenu ses succès les plus marquants en tant qu'arrangeur pour les Impressions de l'époque de Curtis Mayfield et tirait des sons amples de ses formations modestes.

KELLEE PATTERSON
title **MAIDEN VOYAGE** / *year* **1974** /
label Black Jazz / *design* PGM

With barely two dozen titles to their name, every Black Jazz release is a classic, instantly recognizable by the uniform black-and-white artist photo, each one bordered in black. Founded on the outskirts of Chicago by pianist/producer Gene Russell, the label sought to provide a black-owned outlet for the increasingly socially conscious jazz music being conceived in the Midwest and elsewhere. ○
Nicht einmal zwei Dutzend Titel erschienen auf dem Label Black Jazz, und jeder ist ein Klassiker, sofort erkennbar an dem einheitlichen Schwarzweißfoto des Musikers, das in einen schwarzen Rahmen gefasst ist. Black Jazz wurde

am Rand von Chicago vom Pianisten und Produzenten Gene Russell gegründet und sollte als Label im Besitz von Schwarzen eine Plattform für die in steigendem Maße sozialkritische Jazzmusik sein, die im Mittleren Westen und auch anderswo gespielt wurde. ○
Black Jazz ne possède qu'un catalogue d'à peine plus d'une vingtaine de titres, mais chacun de ses albums est un classique, reconnaissable immédiatement grâce à la même photo en noir et blanc de l'artiste, toujours bordée de noir. C'est le pianiste / producteur Gene Russell qui a fondé ce label dans la banlieue de Chicago, pour fournir un appui logistique dirigé par un Noir au jazz créé dans le Midwest ou ailleurs, qui commençait à développer une conscience sociale croissante.

BILLY PAUL

title **WAR OF THE GODS** / *year* **1973** / *label* Philadelphia International / *design* Ed Lee / *illustration* Roger Hane

Billy Paul's *War of the Gods* owes its surreal cover art to the talented Roger Hane, who himself is best known for the fanciful illustrations that grace early paperback editions of the *Chronicles of Narnia* series, as well as notable work for *Esquire*, *Playboy*, and the *Saturday Review*. ○
Die surreale Coverkunst hat Billy Pauls *War of the Gods* dem talentierten Roger Hane zu verdanken. Dieser ist be-

kannt für seine fantasievollen Illustrationen, die die ersten Taschenbuchausgaben der *Chroniken von Narnia* zieren, und außerdem durch seine bemerkenswerten Arbeiten für *Esquire*, *Playboy* und *Saturday Review*. ○
L'album *War of the Gods* de Billy Paul doit sa pochette surréaliste au talentueux Roger Hane, plus connu pour les illustrations pleines d'imagination qui ornent les premières éditions brochées de la série *Le Monde de Narnia*, ainsi que pour son remarquable travail pour *Esquire*, *Playboy* et *Saturday Review*.

BILLY PAUL
title **360 DEGREES OF BILLY PAUL** /
year **1972** / *label* Epic /
photography Don Hunstein

FREDA PAYNE BAND OF GOLD

I LEFT SOME DREAMS BACK THERE
THROUGH THE MEMORY OF MY MIND
DEEPER & DEEPER
The Easiest Way to Fall
Unhooked Generation
Love on Borrowed Time
This Girl Is a Woman Now
The World Don't Owe You a Thing
Now Is The Time to Say Goodbye
Happy Heart
Rock Me in the Cradle

FREDA PAYNE
title **BAND OF GOLD** / *year* **1970** / *label* Invictus

"Band of Gold" was Freda Payne's first and most enduring hit. Written by the songwriting triumvirate of Holland/Dozier/Holland, the song details a marriage in which the flame is all but extinguished by the arrival of Payne's fictionalized wedding night, the solitary evidence of their former love being "a band of gold". **o**

»Band of Gold« war Freda Paynes erster und beständigster Hit. Geschrieben wurde er vom Songwriter-Triumvirat Holland/Dozier/Holland, und der Song handelt von einer Ehe, bei der die Flamme der Liebe praktisch schon erloschen ist, als die Hochzeitsnacht kommt, und dem Paar als einziger Beweis ihrer früheren Liebe das »goldene Band« erhalten bleibt. **o**

Band of Gold a été le premier succès de Freda Payne, et le plus marquant. Écrite par le triumvirat de la composition, Holland, Dozier et Holland, cette chanson décrit un mariage où la flamme s'éteint à l'arrivée de la nuit de noces fictive de Payne. La seule trace qui reste de cet amour disparu est l'anneau d'or du titre.

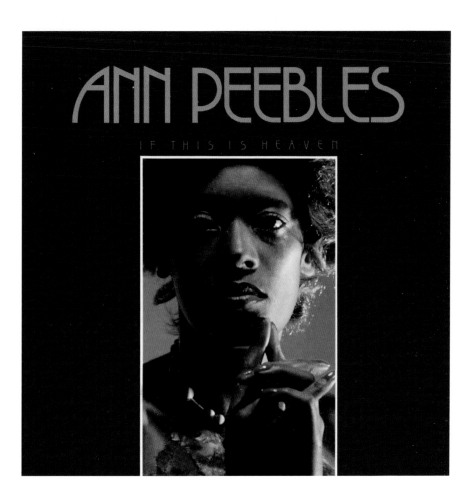

ANN PEEBLES

title **IF THIS IS HEAVEN** / *year* **1977** /
label Hi / *photography* David Scruggs

Best known for her 1973 single *I Can't Stand the Rain*, Ann
Peebles' *If This is Heaven* contains faint, yet recognizable
signs that even Music City, USA was susceptible to disco's
pervasive beat. Memphis photographer David Scruggs
took a handful of photos for Willie Mitchell's Hi Records,
with Ann Peebles, O.V. Wright, and Otis Clay amongst his
soulful subjects. **O**

Ann Peebles wurde bekannt durch ihre 1973 erschienene
Single »I Can't Stand the Rain«. *If This is Heaven* enthält
dezente, aber doch gut erkennbare Anzeichen, dass sogar
Nashville, die »Music City USA«, für den durchdringenden
Beat von Disco empfänglich war. Der Memphis-Fotograf
David Scruggs nahm eine Handvoll Fotos für Willie
Mitchells Hi Records auf, u. a. mit Ann Peebles, O.V. Wright
und Otis Clay als soulige Sujets. **O**

Ann Peebles est plus connue pour son single *I Can't Stand
the Rain* sorti en 1973. Son album *If This is Heaven* renferme
des signes discrets mais identifiables qui indiquent que
même Nashville n'était pas insensible au rythme omniprésent du disco. Le photographe de Memphis David Scruggs
a pris quelques photos pour le label Hi Records de Willie
Mitchell, avec Ann Peebles, O.V. Wright et Otis Clay, pour
ne citer que quelques-uns de ses sujets issus du monde de
la soul. **O**

PEOPLE'S CHOICE

title **WE GOT THE RHYTHM** / *year* **1976** / *label*
Philadelphia International / *design* Ed Lee & Maria De
Oro / *photography* Frank Laffitte / *lettering* Bill Murphy

Frankie Brunson started his singing career in 1951 as "Little
Frankie" out of Buffalo, NY. He recorded with many
different groups until he ended up in Philadelphia in the
mid 1960s. There he met Leon Huff & Kenny Gamble and
People's Choice was born. Ed Lee and Frank Laffitte's
booty-bumping cover art embodied the silky smooth
Gamble & Huff production on this Philly classic. **O**
Frankie Brunson aus Buffalo (New York) begann 1951 seine
Karriere als Sänger unter dem Namen »Little Frankie«. Er
machte mit vielen unterschiedlichen Gruppen Aufnahmen

und landete Mitte der 60er Jahre in Philadelphia. Hier traf
er auf Leon Huff & Kenny Gamble und People's Choice
ward geboren. Das von Ed Lee und Frank Laffitte gestaltete
Cover mit seinen zusammenprallenden Hintern verkör-
perte die seidenweiche Produktion von Gamble & Huff auf
diesem Philly-Sound-Klassiker. **O**
Frankie Brunson a commencé sa carrière de chanteur en
1951 sous le nom de « Little Frankie » à Buffalo, New York.
Il a enregistré avec de nombreux groupes différents jusqu'à
ce qu'il arrive à Philadelphie au milieu des années 1960.
C'est là qu'il a rencontré Leon Huff et Kenny Gamble et
que People's Choice est né. Le carambolage de postérieurs
illustré sur la pochette est l'œuvre d'Ed Lee et de Frank
Laffitte et incarnait la production lisse comme la soie de
Gamble & Huff sur ce classique de Philadelphia.

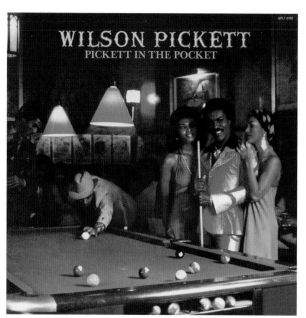

WILSON PICKETT

title **PICKETT IN THE POCKET** /
year **1974** / *label* RCA Victor /
photography Nick Sangiamo /
art direction Acy Lehman

WARDELL PIPER

title **WARDELL PIPER** / *year*
1979 / *label* Midsong International

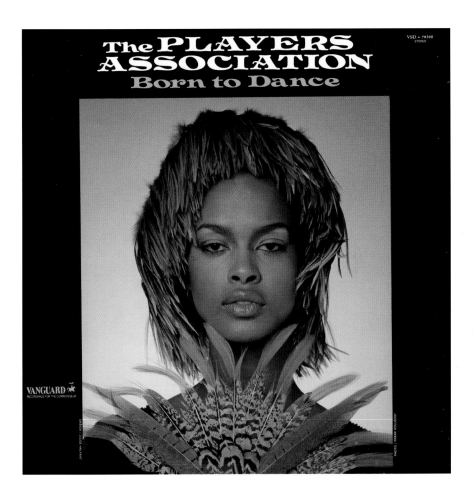

THE PLAYERS ASSOCIATION

title **BORN TO DANCE** / *year* **1977** /
label Vanguard / *photography* Frank
Kolleogy / *design* Jules Halfant

PLEASURE

title **DUST YOURSELF OFF** / *year* **1975** / *label* Fantasy /
art direction Phil Carroll / *illustration* Phil Carroll

Wayne Henderson discovered this outstanding horn-driven funk band in Portland, OR in 1972. He quickly signed them to Fantasy Records and produced their debut (as well as three more of the six records they recorded for the label). Henderson's signature laid-back groove with crackling drums worked perfectly with the band's masterful sound. **○**

Wayne Henderson entdeckte diese hervorragende bläserlastige Funk-Band 1972 in Portland, Oregon. Er ließ sie schnell bei Fantasy Records unterschreiben und produzierte ihr Debütalbum (sowie noch drei weitere der sechs Scheiben, die sie für das Label aufnahmen). Der typische entspannte Groove von Henderson mit seinen knisternden Drums passte perfekt zum meisterhaften Sound der Band. **○**

Wayne Henderson a découvert ce remarquable groupe de funk gonflé aux cuivres à Portland, dans l'Oregon, en 1972. Il s'est empressé de les faire signer chez Fantasy Records et a produit leur premier disque (ainsi que trois autres parmi les six qu'ils allaient enregistrer pour le label). Ce groove décontracté assaisonné de percussions crépitantes, caractéristique de Henderson, fonctionnait à merveille avec le son magistral du groupe.

POCKETS

title **COME GO WITH US** / *year* **1977** / *label* Columbia / *design* Tom Steele / *illustration* Peter Palombi

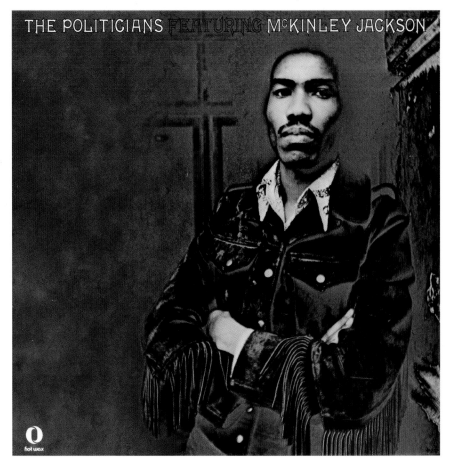

THE POLITICIANS FEATURING McKINLEY JACKSON

THE POLITICIANS FEATURING McKINLEY JACKSON

title **THE POLITICIANS FEATURING MCKINLEY JACKSON** / *year* **1972** / *label* Hot Wax / *design* Glen Christensen / *photography* Hal Wilson

This Detroit quintet served as the backing band for the Invictus/Hot Wax/Music Merchant labels. McKinley Jackson was the house arranger, working on practically every release ever recorded on the family of labels. Hal Wilson's corrosive, solarized portrait of Jackson on the cover to the group's sole release under their own name is an eye-catching homage to this artist who spent most of his career out of the spotlight. **O**
Dieses Detroiter Quintett diente als Backingband für die Label Invictus, Hot Wax und Music Merchant. McKinley

Jackson war der Hausarrangeur und arbeitete praktisch an jeder Veröffentlichung mit, die bei dieser Label-Familie erschienen ist. Hal Wilsons zerfressenes und solarisiertes Porträt von Jackson auf dem Cover, der einzigen Veröffentlichung der Gruppe unter ihrem eigenen Namen, ist eine ins Auge springende Hommage an diesen Künstler, der die meiste Zeit seiner Karriere nicht im Rampenlicht stand. **O**
Ce quintette de Detroit était le groupe d'accompagnement des labels Invictus, Hot Wax et Music Merchant. McKinley Jackson était l'arrangeur résident et a travaillé sur pratiquement tous les disques enregistrés chez cette famille de labels. Le portrait solarisé et corrosif qu'Hal Wilson a réalisé de Jackson sur la pochette du seul album que le groupe ait sorti sous son propre nom est un bel hommage à cet artiste, qui a passé la plus grande partie de sa carrière dans l'ombre.

SUGARHILL RECORDS, LTD.,

POSITIVE FORCE

title **POSITIVE FORCE** / *year* **1980** / *label* Sugarhill /
design Hemu Ghia Aggarwal

This jazzy funk ensemble out of Pennsylvania were
discovered by pianist/organist Nate Edmonds, who was a
writer and producer for Sylvia Robinson's family of labels:
All Platinum, Stang, and Sugarhill Records. The latter was
significant as the group would provide the party ambience
for the Sugarhill Gang's "Rapper's Delight", but were not
credited for the performance. Their debut on the predomi-
nantly rap-oriented label featured the b-boy breakdance
classic "We Got the Funk". **O**

Dieses jazzige Funk-Ensemble aus Pennsylvania wurde vom
Pianisten und Organisten Nate Edmonds entdeckt, der für
die Labels der Sylvia-Robinson-Familie komponierte und

produzierte: All Platinum, Stang und Sugarhill Records. Auf
letzteres Label ist besonders hinzuweisen, weil die Gruppe
die Partyatmosphäre für »Rapper's Delight« von der Sugarhill Gang lieferte, wobei ihr Beitrag allerdings nicht genannt
wurde. Auf ihrem Debüt beim überwiegend am Rap orien-
tierten Label erschien »We Got the Funk« – *der* Klassiker
für B-Boys und Breakdancer. **O**

Cette formation de funk mâtiné de jazz originaire de Penn-
sylvanie a été découverte par le pianiste / organiste Nate
Edmonds, qui écrivait et produisait pour la famille de labels
de Sylvia Robinson: All Platinum, Stang et Sugarhill Records.
Ce dernier a été important, car le groupe allait fournir
l'ambiance festive du *Rapper's Delight* de Sugarhill Gang,
mais n'a pas été crédité pour cette performance. Leur
premier album sur ce label de rap contient le classique de
breakdance *We Got the Funk*.

LLOYD PRICE
title **MR. "PERSONALITY"** /
year **1976** / *label* ABC Paramount

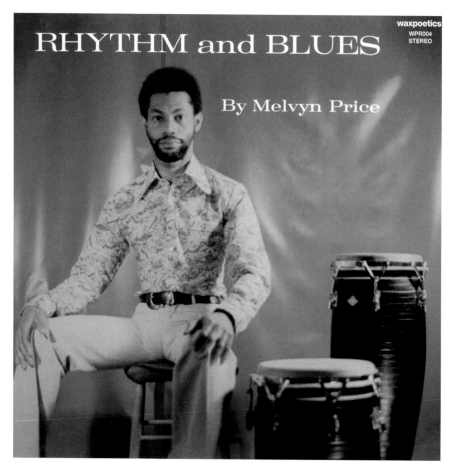

RHYTHM and BLUES

waxpoetics
WPR004
STEREO

By Melvyn Price

MELVYN PRICE
title **RHYTHM AND BLUES** / *year* **1974** /
label Wax Poetics / *design* Beata Bergström

A master conguero and trombonist, Melvyn Price was a
Michigan native who relocated to Sweden in the 1960s.
His third album was a privately-pressed creative explosion.
By incorporating his Motown upbringing and time spent
playing in the freeform Afrikan Folk Ensemble and utilizing
highly trained Swedish players, he was able to finally express himself to his fullest potential. **O**

Der meisterhafte Congaspieler und Posaunist Melvyn Price
stammt aus Michigan und siedelte in den 60er Jahren nach
Schweden um. Sein drittes Album wurde privat gepresst

und war wie eine kreative Explosion. Weil er seine Erfahrungen bei Motown und seine Zeit beim unkonventio-
nellen Afrikan Folk Ensemble mit einfließen ließ und mit
bestens ausgebildeten schwedischen Musikern arbeitete,
konnte er schließlich sein künstlerisches Potenzial voll
ausschöpfen. **O**

Joueur de congas et de trombone hors pair, Melvyn Price
était originaire du Michigan et partit vivre en Suède dans
les années 1960. Son troisième album était une explosion
créative gravée à titre privé. Il a enfin réussi à exprimer
pleinement son potentiel en opérant un mélange issu de sa
formation chez Motown et du temps qu'il a passé à jouer
dans l'orchestre de format libre Afrikan Folk Ensemble, et
en utilisant des musiciens suédois très expérimentés.

PRINCE
title **CONTROVERSY** / *year* **1981** /
label Warner Bros.

PROPHETS OF SOUL
title **"GREGORY JAMES EDITION"** / *year* **1973** /
label Dakar

Forever fly, this Chicago trio produced one of the toughest, most off-kilter jazz funk records ever. Gregory Bibb's keyboards and Farfisa take the lead on most tracks, with James Norris (guitar) and Anthony McAllister (drums) locking into his tight and always surprising grooves. Bibb would go on to work as musical director for the Chi-Sound label with singers Walter Jackson and Gene Chandler. ○
So cool, wie nur Schwarze sein können, produzierte dieses Trio aus Chicago eine außergewöhnlich toughe und sehr, sehr schräge Jazz-Funk-Kuriosität. Die Keyboards und die

Farfisa von Gregory Bibb übernehmen auf den meisten Tracks die Hauptrolle, und James Norris (Gitarre) sowie Anthony McAllister (Drums) klinken sich in seine dichten und stets überraschenden Grooves ein. Bibb fuhr fort, als musikalischer Leiter für das Label Chi-Sound mit den Sängern Walter Jackson und Gene Chandler zu arbeiten. ○
Ce trio de Chicago a produit l'un des disques de jazz funk les plus intransigeants et les plus excentriques. Les claviers et le Farfisa de Gregory Bibb prennent la vedette sur la plupart des morceaux, et James Norris (guitare) et Anthony McAllister (batterie) s'arriment à ses rythmes serrés et toujours surprenants. Bibb allait par la suite travailler comme directeur musical pour le label Chi-Sound, avec les chanteurs Walter Jackson et Gene Chandler.

PUCHO & THE LATIN SOUL BROTHERS

title **DATELINE** / *year* **1969** /
label Prestige / *design* Don Schlitten /
photography Don Schlitten

ORIGINAL MOVIE SOUND TRACK   Performed by BERNARD PRETTY PURDIE

BERNARD PURDIE

title **LIALEH** / *year* **1974** / *label* Bryan /
design Great Scott Advertising

This suggestive still from *Lialeh*, black cinema's first nation-
ally distributed adult film, foretells the sensually funky
soundtrack, produced, composed, and arranged by
drummer Bernard "Pretty" Purdie. Marketed as "the Black
Deep Throat", *Lialeh*'s musical legacy burns bright despite
the cinematic incarnation's brilliant, but brief flash of underground fame. **O**
Diese suggestive Nahaufnahme aus *Lialeh*, dem ersten
USA-weit vertriebenen schwarzen Pornofilm, deutet schon
den sinnlich-funkigen Soundtrack an, der vom Drummer

Bernard »Pretty« Purdie produziert, komponiert und
arrangiert wurde. Dieser Film wurde als »Schwarzer *Deep
Throat*« vermarktet, und das musikalische Erbe von *Lialeh*
strahlt in seiner filmischen Inkarnation hell, trotz seiner
großen, aber nur kurzen Berühmtheit im Underground. **O**
Ce photogramme suggestif tiré de *Lialeh*, le premier film
pour adultes du cinéma noir distribué dans tous les États-
Unis, évoque le funk sensuel de la bande originale produite,
composée et arrangée par le batteur Bernard « Pretty »
Purdie. Le film avait été présenté comme le « *Gorge profonde* noir », et son héritage musical est toujours vivant,
bien que l'œuvre cinématographique en elle-même n'ait
connu qu'une gloire éphémère et confinée aux milieux
underground.

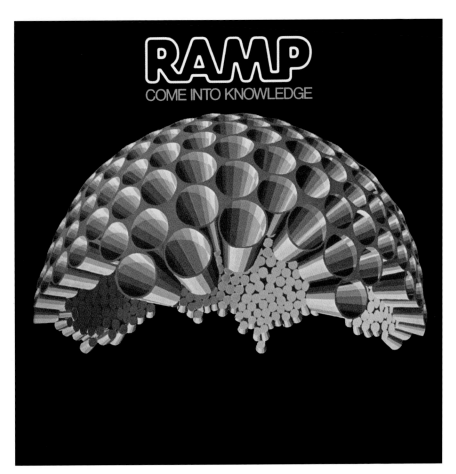

RAMP

title **COME INTO KNOWLEDGE** / *year* **1977** / *label* ABC / *art direction* Kats Abe / *illustration* Masaki Sato

Standing for Roy Ayers Musical Productions, Ramp's sole release is often regarded as one of the best soul jazz records ever. Ayers and frequent collaborator Edwin Birdsong wrote and produced the album which makes great use of a double female vocal style that, coupled with the spaced-out vibes and keyboard sounds, set this masterpiece in a universe of its own. O
Ramp steht für Roy Ayers Musical Productions. Diese einzige Veröffentlichung wird als eine der besten Soul-Jazz-Auf-

nahmen überhaupt betrachtet. Ayers schrieb und produzierte das Album gemeinsam mit Edwin Birdsong, mit dem er viel zusammengearbeitet hatte. Häufig wird darauf die weibliche Stimme doppelt besetzt, was zusammen mit den abgefahrenen Vibraphon- und Keyboardklängen dieses Meisterstück in ein ganz eigenes Universum versetzt. O
L'unique album de Ramp, acronyme de Roy Ayers Musical Productions, est souvent considéré comme l'un des meilleurs albums de soul-jazz de tous les temps. Ayers a écrit et produit cet album avec Edwin Birdsong, un collaborateur fréquent. L'utilisation magistrale de deux voix féminines, ajoutée aux vibrations planantes et aux sons des claviers, donne à ce chef-d'œuvre un univers bien à lui.

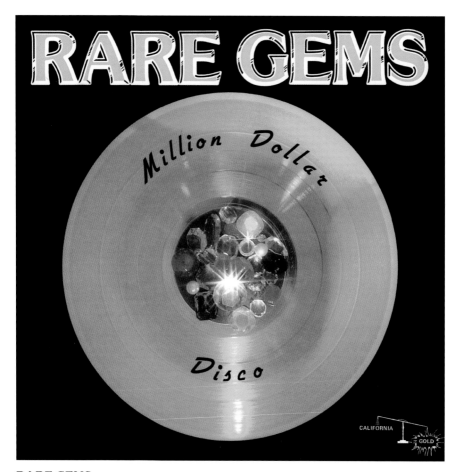

RARE GEMS

title **MILLION DOLLAR DISCO** / *year* **1978** /
label California Gold / *photography* Peg Owens /
art direction Bernard Rollins

This LA group had been around since 1969 and were
known as Black Gems Rare and then Rare Gems Odyssey.
By 1978 they had dropped the Odyssey after they parted
ways with Casablanca Records and recorded this small-
label treasure. Their sound has a funkier west coast combo
vibe than the big-sounding disco records coming out of
New York and Philly. ⊙
Diese Formation aus L.A. gibt es schon seit 1969, erst unter
dem Namen Black Gems Rare und dann Rare Gems Odys-

sey. 1978 kippten sie dann das Odyssey, nachdem sie sich
von Casablanca Records verabschiedet und auf einem kleinen Label diesen Schatz veröffentlicht hatten. Ihr Sound
klingt deutlich funkiger nach Westcoast-Combo als die
groß klingenden Disco-Platten, die aus New York und Philly
stammten. ⊙
Ce groupe de Los Angeles existait depuis 1969. Il avait
d'abord été connu comme les Black Gems Rare, puis
comme les Rare Gems Odyssey. En 1978, le groupe a rac-
courci son nom après s'être séparé de Casablanca Records
et a enregistré ce trésor chez un petit label. L'atmosphère
que dégage la petite formation de la côte ouest est plus
funky que les disques qui viennent de New York ou de
Philadelphie, où l'on emploie pourtant les grands moyens.

CAT 2607/STEREO

RAW SOUL EXPRESS

title **RAW SOUL EXPRESS** / *year* **1976** / *label* Cat /
design Drago / *photography* Joe Elbert

A monster Miami funk rarity produced by George
"Chocolate" Perry. The straight-ahead cover shot by Joe
Elbert evokes the cool southern heat this tight group
serves up. With a keen understanding of jazz in their
changes, their funky tracks are surprisingly fresh and raw. ⭘
Diese monströse Funk-Rarität aus Miami wurde von
George »Chocolate« Perry produziert. Das klar ausgerich-
tete Coverfoto von Joe Elbert erweckt schon die coole
Hitze des Südens, die diese ausdrucksstarke Gruppe hier
serviert. Durch ihr tiefes Verständnis von Jazz sind die
funkigen Tracks in ihren Wechseln überraschend frisch
und ungeschliffen. ⭘
Cet album est un monstre de rareté du funk de Miami
produit par George « Chocolate » Perry. La photo de la
pochette, réalisée par Joe Elbert, illustre bien la chaleur du
Sud qui émane de ce groupe. Ils démontrent une fine
compréhension du jazz, et leurs compositions funky sont
étonnamment originales et authentiques.

STEREO

SOUND
TRIANGLE
ST

ST - 7778

RAY AND HIS COURT

title **RAY AND HIS COURT** / *year* **1973** / *label* Sound Triangle / *design* Mosquera / *photography* Mauricio Mendonza

Ray Fernández was a pioneer in the mixing of traditional Cuban instrumentation and James Brown-style funk. His debut on the Sound Triangle label out of Hialeah, FL has always been a rare and sought-after example of the Latin funk sound that came streaming out of the region because of the influx of immigrants escaping Communist-controlled Cuba. **O**

Ray Fernández war ein Pionier, wenn es darum ging, traditionelle kubanische Instrumentierung mit Funk im Stil von James Brown zu mischen. Sein Debüt auf dem Label Sound Triangle aus Hialeah, Florida, ist schon immer ein seltenes und begehrtes Beispiel des Latin-Funk gewesen. Dieser Musikstil erwuchs dieser Region wegen des Einflusses der Immigranten, die dem kommunistischen Kuba entflohen. **O**

Ray Fernández était un pionnier dans le mélange d'instrumentation cubaine traditionnelle et de funk dans le style de James Brown. Son premier album chez le label Sound Triangle, de la ville de Hialeah en Floride, a toujours été un exemple rare et recherché du funk latin qui inondait la région grâce à l'arrivée des immigrants qui fuyant le régime communiste de Cuba.

VOLT S-413 STEREO

The Soul Album Otis Redding

OTIS REDDING
title **THE SOUL ALBUM** / *year* **1966** / *label* Volt /
design Loring Eutemey / *photography* Peter Levy

It's hard to imagine soul music without Otis Redding.
Although he was known as a great songwriter, this album
consisted mostly of cover songs. His deeply felt vocals
could lend infinite layers of meaning to even the most
trivial lyric. With the mighty Stax sound of Booker T. & the
M.G.'s backing him, the combination was pure soul gold. **O**
Man kann sich Soul ohne Otis Redding kaum vorstellen.
Obwohl er als großartiger Songwriter bekannt ist, besteht
dieses Album hauptsächlich aus Coverversionen. Seine

gefühlvolle Stimme verleiht auch den trivialsten Textzeilen
unendlich viele Bedeutungsebenen. Der mächtige Stax-
Sound von Booker T. & the M.G.'s unterstützte ihn auf
diesem Album, und in dieser Kombination schürften sie
reines Soul-Gold. **O**
On imagine difficilement la musique soul sans Otis
Redding. C'était un grand auteur, mais cet album était
surtout composé de reprises. Son phrasé très expressif
pouvait donner une infinité de significations aux paroles les
plus banales. Avec le son puissant, caractéristique de Stax,
apporté par l'accompagnement de Booker T. & the M.G.'s,
cette combinaison était de l'or soul en barre.

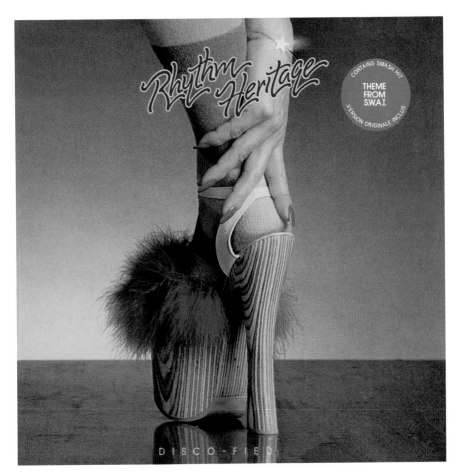

RHYTHM HERITAGE

title **DISCO-FIED** / *year* **1976** / *label* ABC / *design*
Earl Klasky & Tom Wilkes / *photography* Ken Marcus /
art direction Tom Wilkes

Ken Marcus was a long time contributor to *Playboy*, *Penthouse*, and Frederick's of Hollywood. His playful, fetishistic cover photo for Rhythm Heritage's debut LP serves up the humor along with the sex. The brainchild of producer Steve Barri and session keyboardist Michael Omartian, this album is made up of funk instrumentals and TV theme songs that are heavy on the break beats. ○
Ken Marcus hatte schon lange für *Playboy*, *Penthouse* und Frederick's of Hollywood gearbeitet. Sein verspieltes, feti-

schistisches Coverfoto für das Debüt von Rhythm Heritage bedient neben dem Humor ebenso den Sex. Dieses Album ist das geistige Produkt des Produzenten Steve Barri und des Session-Keyboarders Michael Omartian. Es sind darauf Funk-Instrumentalversionen und Fernsehmelodien versammelt, die stark mit Breakbeats arbeiten. ○
Ken Marcus a longtemps travaillé pour *Playboy*, *Penthouse* et la marque de lingerie Frederick's of Hollywood. Sa photo cabotine et fétichiste pour la pochette du premier album de Rhythm Heritage met humour et sexe dans le même panier. Cet album est la création du producteur Steve Barri et du claviériste de studio Michael Omartian. Il est composé de morceaux de funk instrumental et de génériques TV chargés de break beats.

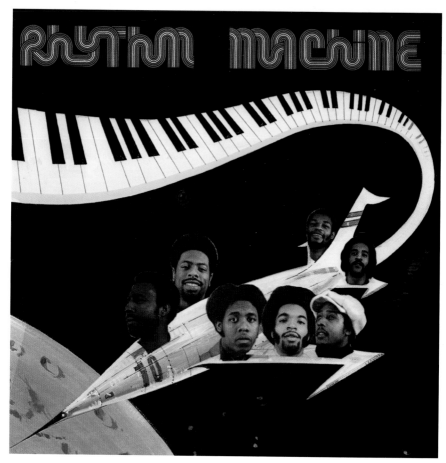

RHYTHM MACHINE

title **RHYTHM MACHINE** / *year* **1976** /
label Lulu / *design* James Cox

This legendary band rose out of the ashes of Indiana's toughest funk outfit, The Highlighters, to create one of the most prized mid-'70s independent funk LPs. The band's spaced-out blend of jazzy horns, hard-hitting funk, and transcendent vocals is balanced perfectly to create a rarity that is well worth its weight in gold. **O**
Diese legendäre Band erhob sich aus der Asche der Highlighters, der schärfsten Funk-Formation von Indiana, um

Mitte der 70er Jahre eine der wertvollsten Independent-Funk-LPs zu schaffen. Die abgespacete Mischung aus jazzigen Bläsern, knallhartem Funk und den überweltlichen Stimmen der Band ist perfekt ausgewogen und sorgt für eine Rarität, die ihr Gewicht in Gold wert ist. **O**
Ce groupe légendaire est né des cendres du groupe de funk le plus authentique de l'Indiana, The Highlighters, pour créer l'un des albums de funk indépendant les plus prisés des années 1970. Ce mélange planant de cuivres jazzy, de funk percutant et de voix transcendantes atteint un équilibre parfait pour créer un moment rare qui vaut largement son pesant d'or.

RIGHT TRACK
title **DESTINATION UNLIMITED** /
year **1978** / *label* True Soul / *design*
L. Anthony / *photography* L. Anthony

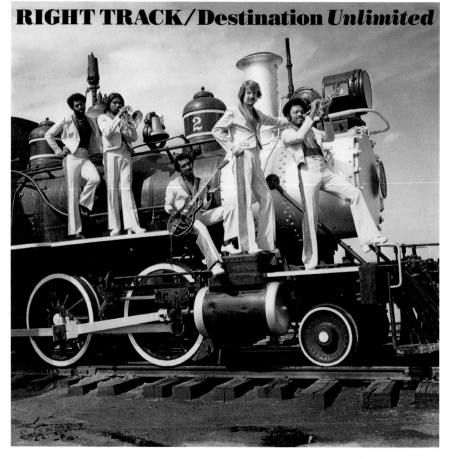

RIGHT TRACK/Destination *Unlimited*

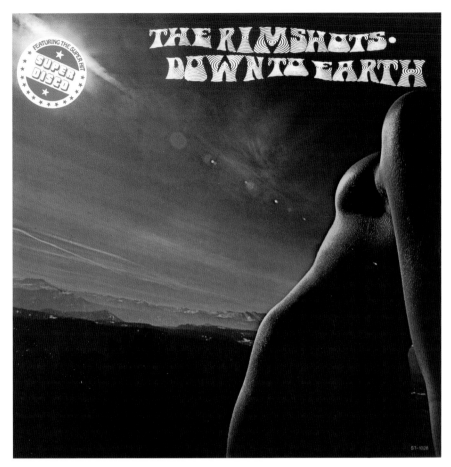

THE RIMSHOTS · DOWN TO EARTH

ST-1028

THE RIMSHOTS

title **DOWN TO EARTH** / *year* **1976** / *label* Stang /
design Dudley Thomas / *art direction* Dudley Thomas

Dudley Thomas' provocative cover for the sophomore
effort from Sylvia Robinson's Stang/All Platinum Records
house-band is a groovy nature-lover's paradise. The photographer mimics the mountainous landscape with the
female form and the rolling typography. The band's proto-
disco has more of a laid-back, elemental funk sound than
the slick disco that was on the horizon. ○
Das provokante Cover von Dudley Thomas für das zweite
Album der Hausband von Sylvia Robinsons Stang/All Platinum Records ist ein Paradies für Liebhaber von Natur-

schönheiten. Der Fotograf setzt die gebirgige Landschaft in
Bezug zu der weiblichen Form und der geschwungenen
Typografie. Der Urdiscosound dieser Band weist eher lässige und elementare Funksounds auf als die sich bereits am
Horizont ankündigende aalglatte Discomusik. ○
La pochette provocante de Dudley Thomas pour le deuxième album de Sylvia Robinson accompagnée du groupe
résident du label Stang/All Platinum Records est un paradis
pour les amants du groove et de la nature. Le photographe
imite le paysage montagneux à l'aide du corps féminin et
de la typographie. L'ébauche de disco que propose le
groupe est fait d'un funk plus décontracté et élémentaire
que le disco lisse qui se profilait à l'horizon.

MINNIE RIPERTON

title **ADVENTURES IN PARADISE** / *year* **1975** / *label* Epic / *design* Ron Coro / *photography* Kenneth McGowan

With her five-and-a-half-octave vocal range Minnie Riperton was one of the most astonishing singers ever. She passed away at the age of 31 from breast cancer, but in her short career she produced some of the most jubilant soul music. Kenneth McGowan photographed many jazz and pop stars of the '70s; his often pensive portraits radiated the cool confidence of his ultra-talented subjects. **O**

Mit ihrem Stimmumfang von fünfeinhalb Oktaven war Minnie Riperton eine der erstaunlichsten Sängerinnen aller Zeiten. Sie starb mit 31 Jahren an Brustkrebs, doch in ihrer kurzen Karriere produzierte sie Kleinode jubilierender Soulmusik. Kenneth McGowan fotografierte viele Jazz- und Popstars der 70er Jahre. Seine oft nachdenklichen Porträts strahlten das coole Selbstvertrauen der ultratalentierten Persönlichkeiten vor seiner Linse aus. **O**

Avec un registre vocal de cinq octaves et demi, Minnie Riperton a été l'une des chanteuses les plus étonnantes de tous les temps. Elle est décédée à l'âge de 31 ans, d'un cancer du sein, mais pendant sa courte carrière elle a chanté quelques-uns des morceaux les plus jubilatoires de la musique soul. Kenneth McGowan a photographié de nombreuses vedettes du jazz et de la pop dans les années 1970. Ses portraits souvent contemplatifs laissaient irradier l'assurance tranquille de ses sujets ultratalentueux.

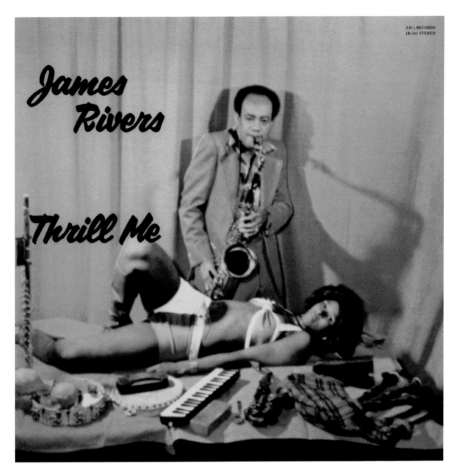

JAMES RIVERS

title **THRILL ME** / *label* J.B.'s / *design* Senator Jones / *photography* Bill Synegal

Senator Jones established several enduring labels in his adopted New Orleans, including Black Patch, Hep' Me, and J.B.'s. "As I got more artists," said the inventive entrepreneur, "I didn't want to go to the radio station with seven records on the same label. The DJs would say 'I can't play all of those records.' So I started new labels and I switched colors on the record labels to make them look different." **O**
Senator Jones gründete in seiner Wahlheimat New Orleans mehrere Plattenfirmen, die sich dauerhaft halten konnten, z. B. Black Patch, Hep' Me und J.B.'s. »Als ich mehr Musiker bekam«, sagte der einfallsreiche Unternehmer, »wollte ich

nicht mit sieben Platten des gleichen Labels zum Radio-sender gehen«. Die DJs sagten dann: »Die kann ich nicht alle spielen«. Also habe ich neue Labels gegründet und die Farben auf den Plattenhüllen verändert, damit sie unter-schiedlich aussehen." **O**
Senator Jones a créé plusieurs labels qui ont marqué l'his-toire dans sa ville d'adoption, la Nouvelle-Orléans, notam-ment Black Patch, Hep' Me et J.B.'s. « Lorsque j'ai commencé à travailler avec un certain nombre d'artistes, raconte cet entrepreneur inventif, je ne voulais pas aller voir les radios avec sept disques provenant du même label. Les DJ au-raient dit qu'ils ne pouvaient pas utiliser tous ces disques. Alors j'ai créé de nouveaux labels et j'ai changé les couleurs pour qu'ils aient l'air différents. »

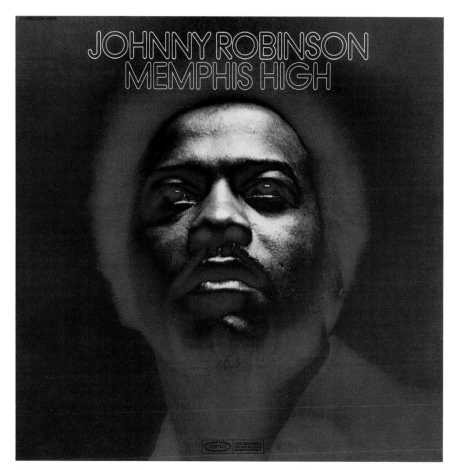

JOHNNY ROBINSON

title **MEMPHIS HIGH** / *year* **1970** / *label* Epic / *design*
Richard Mantel / *photography* Columbia Records Photo
Studios

Over the course of his illustrious career, Push Pin Studios
alumnus Richard Mantel has served as art director for
Columbia, Atlantic, and CTI record companies. He is
responsible for several of Mosaic Records' boxed sets and
anthologies, offering exhaustive accounts of jazz music's
often overlooked acts and comprehensive collections for
jazz completists. **O**
Im Laufe seiner glänzenden Karriere hat Richard Mantel,
der ehemalige Schüler von Push Pin Studios, als Art Direc-

tor bei den Plattenfirmen Columbia, Atlantic und CTI gearbeitet. Er ist verantwortlich für mehrere Sammlerausgaben
und Anthologien bei Mosaic Records. Außerdem erarbeite-
te er erschöpfende Zusammenstellungen von oft übersehe-
nen Acts der Jazzmusik und umfassende Sammlungen für
Jazzfans, die gerne alles komplett haben wollen. **O**
Au cours de son illustre carrière, Richard Mantel de Push
Pin Studios a officié comme directeur artistique pour
Columbia, Atlantic et CTI. Il est responsable de plusieurs
coffrets et anthologies sortis chez Mosaic Records, qui pro-
posent des présentations exhaustives de groupes de jazz
souvent négligés à tort ainsi que des collections complètes
pour les amants du jazz.

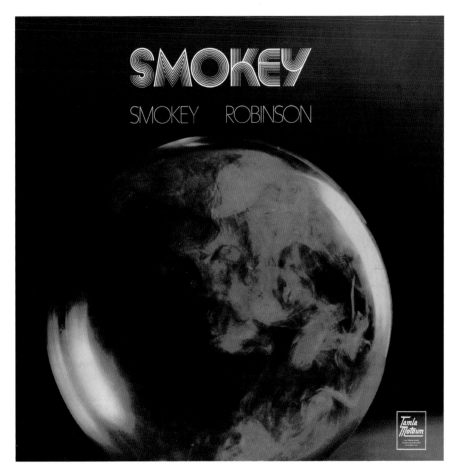

SMOKEY ROBINSON

title **SMOKEY** / *year* **1973** / *label* Tamla Motown /
photography Jim Britt

Smokey Robinson's debut as a solo artist was released a
year after the Miracles broke up. It contained a sweet soul
ode to his former group, "Sweet Harmony", which became
his first hit. Jim Britt had taken over as the art director for
Motown a year before this record came out. He had been
honing his skills with special effects and was a master at
manipulating color images in the dark-room as is evident
with this evocative cover. **O**
Smokey Robinsons Solodebüt erschien ein Jahr, nachdem
sich die Miracles getrennt hatten. Es enthält die liebliche
Soul-Ode an seine frühere Gruppe, »Sweet Harmony«, die

zu seinem ersten Hit wurde. Jim Britt hatte seinen Job als
Art Director bei Motown ein Jahr vor Erscheinen dieser
Platte angetreten. Er hatte sich ausführlich in fotografische
Spezialeffekte eingearbeitet und konnte Farbfotos meister-
lich in der Dunkelkammer bearbeiten, was man diesem
suggestiven Cover ansieht. **O**
Le premier album en solo de Smokey Robinson est sorti un
an après la séparation des Miracles. Il contenait une chanson de sweet soul écrite en pensant à son ancien groupe,
Sweet Harmony, qui est devenue son premier tube. Jim Britt
avait pris le rôle de directeur artistique chez Motown un
an avant la sortie de cet album. Il avait affûté ses connaissances en effets spéciaux et était un maître de la manipulation des images en couleur dans la chambre noire, comme
le montre bien cette pochette évocatrice.

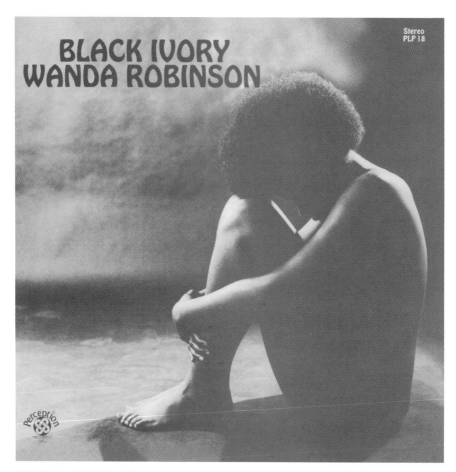

Stereo
PLP 18

BLACK IVORY
WANDA ROBINSON

WANDA ROBINSON

title **BLACK IVORY** / *year* **1971** / *label* Perception / *design* James Martin Stulberger / *photography* Reginald Wickham

Inspired by Arthur Prysock's "This is My Beloved", the 20-year-old poet Wanda Robinson recorded herself reciting some of her work on a tape recorder as she played songs on the stereo behind her. After a local Baltimore DJ, Anthony Davis, played the recordings on his show she was contacted by Perception to make this amazing album. She was allowed to choose music from the label's vault, which she did to great effect. Her clear, righteous voice slides in and out of the funky jazz grooves. ○

Inspiriert von Arthur Prysocks »This is My Beloved« nahm sich die 20-jährige Dichterin Wanda Robinson selbst auf einem Kassettenrecorder auf, während sie einige ihrer Wer-

ke rezitierte und ein paar Songs auf dem Plattenspieler neben sich abspielte. Nachdem Anthony Davis, ein DJ aus Baltimore, diese Aufnahmen in seiner Sendung abspielte, wurde sie von Perception kontaktiert, um dieses erstaunliche Album möglich zu machen. Sie durfte aus dem Tresor des Labels Musik auswählen. Ihre klare Stimme gleitet in die funkigen Jazz-Grooves hinein und wieder hinaus. ○

Wanda Robinson était une poétesse de 20 ans lorsque, inspirée par *This is My Beloved* d'Arthur Prysock, elle s'est enregistrée récitant ses propres compositions sur un fond de musique venant de sa stéréo. Anthony Davis, un DJ de Baltimore, utilisa ces enregistrements lors de son spectacle, à la suite de quoi Perception contacta Robinson pour faire ce superbe album. Elle a été autorisée à choisir sa musique dans les archives du label, ce qu'elle a fait avec un goût très sûr. Sa voix claire et juste glisse sur les rythmes de jazz-funk.

DIANA ROSS
title **DIANA** / *year* **1980** / *label*
Motown / *design* Rita Lewerke /
photography Francesco Scavullo

**DIANA ROSS
& MARVIN GAYE**
title **DIANA** & **MARVIN** /
year **1973** / *label* Tamla Motown /
photography Jim Britt / *art direction*
Katarina Pettersson

*Takin' Care of Business

DIANA ROSS AND THE SUPREMES WITH THE TEMPTATIONS

title **THE ORIGINAL SOUNDTRACK FROM TCB** / *year* **1968** / *label* Tamla Motown / *photography* Edward M. Broussard/NBC-TV / *art direction* Ken Kim

TCB (short for Takin' Care of Business) was a television special, designed to showcase two of Motown's biggest acts. Filmed before a live studio audience, *TCB* featured an assortment of collaborations, covers, and show tunes; the soundtrack soared to number one on the Billboard chart, helping both groups achieve mainstream success. **O**

TCB (das Kürzel steht für *Takin' Care of Business*) war eine Fernsehsondersendung, in der die beiden größten Acts von Motown präsentiert werden sollten. Eine spezielle Auswahl von Gemeinschaftsproduktionen, Covern und Showtunes wurde bei *TCB* vorgestellt und vor einem Studiopublikum live gefilmt. Der Soundtrack rauschte in den Billboard-Charts auf Platz eins und half beiden Gruppen bei ihrem Durchbruch im Mainstream. **O**

TCB (Takin' Care of Business) était une émission spéciale de télévision, conçue pour mettre en valeur deux des plus grands atouts de Motown. Elle a été filmée en public et se composait d'une série de collaborations et de reprises de morceaux connus et d'airs tirés de comédies musicales. La bande originale est montée en flèche jusqu'à la première place des classements et a aidé les deux groupes à atteindre un large public.

ROTARY CONNECTION

title **ROTARY CONNECTION** / *year* **1969** / *label* Cadet Concept / *design* Hurvis, Binzer & Churchill / *photography* Curt Cole Burkhart

Hurvis, Binzer & Churchill designed many award-winning covers for Chess Records in the '60s. When the Cadet Concept subsidiary was started in 1967, the agency called on Curt Cole Burkhart to produce the heavenly kaleidoscopic image that would grace the cover of Rotary Connection's psychedelic soul debut. One of the Chess receptionists, Minnie Riperton, with her astonishing vocal range, turned out to be an invaluable addition to the far-out sound that producer Charles Stepney was concocting on this record. **O** Hurvis, Binzer & Churchill gestalteten für Chess Records in den 60er Jahren viele preisgekrönte Cover. Als 1967 die

Tochterfirma Cadet Concept gegründet wurde, engagierte die Agentur Curt Cole Burkhart für die Produktion des Kaleidoskopbilds für das Cover des psychedelischen Soul-Debütalbums von Rotary Connection. Eine der Empfangsdamen bei Chess war Minnie Riperton. Mit ihrem erstaunlichen Stimmumfang erwies sie sich als unschätzbare Aufwertung des abgefahrenen Sounds, den Produzent Charles Stepney auf dem Album zusammenbraute. **O** Hurvis, Binzer & Churchill ont créé de nombreuses pochettes primées pour Chess Records dans les années 1960. Lorsque la filiale Cadet Concept fut lancée en 1967, l'agence demanda à Curt Cole Buckhart de réaliser l'image céleste kaléidoscopique qui allait orner la pochette des débuts de Rotary Connection dans la soul psychédélique.

ROSE ROYCE

title **IN FULL BLOOM** / *year* **1977** /
label Whitfield / *design* Eric Chan/
Gribbitt! / *art direction* Ed Thrasher /
illustration Shusei Nagaoka

ROSE ROYCE   IN FULL BLOOM

PRODUCED BY NORMAN WHITFIELD

DAVID RUFFIN

title **DAVID RUFFIN** / *year* **1973** / *label* Motown /
design Rod Dyer / *photography* Jim Britt

Although his tenure with The Temptations lasted only four
years, David Ruffin's commanding lead is often considered
central to the influential franchise's enduring legacy.
Unfortunately, financial disputes and egocentricity drove a
wedge between Ruffin and his bandmates, resulting in a
string of solo albums that follow the talented, yet troubled
tenor down a road of drug abuse and industry isolation. **O**
Obwohl seine Zusammenarbeit mit den Temptations nur
vier Jahre währte, wurde die imposante Leadstimme von
David Ruffin von vielen als entscheidend für den fort-
dauernden Erfolg dieses einflussreichen Franchiseunter-

nehmens betrachtet. Leider trieben Egozentrik und finan-
zielle Auseinandersetzungen einen Keil zwischen Ruffin
und seine Bandkollegen, was zu einer Reihe von Soloalben
führte, die den talentierten, aber problembeladenen Tenor
auf seiner Abwärtsspirale von Drogenkonsum und Isolie-
rung begleiteten. **O**
Bien que David Ruffin ne soit resté que quatre ans avec les
Temptations, ses qualités de meneur sont souvent considé-
rées comme un ingrédient essentiel de l'héritage de cette
franchise. Malheureusement, les querelles financières et
l'égocentrisme ont fini par séparer Ruffin et les autres
membres du groupe, et une série d'albums suit ce ténor
talentueux mais torturé sur un chemin pavé de drogue et
d'isolation professionnelle.

DAVID RUFFIN

title **WHO I AM** / *year* **1975** / *label* Motown /
photography Norman Seeff / *art direction* Frank Mulvey

For David Ruffin's 1975 album, Motown enlisted disco
producer and arranger Van McCoy to update the former
Temptation's Motor City sound. Having achieved recent
stardom with his club sensation, "The Hustle", McCoy
finds as much of a musical memoir in *Who I Am* as does
Ruffin. **O**
Für das 1975er-Album von David Ruffin beauftragte Motown den Discoproduzenten und Arrangeur Van McCoy,
den ehemaligen Motor-City-Sound der Temptations aufzu-
möbeln. Nachdem er kurz vorher mit seiner Clubsensation
»The Hustle« zu Ruhm gekommen war, wurde *Who I Am*
für McCoy ebenso zu einer musikalischen Denkschrift wie
für Ruffin. **O**
Pour l'album que David Ruffin a sorti en 1975, Motown
avait engagé le producteur et arrangeur de disco Van
McCoy afin de mettre au goût du jour le son typique de
Detroit de l'ancien membre des Temptations. McCoy venait d'accéder à la célébrité avec *The Hustle*, un phénomène
dans les discothèques, et *Who I Am* est pour lui comme
pour Ruffin une sorte d'autobiographie musicale.

PATRICE RUSHEN

title **BEFORE THE DAWN** / *year* **1975** / *label* Prestige / *photography* Phil Bray / *art direction* Phil Carroll

Patrice Rushen's sophomore effort is primarily an instrumental jazz/funk fusion LP much in the same mode that Herbie Hancock was working in during the early 1970s. Her fantastic keyboard prowess is showcased with aplomb as she works her way through the hard-edged funk and spacious jazz cuts. **O**

Das zweite Werk von Patrice Rushen ist in erster Linie eine instrumentale Jazz/Funk-LP und gleicht in der Art weitge-

hend dem, woran Herbie Hancock Anfang der 70er Jahre gearbeitet hat. Ihr fantastisches Können an den Keyboards stellt sie mit viel Selbstbewusstsein heraus, während sie sich durch kantigen Funk und weitläufige Jazz-Stücke arbeitet. **O**

Le deuxième disque de Patrice Rushen est avant tout un album instrumental de fusion jazz-funk, qui ressemble beaucoup au travail d'Herbie Hancock au début des années 1970. Sa prouesse fantastique au clavier est mise en valeur avec aplomb sur ces morceaux de funk pur et dur et de jazz généreux.

PATRICE RUSHEN

title **PIZZAZZ** / *year* **1979** / *label* Elektra /
photography Norman Seeff / *art direction* Ron Coro

Norman Seeff's photos have a casual elegance that catches
the subjects in a relaxed and natural state. His portrait of
Patrice Rushen for her second release on Elektra highlight-
ed the beauty and confidence of this talented vocalist/
pianist/songwriter. Although she had moved away from
the jazz world with her previous album, and was still
getting a lot of flak for it, her integration of jazz into the
R&B she was producing would leave an enduring mark on
funk in the '80s. ○
Den Fotos von Norman Seeff ist eine lässige Eleganz eigen,
er fängt seine Sujets in einer entspannten und natürlichen
Stimmung ein. Sein Porträt von Patrice Rushen für ihr zwei-

tes Album auf Elektra unterstrich die Schönheit und das
Selbstbewusstsein dieser talentierten Sängerin, Pianistin
und Komponistin. Obwohl sie sich mit ihrem vorigen
Album von der Jazzwelt entfernt hatte und dafür noch
mächtig unter Beschuss stand, sollte ihre Art, Jazz mit R&B
zu integrieren, dauerhafte Spuren im Funk der 80er Jahre
hinterlassen. ○
Les photos de Norman Seeff ont une élégance désinvolte
qui saisit les sujets dans une attitude naturelle et décontractée. Son portrait de Patrice Rushen pour son deuxième
album chez Elektra met en valeur la beauté et l'assurance
de cette chanteuse / pianiste / auteure talentueuse. Elle
s'était éloignée du monde du jazz dans son album précédent, ce qui lui attirait encore beaucoup de critiques, mais
son intégration du jazz dans le R&B allait laisser une empreinte durable sur le funk dans les années 1980.

EDDIE RUSS

title **SEE THE LIGHT** / *year* **1976** /
label Monument / *photography*
Ken Kim / *art direction* Ken Kim

EDDIE RUSS

title **FRESH OUT** / *year* **1974** /
label Soul Jazz / *design* Travis Erby /
photography Palmer James & Curtis
Roger

S.O.S. BAND
title **III** / *year* **1982** / *label* CBS /
design Jones & Armitage/Out Of
Focus / *photography* Diem Jones/
Out Of Focus

Abet 406 Stereo

OLIVER SAIN < BUS STOP

6408

OLIVER SAIN

title **BUS STOP** / *year* **1974** / *label* Abet / *design*
Dan Quest & Associates / *photography* Dan Quest
& Associates

A talented multi-instrumentalist, Oliver Sain's first love was
the alto saxophone, which was all-present on this 1974
album of bumping instrumental funk nuggets. Designer
Dan Quest did a lot of work for James Brown as well as
many country and western covers. Regardless of the genre
his work always had a groovy sensibility. ⊙
Oliver Sain war ein talentierter Multiinstrumentalist, dessen
erste Liebe dem Altsaxophon galt. Also war dieses Instru-

ment auf seinem Album von 1974 voller quirliger instru-
mentaler Funk-Perlen natürlich allgegenwärtig. Der Designer Dan Quest arbeitete viel für James Brown, hatte aber
auch eine Menge Country- und Western-Cover gestaltet.
Egal in welchem Genre er sich tummelte, seine Arbeiten
spiegelten stets ein gutes Gespür für den Groove. ⊙
Oliver Sain était un multi-instrumentiste talentueux. Son
premier amour, le saxophone alto, est omniprésent sur cet
album de 1974, où se bousculent les pépites de funk instrumental. Le graphiste Dan Quest a beaucoup travaillé pour
James Brown et a aussi réalisé de nombreuses pochettes
de country et de western. Quel que soit le genre concerné,
son travail avait toujours une sensibilité groovy.

SALSOUL SZS-5502

THE SALSOUL ORCHESTRA

NICE 'N' NAASTY

DANCE YOUR ASS

THE SALSOUL ORCHESTRA

title **NICE 'N' NAASTY** / *year* **1976** / *label* Salsoul

Vibes master Vince Montana, Jr. arranged, produced, conducted, and wrote practically the entire sophomore outing by the Salsoul Orchestra. The group's musicality shines through in a more inventive and dance-floor-friendly way than that of their debut. Montana created the template for orchestral-style disco with a Latin flavor on this LP, which was often copied but rarely matched. **O**

Der Vibraphon-Meister Vince Montana Jr. arrangierte, produzierte, dirigierte und komponierte praktisch das gesamte zweite Werk des Salsoul Orchestra. Mit ihren musikalischen

Qualitäten fand die Gruppe hier zu einer noch ideenreicheren und tanzbareren Darbietung als bei ihrem Debüt. Montana schuf mit dieser LP die Matrix für eine orchestrale Disco-Musik mit Latin-Einschlag, die oft kopiert, aber selten erreicht wurde. **O**

Le maître du vibraphone Vince Montana Jr. a arrangé, produit, dirigé et écrit pratiquement tout le deuxième album du Salsoul Orchestra. La musicalité du groupe se révèle sous un angle plus inventif et dansant que sur son premier disque. Sur cet album, Montana a créé un modèle de musique disco jouée en orchestre avec une saveur latine. Ce modèle a souvent été copié, mais rarement égalé.

THE SALSOUL ORCHESTRA

title **SALSOUL ORCHESTRA** /
year **1975** / *label* Salsoul / *photography*
Douglas Quackenbush / *art direction*
Richard Lopez

Columbia
Stereo
CB 9927

Twenty-Five Miles
Too Busy Thinking
About My Baby
My Cherie Amour
Proud Mary
Spinning Wheel
We Got Latin Soul
Getting It Out Of
My System
Workin' On A
Groovy Thing
Ain't That Peculiar
It's Your Thing
Get Back

Mongo
Santamaria
Workin'
on a
Groovy
Thing

MONGO SANTAMARIA

title **WORKIN' ON A GROOVY THING** / *year* **1969** /
label Columbia / *photography* Don Hunstein & Fred
Lombardi

This mighty Afro-Cuban Latin jazz percussionist socks it to
the way-out sounds of the '60s with a tight set of popular
covers. This was a trend he had started when his funky,
percussive rendition of Herbie Hancock's "Watermelon
Man" set the groundwork for the Boogaloo movement of
a few years later. **O**

Dieser kraftvolle afrokubanische Latin-Jazz-Perkussionist
räumt zu den abgefahrenen Klängen der 60er mit einem

dichten Set populärer Coverversionen ab. Dieser Trend
wurde von ihm losgetreten, als seine funkige, perkussive
Interpretation von Herbie Hancocks »Watermelon Man«
ein paar Jahre später die Grundlage für die Boogaloo-
Bewegung bildete. **O**

Cet imposant percussionniste de jazz latin afro-cubain
s'en prend aux sons excentriques des années 1960 avec un
album de reprises bien ficelées. C'est une tendance qu'il
avait lancée lorsque sa version funky et percutante du
Watermelon Man de Herbie Hancock avait préparé le terrain au mouvement Boogaloo survenu quelques années
plus tard..

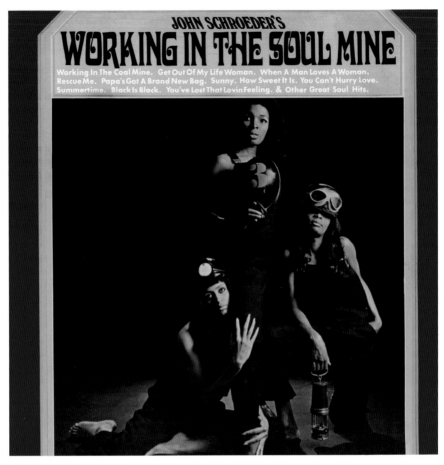

JOHN SCHROEDER
title **WORKING IN THE SOUL MINE** /
year **1966** / *label* Pye

John Schroeder's ascent through the British music industry is the classic mailroom-to-boardroom fairy-tale. For *Working in the Soul Mine*, the successful A&R man excavated several soul boulders from across the pond, giving tracks like "Papa's Got A Brand New Bag" and "Rescue Me" a blue-eyed makeover, tailoring them to an older UK audience, otherwise unfamiliar with this set of funky standards. **O**
John Schroeders Karriere in der britischen Musikbranche ist das klassische Märchen eines Aufstiegs von der Poststelle bis in die Vorstandsetage. Für *Working in the Soul Mine*

grub der erfolgreiche A&R-Mann auf der anderen Seite des großen Teichs mehrere Soul-Brocken aus, überarbeitete Stücke wie »Papa's Got A Brand New Bag« und »Rescue Me« und passte sie für ein älteres Publikum aus Großbritannien an, das bei solchen Funk-Standards ansonsten nicht sonderlich bewandert war. **O**
Le parcours de John Schroeder dans le monde de la musique britannique est un vrai conte de fées de l'ascension sociale. Pour *Working in the Soul Mine*, ce développeur artistique à succès a déniché plusieurs monuments de la soul américaine et a fignolé le relookage de morceaux tels que *Papa's Got A Brand New Bag* et *Rescue Me* pour les adapter à un public britannique mûr, qui ne connaissait pas ces standards du funk.

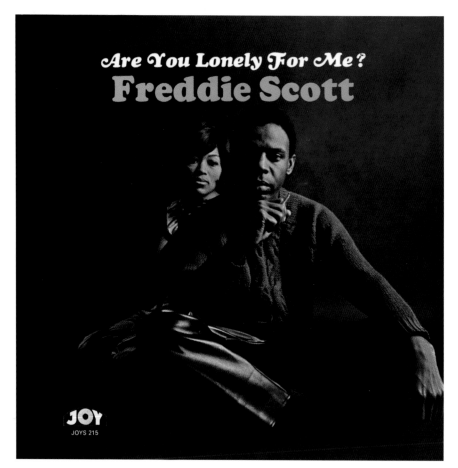

Are You Lonely For Me?
Freddie Scott

JOY
JOYS 215

FREDDIE SCOTT

title **ARE YOU LONELY FOR ME?** / *year* **1967** / *label* Joy

Like many talented performers before him, Freddie Scott received unfavorable marks upon his amateur night debut at Harlem's notoriously picky Apollo Theater. Regardless, Burt Berns, who five years before wrote "Twist and Shout", saw great promise in the Rhode Island native, signing him to his newly minted Shout Records, assembling a tempest of slow-cooked grooves for Scott to christen with his convincing voice. O

Wie viele talentierte Darsteller vor ihm wurde Freddie Scott an seinem Debütabend im Apollo Theater von Harlem mit dem dortigen, notorisch pingeligen Publikum ungünstig bewertet. Doch nichtsdestotrotz betrachtete Burt Berns, der fünf Jahre vorher »Twist and Shout« geschrieben hatte,

den aus Rhode Island stammenden Scott als vielversprechend und nahm ihn bei seinem gerade gegründeten Verlag Shout Records unter Vertrag. Dann stellte er für Scott ein ganzes Bündel langsam gegarter Grooves zusammen, das er dann mit seiner bestechenden Stimme krönte. O

Comme de nombreux autres interprètes talentueux avant lui, Freddie Scott a reçu des critiques cinglantes pour ses débuts lors de l'Amateur Night à l'Apollo Theater de Harlem, dont le public est connu pour être difficile à satisfaire. Mais Burt Berns, qui avait écrit *Twist and Shout* cinq ans plus tôt, a deviné un grand potentiel dans ce natif de Rhode Island. Il lui a offert un contrat avec son label tout neuf Shout Records et a rassemblé un choix de grooves mijotés à feu doux pour que Scott les baptise de sa voix convaincante.

Gloria Scott What Am I Gonna Do

GLORIA SCOTT

title **WHAT AM I GONNA DO** / *year* **1974** / *label*
Casablanca / *design* John & Barbara Casado / *photography*
Sherman & Josyane Weisburd / *art direction* Ed Thrasher

Always taking advantage of each LP's expansive canvas,
art director Ed Thrasher fills this frame with an intimate
portrait of Gloria Scott. After recording with Sylvester
Stewart and performing with Ike and Tina, Scott's dynamic
voice would lead her to Barry White, who would serve as
producer and arranger for this gracefully funky outing. **O**
Der Art Director Ed Thrasher hat es stets verstanden, die
ausgedehnte Leinwand einer LP voll auszunutzen, und er

füllte auch diesen Rahmen mit einem intimen Porträt von
Gloria Scott. Nachdem sie Aufnahmen mit Sylvester Stewart gemacht und mit Ike und Tina aufgetreten war, führte
ihre dynamische Stimme sie zu Barry White, dem Produzenten und Arrangeur dieser anmutigen Funk-Scheibe. **O**
Ed Thrasher aimait tirer parti de la surface généreuse des
pochettes d'album. Ici, il remplit le cadre avec un portrait
intimiste de Gloria Scott. Après avoir enregistré avec
Sylvester Stewart et avoir chanté avec Ike et Tina, la voix
dynamique de Scott allait la conduire à travailler avec Barry
White, qui allait par la suite officier en tant que producteur
et arrangeur pour cette promenade funk élégante.

SHIRLEY SCOTT

title **SOUL SONG** / *year* **1969** / *label*
Atlantic / *design* Stanislaw Zagorski /
illustration Stanislaw Zagorski

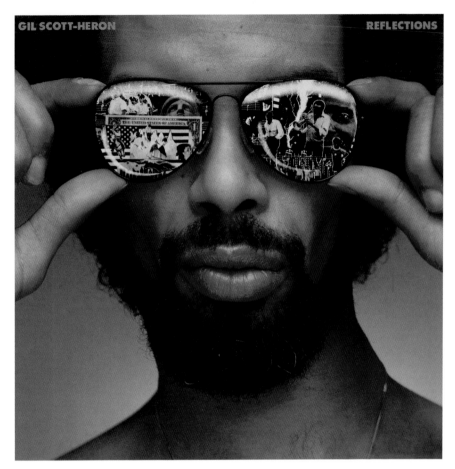

GIL SCOTT-HERON

title **REFLECTIONS** / *year* **1981** / *label* Arista

Poet-activist Gil Scott-Heron makes a visual statement on 1981's *Reflections*. Inside Scott-Heron's spectacles bubbles a collage of topical fodder for the lyricist's social sermons. The police, the Ku Klux Klan, and Ronald Reagan fill the left lens, while staves of music, trumpeter Miles Davis, and an assortment of black individuals fill the right. **◐**

Der Poet und Aktivist Gil Scott-Heron trifft auf *Reflections* (1981) eine starke visuelle Aussage: Aus seinen Brillengläsern sprudelt eine Collage typischer Themen des sozialen Sermons dieses Lyrikers. Polizei, Ku Klux Klan und Ronald Reagan füllen das linke Brillenglas, während auf der rechten Seite Notenlinien, der Trompeter Miles Davis und verschiedene schwarze Personen zu sehen sind. **◐**

Le poète activiste Gil Scott-Heron signe une déclaration visuelle sur *Reflections*, sorti en 1981. Les verres de ses lunettes sont remplacés par un collage des actualités de l'époque, qui nourrissaient les sermons sociaux de ce parolier. La police, le Ku Klux Klan et Ronald Reagan remplissent le verre droit, tandis que des portées de musique, le trompettiste Miles Davis et un assortiment de personnages noirs occupent le verre gauche.

GIL SCOTT-HERON
& BRIAN JACKSON

title **MIDNIGHT BAND: THE FIRST MINUTE
OF A NEW DAY** / *year* **1974** / *label* TVT/Arista /
illustration Iceman

Gil Scott-Heron and Brian Jackson's first record for the Arista label showed commercial promise for the left-of-center songwriting team, making dents in both jazz and pop charts. The primate on the front also appears on the back, armed with an automatic rifle and donning informal military attire; both illustrations are credited to Iceman. ❍
Die erste Aufnahme von Gil Scott-Heron und Brian Jackson für Arista sollte sich für das linksgerichtete Songwriter-Team

kommerziell als vielversprechend erweisen und sorgte in den Jazz- und Popcharts gleichermaßen für Eindruck. Der vorne abgebildete Primat erscheint auch auf der Rückseite, wo er in eine informelle Militärkleidung geschlüpft und mit einem Automatikgewehr bewaffnet ist. Für beide Illustrationen zeichnete Iceman verantwortlich. ❍
Le premier disque de Gil Scott-Heron et Brian Jackson pour le label Arista s'est révélé être un succès commercial pour cette équipe d'auteurs-compositeurs inattendue et a réussi à se nicher dans les classements de jazz et de pop. Le primate du recto de la pochette apparaît également au verso, armé d'un fusil automatique et vêtu d'une tenue militaire informelle. Les deux illustrations sont signées Iceman.

EDDY SENAY

title **HOT THANG** / *year* **1972** /
label Sussex / *photography* Bob
Gruen with The Best of Friends
& Sparky Martin / *art direction* Glen
Christensen

LPS-833
CADET STEREO
CAN ALSO BE PLAYED ON MONO EQUIPMENT

MARLENA SHAW

title **THE SPICE OF LIFE** / *year* **1969** / *label* Cadet /
design Jerry Griffith / *photography* Bob Crawford

Bob Crawford, a Chicago-based photographer who documented urban life in the '60s and '70s, captured this groovy shot of Marlena Shaw looking up and into the distance, with a glint of the setting sun in her eyes. It is a perfect entry to her powerhouse second and final Cadet release. Richard Evans' and Charles Stepney's soft-psychedelic arrangements lift Shaw's earthy, yearning vocals to new heights. ⭘

Der Fotograf Bob Crawford aus Chicago dokumentierte in den 60er und 70er Jahren das urbane Leben. Er machte diese tolle Aufnahme von Marlena Shaw, wie sie nach oben in die Weite schaut und das Glitzern der untergehenden Sonne in ihren Augen trägt. Es ist ein perfekter Einstieg in ihr zweites und letztes Poweralbum bei Cadet. In den soften, psychedelischen Arrangements von Richard Evans und Charles Stepney kann sich die erdige, schmachtende Stimme von Marlena Shaw zu ganz neuen Höhen aufschwingen. ⭘

Bob Crawford, un photographe basé à Chicago qui a documenté la vie urbaine dans les années 1960 et 1970, a pris ce cliché groovy de Marlena Shaw levant les yeux dans le lointain, avec des lueurs du soleil couchant dans le regard. C'est une image idéale pour son deuxième et dernier opus chez Cadet. Les arrangements légèrement psychédéliques de Richard Evans et Charles Stepney font gravir de nouveaux sommets à la voix terrienne et ardente de Shaw.

PE 6603
people
2391 134

CHARLES SHERRELL

title **FOR SWEET PEOPLE FROM SWEET CHARLES** /
year **1974** / *label* People / *photography* Arthur Shardin

Ensconced in a heart-shaped enclave of presumably sweet
people, Nashville native Charles Sherrell earned his sugary
moniker, Sweet Charles, upon his induction into the James
Brown Orchestra. Despite his towering presence, Sherrell's
voice possesses a gentle timbre that perfectly accommo-
dates the generous arrangements created by long-time
Brown collaborators Dave Matthews and Fred Wesley. ⊙
Der aus Nashville stammende Charles Sherrell macht es
sich in einer herzförmigen Enklave mit wahrscheinlich ganz
süßen Leuten gemütlich. Er erhielt seinen zuckrigen Spitz-

namen Sweet Charles beim Eintritt ins James Brown
Orchestra. Trotz seiner hoch aufragenden Präsenz besitzt
Sherrells Stimme ein sanftes Timbre, das perfekt zu den
großzügigen Arrangements passt, die die langjährigen
Mitarbeiter von James Brown, Dave Matthews und Fred
Wesley, geschaffen haben. ⊙
Niché au milieu d'une foule qui forme un cœur, constituée
de gens que l'on suppose charmants, Charles Sherrell,
originaire de Nashville, a reçu son surnom sucré « Sweet
Charles » à son entrée dans le James Brown Orchestra.
Malgré sa grande taille, la voix de Sherrell possède un
timbre doux qui s'harmonise parfaitement avec les arrange-
ments généreux créés par de vieux collaborateurs de
Brown, Dave Matthews et Fred Wesley.

SIDE EFFECT

title **WHAT YOU NEED** / *year* **1976** / *label* Fantasy /
design Jamie Putnam / *photography* Phil Bray & Jerome
Knill / *art direction* Phill Carroll

Side Effect's sophomore release, produced by their mentor
Wayne Henderson, of Crusaders fame, takes a step further
toward the modern soul sound that Henderson was
perfecting. With the help of an all-star roster of jazz and
funk players backing them, this group's fantastic harmonies
soared. **O**

Das zweite Album von Side Effect wurde vom Mentor der
Gruppe Wayne Henderson produziert, bekannt durch die
Crusaders. Es geht einen weiteren Schritt in Richtung eines
modernen Soul-Sounds, der von Henderson perfektioniert
wurde. Der Gruppe zur Seite stand ein All-Star-Aufgebot an
Jazz- und Funkmusikern, deren fantastische Harmonien
sich in ungeahnte Höhen schwingen. **O**

Ce deuxième album de Side Effect, produit par leur mentor
Wayne Henderson, connu pour son travail avec les Crusaders, leur fait franchir un pas supplémentaire vers le son de
soul moderne que Henderson était en train de perfection-
ner. Accompagnées par les meilleurs musiciens du jazz et du
funk, les superbes harmonies du groupe ont pris leur envol.

SIDE EFFECT

title **AFTER THE RAIN** / *year* **1980** /
label Elektra / *design* Denise Minobe /
photography Ron Slenzak / *art direction*
Ron Coro

LABI SIFFRE

title **LABI SIFFRE** / *year* **1970** / *label* Polydor

The 1970 debut from this British singer/songwriter show-cases his clear vocal styling and deft, melodic guitar-picking. It's a breezy affair that nods toward the Cat Stevens school of soft folk-psych, while showing hints of the soul and funk that would crystallize on his masterpiece LP *Remember My Song*. The later LP contains the track "I Got The", which has been sampled by the likes of Jay-Z and Eminem. **O**

Das Debütalbum des britischen Singer/Songwriter von 1970 präsentiert seine klare stimmliche Gestaltung und sein flinkes, melodisches Gitarrenspiel. Diese locker-flockige Produktion verneigt sich vor Cat Stevens und seiner Schule des soften Folk Psych, verweist aber aber auch schon auf den Soul und Funk, der sich auf seiner meisterhaften LP *Remember My Song* herauskristallisieren sollte. Letztere LP enthält den Song »I Got The«, der von Größen wie Jay-Z und Eminem gesampelt wurde. **O**

Le premier album de cet auteur / interprète britannique, sorti en 1970, met à l'honneur son style vocal clair et son jeu habile et mélodique à la guitare. Son atmosphère en-jouée penche vers l'école de folk psychédélique soft de Cat Stevens tout en annonçant les éléments de soul et de funk qui allaient se cristalliser dans son chef-d'œuvre *Remember My Song*. Ce dernier album contient le morceau *I Got The*, qui a plus tard été samplé par des gens tels que Jay-Z et Eminem.

PS-50,000   STEREO

BUNNY SIGLER
LET THE GOOD TIMES ROLL & (FEEL SO GOOD)
LOVEY DOVEY (You're So Fine)

Parkway

BUNNY SIGLER
title **LET THE GOOD TIMES ROLL** & **(FEEL SO GOOD)** / *year* **1967** / *label* Parkway

Bunny Sigler, along with Philadelphia brethren Kenny Gamble and Leon Huff, helped define the Philadelphia Sound. Here, Mr. Emotion poses with another famous bunny, White Rabbit from Central Park's famous *Alice in Wonderland* monument. Jimi Hendrix would photograph his own group here a year later for his own intended, yet sadly unused cover concept for *Electric Ladyland*. **O**
Bunny Sigler definierte gemeinsam mit den Brüdern Kenny Gamble und Leon Huff aus Philadelphia den Philly Sound. Hier posiert »Mr. Emotion« mit einem anderen berühmten Langohr: dem weißen Kaninchen vom berühmten *Alice im Wunderland*-Denkmal im Central Park. Ein Jahr später sollte Jimi Hendrix hier seine Gruppe für sein eigenes geplantes, aber leider nicht umgesetztes Coverkonzept für *Electric Ladyland* fotografieren. **O**
Bunny Sigler, avec ses collègues de Philadelphie Kenny Gamble et Leon Huff, a contribué à la définition du « son de Philadelphie ». Ici, M. Émotion pose avec un autre « bunny » célèbre, le lapin blanc du célèbre monument *Alice au Pays des Merveilles* de Central Park. Un an plus tard, Jimi Hendrix allait photographier son propre groupe ici même pour le concept de pochette qu'il avait imaginé pour *Electric Ladyland*, qui n'a malheureusement pas été utilisé.

Featuring: "Party-Pt.1+2" • "Let Him Go" & "Ain't No Need Of Crying"

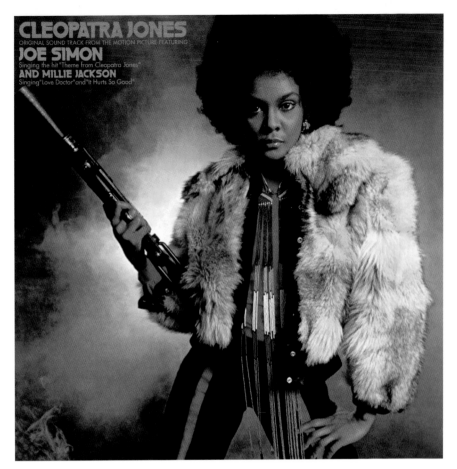

CLEOPATRA JONES
ORIGINAL SOUND TRACK FROM THE MOTION PICTURE FEATURING
JOE SIMON
Singing the hit "Theme from Cleopatra Jones"
AND MILLIE JACKSON
Singing "Love Doctor" and "It Hurts So Good"

JOE SIMON

title **CLEOPATRA JONES** / *year* **1973** / *label* Warner Bros.

Baltimore native Tamara Dobson is best known for her portrayal of Cleopatra Jones, the sexy special agent sent to the Middle East to disrupt a heroin operation in the blaxploitation classic of the same name. As exemplified by this powerful, provocative photograph of the fur-clad actress, the 6'2" beauty enjoyed a successful modeling career through the '60s and '70s. ○
Die aus Baltimore stammende Tamara Dobson war wegen ihrer Darstellung der Cleopatra Jones bekannt. Die sexy Spezialagentin wird in diesem Blaxploitation-Filmklassiker gleichen Namens in den Mittleren Osten geschickt, um ein Heroingeschäft zu vereiteln. Wie durch dieses kraftvolle und provokative Foto der in Pelz gekleideten Schauspielerin deutlich wird, genoss diese 188 cm große Schönheit in den 60er und 70er Jahren eine erfolgreiche Karriere als Model. ○
Tamara Dobson, originaire de Baltimore, est surtout connue pour son interprétation de Cleopatra Jones, l'agent spécial sexy envoyé au Moyen-Orient pour arrêter une opération de trafic d'héroïne dans le classique du cinéma de blaxploitation éponyme. Cette photographie intense et provocante de l'actrice en fourrure montre un échantillon de la carrière réussie que cette beauté d'un mètre quatre-vingt-huit a menée dans le mannequinat dans les années 1960 et 1970.

Valerie Simpson

Keep It Comin'

T6-85

VALERIE SIMPSON

title **KEEP IT COMIN'** / *year* **1977** / *label* Tamla /
design Stan Martin

This was a compilation of tracks from Valerie Simpson's
two solo LPs for Motown. Along with her partner Nick
Ashford she wrote some of the most influential soul songs
of the '60s and '70s including hits like "Ain't No Mountain
High Enough", "Let's Go Get Stoned", and "California Soul".
The couple married in 1974 and began recording their own
songs for Warner Bros., becoming top-selling performers in
their own rights through the 1980s. **O**
Dies war eine Compilation von Stücken aus den beiden
Solo-LPs von Valerie Simpson für Motown. Zusammen mit
ihrem Partner Nick Ashford schrieb sie einige der einflussreichsten Soul-Songs der 60er und 70er Jahre, darunter Hits
wie »Ain't No Mountain High Enough«, »Let's Go Get
Stoned« und »California Soul«. Das Paar heiratete 1974
und begann damit, eigene Songs für Warner Bros. aufzunehmen. Sie wurden in den 80er Jahren zu hoch vergüteten
Live-Acts. **O**
Ce disque est une compilation de morceaux sortis sur deux
albums en solo de Valerie Simpson chez Motown. Avec
son partenaire Nick Ashford, elle a écrit quelques-unes des
chansons de soul les plus marquantes des années 1960 et
1970, notamment des tubes tels que *Ain't No Mountain
High Enough*, *Let's Go Get Stoned* et *California Soul*. Le
couple s'est marié en 1974, a commencé à enregistrer
ses propres chansons pour Warner Bros. et a rencontré
un grand succès dans les années 1980.

SINS OF SATAN

title **THOU SHALT BOOGIE FOREVER** / *year* **1976** / *label* Buddah / *illustration* Jim O'Connell / *packaging* Milton Sincoff

Jim O'Connell's cover illustration is an anomaly in the annals of disco. By using an iconography that could be seen on many secular recordings of the time he made a closer connection than most to the gospel leanings of the burgeoning dance music. Jimmy Roach was the mastermind behind this Detroit ensemble and leads them through a tight set of funky disco. **O**
Jim O'Connells Coverillustration ist in den Disco-Annalen eine Ausnahmeerscheinung. Durch den Einsatz einer

Bildersprache, die man auf vielen säkularen Aufnahmen jener Zeit fand, knüpfte er an die Gospel-Tendenzen dieser aufkeimenden Tanzmusik enger an als die meisten anderen. Jimmy Roach war der Kopf dieses Detroiter Ensembles, das er durch einen sprühenden Set mit funkiger Disco führte. **O**
L'illustration de Jim O'Connell pour cette pochette est une anomalie dans les annales du disco. En utilisant une iconographie que l'on pouvait voir sur de nombreux enregistrements de l'époque, il établit une connexion plus étroite que les autres avec les penchants que le disco balbutiant montrait pour le gospel. Jimmy Roach était le cerveau de ce groupe de Detroit, et sur ce disque il conduit une série bien ficelée de morceaux de disco funk.

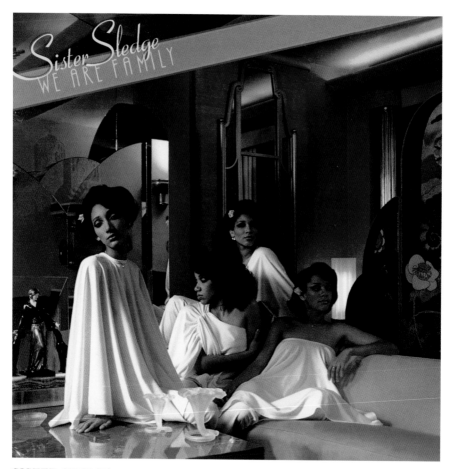

SISTER SLEDGE

title **WE ARE FAMILY** / *year* **1979** / *label* Cotillion /
photography Jim Houghton / *art direction* Bob Defrin

This North Philadelphia family group had released two
albums with little success when Chic's hit-making team of
Bernard Edwards and Nile Rodgers took over the production reins. The mix of tight funk instrumentation with the
gospel inflection of the sisters' sweet singing made for a
powerful collection of late disco classics. Jim Houghton's
art deco-inspired cover shot adds a nice touch of class to
the package. **O**
Diese Familienband aus North Philadelphia hatte zwei
Alben mit geringem Erfolg veröffentlicht, als Chics Hit-
Macher-Team Bernard Edwards und Nile Rodgers bei der
Produktion die Zügel übernahm. Die Mischung aus dichter
Funk-Instrumentierung und dem wunderschönen Gesang
der Schwestern mit ihren Gospel-Einsprengseln führten zu
dieser Sammlung von späteren Disco-Klassikern. Für sein
Foto ließ sich Jim Houghton vom Art déco inspirieren, um
der Plattenhülle ein elegantes Flair zu verleihen. **O**
Ce groupe familial du nord de Philadelphie avait sorti deux
albums qui n'avaient rencontré qu'un succès très relatif
lorsque l'équipe d'accoucheurs de tubes de Chic, Bernard
Edwards et Nile Rodgers prirent les rênes de la production.
L'instrumentation funky impeccable et les accents de gospel des voix harmonieuses des sœurs ont donné une collection solide de classiques du disco. Le style Art déco de la
photo de la pochette, un cliché de Jim Houghton, ajoute à
l'ensemble une touche de classe.

GSF-S-1011
STEREO

SKULL SNAPS

title **SKULL SNAPS** / *year* **1973** / *label* GSF /
art direction Michael Mendel/Maurer Productions

Michael Mendel's work with Maurer Productions often relied on the idea of collage or breaking the space into separate planes to show an action occurring simultaneously across the cover. His spooky design for the Skull Snaps' sole LP has certainly helped solidify its place as a classic. The group had been known as the Diplomats before teaming up with George Kerr and Bert Keyes to produce this monster album full of sweet harmonies and hard-hitting drums. **O**

Michael Mendels Arbeit für Maurer Productions beruhte oft auf dem Konzept einer Collage oder auf einer Aufteilung des zur Verfügung stehenden Raums in mehrere Bereiche, um auf dem Cover verteilt eine simultane Aktion zei-

gen zu können. Seine gruselige Gestaltung für die einzige LP der Skull Snaps hat sicher dabei geholfen, dass sie ihren Platz unter den Klassikern bekam. Die Gruppe war vorher unter dem Namen Diplomats bekannt, bevor sie sich mit George Kerr und Bert Keyes zusammentat, um dieses Monsteralbum zu produzieren. **O**

Le travail de Michael Mendel avec Maurer Productions reposait souvent sur l'idée du collage ou de séparation de l'espace en différents plans pour montrer une action qui se déroule simultanément en plusieurs endroits de la pochette. La pochette sinistre qu'il a réalisée pour le seul album des Skull Snaps a certainement contribué à son statut de classique. Le groupe s'était fait connaître sous le nom des Diplomats avant de faire équipe avec George Kerr et Bert Keyes pour produire ce monstre d'album rempli d'harmonies mélodieuses et de percussions qui frappent dur.

SKY

title **SKYPORT** / *year* **1980** / *label* Salsoul / *design* Jim O'Connell / *photography* Marlis Mathews

SLAVE

title **STONE JAM** / *year* **1980** / *label* Cotillion /
design Bob Heimall / *art direction* Bob Heimall /
illustration De Es Schwertberger

San Francisco heavy funk ensemble Slave was born out of
two former Ohio bands, the Young Mystics and Black Satin
Soul. Cover artist De Es Schwertberger, an Austrian painter,
began his Stone Period in the early '70s. His work dealt with
the strength of his Stoneman characters and the light that
helped them transcend the limitations of their world. ❍
Das Ensemble Slave aus San Francisco spielte Heavy Funk.
Es setzte sich aus zwei ehemaligen Bands aus Ohio zusam-

men: den Young Mystics und Black Satin Soul. Der Covergestalter De Es Schwertberger, ein österreichischer Maler,
begann in den frühen 70er Jahren mit seiner »Stein-Phase«.
In seiner Arbeit beschäftigte er sich mit der kraftvollen Ausstrahlung seines Steinmenschen und dem Licht, das ihm
half, die Begrenzungen seiner Welt zu überwinden. ❍
Cette formation de heavy funk de San Francisco est née de
l'union de deux anciens groupes de l'Ohio, les Young Mystics et Black Satin Soul. L'illustrateur de la pochette est De
Es Schwertberger, un peintre autrichien qui était entré dans
sa période « pierre » au début des années 1970. Il cherchait
à exprimer la force de ses hommes de pierre et la lumière
qui les aidait à transcender les limites de leur monde.

SLY & THE FAMILY STONE

title **DANCE TO THE MUSIC** /
year **1968** / label Epic

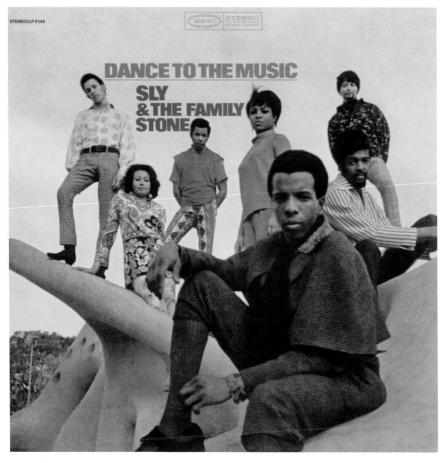

SLY & THE FAMILY STONE

title **FRESH** / *year* **1973** / *label* Epic / *design* John Berg / *photography* Richard Avedon

John Berg designed over 5,000 record covers and won four Grammys as Art Director for Columbia Records. His ability to tell the story of an album before the listener ever got the disc to the turntable helped produce some of the most iconic images of the 20th century. For Sly's sixth album Berg brought in frequent collaborator photographer Richard Avedon to set the tone of freewheeling, exuberant funk. ◐

John Berg gestaltete mehr als 5.000 Plattenhüllen und gewann als Art Director von Columbia Records vier Grammys. Er war in der Lage, die Geschichte eines Albums schon erzählt zu haben, bevor der Hörer die Platte überhaupt auf

den Plattenteller legte, und schuf einige der symbolträchtigsten Bilder des 20. Jahrhunderts. Für Slys sechstes Album brachte Berg den Fotografen Richard Avedon ins Spiel, mit dem er häufig zusammenarbeitete, um schon auf dem Cover die Atmosphäre von ausgelassenem und überschäumendem Funk zu vermitteln. ◐

John Berg a créé plus de 5000 pochettes de disque et a remporté quatre prix Grammy comme directeur artistique pour Columbia Records. Sa capacité à raconter l'histoire d'un album avant même que le disque ait pu être posé sur la platine de l'acheteur a contribué à créer quelques-unes des images les plus emblématiques du XXᵉ siècle. Pour le sixième album de Sly, Berg a fait intervenir le photographe Richard Avedon, qui avait souvent travaillé avec lui, pour rendre l'atmosphère d'un funk libre et exubérant.

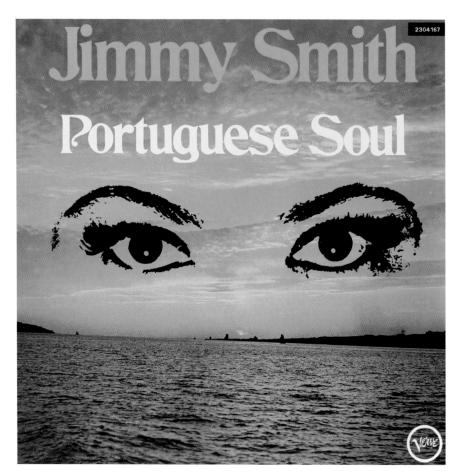

JIMMY SMITH

title **PORTUGUESE SOUL** / *year* **1973** / *label* Verve

In Jimmy Smith's apparent ode to Portugal, the versatile
organist conquers complicated terrain as conductor Thad
Jones navigates a capable orchestra through a series of
tempo changes, mood swings, and other compositional
curiosities. The majority of the long-player consists of
multiple movements of the title track, concluding with the
bitter-sweet "Farewell to Lisbon Town". **O**

Bei Jimmy Smiths offenkundiger Ode an Portugal erobert
der vielseitige Organist ein kompliziertes Terrain, während
Thad Jones sein fähiges Orchester durch eine Reihe von
Tempowechseln, Stimmungswechseln und anderen kompositorischen Kuriositäten lotst. Der Großteil der Langspielplatte besteht aus verschiedenen Sätzen des Titelstücks
und schließt mit dem bittersüßen »Farewell to Lisbon
Town« ab. **O**

Dans cette ode que Jimmy Smith consacre au Portugal,
l'organiste aux talents multiples conquiert un terrain difficile tandis que le chef d'orchestre Thad Jones dirige des
musiciens compétents à travers une série de changements
de tempo et d'humeur, entre autres curiosités de la composition. La plus grande partie de ce disque longue durée est
formée des différents mouvements du morceau-titre, qui
se concluent par le doux-amer *Farewell to Lisbon Town*.

JIMMY SMITH

title **SIT ON IT!** / *year* **1977** / *label* Mercury / *photography* Antonin Kratochvil / *art direction* Mike Doud/AGI

Although Czech-born photographer Antonin Kratochvil has had his share of musical subjects, his most evocative work has been generated documenting global hardship. Though this cover shows a young woman sitting on Jimmy's organ happily having her dress blow in the breeze, Kratochvil's harrowing work in the field of photojournalism has rendered numerous photo essays on multi-dimensional matters. **O**
Der in Tschechien geborene Fotograf Antonin Kratochvil hat eine ganze Menge musikalischer Sujets abgelichtet,

doch seine bewegendsten Arbeiten entstanden, als er das globale Elend dokumentierte. Auf diesem Cover sitzt eine junge Frau auf Jimmys Orgel und lässt sich fröhlich den Rock hochpusten – unterdessen haben die erschütternden Arbeiten Kratochvils im Bereich des Fotojournalismus zu zahlreichen Fotoessays mit vielfältigsten Themen geführt. **O**
Le photographe tchèque Antonin Kratochvil a eu son quota de sujets musicaux, mais son travail le plus évocateur a vu le jour en documentant les misères du monde. Sur cette pochette, on ne voit qu'une jeune femme assise sur l'orgue de Jimmy, s'amusant de sa robe emportée par la brise, mais les photographies poignantes que Kratochvil a réalisées sur le terrain ont donné lieu à des photoreportages sur des sujets complexes et multidimensionnels.

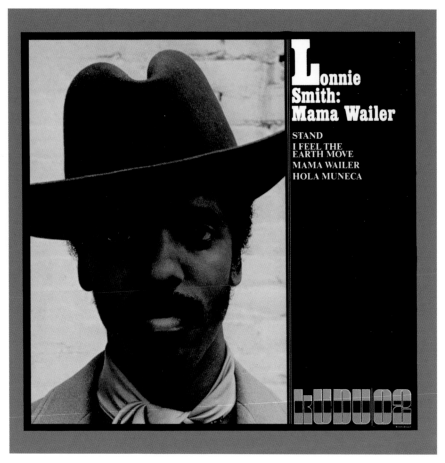

LONNIE SMITH

title **MAMA WAILER** / *year* **1971** / *label* Kudu /
design Bob Ciano / *photography* Duane Michals

Lonnie Smith's sole outing for Creed Taylor's Kudu label
finds the doctor of the Hammond B3 in rare form. Backed
by an ensemble of Taylor regulars, this is a swinging affair
that easily roams between post-bop jazz improvisations,
Latin grooves, and down & dirty '70s funk. Duane Michals'
enigmatic portrait served as inspiration to painter Bob
Grossé for the psychedelic cover to the keyboardist's next
LP, *When the Night is Right*. ○

Bei seinem einzigen Ausflug zu Creed Taylors Label Kudu
befindet sich der Doktor der Hammond B3 in selten guter
Form. Vor dem Hintergrund eines Ensembles mit Stammmusikern von Creed Taylor wechselt diese Swinging Affair

mit Leichtigkeit zwischen Post-Bop-Jazzimprovisationen,
Latin-Groove und knallhartem 70er-Jahre-Funk hin und her.
Das enigmatische Porträt von Duane Michals diente dem
Maler Bob Grossé als Inspiration für das psychedelische
Coverbild der nächsten LP des Keyboarders: *When the
Night is Right*. ○

Le seul opus de Lonnie Smith pour le label Kudu de Creed
Taylor révèle le docteur du Hammond B3 en grande forme.
L'accompagnement est assuré par des fidèles de Taylor, et
cette aventure swing navigue sans effort entre les improvisations de jazz post-bop, les grooves latins et le funk brut
des années 1970. Le portrait énigmatique de Duane
Michals a inspiré le peintre Bob Grossé pour la pochette
psychédélique de l'album suivant du claviériste, *When the
Night is Right*.

JAKE SOLLO
title **JAKE SOLLO** / *year* **1979** /
label Pye

SOUL CHILDREN

title **CHRONICLE** / *year* **1979** / *label* Stax / *photography* William R. Eastbrook / *art direction* Phil Carroll

SOUL STRINGS & A FUNKY HORN

title **SOUL STRINGS** & **A FUNKY HORN** / *year* **1968** / *label* Solid State

SPARKS! MELVIN SPARKS

VIRGIL JONES / HOUSTON PERSON / JOHN MANNING / LEON SPENCER JR. / IDRIS MUHAMMAD

MELVIN SPARKS

title **SPARKS!** / *year* **1970** / *label* BGP /
design Don Schlitten / *photography* Al Johnson

Melvin Sparks was one of the funkiest jazz guitarists to
record in the '60s and '70s. He honed his chops as a member of the show band the Upsetters, backing singers like
Sam Cooke, and Little Richard, and moved toward jazz
with a stint in Jack McDuff's band. His debut harks back to
his R&B roots with covers of some popular soul cuts, but
the remarkable improvisatory playing by him and his group
for this session keeps the jazz well ahead of the pop. **O**
Melvin Sparks war einer der besten Funk-Jazz-Gitarristen.
Er verfeinerte sein Gitarrenspiel als Mitglied der Showband
The Upsetters, die mit Sängern wie Sam Cooke und Little
Richard auftraten, und arbeitete sich nach einem kurzen

Abstecher zu Jack McDuffs Band in Richtung Jazz vor. Bei
seinem Debüt griff er auf seine R&B-Wurzeln zurück. Er
nahm ein paar Coverversionen bekannter Soulstücke auf,
doch in dieser Session rückt durch sein bemerkenswertes
Improvisationstalent und das seiner Gruppe der Jazz deutlich vor den Pop. **O**
Melvin Sparks a été l'un des guitaristes de jazz les plus
funky. Il s'est fait les dents comme membre du groupe
d'accompagnement les Upsetters, qui ont joué avec des
chanteurs tels que Sam Cooke et Little Richard, et s'est
rapproché du jazz avec une incursion dans le groupe de
Jack McDuff. Ce premier album revient sur ses racines R&B,
avec des reprises de quelques morceaux de soul populaires,
mais le remarquable jeu d'improvisation dont lui et son
groupe font preuve lors de cette session donne un poids
bien plus important au jazz qu'à la pop.

SPIRITUAL CONCEPT

title **SPIRITUAL CONCEPT** / *year* **1973** / *label* Philadelphia International / *photography* Don Hunstein / *art direction* Ed Lee

Ed Lee and Don Hunstein went all out on the cover to this unusual Philadelphia International release. Lee used Hunstein's wide, long-distance photo of the group to balance them between the heavens and the earth, evoking a Japanese rock garden. This tranquil approach is mirrored in the group's rarefied sound that wells up with airy jazz flourishes and hits hard with earthy Latin funk hooks. **O**

Ed Lee und Don Hunstein legten sich für das Cover dieser ungewöhnlichen Veröffentlichung bei Philadelphia International richtig ins Zeug. Lee verwendete ein breitformatiges

Foto der Gruppe, auf dem die Musiker dank eines Teleobjektivs zwischen Himmel und Erde gut ausbalanciert sind und die Anmutung eines japanischen Steingartens heraufbeschwören. Diesem friedvollen Ansatz stehen die exklusiven Klänge der Gruppe gegenüber, bei denen luftige Jazz-Fanfaren hart auf erdigen Latin Funk treffen. **O**

Ed Lee et Don Hunstein ont employé les grands moyens pour la pochette de cet album inhabituel sorti chez Philadelphia International. Lee a utilisé la photo à cadrage large de Hunstein pour faire flotter le groupe entre les cieux et la terre et évoquer un jardin de pierres japonais. Cette approche zen se retrouve dans le son très original du groupe, qui se remplit d'ornements jazzy aériens et frappe fort avec des crochets de funk latin très terrestres.

STAIRSTEPS

title **2ND RESURRECTION** / *year* **1976** / *label*
Dark Horse / *design* Chuck Beeson / *photography*
Fred Valentine / *art direction* Roland Young

Chicago's Burke Family was the reigning "First Family of Soul" before forfeiting the familial moniker to their Gary, Indiana neighbors, the Jacksons, in the late '70s. Best known for their childhood chart-topper "O-o-h Child", the Burke brothers are captured on *2nd Resurrection* in a more mature mode of operation, assembling a nuclear bomb of sophisticated soul for Beatle George Harrison's Dark Horse label. **O**
Die Burke-Familie aus Chicago führte den Titel der »First Family of Soul«, bevor sie diesen vertrauten Spitznamen

Ende der 70er Jahre an die Jacksons, ihre Nachbarn aus Gary, Indiana, abtreten musste. Sie wurde vor allem durch ihren Chartbreaker »O-o-h Child« bekannt, aber die Platte *2nd Resurrection* offenbart eine ausgereiftere Arbeitsweise der Burke-Brüder. Diese raffinierte Soul-Bombe erschien auf dem Label Dark Horse des Beatles George Harrison. **O**
À Chicago, la famille Burke était la « Première famille de la soul » et régnait sur ce territoire avant de céder la place à la fin des années 1970 à ses voisins les Jackson, de la ville de Gary, dans l'Indiana. Surtout connus pour le numéro un de leur enfance *O-o-h Child*, sur cet album les frères Burke sont représentés sur le mode de la maturité et assemblent une bombe atomique de soul sophistiquée pour le label Dark Horse de George Harrison, des Beatles.

THE STAPLE SINGERS
title **HAMMER AND NAILS** /
year **1962** / *label* Riverside / *design*
Ken Deardoff / *photography* Steve
Schapiro

THE STAPLE SINGERS

title **BEALTITUDE: RESPECT YOURSELF** / *year* **1971** / *label* Stax / *photography* Jerry Griffith / *art direction* David Krieger/The Graffiteria

Jerry Griffith perched this gospel soul family jovially on the lip of a jet engine, which seems prophetic since this was the album that took their sound to new heights. Al Bell replaced Steve Cropper as the group's producer and he took them to the Muscle Shoals studio to inject some serious funk into the mix and gave them the biggest hits of their career. **O**

Jerry Griffith hieß diese Gospel-Soul-Familie sich fröhlich in eine Turbine setzen. Das erscheint prophetisch, denn es war dieses Album, das ihren Sound zu neuen Höhen bringen sollte. Al Bell ersetzte Steve Cropper als Produzent der Gruppe und nahm sie mit ins Studio Muscle Shoals, um knochentrockenen Funk in den Mix zu injizieren. So erlangten sie die größten Hits ihrer Karriere. **O**

Jerry Griffith a juché cette famille de gospel soul tout sourire sur un moteur d'avion, ce qui semble presque prophétique puisque cet album a propulsé leur son vers de nouvelles hauteurs. Al Bell a remplacé le producteur Steve Cropper et a emmené le groupe au studio Muscle Shoals afin de lui faire une petite injection de funk, ce qui a donné le plus grand succès de sa carrière. **O**

STARFIRE

title **DANCING AND SINGING FOR YOU** / *year* **1978** /
label Dynamic Artists / *design* Joe Carter

Billed as "the baddest 5 stars in the galaxy", this obscure
Richmond, VA band deliver the goods. This talented band
makes no effort to hide their debt to Earth, Wind & Fire,
from the spaced-out cover imagery, contributed by producer Joe Carter, to the mix of spaced-out funk and modern soul. **○**

Angekündigt als »die 5 miesesten Sterne der Galaxie« hat's
diese obskure Band aus Richmond, Virginia, doch tatsächlich gebracht. Diese talentierte Band gibt sich nicht damit
ab zu verbergen, was sie Earth, Wind & Fire alles zu verdanken hat: von der abgespaceten Covergestaltung, die der
Produzent Joe Carter lieferte, bis hin zum Mix aus ebenso
abgespacetem Funk und Modern Soul. **○**

La pochette annonce que ce groupe obscur de Richmond,
en Virginie, est composé des « 5 étoiles les plus redoutables
de la galaxie » et tient ses promesses. Ces musiciens talentueux ne font aucun effort pour dissimuler leur admiration
pour Earth, Wind & Fire, depuis l'image cosmique de la
pochette, fournie par le producteur Joe Carter, jusqu'au
mélange de funk galactique et de soul moderne.

STARGARD

title **STARGARD** / *year* **1978** /
label MCA / *design* Norman Moore /
photography Jennifer Griffiths /
art direction George Osaki

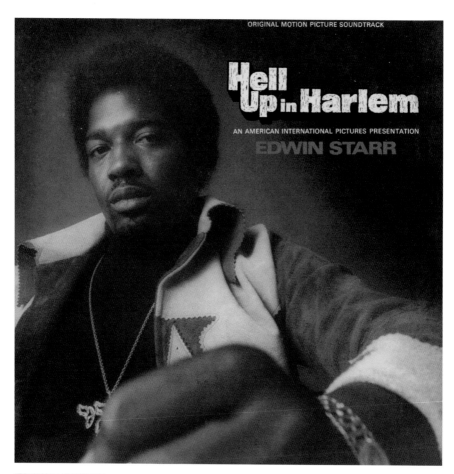

Hell Up in Harlem

AN AMERICAN INTERNATIONAL PICTURES PRESENTATION

EDWIN STARR

EDWIN STARR

title **HELL UP IN HARLEM** / *year* **1974** / *label* Motown / *design* Jim Britt / *photography* Jim Britt

Although James Brown was originally commissioned to compose and perform the soundtrack to this *Black Caesar* sequel, it would be Edwin Starr who would provide Motown sounds for this Uptown gangster classic. Photographer Jim Britt adds this snapshot to his portfolio of simple, yet effective soul portraits from the '70s. **O**
Obwohl eigentlich James Brown den Auftrag hatte, den Soundtrack zu diesem Nachfolger von *Black Caesar* zu komponieren und aufzunehmen, sollte es Edwin Starr sein,
der für diesen klassischen Uptown-Gangsterfilm die Motown-Sounds lieferte. Der Fotograf Jim Britt ergänzte mit diesem Schnappschuss sein gewaltiges Portfolio voller simpler und doch effektiver Soul-Porträts aus den 70er Jahren. **O**
À l'origine, c'est James Brown qui avait été chargé de composer et d'interpréter la bande originale de cette suite de *Black Cesar, le parrain de Harlem*, mais c'est Edwin Starr qui allait donner à Motown la musique de ce classique des films de gangsters des quartiers chics. Le photographe Jim Britt ajoute ce cliché à son portfolio débordant de portraits simples mais efficaces du monde de la soul dans les années 1970.

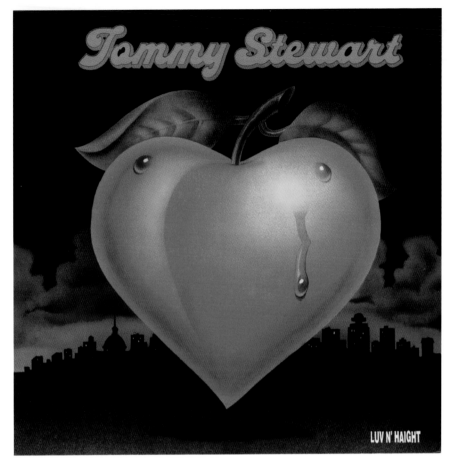

LUV N' HAIGHT

TOMMY STEWART

title **TOMMY STEWART** / *year* **2003** / *label* Luv N'
Haight / *design* Reagan Wilson & Gordon Smith/Creative
Services / *art direction* John Salston & Marlin McNichols

Hotlanta was never hotter than when Tommy Stewart
spread the love on his self-titled solo LP in 1976. Reagan
Wilson and Gordon Smith supplied the luscious cover
illustration of a perspiring heart-shaped Georgia peach. The
fiery glow of the sunset over the silhouetted Atlanta skyline
seems to propose a night on the town where the dance-
floor classic "Bump and Hustle" never stops playing. **O**
Hotlanta war niemals so heiß wie zu der Zeit, als Tommy
Stewart 1976 seine Liebe auf seiner gleichnamigen LP
ausgoss. Reagan Wilson und Gordon Smith lieferten diese

saftige Cover-Illustration eines herzförmigen Georgia-
Pfirsichs mit Schweißtropfen. Der feurige Glanz des
Sonnenuntergangs über der Silhouette der Skyline von
Atlanta verspricht eine atemberaubende Nacht in der
Stadt, wo der Dancefloor-Klassiker »Bump and Hustle«
scheinbar nie verklingt. **O**
« Hotlanta » n'a jamais été aussi chaude que lorsque Tommy
Stewart prêchait l'amour sur son album solo éponyme de
1976. Reagan Wilson et Gordon Smith ont fourni la somp-
tueuse illustration de la pochette, une pêche juteuse de
Géorgie en forme de cœur. Le rougeoiement du soleil couchant sur la ligne des toits d'Atlanta semble inviter à une
virée en ville, où le classique *Bump and Hustle* est joué en
boucle sur les pistes de danse.

THE STRIKERS

title **THE STRIKERS** / year **1981** /
label Rams Horn / photography Trudy
Schlachter / art direction R. Robbins

SYLVIA STRIPLIN

title **GIVE ME YOUR LOVE** / *year* **1981** / *label* Uno
Melodic / *photography* Charles Robinson/Lumina /
art direction Dennis Armstead/Yellow Go-Rilla

Dennis Armstead founded Yellow Go-Rilla, one of the first
black-owned production companies handling jazz in
New York. Roy Ayers was involved with the company from
the start. The soft, hand-colored look of Charles Robinson's
cover photo mirrors Sylvia Striplin's sensual vocals and
Ayers' lush production for his Uno Melodic label. ○
Dennis Armstead gründete in New York den Musikverlag
Yellow Go-Rilla, eine der ersten Jazz-Produktionsfirmen im

Besitz von Afroamerikanern. Roy Ayers war von Anfang an
bei der Firma mit im Spiel. Der weiche, handkolorierte Look
des Coverfotos von Charles Robinson spiegelt die sinnliche
Stimme von Sylvia Striplin und die üppige Produktion von
Ayers für sein Label Uno Melodic. ○
Dennis Armstead est le fondateur de Yellow Go-Rilla, l'une
des premières sociétés de production noires s'occupant de
jazz à New York. Roy Ayers a travaillé avec cette société dès
le début. La photo colorée à la main de Charles Robinson
dégage une douceur qui évoque la voix sensuelle de Sylvia
Striplin et la magnifique production d'Ayers pour son label
Uno Melodic.

THE STYLISTICS

title **LET'S PUT IT ALL TOGETHER** / *year* **1974** /
label Avco / *art direction* Michael Mendel/Maurer
Productions / *illustration* Doug Johnson/Jim O'Connell

The softly psychedelic surrealism and muted tones on the
cover to The Stylistics' fourth LP capture the kings of sweet
modern soul at their zenith. Although they had recently
split from mastermind writer/producer Thom Bell, his one
last gift to the group would be the album's moving ballad
"You Make Me Feel Brand New". With Russell Thompkins
Jr.'s soaring falsetto leading the way, it would prove to be
their biggest hit. **O**
Das Cover der vierten LP der Stylistics bettet die Meister
des harmonischen modernen Souls in sanften, psychedeli-

schen Surrealismus und gedeckte Farben. Obwohl sie sich
kurz vorher von dem genialen Texter und Produzenten
Thom Bell getrennt hatten, war die bewegende Ballade
»You Make Me Feel Brand New« auf diesem Album sein
letztes Geschenk an die Gruppe. Getragen von dem hoch-
fliegendem Falsetto von Russell Thompkins Jr., sollte sie zu
ihrem größten Hit werden. **O**
Le surréalisme doucement psychédélique et les couleurs
rabaissées de la pochette du quatrième album des Stylistics
illustrent les rois de la sweet soul moderne à leur zénith. Ils
venaient de se séparer de l'auteur / producteur et cerveau
du groupe, Thom Bell, mais son dernier cadeau pour le
groupe allait être l'émouvante ballade *You Make Me Feel
Brand New*. Le *falsetto* de Russell Thompkins Jr. allait en
faire leur plus grand succès.

THE STYLISTICS

title **THANK YOU BABY** / *year*
1975 / *label* Avco / *photography* Si Chi
Ko / *art direction* Michael Mendel/
Maurer Productions

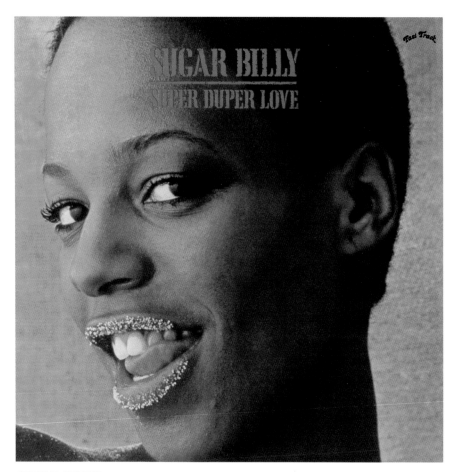

SUGAR BILLY

title **SUPER DUPER LOVE** / *year* **1975** / *label* Fast Track / *design* The Graffiteria / *photography* Joel Brodsky

The Graffiteria design firm was working here in a slightly more subdued manner than some of their more psychedelic covers from a few years earlier, although the provocative cover-shot by the always reliable Joel Brodsky does show the sense of humor they so often exhibited. Sugar Billy, a.k.a. Willie Garner, delivers a set of funk that owes as much to the laid-back groove of the south as it does the snappy beat of the north, due as much to his raw vocals as to Jimmy Roach's deft arrangements. ○

Die Designagentur Graffiteria lieferte hier, verglichen mit einigen sehr psychedelischen Covern in früheren Jahren, eher eine dezentere Arbeit ab, obwohl der provokative Cover-Shot des stets zuverlässigen Joel Brodsky doch genau jenen Sinn für Humor zeigt, den sie so oft zur Schau gestellt hat. Sugar Billy alias Willie Garner liefert hier eine Funk-Scheibe ab, die dem lässigen Groove des Südens genauso viel zu verdanken hat wie dem schmissigen Beat des Nordens. Seine raue Stimme hat daran einen ebenso großen Anteil wie die geschickten Arrangements von Jimmy Roach. ○

La société de graphisme Graffiteria a travaillé ici avec plus de sobriété que sur certaines de ses pochettes antérieures plus psychédéliques, bien que la photographie provocante de Joel Brodsky, toujours efficace, soit bien dans le ton humoristique habituel de la maison. Sugar Billy, également connu sous le nom de Willie Garner, livre ici un album de funk qui empreinte autant au groove décontracté du Sud qu'aux rythmes nerveux du Nord, que ce soit dans sa voix ou dans les arrangements habiles de Jimmy Roach.

SUGARHILL GANG

title **SUGARHILL GANG** / *year* **1979** / *label* Sugarhill /
design Christopher Rohn / *photography* James Dargan /
art direction Novigraphics

Producer and label owner Sylvia Robinson scored big when
she took three local Englewood, New Jersey MCs into the
studio and had them rap over a music track that was basically a snippet of Chic's hit "Good Times" played by session
musicians, the future Living Colour bassist, Doug Wimbish,
guitarist Little Axe, and drummer Keith LeBlanc. The result,
"Rapper's Delight", was one of the first hip-hop tracks ever
cut and the first to become a gold record. **O**
Die Produzentin und Label-Inhaberin Sylvia Robinson landete einen Volltreffer, als sie drei MCs aus Englewood, New
Jersey, ins Studio holte und sie zu einem Musiktrack rappen

ließ. Es war im Grunde ein Ausschnitt aus dem von Sessionmusikern eingespielten Chic-Hit »Good Times«, und
zwar von Doug Wimbish, dem Gitarristen Little Axe und
dem Drummer Keith LeBlanc. Das Ergebnis kam als
»Rapper's Delight« weltweit zu Ruhm und war einer der
ersten Hiphop-Tracks überhaupt und der erste, der mit
einer Goldenen Schallplatte ausgezeichnet wurde. **O**
La productrice et propriétaire de label Sylvia Robinson a vu
juste lorsqu'elle a décidé de faire entrer trois MC d'Englewood (New Jersey) dans un studio et de les faire rapper sur
un fond musical qui n'était rien d'autre qu'un fragment du
succès *Good Times* de Chic joué par des musiciens de studio, le futur bassiste de Living Colour, Doug Wimbish, le
guitariste Little Axe et le batteur Keith LeBlanc. Le résultat,
Rapper's Delight, a été l'un des premiers morceaux de hip-
hop jamais gravé, et le premier à recevoir un disque d'or.

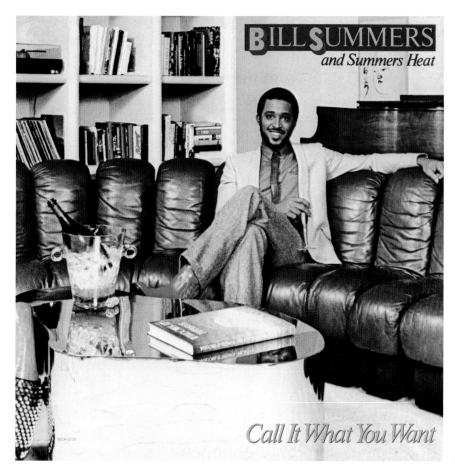

BILL SUMMERS
AND SUMMERS HEAT
title **CALL IT WHAT YOU WANT** / *year* **1981** /
label MCA

Bill Summers is best known in funk factions for the percussive role he played in Herbie Hancock's revolutionary unit, the Head Hunters. At the beginning of the '80s, Summers endured the rising heat, fabricating a respectable body of dance music in the tradition of Quincy Jones, with whom the percussionist collaborated on the score for *Roots'* televised incarnation. **O**

Bill Summers wurde in der Funk-Fraktion vor allem als Perkussionist in Herbie Hancocks revolutionärer Formation Head Hunters bekannt. Anfang der 80er Jahre hielt Summers der steigenden Hitze stand und fabrizierte ein respektables Werk mit Tanzmusik in der Tradition von Quincy Jones, mit dem er zusammen die Musik für den Film *Roots* für das Fernsehen überarbeitete. **O**

Bill Summers est connu dans les cercles du funk pour le rôle qu'il a joué aux percussions dans le groupe révolutionnaire de Herbie Hancock, les Head Hunters. Au début des années 1980, il a supporté la chaleur montante en produisant une œuvre respectable de musique de danse dans la tradition de Quincy Jones, avec qui il a travaillé sur la bande originale de l'adaptation télévisée de *Racines*.

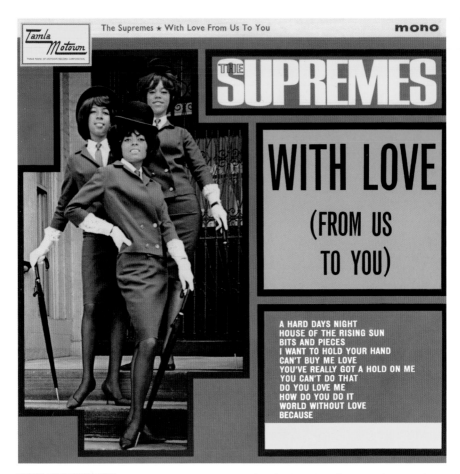

**THE SUPREMES

WITH LOVE

(FROM US
TO YOU)**

A HARD DAYS NIGHT
HOUSE OF THE RISING SUN
BITS AND PIECES
I WANT TO HOLD YOUR HAND
CAN'T BUY ME LOVE
YOU'VE REALLY GOT A HOLD ON ME
YOU CAN'T DO THAT
DO YOU LOVE ME
HOW DO YOU DO IT
WORLD WITHOUT LOVE
BECAUSE

THE SUPREMES

title **WITH LOVE (FROM US TO YOU)** / *year* **1964** / *label* Tamla Motown / *design* Bernard Yeszin & Wallace Mead

This was the UK pressing of the album entitled *A Bit Of Liverpool*. The best thing about this record is the amazing mod cover by Bernard Yeszin and Wallace Mead. Their use of geometric shapes, playful type, and the subdued green background color that mimics the chic outfits the group is wearing contribute to the modern look. Unfortunately the pedestrian cover versions of British Invasion do not do either the singers or the songs a great service. **O**
Dies war die Pressung des Albums *A Bit Of Liverpool* für den britischen Markt. Das Beste an dieser Platte ist das

atemberaubende Mod-Cover von Bernard Yeszin und Wallace Mead. Ihre Verwendung geometrischer Formen und verspielter Schrift vor dem gedämpft grünen Hintergrund, der die schicken Kostüme der Gruppe aufgreift, trägt zum modernen Look bei. Leider erweisen die langweiligen Cover-Versionen der British Invasion weder den Sängerinnen noch den Songs einen sonderlich guten Dienst. **O**
Ceci était l'édition britannique de l'album intitulé A Bit Of Liverpool. Le meilleur ingrédient de ce disque est la superbe pochette mod de Bernard Yeszin et Wallace Mead. Leur utilisation des formes géométriques, leur jeu sur la typographie et le fond vert qui fait écho aux tenues chics du groupe contribuent à créer un look moderne. Malheureusement, la platitude à ces versions de tubes anglais de l'époque ne fait honneur ni aux chanteuses, ni aux chansons.

THE SUPREMES

title **THE SUPREMES** / year **1964** /
label Tamla Motown

The Supremes

TMLF 101

Photo X...

WHERE DID OUR LOVE GO●
I'M GIVING YOU YOUR FREE-
DOM ● (THE MAN WITH THE)
ROCK AND ROLL BANJO
BAND ● I'M STANDING AT
THE CROSS ROADS OF LOVE
●●RUN, RUN, RUN ●● BABY
LOVE ● COME SEE ABOUT
ME ●●● ASK ANY GIRL●●
WHEN THE LOVE LIGHT
STARTS SHINING THROUGH
HIS EYES ● YOU CAN'T DO
THAT ●●●● I'M IN LOVE
AGAIN ●●●●●●●● STOP!
IN THE NAME OF LOVE●●

ST 190

THE SOUL VIEW NOW! BETTYE SWANN

BETTYE SWANN

title **THE SOUL VIEW NOW!** / *year* **1968** / *label* Capitol / *photography* Ed Simpson/Capitol Photo Studios

Bettye Swann crafted a creative mode of soul that, if not country, was at the very least rural. Born in Shreveport, Louisiana, Swann's music straddled the Mason-Dixon line, striking a balance between the swing of Stax and the soul of Motown. She was influenced by equal parts Elvis Presley and Ray Charles, and performed unique interpretations of country compositions during her recorded career. **○**
Bettye Swann schuf eine kreative Spielart des Soul, die, wenn schon nicht Country, dann zumindest ländlich war. Sie wurde in Shreveport, Louisiana, geboren. Ihre Musik

liegt auf der Mason-Dixon-Linie und findet einen Mittelweg zwischen dem Swing von Stax und dem Soul von Motown. Sie wurde zu gleichen Teilen von Elvis Presley und Ray Charles beeinflusst und nahm in ihrer Zeit viele einzigartige Interpretationen von Country-Songs auf. **○**
Bettye Swann a inventé un style de soul créative qui, sans être country, est quand même bien rurale. Swann est née à Shreveport, en Louisiane, et sa musique voyage sur la ligne Mason-Dixon, à la frontière entre les États du Nord et les États du Sud, pour trouver un équilibre entre le swing de Stax et la soul de Motown. Ses influences lui viennent autant d'Elvis Presley que de Ray Charles, et au cours de sa carrière elle a donné des interprétations singulières de compositions de country.

THE SYLVERS

title **THE SYLVERS II** / *year* **1973** / *label* Pride / *design* Ron Raffaelli / *photography* Ron Raffaelli / *art direction* Saul Saget

An outstanding use of afros and silver metallic paper from famed rock 'n' roll photographer Ron Raffaelli and MGM art director Saul Saget for the sophomore effort from this sweet soul family group. The silver cover is an obvious allusion to the name of the group, but the floating head portraits and shining material prefigure the heavenly sounds held within. **o**

Für das zweite Werk dieser harmonischen Soulfamilie setzen der berühmte Rock'n'Roll-Fotograf Ron Raffaelli und Saul Saget, der Art Director von MGM, auffallende Afros und Silbermetallicpapier ein. Das Silbercover ist eine offensichtliche Anspielung auf den Gruppennamen, die schwebenden Gesichter und das glänzende Material künden von den himmlischen Klängen des Albums. **o**

Le célèbre photographe du rock'n'roll Ron Raffaelli et le directeur artistique de MGM Saul Saget font ici une utilisation remarquable de la coiffure afro et du papier argenté pour le deuxième album de ce groupe familial de sweet soul. La pochette couleur argent fait bien sûr allusion au nom du groupe, mais les portraits sous forme de têtes flottantes et le papier brillant annoncent les sons célestes qui sont renfermés à l'intérieur. **o**

SYREETA

title **ONE TO ONE** / *year* **1977** / *label* Motown /
art direction Carl Overr / *illustration* Bob Hickson

The former Mrs. Stevie Wonder's third LP is the only one to
feature a painted cover. Famed California airbrush-artist Bob
Hickson was hired by Motown to do the action-packed
hair piece. Because of the costly and time-consuming nature of braids, Hickson's artist impression was the perfect
alternative. Although their marriage was short lived, Syreeta
and Stevie were frequent co-writers. This album contains
their final collaboration, the exquisite "Harmour Love". **O**
Die dritte LP der ehemaligen Mrs. Stevie Wonder ist die
einzige mit einem gemalten Cover. Der berühmte Airbrush-
Künstler Bob Hickson aus Kalifornien wurde von Motown

angeheuert, dieses dynamische Haarteil zu schaffen. Weil
Zöpfe kostspielig und zeitraubend sind, war eine künstlerische Interpretation von Hickson die perfekte Alternative.
Obwohl ihre Ehe nur zwei Jahre hielt, haben Syreeta und
Stevie viele Songs zusammen geschrieben. Dieses Album
enthält ihr letztes gemeinsames Werk: das exquisite »Harmour Love«. **O**
Le troisième album de l'ex-épouse de Stevie Wonder est le
seul à être illustré d'un tableau. Motown a chargé le célèbre
peintre aérographiste californien Bob Hickson de créer cette
coiffure dynamique. Les tresses étant chères et longues à
réaliser, le rendu artistique de Hickson était la solution idéale.
Bien que leur mariage n'ait pas duré longtemps, Syreeta et
Stevie écrivaient souvent ensemble. Cet album contient
leur dernière collaboration, l'excellent *Harmour Love*.

STEREO/2325 001

**BOOKER T.
AND THE M.G.'S
SOUL LIMBO**

LA LA MEANS I LOVE YOU
OVER EASY
ELEANOR RIGBY
AND OTHERS

BOOKER T. AND THE M.G.'S

title **SOUL LIMBO** / *year* **1968** / *label* Stax / *photography*
George Whiteman / *art direction* Christopher Whorf

Bandleader Booker T. Jones and his combo were a long way
from their Memphis home when they shot the seaside
cover for *Soul Limbo*. They were one of the first racially
integrated bands from the South, and this cover photo
was a valuable reminder to soul fans nationwide that the
Memphis Sound was indeed a sound and not a color. **O**
Der Bandleader Booker T. Jones war mit seiner Combo ganz
weit weg von seinem Zuhause in Memphis, als diese Auf-

nahmen am Meer für das Cover von *Soul Limbo* geschossen
wurden. Im Süden war dies eine der ersten Bands, in der
mehrere Rassen integriert waren, und dieses Foto erinnerte
die Soulfans der Nation nachdrücklich daran, dass der Mem-
phis-Sound tatsächlich ein Sound war und keine Farbe. **O**
Le leader de groupe Booker T. Jones et sa formation musicale étaient bien loin de leur Memphis natal lorsqu'ils po-
sèrent sur la plage pour la pochette de *Soul Limbo*. C'était
l'un des premiers groupes du sud des États-Unis à compter
des membres noirs et blancs, et cette photo rappelait aux
fans de soul de tout le pays que le son de Memphis était
bien un son, et non une couleur.

GRADY TATE

title **SHE IS MY LADY** / *year*
1972 / *label* Janus / *photography* Joel
Brodsky / *art direction* David Krieger

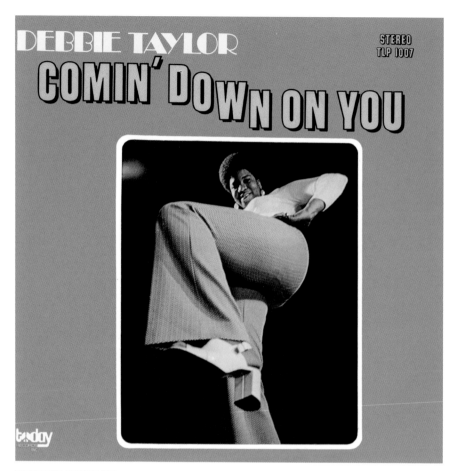

DEBBIE TAYLOR
title **COMIN' DOWN ON YOU** / *year* **1972** / *label* Today / *design* Fred Stark / *photography* Reginald Wickham

Before he began masterminding some of the era's most inventive disco, producer Patrick Adams was working diligently within the confines of soul music's established parameters, producing and recruiting for some of Manhattan's most industrious indie labels. Debbie Taylor's lone full-length LP transcends soul, funk, and Northern boundaries – a phenomenal feat for Adams and songwriter David Jordan. ⊙
Bevor sich der Produzent Patrick Adams hinter einige der einfallsreichsten Tracks der Disco-Ära klemmte, arbeitete

er genau und sorgfältig innerhalb der engen Grenzen etablierter Parameter der Soulmusik und produzierte und rekrutierte für einige der produktivsten Indie-Labels von Manhattan. Debbie Taylors einzige Langspielplatte transzendiert Soul-, Funk- und Northern-Grenzen – eine phänomenale Heldentat für Adams und seinen Songwriter David Jordan. ⊙
Avant de devenir le cerveau des manifestations les plus inventives du disco de l'époque, Patrick Adams travaillait avec diligence dans les paramètres définis de la musique soul et s'occupait de la production et du recrutement pour les labels indépendants les plus productifs de Manhattan. L'unique album de Debbie Taylor transcende les frontières de la soul, du funk et du Nord, un exploit phénoménal pour Adams et pour le compositeur David Jordan.

JOHNNIE TAYLOR

title EARGASM / *year* 1976 /
label CBS

John·nie Tay·lor *(Jŏn'ēē*
Tā'lōr) (see eargasm; earful)

ear·ful *(ēr'ful)* n-s. **1.a.** an astonishing unexpected aural re-
sponse **b:** an outpouring of news
or gossip **2:** a sharp reprimand
3: the music of Johnnie Taylor

ear·ga·sm *(ēr'gaz·ĕm)* n-s:
a paroxysm of emotional and
auditory excitation or instance
or climax of such excitement
sufficient to cause release of tension and a state of beatitude

ear·gas·mic *(ēr'gaz·mik)* adj.
1: like or suggestive of an eargasm **2:** tending to produce an
eargasm

ear·ing *(ēr'ing)* n-s: a line used
to fasten a corner of a sail to the
yard or gaff to haul a reef cringle
to the yard.

FEATURING
THE SMASH HIT
SINGLE
"DISCO LADY"

STEREO
GS949

SLAVE
HEY JUDE
IT'S YOUR THING
I CAN'T GET NEXT TO YOU
MESSAGE FROM A BLACK MAN
DON'T LET THE JONESES GET YOU DOWN

GS949

THE TEMPTATIONS

title **PUZZLE PEOPLE** / *year* **1969** / *label* Tamla Motown / *design* Curtis McNair / *photography* P. Bass

Curtis McNair's groovy, hip covers captured Motown during its high-water mark from 1968 to 1972. As the label turned toward the psychedelic soul productions of Norman Whitfield, McNair seized the opportunity to push the boundaries of his designs. The marriage of The Temptations' most socially-conscious record with the playful visual pun of the cover created a perfect balance for where the group was at the time. **O**

Die kultigen, hippen Cover von Curtis McNair spiegeln Motown in der Blütezeit des Labels von 1968 bis 1972. Als sich Motown den psychedelischen Soulproduktionen von

Norman Whitfield zuwandte, ergriff McNair die Gelegenheit, die Grenzen seiner Gestaltungskunst zu erweitern. Die Verbindung dieser sozialkritischen Scheibe der Temptations mit den verspielten visuellen Anspielungen des Covers ist perfekt ausbalanciert und dokumentiert den damaligen Status quo der Gruppe. **O**

Les pochettes branchées et groovy de Curtis McNair dépeignent Motown au sommet de sa gloire, entre 1968 et 1972. À l'époque où le label se tournait vers la soul psychédélique de Norman Whitfield, McNair a saisi cette occasion pour repousser les limites de ses créations graphiques. Le disque des Temptations à la conscience sociale la plus aiguë, allié au jeu de mots visuel de la pochette, crée un équilibre parfait pour décrire le groupe tel qu'il était à l'époque.

THE TEMPTATIONS
title **ALL DIRECTIONS** / *year* **1972** /
label Tamla Motown

Although the marquee leads of recently departed David
Ruffin and Eddie Kendricks are absent here, *All Directions*
fires on all pistons, thanks largely to the compositional
prowess of producer in shining armor Norman Whitfield,
whose "Papa Was A Rollin' Stone" became an instant
smash and a certified Temptations standard. **O**
Obwohl hier die Schlüsselstimmen der kurz vor der Aufnahme ausgeschiedenen Sänger David Ruffin und Eddie

Kendricks fehlen, wird auf *All Directions* aus allen Rohren
geschossen. Das ist weitgehend dem kompositorischen
Können von Norman Whitfield zu verdanken, diesem
Produzenten ohne Furcht und Tadel, dessen »Papa Was
A Rollin' Stone« sofort zu einem Riesenerfolg und einem
amtlichen Temptations-Standard wurde. **O**
Bien que privé des voix des chanteurs principaux David
Ruffin et Eddie Kendricks, qui venaient de quitter le groupe,
All Directions roule à toute vapeur, en grande partie grâce
aux prouesses de composition du producteur Norman
Whitfield, responsable de l'énorme succès *Papa Was A
Rollin' Stone*, un grand classique des Temptations.

THE TEMPTATIONS

title **SOLID ROCK** / *year* **1971** / *label*
Tamla Motown / *photography* James
Hendin / *art direction* Curtis McNair /
cover concept Norman Whitfield

LEON THOMAS

title **BLUES AND THE SOULFUL
TRUTH** / *year* **1972** / *label* Flying
Dutchman / *design* Haig Adishian /
photography Giuseppe Pino

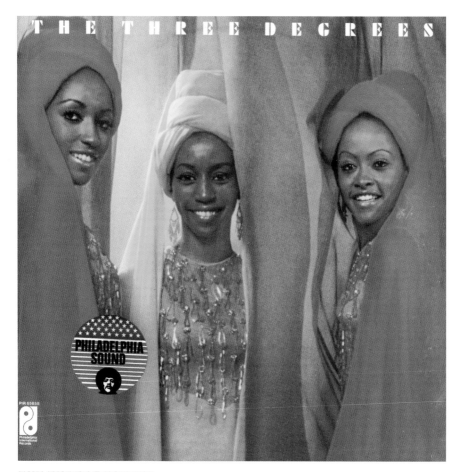

THE THREE DEGREES

title **THE THREE DEGREES** / *year* **1973** /
label Philadelphia International / *design* Ed Lee /
photography Owen Brown

Owen Brown's exotic photo of the sweet young girls in
flowing head wrappings on the front cover to the Three
Degrees' debut on Philadelphia International is hiding a
secret on the inside of the gatefold cover where the sheer
body-suits are completely see-through. This was much
like the women's music, which was syrupy sweet on the
outside but once you listened a little closer there was a
definite undercurrent of sexuality. **O**
Owen Browns exotisches Foto der süßen Mädels in fließen-
den Kopftüchern auf dem Frontcover ihres Debüts auf

Philadelphia International verbirgt ein Geheimnis, das erst
bei ausgeklapptem Cover gelüftet wird: Die dünnen Body-
suits sind vollständig durchsichtig. Das passte sehr gut zur
Musik dieser Frauen, die oberflächlich sirupartig süß war,
doch wenn man ein wenig genauer hinhörte, gab es eindeutig sexuelle Unterströmungen. **O**
La photo exotique d'Owen Brown mettant en scène trois
jeunes filles en turbans fluides sur la pochette du premier
album des Three Degrees chez Philadelphia International
cache un secret : à l'intérieur, les justaucorps sont complètement transparents. Ce concept reflète assez fidèlement la
musique de ces femmes, sirupeuse au premier abord, mais
parcourue d'un courant sous-jacent de sensualité dès que
l'on écoute les paroles.

BOBBY THURSTON
title **THE MAIN ATTRACTION** /
year **1981** / *label* Prelude /
photography Trudy Schlachter

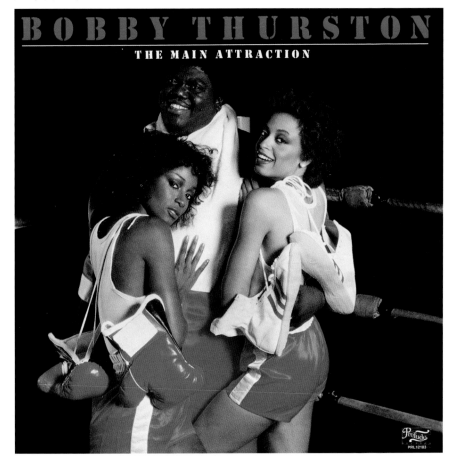

TIMELESS LEGEND

title **SYNCHRONIZED** / *year* **1976** / *label* Escrow /
design Darlene Scales / *photography* John Ellis /
art direction Darlene Scales

The design for the cover of this incredibly rare LP is quite
inventive in its presentation of a visual pun. The hour-
glasses on either side of the grandfather clock break the
cover plane into four symmetrical spaces that are each
filled with one of the singers of this sweet soul group from
Columbus, Ohio. The designer even went so far as to break
the title in half to emphasize the idea of synchronization. **O**
Die Gestaltung der Hülle dieser exzeptionellen LP präsentiert ihren visuellen Gag sehr einfallsreich. Die Sanduhren
auf beiden Seiten der Standuhr teilen die Fläche des Covers
in vier symmetrische Bereiche auf, die jeweils mit einem der
Sänger dieser harmonischen Soul-Gruppe aus Columbus,
Ohio, besetzt sind. Der Gestalter ging sogar so weit, den
Titel aufzuteilen, um das Konzept der Synchronisierung zu
unterstreichen. **O**
La pochette de cet album incroyablement rare fait preuve
d'une belle inventivité pour illustrer un jeu de mots visuel.
De chaque côté de la vieille horloge, les sabliers découpent
l'espace en quatre sections symétriques occupées par les
chanteurs de ce groupe de sweet soul originaire de Columbus, dans l'Ohio. Le graphiste est allé jusqu'à couper le titre
en deux pour souligner l'idée de synchronisation.

TONI TORNADO

title **TONI TORNADO** /
year **1972** / *label* Odeon /
design Joselito

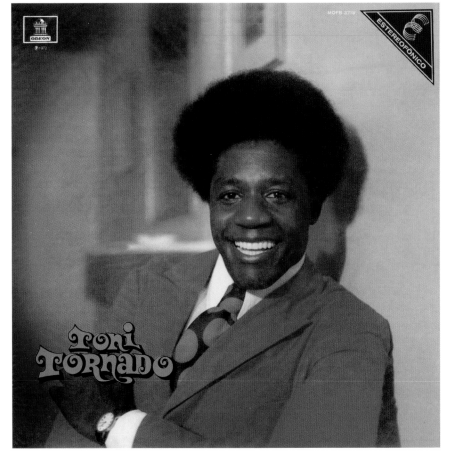

TOUCH OF CLASS
title **I'M IN HEAVEN** / *year* **1976** /
label Midland International /
art direction Acy Lehman & Dick
Smith / *illustration* Richard Sparks

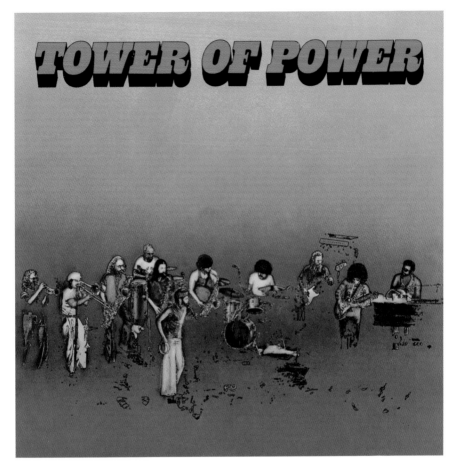

TOWER OF POWER

title **TOWER OF POWER** / *year* **1973** / *label* Warner Bros. / *design* Bruce Steinberg / *photography* Bruce Steinberg / *illustration* Bruce Steinberg

The brass-powered funk of this Oakland, CA band had been laying down stone-cold grooves for a couple of albums, but when singer Lenny Williams joined the mix it took them to another level. San Francisco Bay Area photographer Bruce Steinberg captured some of the greatest moments of his home town's music scene from the mid-'60s onward. His solarized color shot for this cover captured the electrifying energy of the band at the height of their power. **O**

Mit ihrem bläserlastigen Funk hatte diese Band aus dem kalifornischen Oakland schon auf mehreren Alben knochenharte Grooves abgeliefert, doch als Lenny Williams als Sänger zu diesem Mix stieß, hoben sie auf ganz andere Ebenen ab. Der Fotograf Bruce Steinberg aus der San Francisco Bay Area hielt ab Mitte der 60er Jahre viele besondere Momente aus der Musikszene seiner Heimatstadt fest. Sein solarisiertes Farbfoto für dieses Cover fängt die elektrisierende Energie der Band am Höhepunkt ihrer Kraft ein. **O**

Ce groupe d'Oakland (Californie) au funk très cuivré avait déjà gravé des grooves puristes sur quelques albums, mais l'arrivée du chanteur Lenny Williams leur ouvrit de nouveaux horizons. Le photographe Bruce Steinberg, actif dans la région de la baie de San Francisco, a fixé sur la pellicule quelques-uns des plus grands moments de la scène musicale de sa ville à partir du milieu des années 1960. Pour cette pochette, sa photo en couleur solarisée transmet l'énergie électrisante du groupe au sommet de son art.

TRAMMPS

title **THE LEGENDARY ZING ALBUM FEATURING THE FABULOUS TRAMMPS** / year **1975** / label Buddah / photography J. Paul Simone / packaging Milton Sincoff

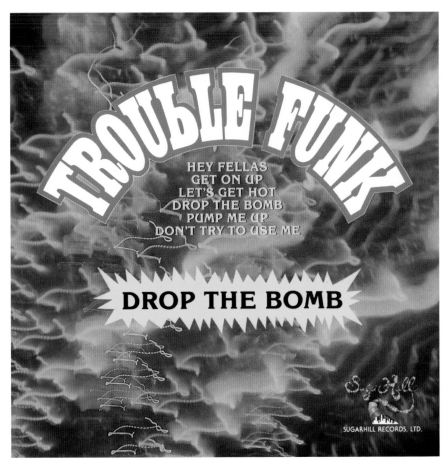

HEY FELLAS
GET ON UP
LET'S GET HOT
DROP THE BOMB
PUMP ME UP
DON'T TRY TO USE ME

DROP THE BOMB

SUGARHILL RECORDS, LTD.

TROUBLE FUNK

title **DROP THE BOMB** / *year* **1982** / *label* Sugarhill / *design* AQ Graphics Inc. / *photography* Hemu Aggarwal

Taking their cue from Chuck Brown and the Soul Searchers, this Washington, D.C. outfit let loose a nitro-powered version of their indigenous go-go music. Punctuated by a syncopated rhythm created by an unusual assortment of percussion instruments, "Pump Me Up" gave this group one of the musical form's biggest hits. **o**
Diese Truppe aus Washington, D.C., nahm sich Chuck Brown und seine Soul Searchers zum Vorbild und zündete

eine nitrogetränkte Version ihrer ureigenen Go-Go-Musik. Akzentuiert durch den synkopierten Rhythmus einer ungewöhnlichen Ansammlung von Percussion-Instrumenten wurde das »Pump Me Up« dieser Gruppe einer der größten Hits dieser Musikform. **o**
Sur les traces de Chuck Brown and the Soul Searchers, ce groupe de Washington, D.C. a lancé une version nitro-propulsée de leur musique go-go. Ponctué par un rythme syncopé fait d'un assortiment inhabituel de percussions, *Pump Me Up* a donné à Trouble Funk l'un de ses plus grands succès.

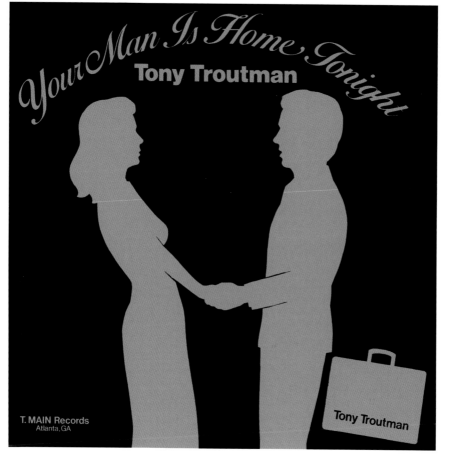

ACT 1
TURNER BROS.

LUV N' HAIGHT

TURNER BROS.

title **ACT I** / *year* **1999** / *label* Luv N' Haight /
photography Harvey C. Riedel

This late '90s reissue of the Turner Bros.' ultra-rare self-
released LP is brimming with raw funk. The group hailed
from Indianapolis and toured the Chitlin' Circuit for years
before they got it together to put this record out. On its
strength they were able to book tours opening for the likes
of Rufus Thomas, The Chi-Lites, and The Ohio Players,
among others. **O**

Diese Ende der 90er Jahre erschienene Neuauflage der ultra-
seltenen, im Selbstverlag veröffentlichten LP der Turner Bros.
ist vollgepackt mit rauem Funk. Die Gruppe stammt aus
Indianapolis und tourte jahrelang im Chitlin' Circuit (eine
Reihe von Musiktheatern, in denen während der Rassen-
trennung in den USA Künstler afroamerikanischer Herkunft
sicher auftreten konnten), bevor sie sich aufrafften, diese
Platte herauszubringen. Mit dem Rückenwind dieser Veröffentlichung durften sie als Vorgruppe für Künstler wie Rufus
Thomas, The Chi-Lites und die Ohio Players auftreten. **O**

La réédition sortie dans les années 1990 de cet album autoproduit ultrarare est débordante de funk brut. Les Turner
Bros, originaires d'Indianapolis, ont tourné pendant des
années sur le circuit « Chitlin' » des établissements ouverts
aux Afro-Américains du sud et de l'est des États-Unis avant
de réussir à sortir cet album. C'est grâce à lui qu'ils ont pu
faire la première partie d'artistes tels que Rufus Thomas,
The Chi-Lites et The Ohio Players, entre autres.

IKE & TINA TURNER

NUTBUSH CITY LIMITS

IKE & TINA TURNER

title **NUTBUSH CITY LIMITS** / *year* **1973** / *label* United Artists / *design* Lloyd Ziff / *photography* Fred Valentine / *art direction* Mike Salisbury / *illustration* Dave Willardson

Although it's unclear how many Chevy trucks Tina kicked during her days in Nutbush, Tennessee, many of the landmarks mentioned in this semi-autobiographical song are pictured in this whimsical illustration of Turner's hometown. Whether the building on the left is a schoolhouse or a gin house, we can be quite certain the building opposite is an outhouse. ◐

Zwar ist nicht ganz klar, wie vielen Chevy-Trucks Tina Turner in ihrer Zeit in Nutbush, Tennessee, vor den Kühler trat,

doch die skurrile Illustration von Tinas Heimatstadt zeigt viele der Sehenswürdigkeiten aus diesem halbautobiografischen Song. Wir wissen nicht, ob es sich bei dem Haus links um ein Schulgebäude oder ein Gin House handelt, aber gegenüber steht ganz sicher das Plumpsklo. ◐

On ne sait pas combien de coups de pied Tina a donnés à des pick-ups Chevrolet lorsqu'elle vivait à Nutbush, dans le Tennessee, mais cette illustration humoristique de la ville natale de Turner réunit un bon nombre des éléments décrits dans cette chanson autobiographique. Que le bâtiment de gauche soit une école ou un bar, on peut parier que celui qui est en face sert de toilettes de campagne.

IKE & TINA TURNER
title **RIVER DEEP – MOUNTAIN HIGH** / *year* **1966** /
label A&M / *photography* Dennis Hopper

Actor Dennis Hopper, who has always maintained an
active interest in photography, composed this Ike and Tina
cover from two informal shoots. An enormous movie
poster from a Hollywood sign-shop provided a feminine
backdrop for the photo on the right, while an advertise-
ment for a nearby gas company supplied the oversized
flame used for the close-up on the left. **O**
Der Schauspieler Dennis Hopper hatte stets ein aktives
Interesse an der Fotografie und komponierte dieses Cover

für Ike und Tina aus zwei informellen Shootings. Ein riesiges
Filmplakat aus einem Posterladen in Hollywood bot die
feminine Kulisse für das Foto rechts, während das Werbe-
plakat eines nahe gelegenen Gasunternehmens für die
Flamme in Übergröße sorgte, die bei der Nahaufnahme
links eingesetzt wurde. **O**
L'acteur Dennis Hopper, qui s'est toujours intéressé activement à la photographie, a composé cette pochette pour
Ike et Tina à partir de deux clichés informels. Une énorme
affiche de cinéma provenant d'une boutique de Hollywood
donne un fond féminin à la photo de droite, tandis qu'une
publicité pour une société pétrolière a fourni la flamme
surdimensionnée utilisée pour le gros plan de gauche.

STANLEY TURRENTINE
title **THE BADDEST TURRENTINE** / *year* **1974** / *label* CTI / *design* Bob Ciano / *photography* Alen MacWeeney

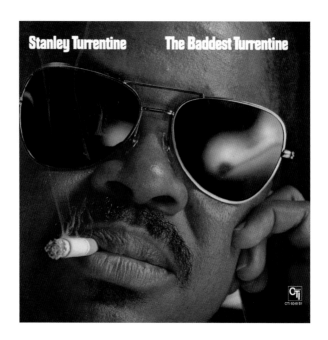

TWENNYNINE FEATURING LENNY WHITE
title **BEST OF FRIENDS** / *year* **1979** / *label* Elektra

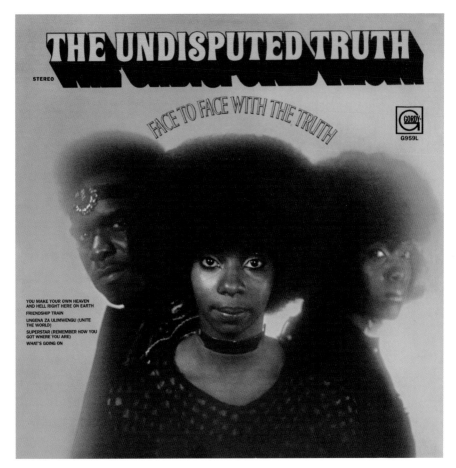

THE UNDISPUTED TRUTH

title **FACE TO FACE WITH THE TRUTH** / *year* **1971** / *label* Gordy / *photography* James Hendin / *art direction* Curtis McNair / *cover concept* Norman Whitfield

James Hendin was one of the great photographers in the trenches at Motown during the label's heyday. The long exposure on this confrontational portrait of the band gives it a hazy quality, which reflects the psychedelic soul that producer Norman Whitfield was popularizing at the time. ❍

James Hendin war einer der großen Motown-Fotografen in der Blütezeit des Labels. Die lange Belichtungszeit verleiht diesem konfrontativen Porträt der Band seine verschleierte Qualität, die dem vom Produzenten Norman Whitfield zu jener Zeit popularisierten psychedelischen Soul entspricht. ❍

James Hendin était l'un des grands photographes de Motown pendant l'âge d'or du label. Sur ce portrait qui met le spectateur face à face avec le groupe, l'exposition longue produit un halo qui évoque la soul psychédélique que le producteur Norman Whitfield cherchait à populariser à l'époque.

UNIVERSAL ROBOT BAND
title **DANCE AND SHAKE YOUR TAMBOURINE** /
year **1977** / *label* Panther

Prolific New York producers Patrick Adams and Greg
Carmichael are joined by Leroy Burgess (of Black Ivory
fame), Gregory Tolbert, and Woody Cunningham on this
spaced-out, Moog-filled disco odyssey. Originally released
on Carmichael's Red Greg label, the beat-driven title cut
was a disco classic that became a popular track for breakdancers. **O**
Die überaus produktiven New Yorker Produzenten Patrick
Adams und Greg Carmichael werden bei dieser abgespaceten Disco-Odyssee voller Moog-Klänge unterstützt von
Leroy Burgess (bekannt durch Black Ivory), Gregory Tolbert
und Woody Cunningham. Der Titelsong wurde ursprünglich auf Carmichaels Label Red Greg veröffentlicht. Sein
treibender Beat machte ihn zum Disco-Klassiker und zu
einem beliebten Stück für Breakdancer. **O**
Les prolifiques producteurs new-yorkais Patrick Adams et
Greg Carmichael font équipe avec Leroy Burgess (de Black
Ivory), Gregory Tolbert et Woody Cunningham sur cette
odyssée disco planante qui marche au synthétiseur Moog.
Le morceau-titre très rythmé, initialement édité chez le
label Red Greg de Carmichael, était un classique du disco
et est devenu très populaire chez les breakdancers.

UPCHURCH/TENNYSON

PHIL UPCHURCH & TENNYSON STEPHENS

title **UPCHURCH / TENNYSON** / *year* **1975** / *label* Kudu / *design* Bob Ciano / *photography* Victor Skrebneski

Phil Upchurch was one of the hardest-working musicians on the Chicago scene. His funky guitar and bass playing can be heard on a large number of the blues, jazz, and R&B sessions coming out of the Windy City from the '50s onward. Award-winning art director Bob Ciano's stark cover design lends an air of cool mystery to this sophisticated funk outing. **O**

Phil Upchurch war einer der am härtesten arbeitenden Musiker der Chicagoer Szene. Sein funkiges Gitarren- und Bassspiel findet sich auf einer großen Zahl von Blues-, Jazz- und R&B-Sessions, die seit den 50er Jahren in der Windy City erschienen waren. Der preisgekrönte Art Director Bob Ciano schmückt durch seine ungewöhnliche Covergestaltung diese ausgefeilte Funk-Aufnahme mit dem Flair eines coolen Mysteriums. **O**

Phil Upchurch était l'un des musiciens les plus actifs sur la scène de Chicago. On peut entendre le jeu funky de sa guitare et de sa basse sur de nombreuses sessions de blues, de jazz et de R&B enregistrées dans cette ville à partir des années 1950. La pochette austère du directeur artistique primé Bob Ciano prête un air de mystère et de classe à cet album de funk sophistiqué.

STAX RECORDS STEREO SXD 103

SWEET SWEETBACK'S BAADASSSSS SONG

MELVIN VAN PEEBLES
title **SWEET SWEETBACK'S BAADASSSSS SONG** /
year **1971** / *label* Stax

A pioneer not only in film, Melvin Van Peebles blazed the
trail for the movie soundtrack. In 1971 he had no budget
for advertising on his first, independently produced film.
Van Peebles had composed the music, but needed a band
to play it. His secretary was going out with a member of
the as-yet-undiscovered group, Earth, Wind & Fire. In a
stroke of genius he released the soundtrack first as a way to
get word out about the film before anyone had seen it. **O**
Melvin Van Peebles war nicht nur im Film ein Pionier, sondern bahnte auch den Weg für den Filmsoundtrack. 1971
hatte er für seinen ersten selbst produzierten Independent-
Film keinen Werbeetat. Van Peebles hatte die Musik kom-

poniert und brauchte eine Band, die sie spielte. Seine Sekre-
tärin ging mit einem Mitglied der damals noch unbekannten
Gruppe Earth, Wind & Fire aus. Sein genialer Einfall war,
zuerst den Soundtrack herauszubringen, um den Film ins
Gespräch zu bringen, noch bevor ihn überhaupt jemand
gesehen hatte. **O**
Melvin Van Peebles n'était pas seulement un pionnier du
film, il a également débroussaillé la voie pour les bandes
originales de films. En 1971, il n'avait pas de budget publici-
taire pour son premier film indépendant. Van Peebles avait
composé la musique, mais avait besoin d'un groupe pour la
jouer. Sa secrétaire sortait avec un membre d'Earth, Wind &
Fire, un groupe encore inconnu à l'époque. Sur un coup de
génie, il sortit la bande sonore en premier afin de faire parler du film avant que quiconque ait eu l'occasion de le voir.

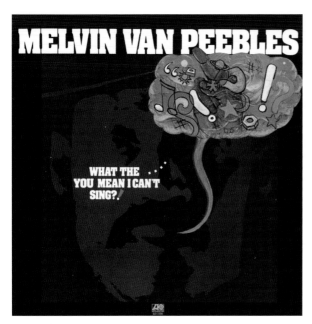

MELVIN VAN PEEBLES
title **WHAT THE ... YOU MEAN I CAN'T SING?!** / *year* **1974** / *label* Atlantic / *design* David & Mark Rubin / *art direction* Abdul Rahman

VARIOUS
title **LET'S CLEAN UP THE GHETTO** / *year* **1977** / *label* Philadelphia International / *design* Ed Lee / *photography* John Pinderhughes

THE VOICES OF EAST HARLEM

title **RIGHT ON BE FREE** / *year* **1970** / *label* Elektra /
photography Jan Blom, Bruce Davidson & Carl Samrock

A highly energetic youth choir whose ages ranged from 12
to 21, the Voices were often 20-strong as they clapped and
stomped their way through a set of gut funky gospel soul.
The stark, black & white cover is appropriately balanced
between its socio-political imagery and the type, which
keeps the buoyant side of the affair in equal measure. **O**
Die Voices waren ein höchst energetischer Jugendchor im
Alter zwischen 12 und 21, und oft waren sie 20 Mann stark,

wenn sie sich den Weg durch ihren Set mit funkigem
Gospel-Soul klatschten und stampften. Das sachliche
Schwarzweiß-Cover balanciert ganz angemessen zwischen
soziopolitischer Bildsprache und Schrift, wodurch die
beschwingte Seite der Angelegenheit ebenso gewürdigt
wird. **O**
The Voices, un chœur plein d'énergie composé de chanteurs âgés de 12 à 21 ans, était souvent fort de 20 membres
tapant des mains et des pieds sur de la soul gospel funky à
souhait. La pochette sobre en noir et blanc trouve un équilibre entre l'image sociopolitique et le côté léger de l'album,
représenté par la typographie.

DAVID T. WALKER

title **DAVID T. WALKER AND THE
REAL T.** / *year* **1973** / *label* Ode /
design Chuck Beeson / *photography*
Jim McCrary / *art direction* Roland
Young

DEXTER WANSEL

title **LIFE ON MARS** / *year* **1976** / *label* CBS / *design*
Chris Peterson & Gerard Huerta / *photography* Eric Meola
& Danny Wong / *art direction* Ed Lee

One of many credits for Gerard Huerta, a Southern
California designer who works mostly in letter-forms.
A graduate of the Art Center College of Design, Huerta
has created lasting logos for rockers Ted Nugent, Boston
soul luminaries The Isley Brothers, Harold Melvin and
the Blue Notes, and jazzers George Benson and Ramsey
Lewis. **O**

Eine der vielen Arbeiten des Grafikdesigners Gerard Huerta
aus Südkalifornien, der vor allem mit Buchstabenformen
arbeitet. Er besuchte das Art Center College of Design und
hat langlebige Logos für Rockstars wie Ted Nugent und
Boston, Soulgestirne wie die Isley Brothers und Harold
Melvin and the Blue Notes und Jazzer wie George Benson
und Ramsey Lewis geschaffen. **O**

Le graphiste de Californie du Sud Gerard Huerta travaille
principalement sur les lettres. Diplômé de l'Art Center
College of Design, il a créé des logos pour les rockers Ted
Nugent et Boston, les maîtres de la soul des Isley Brothers,
Harold Melvin and the Blue Notes, et les jazzmen George
Benson et Ramsey Lewis.

WAR

title **GALAXY** / *year* **1977** / *label* MCA / *photography*
Tom Bert / *art direction* Lee Oskar, Larry Marmorstein
& George Osaki

Tom Bert's darkly humorous cover for War's last LP with
its classic line-up hints at the group's future – they are on
the street with their gear and logo ready to move on to
the next gig – while touching on the group's eclectic,
politically-charged past. This powerhouse band's ability to
build densely-packed grooves from Latin, jazz, and funk
bases is as strong as ever, even when they try their hands
at disco as with the title cut. **O**

Schwarzer Humor prägt das Cover von Tom Bert für die
letzte LP von War in ihrer klassischen Besetzung – es
deutet die Zukunft der Band an: Sie stehen mit gepackten

Sachen und ihrem Logo auf der Straße und sind bereit,
zum nächsten Gig aufzubrechen. Gleichzeitig greift es die
vielseitige, politisch aktive Vergangenheit der Band auf.
So kraftvoll wie eh und je vermag diese Powerband, dicht-
gepackte Grooves aus Latin, Jazz und Funk zu zimmern,
auch wenn sie es wie beim Titelsong diesmal mit Disco
probieren. **O**

L'humour noir de la pochette de Tom Bert pour le dernier
album de War avec tous ses membres d'origine présage de
l'avenir du groupe (ils sont dans la rue, avec leur matériel et
leur logo, prêts à aller donner un concert) tout en faisant
allusion à son passé éclectique et politique. Ce groupe explosif n'a rien perdu de sa capacité à composer des rythmes
denses sur des bases de musique latine, de jazz et de funk,
même lorsqu'ils s'essaient au disco, par exemple avec le
morceau-titre.

© 1975 Far Out Productions

WAR

title **WHY CAN'T WE BE FRIENDS?** / *year* **1975** /
label United Artists / *illustration* Howard Miller /
cover concept Lee Oskar

The simple graphic depiction of a grinning face with one
gold tooth is a fitting one for the joyfully sweaty grooves
contained in this, one of War's biggest records. From the
title cut to the massive Chicano funk hit, "Low Rider", the
band's signature bouillabaisse of multi-cultural sounds was
never better. **O**

Die einfache grafische Darstellung eines grinsenden
Gesichts mit Goldzahn passt ausgezeichnet zu den fröh-
lich-schwitzigen Grooves dieser Platte – eine der größten
Aufnahmen von War. Vom Titelstück bis zum massiven
Chicano-Funk-Hit »Low Rider« war die typische Bouillabaisse der Band aus multikulturellen Klängen nie besser. **O**
Le graphisme simple de ce visage à large sourire et à dent
en or convient parfaitement aux grooves moites et enjoués
de cet album, l'un des plus grands de War. Du morceau-
titre à l'énorme tube de funk chicano *Low Rider*, le mélange
de sons multiculturels caractéristique du groupe n'a jamais
été meilleur que sur ce disque.

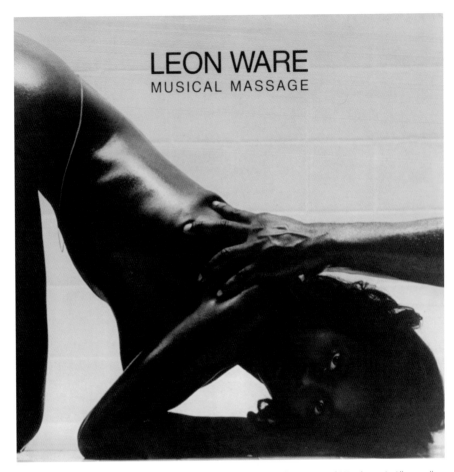

LEON WARE
MUSICAL MASSAGE

LEON WARE

title **MUSICAL MASSAGE** / *year* **1976** / *label* Motown /
photography Sam Emerson / *art direction* Frank Mulvey

Frank Mulvey's clean design for this cover forgoes sub-text
and reaches right out to touch you, much like Leon Ware's
sex-filled compositions. Ware had written an album's-
worth of sensual soul that he intended to record himself,
but was "persuaded" by Berry Gordy to give the songs to
Marvin Gaye in exchange for a chance to produce the
album *I Want You*. When he refused to give up his next
batch of tunes, Gordy let him record this LP, but yanked
the promotion budget. **O**
Das klare Coverdesign von Frank Mulvey verzichtet auf
unterschwellige Botschaften und wendet sich direkt an den
Betrachter, um ihn anzurühren – so wie Leon Wares Kom-

positionen voller Sex-Appeal. Ware hatte ein Album voller
sinnlicher Soulmusik geschrieben, das er eigentlich selbst
aufnehmen wollte. Berry Gordy »überredete« ihn aber, die
Songs Marvin Gaye zu überlassen, um im Gegenzug das
Album *I Want You* produzieren zu können. Als er sich weigerte, seinen nächsten Schwung Songs abzutreten, ließ Gordy ihn diese LP aufnehmen, kappte aber den Werbeetat. **O**
Le design de Frank Mulvey pour cette pochette renonce au
sous-texte et entreprend de toucher directement le spectateur, à l'instar des compositions très érotiques de Leon Ware.
Ware avait écrit un album regorgeant de soul sensuelle qu'il
voulait enregistrer lui-même, mais Berry Gordy le « persua-
da » de donner les chansons à Marvin Gaye en échange de
l'opportunité de produire l'album *I Want You*. Lorsqu'il refu-
sa de céder le lot suivant de mélodies, Gordy le laissa enregistrer cet album, mais massacra le budget promotionnel.

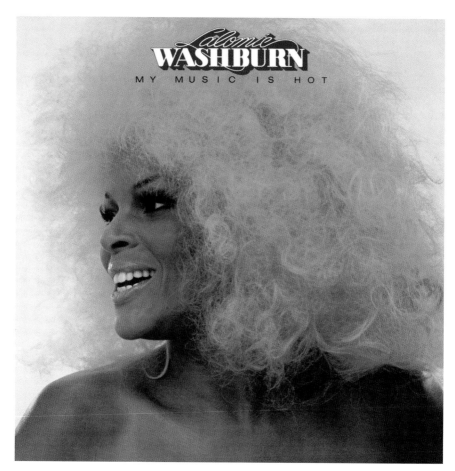

LALOMIE WASHBURN

title **MY MUSIC IS HOT** / *year* **1977** / *label* Parachute / *design* Gribbitt! / *photography* Gary Heery / *art direction* Phillis Chotin

Gribbitt! was formed in 1972 by George Whiteman and Dennis Lidtke as a small and speedy, 24/7 design studio that was set up to be an adjunct to a record company's art department. By the time disco came to the forefront they had grown exponentially with projects by superstars like Donna Summer, and Parliament. Besides being a powerful performer, Lalomie Washburn wrote and collaborated with acts like Rufus, Stevie Wonder, and Quincy Jones. **O**
Gribbitt! wurde 1972 von George Whiteman und Dennis Lidtke als kleines und flottes Designstudio gegründet, das rund um die Uhr geöffnet hat und den Kreativabteilungen von Plattenfirmen zuarbeitet. Beim Aufkommen von Disco wuchs die Agentur durch Projekte von Superstars wie Donna Summer und Parliament exponentiell. Neben ihren kraftvollen Auftritten auf der Bühne komponierte Lalomie Washburn und arbeitete mit Acts wie Rufus, Stevie Wonder und Quincy Jones zusammen. **O**
George Whiteman et Dennis Lidtke ont créé Gribbitt! en 1972. C'était un petit studio de design très réactif, ouvert 24 heures sur 24, pensé pour relayer le service artistique d'une maison de disques. À l'époque où le disco a pris le devant de la scène, le studio a connu une croissance exponentielle avec des projets pour des superstars telles que Donna Summer et Parliament. En plus d'être une artiste impressionnante à voir en action, Lalomie Washburn a écrit et collaboré avec des pointures comme Rufus, Stevie Wonder et Quincy Jones.

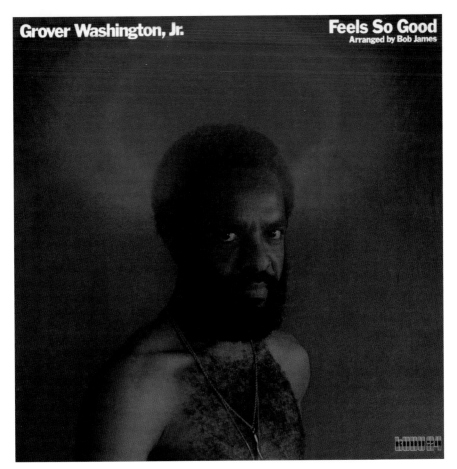

Grover Washington, Jr.

Feels So Good
Arranged by Bob James

GROVER WASHINGTON, JR.

title **FEELS SO GOOD** / *year* **1975** / *label* Kudu /
design Richard Mantel / *photography* Alen MacWeeney /
art direction Richard Mantel

Following the near-perfect formula forged on 1974's
Mr. Magic, Grover Washington, Jr. and arranger Bob James
returned to Rudy Van Gelder's New Jersey jazz sanctuary
to further advance their collaborative soul-jazz vision. Alen
MacWeeney again photographed a shirtless Washington
for the cover, this time favoring the studio to the swim-
ming pool. **O**
Grover Washington Jr. und der Arrangeur Bob James folg-
ten der fast perfekten Formel, die sie 1974 für *Mr. Magic*

ersonnen hatten, und kehrten in Rudy Van Gelders Jazz-
Heiligtum in New Jersey zurück, um ihre gemeinsame
Vision eines Soul-Jazz noch weiter zu verfeinern. Alen
MacWeeney fotografierte für das Cover wieder einen bar-
brüstigen Washington und zog diesmal den Swimming-
pool dem Studio vor. **O**
Suivant la formule presque parfaite forgée sur *Mr. Magic* en
1974, Grover Washington Jr. et l'arrangeur Bob James sont
retournés au sanctuaire du jazz de Rudy Van Gelder dans
le New Jersey pour faire progresser leur vision collaborative
du soul-jazz. Alen MacWeeney a encore une fois photographié Washington sans sa chemise pour la pochette, mais
cette fois il a préféré le studio à la piscine.

JOHNNY "GUITAR" WATSON
title **FUNK BEYOND THE CALL OF DUTY** / *year* **1977** / *label* DJM / *photography* Jim McCrary / *art direction* David Krieger/DFK

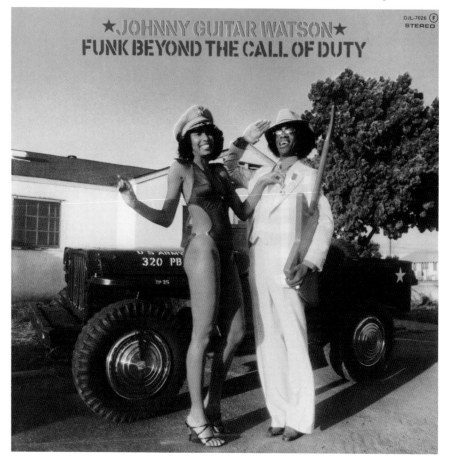

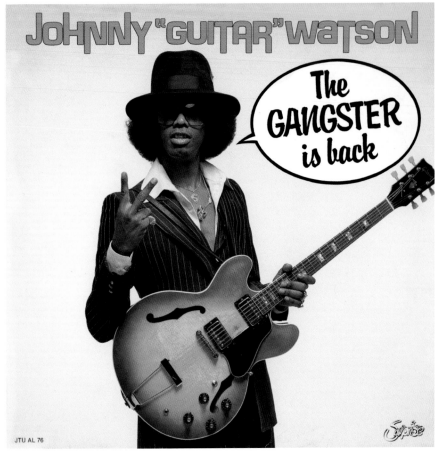

JTU AL 76

JOHNNY "GUITAR" WATSON
title **THE GANGSTER IS BACK** / year **1975** /
label Surprise

A pompadoured Johnny "Guitar" Watson debuted his raucous brand of blues in 1957 with "Gangster of Love". His often unorthodox guitar-playing would influence Frank Zappa and Stevie Ray Vaughan, among others. As the Houston-born Watson was on the verge of a full-fledged funk crossover, The *Gangster is Back* was released to educated audiences unfamiliar with the influential guitarist's bluesy roots. **o**

Johnny »Guitar« Watson trug zu seinem Debüt ein Haarstyling à la Pompadour und brachte 1957 mit seinem „Gangster of Love" seine ganz eigene heisere Bluesmarke

heraus. Sein oft unorthodoxes Gitarrenspiel sollte neben Frank Zappa auch Stevie Ray Vaughan und andere beeinflussen. Als der aus Houston stammende Watson sich kurz vor einem kompletten Funk-Crossover befand, kam *The Gangster is Back* heraus, damit sich das Publikum mit den Blueswurzeln des einflussreichen Musikers vertraut machen konnte. **o**

C'est un Johnny « Guitar » Watson coiffé d'une banane qui avait lancé son style de blues tapageur en 1957 avec *Gangster of Love*. Son jeu de guitare souvent anticonformiste allait influencer Frank Zappa et Stevie Ray Vaughan, entre autres. Alors que ce natif de Houston était sur le point de passer corps et âme du côté du funk, il a sorti *The Gangster is Back* pour éduquer le public qui ne connaissait pas les racines de ce guitariste influent nourri au blues.

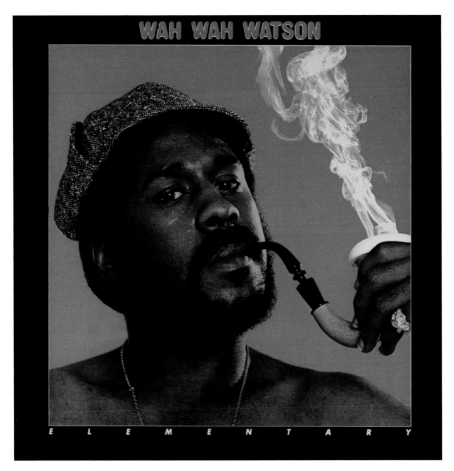

WAH WAH WATSON

ELEMENTARY

WAH WAH WATSON
title **ELEMENTARY** / *year* **1976** / *label* Columbia /
photography Herb Greene

Herb Greene's humorous portrait for the cover to Melvin
"Wah Wah Watson" Ragin's sole LP as a leader is fitting
on many levels. It's not only a funky take on the classic
Sherlock Holmes wingman, but it tells the tale of a musical
sidekick to many of the funk world's greatest geniuses.
Watson's signature guitar style can be heard on a plethora
of Motown hits including The Temptations' "Papa Was a
Rollin' Stone". **O**
Das humorvolle Porträt von Herb Greene für das Cover der
einzigen LP von Melvin »Wah Wah Watson« Ragin als
Bandleader ist in vielerlei Hinsicht stimmig. Es spielt nicht
nur humorvoll auf den klassischen Partner von Sherlock

Holmes an, sondern erzählt auch die Geschichte eines musikalischen Mitstreiters für viele der weltweit größten Ge-
nies des Funk. Watson ist mit seinem unverwechselbaren
Gitarrenspiel auf einer Vielzahl von Motown-Hits zu hören,
unter anderem auch bei »Papa Was a Rollin' Stone« von
den Temptations. **O**
Le portrait humoristique réalisé par Herb Greene pour la
pochette du seul album de Melvin « Wah Wah Watson »
Ragin en tant que leader met dans le mille à plusieurs titres.
Ce n'est pas seulement une interprétation funky du célèbre
compagnon de Sherlock Homes, car Wah Wah Watson a
également été l'acolyte des plus grands génies mondiaux
du funk. La guitare caractéristique de Watson se retrouve
sur une pléthore de succès de Motown, notamment
« Papa Was a Rollin' Stone » des Temptations.

THE WATTS 103rd
STREET RHYTHM BAND

title **IN THE JUNGLE, BABE** / *year* **1969** / *label* Warner
Bros. / *photography* Ivan Nagy / *art direction* Ed Thrasher

Art director Ed Thrasher was important in bringing the
art-form of cover graphics to the forefront in the 1960s.
There was a shift in this period from record covers being
something to protect the record to becoming a pre-MTV
way of representing the artist to the public in a new and
exciting way. *In The Jungle, Babe* was the third release from
Charles Wright and his outstanding L.A. funk group who
worked in a loose, improvisational style. **O**
Der Art Director Ed Thrasher hatte einen wesentlichen
Anteil daran, als die Covergestaltung in den 60er Jahren zur
Kunstform avancierte. In dieser Zeit wandelte sich die Be-

deutung des Covers von der Schutzhülle zu einer Art MTV-
Vorläufer: Der Künstler wurde dem Publikum auf eine neue
und spannende Weise vorgestellt. *In The Jungle, Babe* war
die dritte Veröffentlichung von Charles Wright und seiner
herausragenden Funk-Truppe aus L.A., die in einem lockeren, improvisierenden Stil arbeitete. **O**
Le directeur artistique Ed Thrasher a joué un rôle considé-
rable dans l'évolution des pochettes dans les années 1960.
C'est à cette époque qu'elles ont cessé d'être un simple
moyen de protéger le disque et sont devenues les ancêtres
de MTV, dans la mesure où elles ont commencé à servir à
présenter les artistes au public avec créativité. *In The Jungle,
Babe* était le troisième album de Charles Wright et de son
excellent groupe de funk de Los Angeles, qui ont travaillé
dans un esprit d'improvisation libre.

**THE WATTS 103rd
STREET RHYTHM
BAND**

title **TOGETHER** / *year* **1968** / *label*
Warner Bros. / *design* Bob Zoell /
photography George Whiteman /
art direction Ed Thrasher

JUNIOR WELLS
title **YOU'RE TUFF ENOUGH** / *year* **1968** /
label Mercury / *design* Mark Weinberg

Junior Wells was the James Brown of Chicago blues, injecting his own soulful laments with heavy doses of funk, trading off between grisly vocals and broad strokes of harmonica. Keeping the casual compositions in order was Chicago arranger Charles Stepney, who was responsible for much of Earth, Wind & Fire's most elegant output. ○ Junior Wells war der James Brown des Chicago-Blues. Er peppte seine eigenen souligen Lamenti hochdosiert mit Funk auf und wechselte zwischen grimmigem Gesang und ausgedehnten Ausbrüchen mit der Mundharmonika. Zur Aufgabe von Charles Stepney, dem Arrangeur aus Chicago, gehörte es, diese lockeren Kompositionen in Ordnung zu halten. Er zeichnet auch für vieles vom elegantesten Schaffen der Band Earth, Wind & Fire verantwortlich. ○ Junior Wells était le James Brown du blues de Chicago, et injectait des doses massives de funk dans ses propres lamentations en clé de soul, allant et venant entre les vocalises sinistres et les brassées d'harmonica. L'arrangeur Charles Stepney veillait à maintenir l'ordre dans ces compositions informelles. C'est à lui que l'on doit une bonne partie des productions les plus élégantes d'Earth, Wind & Fire.

WHATNAUTS

title **WHATNAUTS ON THE ROCKS** / *year* **1972** / *label* Stang / *design* Martin Bough

The title, *On the Rocks*, assumes abundant significance for the Baltimore trio as they sit atop a pile of boulders, super-imposed delicately on the inside of a cocktail glass. Perhaps the original intent of the title refers to the album's wealth of soulful laments, the most impressive of which were penned by in-house writer and arranger, George Kerr. ⭘ Der Titel *On the Rocks* unterstellt für das Trio aus Baltimore opulente Signifikanz, während sie auf einem filigran ins

Innere eines Cocktailglases eingepassten Felshaufen sitzen. Vielleicht bezieht sich die ursprüngliche Absicht des Titels auf die Überfülle an souligen Lamenti, von denen die beeindruckendsten vom hauseigenen Komponisten und Arrangeur George Kerr geschrieben wurden. ⭘ Le titre *On the Rocks* prend une tout autre signification pour ce trio de Baltimore, assis sur une pile de rochers placés délicatement à l'intérieur d'un verre à cocktail. À l'origine il fait peut-être référence aux lamentations expressives que renferme l'album, dont les plus impressionnantes ont été écrites par George Kerr, également arrangeur.

CLARENCE WHEELER
& THE ENFORCERS

title **DOIN' WHAT WE WANNA** / *year* **1970** / *label*
Atlantic / *design* Haig Adishian / *photography* Mel Kaspar

A stone-cold Clarence Wheeler is featured prominently on
this sizeable slab of Chicago organ funk. This group portrait
is typical of Atlantic designer Haig Adishian's work from the
early '70s, characterized by tightly-cropped artist portraits
set against black or unfocused backgrounds. **O**
Auf dem Cover dieser beachtlichen Scheibe voller Orgel-
Funk aus Chicago steht in der ersten Reihe ein eiskalt drein-

schauender Clarence Wheeler. Dieses Bandporträt ist
typisch für Haig Adishians Arbeiten aus den frühen 70er
Jahren. Er war Gestalter bei Atlantic und stellte gerne stark
angeschnittene Künstlerporträts vor einen schwarzen oder
unspezifischen Hintergrund. **O**
Cette belle tranche de funk assaisonné à l'orgue de Chicago
met en vedette un Clarence Wheeler au sommet de sa
forme. Le portrait de groupe de la pochette est caractéristique du travail du graphiste d'Atlantic Haig Adishian au
début des années 1970, qui aimait cadrer les artistes de près
sur un fond noir ou flou.

BARRY WHITE

title **THE MESSAGE IS LOVE** / *year* **1979** /
label Unlimited Gold / *design* Andy Engel /
art direction Tony Lane

For his first release on his own Unlimited Gold Records,
the Man with the Velvet Voice enlisted Andy Engel to
combine many elements indicative of White's brand of
sophisticated soul. The conductor's baton and white baby
grand piano no doubt allude to *The Message is Love*'s
compositional strength and rich orchestral presence. **O**
Für die erste Veröffentlichung auf seinem eigenen Label
Unlimited Gold Records engagierte der Mann mit der
Samtstimme Andy Engel, der die vielen Elemente kom-
binieren sollte, die als Markenzeichen für Barry Whites
raffinierten Soul gelten. Der Taktstock des Dirigenten und
der weiße Flügel spielen zweifellos auf die kompositorische
Strenge und die reichhaltige orchestrale Präsenz von *The
Message is Love* an. **O**
Pour son premier album sous son propre label Unlimited
Gold Records, l'Homme à la voix de velours a recruté Andy
Engel pour combiner les divers éléments qui caractérisent
sa soul sophistiquée. Le bâton de chef d'orchestre et le piano à queue blanc font sans aucun doute référence à la solide composition et à la riche orchestration de *The Message
is Love*.

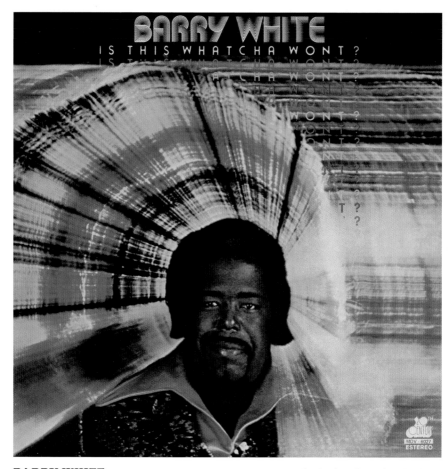

BARRY WHITE

title **IS THIS WHATCHA WONT?** / *year* **1976** /
label 20th Century / *design* Len Freas, Van Noy & Co. /
photography Gene Brownell

Using sci-fi effects and filters, Grammy award-winning photographer Gene Brownell makes Barry White look as much like Doctor Who as the Sultan of Smooth Soul in this psychedelic snapshot. For designer Len Freas, winning first prize in *Scholastic* magazine's National Art Contest at age 15 was just the start of a bountiful career in fine art. ✪
Unter Einsatz von Science-Fiction-Effekten und Filtern lässt der mit Grammys ausgezeichnete Fotograf Gene Brownell Barry White auf diesem psychedelischen Schnappschuss

wie einen Doctor Who als Sultan of Smooth Soul wirken. Für den Designer Len Freas, der im *National Painting*-Wettbewerb des Magazins *Scholastic* schon mit 15 den ersten Preis gewann, war dies der Beginn einer erfolgreichen Gestaltungskarriere. ✪
Le photographe Gene Brownell avait déjà gagné un prix Grammy lorsque, à l'aide d'effets de science-fiction et de filtres, il a réalisé ce portrait psychédélique de Barry White qui le fait ressembler à Doctor Who autant qu'au Sultan de la smooth soul. Pour le graphiste Len Freas, remporter le premier prix du concours national de peinture du magazine *Scholastic* à l'âge de 15 ans ne fut que le début d'une brillante carrière dans les beaux-arts.

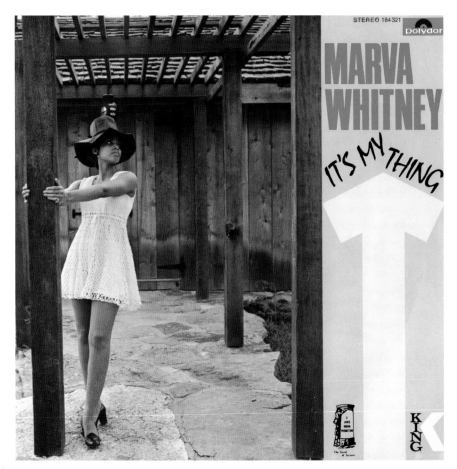

MARVA WHITNEY

title **IT'S MY THING** / *year* **1969** / *label* Polydor /
design Dan Quest Art Studio / *photography* Dan Quest
Art Studio

Perhaps the funkiest woman ever, Marva Whitney was
dubbed "Soul Sister #1". She toured with the James Brown
Revue from 1967–1969 and in that short time she recorded
some of the toughest funk cuts ever laid onto wax. She
easily stood toe to toe with the Godfather of Soul and had
a handful of hits, yet her debut full-length album did not
do well in the charts. **O**

Marva Whitney war wohl die funkigste Frau überhaupt,
weshalb ihr der Spitzname »Soul Sister # 1« verliehen
wurde. Sie tourte von 1967 bis 1969 mit der James Brown

Revue, und in dieser kurzen Zeit nahm sie ein paar der
schärfsten Funk-Cuts auf, die je auf Vinyl festgehalten wurden. Sie hielt mit Leichtigkeit mit dem Godfather of Soul
mit und hatte eine Handvoll Hits, aber in den Charts kam
ihr Debütalbum nicht sonderlich gut an. **O**

Marva Whitney est peut-être la femme la plus funky qui ait
jamais vécu, et elle a reçu le surnom de « Première Sœur de
la soul ». Elle est partie en tournée avec la James Brown
Revue de 1967 à 1969, et lors de cette courte période elle
a enregistré quelques-uns des morceaux de funk les plus
intransigeants jamais gravés dans la cire. Elle prenait sans
peine sa place à côté du Parrain de la soul sur un pied
d'égalité, et elle a eu une poignée de tubes, pourtant son
premier album n'a pas bien marché dans les classements.

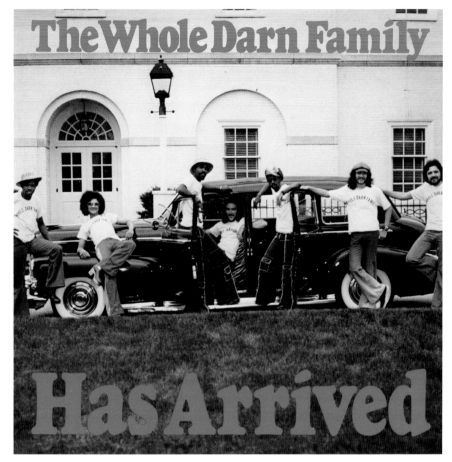

THE WHOLE DARN FAMILY

title **THE WHOLE DARN FAMILY HAS ARRIVED** /
year **1976** / *label* Soul International / *art direction*
August Moon

The laid-back funk of The Whole Darn Family, hailing from
Atlanta, GA, rolls along on a bed of rumbling bass-lines and
is held high by floating keys and a swinging horn section.
The sound is epitomized on "Seven Minutes of Funk", a
track that has been heavily sampled by the likes of EPMD
and Jay-Z. **o**
Der lässige Funk der Whole Darn Family aus Atlanta,
Georgia, rollt auf einem Fundament aus polterenden Bass-

linien herein und wird von schwebenden Pianoklängen und
der swingenden Bläsersektion unterstützt. Dieser Sound
wird von »Seven Minutes of Funk« versinnbildlicht, einem
Stück, das vielfach gesampelt wurde, z. B. von solchen Größen wie EPMD und Jay-Z. **o**
Le funk décontracté des Whole Darn Family, originaires
d'Atlanta, en Géorgie, roule sur des lignes de basse gron-
dantes et est tiré vers le haut par des claviers flottants et
des cuivres qui n'arrêtent pas de swinguer. *Seven Minutes
of Funk*, un morceau qui a été copieusement samp20é par
EPMD, Jay-Z et de nombreux autres illustre parfaitement
le son de l'album.

WILD CHERRY

title **WILD CHERRY** / *year* **1976** /
label CBS / *photography* Frank
Laffitte / *cover concept* Bob Rath

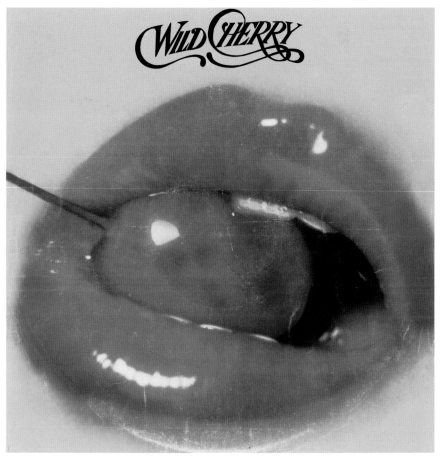

THE WILD MAGNOLIAS WITH THE NEW ORLEANS PROJECT

title **THE WILD MAGNOLIAS** / *year* **1974** / *label* Polydor / *design* Ted Pettus/Kameny Associates / *photography* Michael P. Smith / *illustration* Joseph "Monk" Boudreaux

In 1964, Bo Dollis became Big Chief of the Mardi Gras Indian marching group the Wild Magnolias. They had been involved in the local "Indian masking" tradition of New Orleans since the 1950s, but this was their debut album. Backed by a slew of New Orleans funk stalwarts this is a rocking party album. Co-leader of the group Joseph "Monk" Boudreaux contributed the bead design on the cover. **O** 1964 wurde Bo Dollis zum Big Chief der Mardi Gras Indian Marching Group namens The Wild Magnolias ernannt. Sie

beschäftigten sich seit den 50er Jahren mit der »Indian Masking«-Tradition von New Orleans, doch dies war ihr Debütalbum. Mit Unterstützung einer Bande Funk-Fans aus New Orleans schufen sie ein rockendes Party-Album. Der Co-Leiter der Gruppe, Joseph »Monk« Boudreaux, sorgte für das Glasperlendesign des Covers. **O** En 1964, Bo Dollis est devenu Grand chef de la fanfare indienne de Mardi Gras, The Wild Magnolias. Le groupe participait à la tradition locale de la mascarade indienne de la Nouvelle-Orléans depuis les années 1950, mais ceci était leur premier album. Soutenu par une pléthore d'inconditionnels du funk de la Nouvelle-Orléans, c'est un disque pour faire la fête. Le tableau en perles de la pochette est une réalisation du co-leader du groupe, Joseph « Monk » Boudreaux.

BOBBY WILLIAMS
title **"FUNKY SUPER FLY"** /
year **1974** / *label* R&R / *design*
Guy Norman & Dr. Bob Blow /
photography Jimmie Zilliner

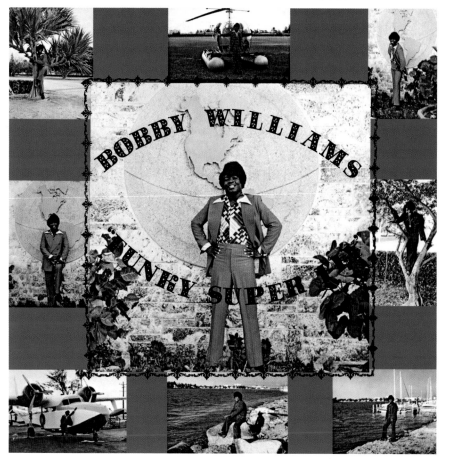

DENIECE WILLIAMS

title **THIS IS NIECY** / *year* **1976** / *label* CBS / *design* Ron Coro & Norm Ung / *photography* Ethan Russell

Accompanied by the Earth, Wind & Fire rhythm section and produced by Charles Stepney, songbird Deniece Williams makes a stunning debut with *This is Niecy*. American photographer Ethan Russell holds the distinct honor of shooting album covers for The Beatles, The Rolling Stones, and The Who. ⭘

Deniece Williams wird auf ihrem atemberaubenden Debüt *This is Niecy* von der Rhythm-Section von Earth, Wind &

Fire begleitet (produziert von Charles Stepney). Der amerikanische Fotograf Ethan Russell hatte die besondere Ehre, Albumcover für die Beatles, die Rolling Stones und The Who fotografiert zu haben. ⭘

Accompagnée par la section rythmique d'Earth, Wind & Fire et produite par Charles Stepney, Deniece Williams fait des débuts très remarqués avec *This is Niecy*. Le photographe américain Ethan Russell a eu l'insigne honneur de travailler sur des pochettes d'album des Beatles, des Rolling Stones et des Who.

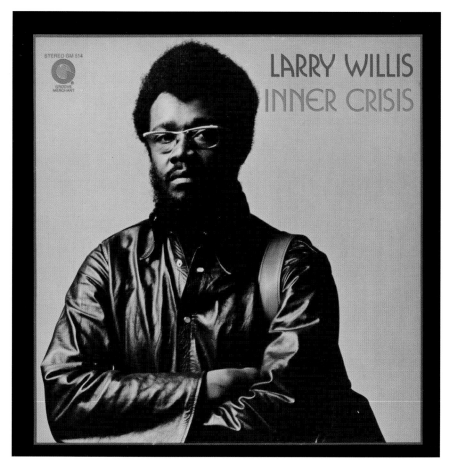

LARRY WILLIS

title **INNER CRISIS** / *year* **1974** / *label* Groove Merchant /
photography Chuck Stewart / *art direction* Sam Alexander

Larry Willis was well known in jazz circles as Jackie McLean's
keyboardist and had already begun a long stint with the
rock band Blood, Sweat & Tears by the time he released
this LP. It sits well above as one of the funkiest jazz records
ever released on the Groove Merchant label. The sounds
within easily live up to the defiant, even slightly militant
portrait by long-time jazz photographer Chuck Stewart. **O**
Larry Willis war in Jazzkreisen als Keyboarder von Jackie
McLean bekannt und hatte bereits eine lange Phase bei der
Rockband Blood, Sweat & Tears hinter sich, als er diese LP
herausbrachte. Sie kann mit Fug und Recht als eine der

funkigsten Jazzplatten bezeichnet werden, die je auf dem
Label Groove Merchant erschienen sind. Die hier versam-
melten Klänge machen dem aufsässigen, sogar leicht mili-
tanten Porträt vom langjährigen Jazzfotografen Chuck
Stewart alle Ehre. **O**
Au moment où cet album est sorti, Larry Willis était connu
dans le milieu du jazz en qualité de claviériste de Jackie
McLean et avait déjà commencé ce qui allait être une
longue collaboration avec le groupe de rock Blood, Sweat
& Tears. *Inner Crisis* est sans aucun doute l'un des disques
de jazz les plus funky jamais sortis chez le label Groove
Merchant. Les sons qu'il renferme ressemblent au portrait
défiant, et même légèrement militant, créé par le photographe de jazz Chuck Stewart.

JACKIE WILSON
title **I'LL BE SATISFIED** / *year* **1959** /
label Coral

THE SOUND OF
CORAL
RECORDS
HIGH-FIDELITY

94162 EPC  HI-FI

I'll Be Satisfied

**Each Time
You Better Know It
Come Back To Me**

Jackie Wilson

REUBEN WILSON
AND THE COST OF LIVING

title **GOT TO GET YOUR OWN** / *year* **1975** / *label* Cadet / *design* Joel Brodsky / *art direction* Neil Terk / *photography* Joel Brodsky

Reuben Wilson had been slugging away at some nice Hammond B3 organ releases for Blue Note and Groove Merchant for the better part of a decade when he found his way to Chess and its jazz subsidiary Cadet for this monstrously funky release. His sole outing for the label is an all-out onslaught of funk. Joel Brodsky's effusive cover photo captures the spirit of the session. **O**
Reuben Wilson hatte den größeren Teil des Jahrzehnts an ein paar schönen Releases mit der Hammond-B3-Orgel für

Blue Note und Groove Merchant herumgefeilt, als er für diese mächtig funkige Platte den Weg zu Chess und deren Jazz-Dependance Cadet fand. Seine einzige Exkursion zu diesem Label ist ein kompromissloser Angriff auf den Funk. Das überschwängliche Coverfoto von Joel Brodsky fängt die Stimmung der Session gut ein. **O**
Reuben Wilson frappait joyeusement sur des orgues Hammond B3 depuis presque dix ans pour de beaux albums sortis chez Blue Note et Groove Merchant lorsqu'il se retrouva chez Chess et sa filiale de jazz Cadet pour cet album monstrueusement funky. C'est le seul qu'il ait réalisé pour ce label, et c'est un bombardement sauvage de funk. La photo exubérante de Joel Brodsky pour la couverture saisit bien l'esprit de la session d'enregistrement.

SPANKY WILSON

title **SPECIALTY OF THE HOUSE** / *year* **1975** / *label* Westbound / *design* Joel Brodsky / *photography* Joel Brodsky

Joel Brodsky's sultry cover-shot of Spanky Wilson jives with her move to the Westbound label and a more straight-ahead sound than her previous, grittier records. Her rich vocals are paired with a sophisticated set of arrangements that, while not as adventurous as her earlier work, are a great showcase for her prowess behind the mic. ⭘
Joel Brodskys heißblütiges Coverfoto von Spanky Wilson swingt regelrecht, nachdem sie zum Westbound-Label gewechselt war und nun einen geradlinigeren Sound hat als bei ihren frühen, raueren Aufnahmen. Ihre volle Stimme fügt sich nahtlos in die anspruchsvollen Arrangements ein, die vielleicht nicht so abenteuerlich sind wie ihre früheren Arbeiten, doch einen hervorragenden Beweis für ihr Können am Mikro liefern. ⭘
Le portrait sensuel que Joel Brodsky a réalisé de Spanky Wilson illustre son passage au label Westbound et à un son plus épuré que sur ses disques précédents, plus abrasifs. Sa voix riche s'allie à des arrangements sophistiqués qui, bien qu'ils ne soient pas aussi aventureux que son travail antérieur, mettent superbement en valeur ses prouesses derrière le micro.

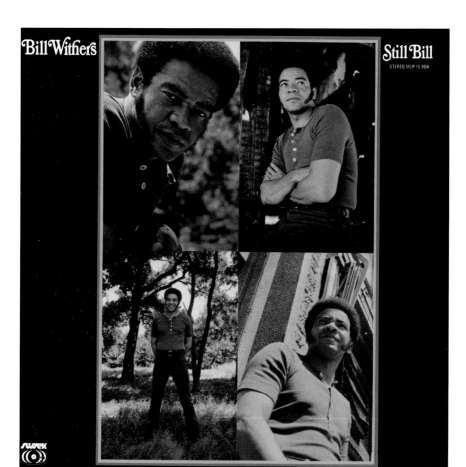

BILL WITHERS

title **STILL BILL** / *year* **1972** / *label* Sussex /
photography Hal Wilson

For Bill Withers' sophomore release, photographer Hal
Wilson captured the West Virginia native in numerous
poses, set in both natural and urban environments.
Hal Wilson's simple snapshots also grace the covers of
Sixto Rodriguez's *Coming From Reality* and Dennis Coffey's
Goin' for Myself, all released on Sussex within a one-year
period. **O**

Für die zweite LP von Bill Withers fotografierte Hal Wilson
den Mann aus West Virginia in verschiedenen Posen und
stellte ihn dafür in ländliche und auch städtische Umge-
bungen. Hal Wilsons einfache Schnappschüsse zieren auch
die Cover von Sixto Rodriguez' *Coming From Reality* und
Goin' for Myself von Dennis Coffey. Alle diese Alben erschienen innerhalb eines Jahres auf Sussex. **O**

Pour le deuxième album de Bill Withers, le photographe
Hal Wilson a mitraillé ce natif de la Virginie de l'Ouest
dans de nombreuses poses, en ville et à la campagne. Ces
clichés simples ornent également les pochettes de *Coming
From Reality* de Sixto Rodriguez et *Goin' for Myself* de
Dennis Coffey, sortis chez Sussex sur une période d'un an.

ORIGINAL MOTION PICTURE SCORE

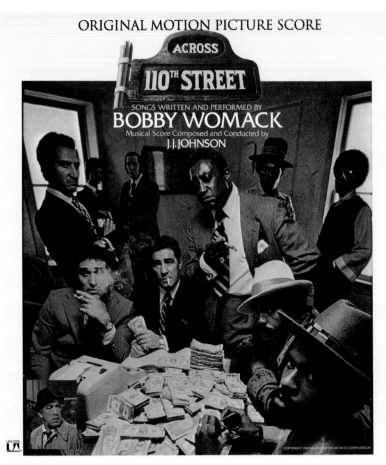

BOBBY WOMACK

title **ACROSS 110TH STREET** / *year* **1972** /
label United Artists

Across 110th Street is a classic crime-drama with a stellar
soundtrack by Bobby Womack. The cover photo captures
a definitive image from the movie, one central to the
film's over-arching plot – the flagrant robbery of a mob-
controlled bank in Harlem, whose southern-most boun-
dary is formed by the movie's namesake street. **O**

Across 110th Street ist ein klassisches Krimidrama mit einem
brillanten Soundtrack von Bobby Womack. Das Coverfoto

zeigt eine maßgebliche, für den gesamten Spannungsbogen
sehr wichtige Szene aus dem Film: der schamlose Überfall
auf eine von der Mafia kontrollierte Bank in Harlem.
Jene Straße, die dem Film seinen Namen gab, bildet die
südlichste Grenze dieses Bezirks. **O**

Across 110th Street est un film policier classique pourvu
d'une sublime bande originale de Bobby Womack. La photo de la pochette représente une scène clé pour l'intrigue
principale du film, le cambriolage d'une banque de Harlem
contrôlée par la mafia, dont la limite située le plus au sud
est marquée par la rue qui donne son nom au film.

STEVIE WONDER
title **MY CHERIE AMOUR** /
year **1969** / *label* Tamla Motown /
art direction Curtis McNair

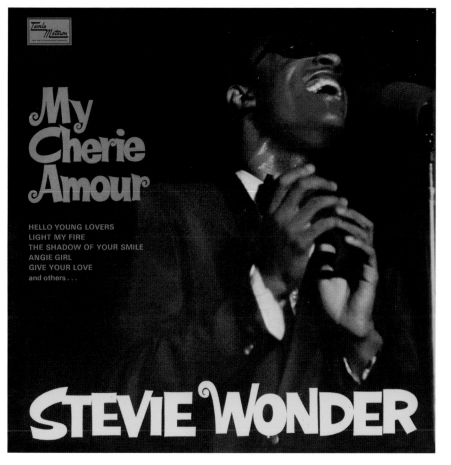

STEVIE WONDER

TALKING BOOK

STEVIE WONDER

title **TALKING BOOK** / *year* **1972** / *label* Motown /
photography R. Margouleff

Sitting securely in the center of his classic '70s run of outstanding records, this LP shows Stevie Wonder flexing his
musical muscles. He experiments freely with the layering of
his keyboard arsenal and while it contains some of his
heaviest funk to date with "Superstition" and "Maybe Your
Baby", its bookends, "You Are the Sunshine of My Life" and
"I Believe (When I Fall in Love It Will Be Forever)", are some
of his most soulful yearnings. ○

Auf dieser hervorragenden Aufnahme lässt Stevie Wonder
geschickt seine musikalischen Muskeln spielen. Die Scheibe
nimmt inmitten seiner klassischen Serie ausgezeichneter
Aufnahmen aus den 70er Jahren einen Ehrenplatz ein. Er

experimentiert frei mit seinem übereinandergeschichteten
Keyboard-Arsenal. Zwar enthält das Album mit »Superstition« und »Maybe Your Baby« ein paar seiner bis dato
mächtigsten Funk-Bomben, doch mit dem Intro »You Are
the Sunshine of My Life« und dem Outro »I Believe (When
I Fall in Love It Will Be Forever)« finden sich hier auch zwei
seiner sehnsuchtsvollsten Soul-Stücke. ○

Confortablement niché au milieu de sa série de classiques
des années 1970, cet album montre un Stevie Wonder au
sommet de ses talents musicaux. Il expérimente en toute
liberté sur la superposition de son arsenal de claviers et,
bien que le disque contienne certains de ces morceaux les
plus funky, avec *Superstition* et *Maybe Your Baby*, il commence et finit par *You Are the Sunshine of My Life* et *I Believe (When I Fall in Love It Will Be Forever)*, qui font partie
de ses chansons les plus soul.

Collector's Album
Includes Two Records
A Something's Extra
Bonus Record
24-Page
Lyric Booklet

STEVIE WONDER

title **SONGS IN THE KEY OF LIFE** / *year* **1976** /
label Motown / *illustration* Tony Warren

A highlight in a career full of highs, this was the fifth and final record from Stevie Wonder's classic mid-'70s period. The double LP was the first American record ever to enter the Billboard charts at #1. A funky stew of soul and jazz sounds, which culminated in Wonder's biggest hit to date, "Sir Duke". ○

Dieses fünfte und letzte Album aus Stevie Wonders klassischer Phase Mitte der 70er Jahre ist ein weiteres Highlight seiner an Höhepunkten nicht armen Karriere. Dieses Dop-

pelalbum war die erste amerikanische Platte, die in den Billboard-Charts gleich auf Platz 1 landete. Der funkige Cocktail aus Soul- und Jazzklängen kulminierte im bis dato größten Hit von Stevie Wonder: »Sir Duke«. ○

Ce cinquième et dernier disque de la période classique de Stevie Wonder au milieu des années 1970 marque un temps fort dans une carrière pleine de sommets. Ce double album était le premier disque américain de l'histoire à entrer au classement du Billboard directement en première place. C'est une fricassée de sons de soul et de jazz, dont l'ingrédient phare est le plus grand succès de Wonder à ce jour, *Sir Duke*.

STEVIE WONDER

title **INNERVISIONS** / *year* **1973** / *label* Motown /
illustration Efram Wolff

Los Angeles native Efram Wolff began illustrating profes-
sionally in the early '70s for a number of clients, including
the newly relocated Motown, and local jazz indie, Contemporary Records. He presently lives in Washington state
where he maintains a studio on Vashon Island, southwest
of Seattle in the Puget Sound. **O**
Der aus Los Angeles stammende Efram Wolff begann seine
Profilaufbahn Anfang der 70er Jahre mit Illustrationen für

verschiedene Auftraggeber, z. B. für das gerade umgezogene
Label Motown und das Independent-Label für Jazz Contemporary Records. Heute lebt er im Staat Washington,
wo er südwestlich von Seattle auf Vashon Island im Puget
Sound sein Studio betreibt. **O**
Efram Wolff, natif de Los Angeles, a commencé sa carrière
d'illustrateur au début des années 1970 avec, parmi ses
clients, le label Motown qui venait de déménager, et le label
local de jazz indépendant, Contemporary Records. Il vit
actuellement dans l'État de Washington où il a un studio sur
Vashon Island, au sud-ouest de Seattle dans le Puget Sound.

WOOD, BRASS & STEEL

title **WOOD, BRASS & STEEL** / *year* **1976** / *label* Turbo /
art direction Dudley Thomas / *illustration* Nick Caruso

Nick Caruso's fantastical illustration of a turbo-powered
schooner incorporates the three physical components of
this band with the fast-sailing feeling of their funky sound.
Doug Wimbish and Skip "Little Axe" McDonald would go
on to back the Sugarhill house-band and many early rap
acts. **O**
Die fantastische Illustration eines turbogetriebenen Scho-
ners von Nick Caruso setzt die drei physischen Komponen-

ten dieser Band bildlich um und kombiniert sie mit einem
Funk-Feeling unter vollen Segeln. Doug Wimbish und Skip
»Little Axe« McDonald machten als Backgroundmusiker
für die Sugarhill Gang und viele frühe Rap-Acts weiter. **O**
Cette goélette à turbomoteurs fantasmagorique, dessinée
par Nick Caruso, réunit les trois matériaux qui composent
ce groupe et reproduit l'impression de naviguer avec le
vent dans les voiles que leur son funky transmet à l'auditeur. Doug Wimbish et Skip « Little Axe » McDonald
allaient par la suite accompagner le groupe résident de
Sugarhill et participer activement aux débuts du rap.

THE LYMAN WOODARD ORGANIZATION

title **"SATURDAY NIGHT SPECIAL"** / *year* **1975** /
label Strata / *design* John Sinclair & Lyman Woodard /
art direction John Sinclair

This record has always had a certain mystique about it beginning with the cover's evocation of the seedy streets of Detroit in the early 1970s and flowing through the soulful jazz of Lyman Woodard's organ-driven funk. Far more sophisticated than John Sinclair's gritty cover design would suggest, the music within delivers a deeply textured world of smoldering intensity. **O**

Diese Aufnahme besaß immer einen gewissen Mystizismus. Das begann schon mit dem Heraufbeschwören der zwie-

lichtigen Straßen Detroits in den frühen 70ern und setzte sich fort in dem souligen Jazz von Lyman Woodards orgellastigem Funk. Die Musik auf der Platte ist sehr viel ausgefeilter, als man beim grobkörnigen Coverdesign von John Sinclair annehmen würde, und liefert eine tief durchdachte Klangwelt von glühender Intensität. **O**

Ce disque a toujours dégagé une certaine aura mystique, en commençant par la pochette qui évoque les rues mal famées de Detroit au début des années 1970. Le funk aux accents de jazz et de soul qui sort de l'orgue de Lyman Woodard n'y est pas étranger non plus. Bien plus sophistiquée que le graphisme cru du John Sinclair ne le laisse imaginer sur la pochette, la musique fait plonger l'auditeur dans un monde d'une sourde intensité à la texture très travaillée.

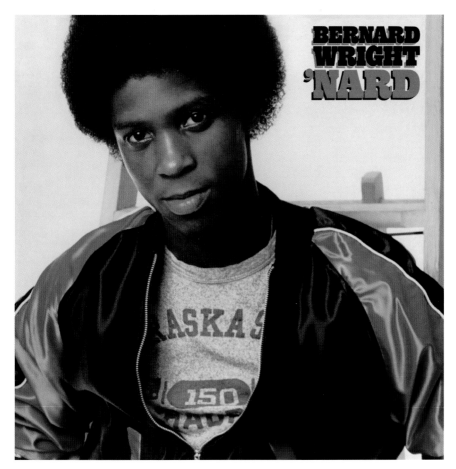

BERNARD WRIGHT

title **'NARD** / *year* **1981** / *label* GRP/Arista /
design Howard Fritzson / *photography* John Ford /
art direction Donn Davenport

Bernard Wright was still a teenager when he recorded this
remarkable debut for Dave Grusin and Larry Rosen's GRP
Records. Although the back photograph reveals that 'Nard
has the pants to match this stylish windbreaker, he has
swapped the athletic gray Nebraska T-shirt for a black
sweat-shirt with "STRAIGHT AHEAD" emblazoned across
the chest in red iron-on letters. ●
Bernard Wright war noch ein Teenager, als er dieses bemerkenswerte Debütalbum für das Label GRP Records von

Dave Grusin und Larry Rosen aufnahm. Obwohl das Foto
auf der Rückseite enthüllt, dass 'Nard die passende Hose
zu diesem stylishen Windbreaker besitzt, hat er das sport-
lich-graue Nebraska-T-Shirt gegen ein schwarzes Sweatshirt
getauscht, auf dem in roter Schrift auf der Brust
»STRAIGHT AHEAD« aufgebügelt ist. ●
Bernard Wright était encore un adolescent lorsqu'il a enregistré ce remarquable premier album pour le label GRP
Records de Dave Grusin et Larry Rosen. La photo du dos
de la pochette révèle que 'Nard avait le pantalon assorti à
son coupe-vent stylé, mais il y troque son t-shirt de sport
gris Nebraska contre un sweat-shirt noir orné des mots
« STRAIGHT AHEAD » (« Droit devant ») en grandes
lettres rouge feu en travers du torse.

BETTY WRIGHT

title **I LOVE THE WAY YOU LOVE** / *year* **1972** / *label* Alston / *design* Drago / *photography* Bruce MacCallum

A prominent member of Henry Stone's soul dynasty, Betty Wright made a sizable impression with *I Love the Way You Love*, which featured the frequently sampled "Clean Up Woman". Emphasizing the teenager's commendable Afro and child-like grin, the backlighting and red toning of the cover image complement the fiery soul portrayed here by the Miami native. **O**

Betty Wright war ein prominentes Mitglied der Soul-Dynastie von Henry Stone. Sie machte mit *I Love the Way* *You Love* mächtig Eindruck. Auf diesem Album wurde das häufig gesampelte »Clean Up Woman« vorgestellt. Das Hintergrundlicht und die rötliche Tönung des Coverfotos betonen ihren beachtlichen Afro sowie ihr kindliches Lächeln und unterstreichen den feurigen Soul, den diese Frau aus Miami hier entzündet. **O**

Membre émérite de la dynastie de la soul de Henry Stone, Betty Wright a fait grande impression avec *I Love the Way You Love*, qui contenait le morceau souvent samplé *Clean Up Woman*. Le contre-jour et les tons rouges de la photo de la pochette mettent en valeur la coiffure afro et le sourire enfantin de l'adolescente, et complètent la soul incandescente de cette chanteuse originaire de Miami.

MILTON WRIGHT

FRIENDS and BUDDIES

MILTON WRIGHT

title **FRIENDS AND BUDDIES** / *year* **1975** /
label Alston / *design* Drago / *illustration* Ann Merritt

Ann Merritt's striking portrait captures the duality of the
graceful funk that Milton Wright exuded. His unique blend
of synthesized, spaced-out sounds and acoustic guitar
balladry did not find great success when this LP was
released in 1975, but has come to be a cherished gem of
the Modern Soul movement. **O**
Ann Merritts eindrucksvolles Porträt fängt die Dualität des
anmutigen Funk ein, den Milton Wright verströmte. Seiner
einzigartigen Mischung aus synthetischen, abgefahrenen
Sounds und akustischen Gitarrenballaden war 1975 bei
Erscheinen dieser LP wenig Erfolg beschieden. Später sollte
sie zu einem besonders verehrten Juwel der Modern-Soul-
Bewegung werden. **O**
Le portrait saisissant d'Ann Merritt illustre la dualité du
funk élégant qui émanait de Milton Wright. Son mélange
original de sons synthétisés planants et de ballades à la
guitare acoustique n'a pas rencontré un grand succès à la
sortie de cet album en 1975, mais est depuis devenu un
joyau très apprécié du mouvement de la modern soul.

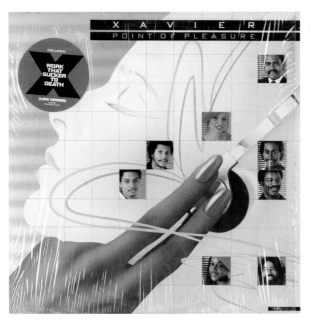

XAVIER

title **POINT OF PLEASURE** /
year **1981** / label Liberty / design
Roy R. Gutzman / photography
John Ford & Tom "Snoopy"
Gibson / art direction W. M. Burks

TOMMIE YOUNG

title **DO YOU STILL FEEL THE
SAME WAY** / year **1973** /
label Soul Power / photography
Skipworth

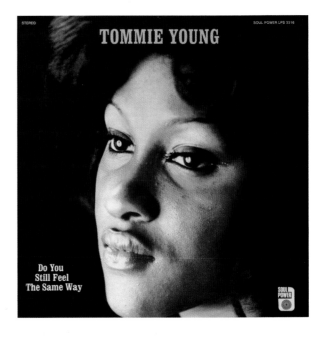

KZ 32405
GAMBLE

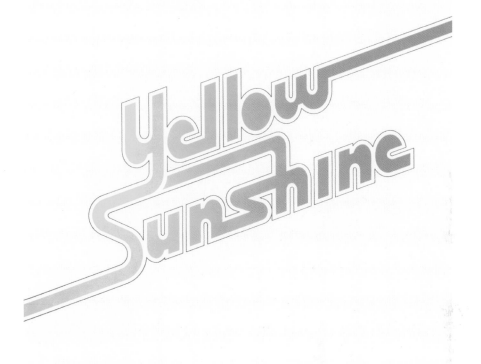

YELLOW SUNSHINE

title **YELLOW SUNSHINE** / *year* **1973** / *label* Gamble / *art direction* Ed Lee / *lettering* Keith Sheridan

Brothers Karl (drums) and Roland Chambers (guitar) founded this tough funk ensemble that included Dexter Wansel on keyboards. The bright, clean graphics by Keith Sheridan on the cover of their sole LP speaks to the polished sound these Philly sons were serving up. **O**
Die Brüder Karl (Drums) und Roland Chambers (Gitarre) gründeten dieses toughe Funk-Ensemble, zu dem auch

Dexter Wansel an den Keyboards zählte. Der leuchtende und klare Schriftzug von Keith Sheridan auf dem Cover ihrer einzigen LP entspricht dem polierten Sound, den diese Söhne des Philly Sound hier servieren. **O**
Les frères Karl (batterie) et Roland Chambers (guitare) ont créé cette formation de funk qui comptait également Dexter Wansel aux claviers. Le graphisme vif et net de Keith Sheridan sur la pochette de leur seul album fait écho au son soigné, concocté par ces enfants de Philadelphie.

SOULFUL STRUT

WHO'S MAKING LOVE / JUST AIN'T NO LOVE / LOVE MAKES A WOMAN / LITTLE GREEN APPLES

THE YOUNG-HOLT UNLIMITED

THE YOUNG-HOLT UNLIMITED

title **SOULFUL STRUT** / *year* **1968** / *label* Brunswick / *photography* Hal Buksbaum

Bassist Eldee Young and drummer Isaac "Red" Holt kept legendary time for Ramsey Lewis as the classically-trained pianist transformed countless pop standards into instrumental hits. Although the album contains some Lewis-style reinterpretations, Eugene Record of the Chi-Lites wrote most of the new fare featured herein, including the enduring title track. **O**
Der Bassist Eldee Young und der Schlagzeuger Isaac »Red« Holt hielten auf legendäre Weise den Takt für Ramsey

Lewis, als dieser klassisch ausgebildete Pianist unzählige Popstandards in Instrumentalhits verwandelte. Das Album enthält einige Neuinterpretationen in Lewis' Stil, aber der Löwenanteil einschließlich des langlebigen Titelstücks wurde von Eugene Record von den Chi-Lites verfasst. **O**
Le bassiste Eldee Young et le batteur Isaac « Red » Holt ont suivi des rythmes légendaires pour Ramsey Lewis tandis que ce pianiste de formation classique transformait d'innombrables standards de la pop en succès instrumentaux. L'album renferme quelques reprises dans le style de Lewis, mais Eugene Record et les Chi-Lites ont écrit la plupart des nouveautés de ce disque, notamment le morceau-titre, qui a marqué son temps.

ZAPP

title **ZAPP III** / *year* **1983** / *label*
Warner Bros. / *design* Laura LiPuma /
art direction Simon Levy / *illustration*
Dan Chapman

DJs' TOP-10 LISTS

PARLIAMENT
title **MOTHERSHIP**
CONNECTION / *year* **1975** /
label Casablanca / *design* Gribbitt! /
art direction Gribbitt!

STEINSKI

www.steinski.com

Steinski – DJ, producer, and record collector – is a pioneer of the cut-and-paste technique in production. He emerged in the '80s with the creation of *Lesson 1: The Pay-Off Mix*. In the course of three albums, Steinski and his partner Double Dee used juxtaposed funk breakbeats with samples of originals, not only from funk but also films, television, and cartoons, making a clear reference to pop culture as raw material for their musical adventures. The result introduced new techniques to producers' and DJs' range, at the same time enlarging the aesthetics of hip-hop.

Steinski ist nicht nur DJ, Produzent und Plattensammler, sondern auch Sample-Pionier. Mit *Lesson 1: The Pay-Off Mix* erschien er in den 80er Jahren auf der Szene. Zusammen mit Double Dee stellt Steinski auf drei gemeinsamen Alben Funk-Breakbeats den Samples von Originalen gegenüber. Dabei stammt das Material nicht nur vom Funk, sondern auch aus dem Fernsehen oder Kino- und Trickfilmen. So verweisen die beiden eindeutig auf die Popkultur als Rohmaterial ihrer musikalischen Streifzüge. Durch ihre Arbeiten schaffen sie für Produzenten und DJs neue Spielräume und Techniken und bauen gleichzeitig die Ästhetik des Hiphop aus.

Steinski, DJ, producteur et collectionneur de disques, est un pionnier de la technique de production du copier-coller. Il a fait surface dans les années 1980 avec la création *Lesson 1: The Pay-Off Mix*. Sur leurs trois albums, Steinski et son partenaire Double Dee ont utilisé des breakbeats de funk juxtaposés à des samples de morceaux originaux, non seulement de funk mais aussi de musiques de films, de génériques de télévision et de dessins animés. Ils font clairement référence à la culture pop et en font la matière première de leurs aventures musicales. Le résultat a ajouté de nouvelles techniques à l'arsenal des producteurs et des DJ, tout en élargissant l'esthétique du hip-hop.

1. THE METERS
REJUVENATION Reprise/1974

2. PARLIAMENT
MOTHERSHIP CONNECTION Casablanca/1975

3. STEVIE WONDER
MUSIC OF MY MIND Motown/1972

4. DYKE & THE BLAZERS
SO SHARP! Kent/1983

5. THE SPINNERS
THE BEST OF THE SPINNERS Atlantic/1978

6. AWB
CUT THE CAKE Atlantic/1975

7. SLY & THE FAMILY STONE
STAND! Epic/1969

8. TROUBLE FUNK
DROP THE BOMB Sugar Hill/1982

9. THE WILD TCHOUPITOULAS
THE WILD TCHOUPITOULAS Island/1976

10. JAMES BROWN
SEX MACHINE (LIVE AT HOME IN AUGUSTA GA) Polydor/1970

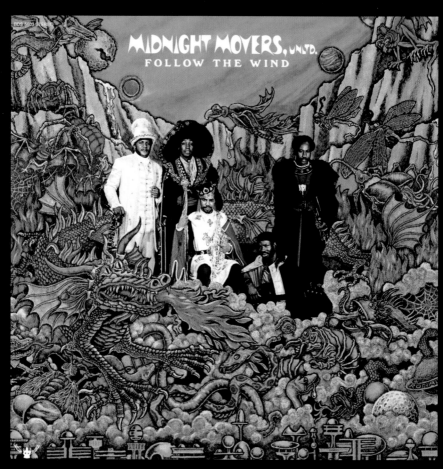

MIDNIGHT MOVERS
title **FOLLOW THE WIND** /
year **1974** / *label* Buddah

DANNY KRIVIT

www.dannykrivit.net

A living legend of DJing. He crossed the '70s alongside names like Larry Levan, David Mancuso, and François Kevorkian. The DJ as central figure was created in this generation. Danny Krivit is a vinyl collector, soul-funk-disco-lover, and a dance-floor master – even for the most demanding! From his long professional journey, his re-editions should also be mentioned, in the course of which Krivit reinvented classical pieces, re-arranging the originals.

Diese Legende unter den DJs war in den 70ern gemeinsam mit solchen Größen wie Larry Levan, David Mancuso und François Kevorkian unterwegs. Der DJ als zentrale Figur erschien erstmals in dieser Generation. Danny Krivit sammelt Vinyl-Platten, liebt Soul, Funk und Disco und ist ein Meister des Dancefloor – auch für allerhöchste Ansprüche!

Unbedingt erwähnenswert aus seiner langen Reise als Profi sind seine »Re-Editions«: Hier erfindet Krivit klassische Stücke ganz neu, indem er die Originale neu arrangiert.

Une légende vivante chez les DJ. Il a traversé les années 1970 aux côtés de noms tels que Larry Levan, David Mancuso et François Kevorkian. C'est cette génération qui a créé le DJ comme figure centrale. Danny Krivit est un collectionneur de vinyles, un amoureux du soul-funk-disco et un maître de la piste de danse, même pour les plus exigeants ! Dans son long parcours professionnel, il faut également citer ses rééditions, dans lesquelles il a réinventé des morceaux classiques en réarrangeant les originaux.

1. THE EMOTIONS
FLOWERS Columbia/1976

2. THE FATBACK BAND
KEEP ON STEPPIN' Southbound/1974

3. THE J.B.'S
FOOD FOR THOUGHT People/1972

4. FUNKADELIC
FREE YOUR MIND... AND YOUR ASS WILL FOLLOW Westbound/1970

5. AL GREEN
I'M STILL IN LOVE WITH YOU London/1972

6. LABELLE
PHOENIX Epic/1975

7. MINNIE RIPERTON
ADVENTURES IN PARADISE Epic/1975

8. RUFUS & CHAKA KHAN
RUFUSIZED MCA/1974

9. MIDNIGHT MOVERS
FOLLOW THE WIND Buddah/1974

10. DENIECE WILLIAMS
THIS IS NIECY CBS/1976

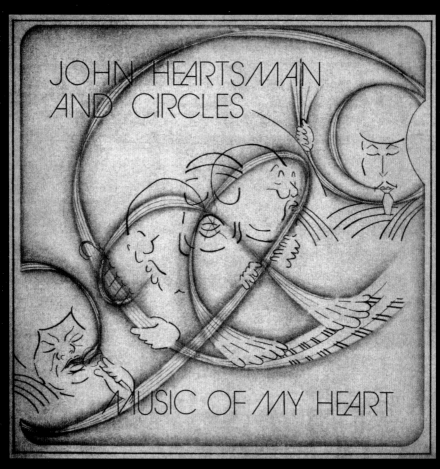

**JOHN HEARTSMAN
& CIRCLES**
title **MUSIC OF MY HEART** /
year **1976** / *label* Private Press

EGON

www.nowagainrecords.com

Egon is a hard digger. Tireless researcher of rare and obscure gems of funk, soul, jazz, Africa, he travels the world to show his precious findings. He is one of the most influential musical personalities of our time through his work as a label manager for Stones Throw and as founder of Now-Again.

Egon ist unter den musikalischen Goldgräbern ein echter Schwerarbeiter. Er forscht unermüdlich nach seltenen und obskuren Schätzen aus Funk, Soul, Jazz und afrikanischer Musik. Auf Reisen durch die ganze Welt lässt er alle an seinen kostbaren Fundstücken teilhaben. Als Label Manager für

Stones Throw und Gründer von Now-Again gilt er heutzutage als eine der einflussreichsten Persönlichkeiten der Musikszene.

Egon est un chercheur d'or musical invétéré. Il explore inlassablement, à la recherche de perles rares et obscures de funk, soul, jazz et musique africaine, et il voyage dans le monde entier pour montrer ses précieuses trouvailles. C'est l'un des personnages les plus influents dans le domaine de la musique actuellement, grâce à son travail comme manager de label pour Stones Throw et comme fondateur de Now-Again.

1. JOHN HEARTSMAN & CIRCLES
MUSIC OF MY HEART Private Press 2LP/1976

2. UNIVERSOULS
NEW GENERATION Tener Custom/1971

3. STONE COAL WHITE
YOU KNOW Shur'n'tell/1971

4. GALT MacDERMOT
WOMAN IS SWEETER Kilmarnock/1969

5. CARLEEN & THE GROOVERS
CAN WE RAP Now-Again Records/2004

6. SOUL EXPEDITION
SOUL EXPEDITION Amherst/1976

7. KASHMERE STAGE BAND
THUNDER SOUL Kram/1971

8. HOT CHOCOLATE
HOT CHOCOLATE Co-Co Cleveland/1971

9. KEY & CLEARY
WHAT IT TAKES TO LIVE Soul-Cal/1976

10. L.A. CARNIVAL
COLOR Stones Throw Records, Now-Again Records/2002

FRED WESLEY &
THE J.B.'S
title **DAMN RIGHT I AM**
SOMEBODY / *year* **1974** /
label People

ANDY SMITH

www.djandysmith.com

Though Andy Smith is most widely known as the "Portishead DJ", he is a remarkable talent in his own right. England's Andy Smith started spinning Northern Soul – a dance-floor-driving sub-genre of vintage American soul music – in the '80s before being swept up in hip-hop in the early '90s. Around that time, a nascent trip-hop group called Portishead enlisted the DJ as its opening act on the road. After two world tours, as well as credits as a supplier of samples on Portishead's first two groundbreaking albums, Smith got back to his soul roots.

Vor allem als »Portishead-DJ« bekannt, ist der Engländer Andy Smith aber auch selbst ein bemerkenswertes Talent. Andy Smith legte schon in den 80er Jahren Northern Soul auf, ein absolut tanzbares Subgenre altmodischer amerikanischer Soulmusik, bevor er sich Anfang der 90er voll auf Hiphop konzentrierte. Etwa zu jener Zeit verpflichtete eine aufkeimende Triphop-Band namens Portishead

diesen DJ als Act bei ihren Tourneen. Nachdem er Portishead auf zwei Welttourneen begleitet und die Gruppe auf ihren beiden bahnbrechenden ersten Alben mit Samples versorgt hatte, kehrte Smith zu seinen Soul-Wurzeln zurück.

Bien qu'Andy Smith soit plus connu du grand public comme le « DJ de Portishead », son talent personnel est remarquable. Cet Anglais a commencé à faire tourner de la Northern Soul (un sous-genre qui reprenait de vieux morceaux de soul américaine et qui faisait fureur sur les pistes de danse) sur ses platines dans les années 1980 avant de se faire happer par le hip-hop au début des années 1990. C'est à cette époque qu'un tout jeune groupe de trip-hop, Portishead, le recruta pour faire sa première partie en tournée. Après deux tournées mondiales, et après avoir fourni au groupe des samples pour ses deux premiers albums révolutionnaires, Smith est retourné à ses racines soul.

1. FRED WESLEY & THE J.B.'S
DAMN RIGHT I AM SOMEBODY People/1974

2. BILL WITHERS
STILL BILL Sussex/1972

3. GLORIA SCOTT
WHAT AM I GONNA DO Casablanca/1974

4. CHUCK JACKSON
THROUGH ALL TIMES ABC/1973

5. JAMES BROWN
THE PAYBACK Polydor/1973

6. TOM BROCK
I LOVE YOU MORE AND MORE 20th Century/1974

7. THE METERS
THE METERS Josie/1969

8. VICKI ANDERSON
MESSAGE FROM A SOUL SISTER Famous Flame

9. MARVIN GAYE
WHAT'S GOING ON Motown/1971

10. THE FOUR TOPS
KEEPER OF THE CASTLE Probe/1972

MUSTAFA ÖZKENT
title **GENÇLIK ILE ELELE** /
year **1972** / *label* Evren

QUANTIC

www.quantic.org

William Holland, aka Quantic, is a British multi-instrumentalist, producer, and DJ who settled in Colombia and has been dedicating himself to the research and study of the sounds of Latin America. His sound crosses elements of salsa, bossa nova, soul, funk, and jazz and he records under a wide range of projects: as The Quantic Soul Orchestra, Quantic and his Combo Bárbaro, or The Limp Twins.

William Holland alias Quantic ist ein britischer Multiinstrumentalist, Produzent und DJ. Er ließ sich in Kolumbien nieder und widmet sich dort seinen Forschungen und Studien über lateinamerikanische Musik. In seinem Sound vermischen sich Elemente von Salsa, Bossa Nova, Soul, Funk und Jazz. Bei verschiedensten Projekten wie The Quantic Soul Orchestra, Quantic and his Combo Bárbaro oder The Limp Twins bringt er seine Aufnahmen heraus.

William Holland, également connu sous le nom de Quantic, est un multi-instrumentiste, producteur et DJ britannique qui s'est installé en Colombie et s'est consacré à la recherche et à l'étude des sons latino-américains. Il croise des éléments de salsa, bossa-nova, soul, funk et jazz, et il enregistre pour un large éventail de projets : sous les noms de The Quantic Soul Orchestra, Quantic and his Combo Bárbaro ou The Limp Twins.

1. SOUL FANTASTICS
LOS NUEVOS Taboga/1968

2. ORQUESTA RIVERSIDE
ORQUESTA RIVERSIDE Areito

3. BYRON LEE & THE DRAGONAIRES
GOING PLACES Dynamic/1970

4. MUSTAFA ÖZKENT
GENÇLIK ILE ELELE Evren/1972

5. LUIS SANTI Y SU CONJUNTO
EL BIGOTE Sound Triangle/1975

6. DR JOHN
THE NIGHT TRIPPER Atco/1970

7. THE EXCITERS
CONOZCO A LOS DOS Loyola

8. PIOTR
PIOTR Pronit/1970

9. LITO MIGRE
LITO MIGRE Carnival

10. JULIAN Y SU COMBO
NOCHE DE FIESTA INS/1975

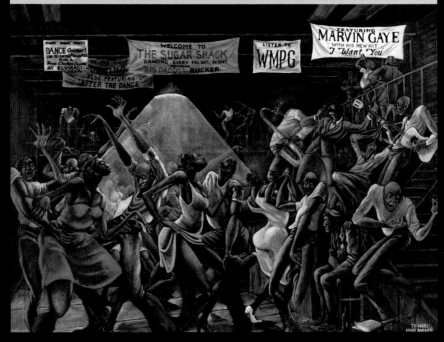

MARVIN GAYE
title **I WANT YOU** / *year* **1976** /
label Motown

KALAF

www.enchufada.com

From Portugal to the world, Buraka Som Sistema has been setting fire to stages and dance floors all over the place. It's an adventure that starts in Africa and goes out to the brand new sounds of dance music. Buraka Som Sistema is a collective exploring the boundaries of groove and Kalaf is the poet, lead singer, and agitator of the band whose musical matrices are found in soul and funk.

Aus Portugal in die ganze Welt: Buraka Som Sistema steckt Bühnen und Dancefloors in aller Welt in Brand. Dieses Abenteuer beginnt in Afrika und erstreckt sich bis in die brandaktuelle Dancemusic. Buraka Som Sistema baut als Kollektiv sein musikali-sches Grundgerüst auf Soul und Funk. Sie erforschen die Grenzen des Groove, und Kalaf gehört als Poet, Leadsänger und Agitator zur Band.

Origine : Portugal. Destination : le monde. Buraka Som Sistema passe son temps à mettre le feu aux scènes et pistes de danse du monde entier. C'est une aventure qui commence en Afrique et qui va jusqu'aux tout nouveaux sons de la musique de danse. Buraka Som Sistema est un collectif qui explore les limites du groove, et Kalaf est le poète, chanteur et agitateur du groupe, dont les matrices musicales se trouvent dans la soul et le funk.

1. MINNIE RIPERTON
COME TO MY GARDEN GRT/1971

2. GIL SCOTT-HERON
PIECES OF A MAN RCA/1971

3. ROBERTA FLACK
FIRST TAKE Atlantic/1969

4. CYMANDE
RENEGADES OF FUNK Newhouse/2005

5. LONNIE LISTON SMITH
EXPANSIONS RCA/1979

6. TIM MAIA
RACIONAL VOL. 1 Seroma/1974

7. D'ANGELO
VOODOO EMI/2000

8. MICHAEL JACKSON
OFF THE WALL Epic/1979

9. MARVIN GAYE
I WANT YOU Motown/1976

10. CURTIS MAYFIELD
CURTIS Curtom/1970

CHANGE

THE GLOW OF LOVE

**CHANGE FEATURING
LUTHER VANDROSS**
title **THE GLOW OF LOVE** /
year **1980** / *label* WEA

KON

www.playin4keeps.blogspot.com

Kon is a musical archeologist who is always following the path of the darkest records, of the endless and fascinating connections between Soul Funk and Afro-Jazz. Together with his friend Amir, he forms one of the most extraordinary partnerships in DJing as well as in the work of production and research, as shown in the compilation series *Off Track*, which already has cult status. Not surprisingly, Kon is among the most legendary diggers who put in thousands of hours sunk deep in record shops in the strangest places – all of this in search of the Groove, for a never-before-heard record.

Kon erkundet als musikalischer Archäologe die Pfade zu dunkelsten Aufnahmen, den endlos verschlungenen und faszinierenden Verbindungen zwischen Soul Funk und Afro-Jazz. Zusammen mit seinem Freund Amir stellt er eine der außergewöhnlichsten Partnerschaften – nicht nur in der DJ-Szene, sondern auch bei Produktion und Recherche. Das

beweist die Compilation-Serie *Off Track*, die bereits Kultstatus erlangt hat. Nicht überraschend, dass Kon zu den legendärsten Ausgräbern gehört und sich bereits Tausende von Stunden an den seltsamsten Orten in Plattenläden vergraben hat – all das auf der Suche nach »dem Groove«, nach ungeahnten und ungehörten Platten.

Kon est un archéologue musical qui suit toujours le chemin des disques les plus sombres, des connexions infinies et fascinantes entre le soul funk et l'afro-jazz. Il forme avec son complice Amir un partenariat extraordinaire de DJ-ing, de production et de recherche, comme le montre la série de compilations *Off Track*, déjà culte. Il n'est pas surprenant que Kon fasse partie des collectionneurs les plus légendaires, qui passent des milliers d'heures plongés dans les magasins de disques aux adresses les plus étranges, à la recherche du Groove, d'un disque que personne n'a encore jamais entendu.

1. JAMES BROWN
LIVE AT THE APOLLO Polydor/1968

2. MARVIN GAYE
I WANT YOU Motown/1976

3. THE EDGE OF DAYBREAK
EYES OF LOVE Bohannon's/1979

4. EARTH, WIND & FIRE
THAT'S THE WAY OF THE WORLD CBS/1975

5. BRIEF ENCOUNTER
BRIEF ENCOUNTER Seventy Seven/1970

6. CHANGE FEATURING LUTHER VANDROSS
THE GLOW OF LOVE WEA/1980

7. KOOL & THE GANG
KOOL & THE GANG Polygram/1969

8. SKULL SNAPS
SKULL SNAPS GSF/1973

9. STEVIE WONDER
SONGS IN THE KEY OF LIFE Motown/1976

10. GIL SCOTT-HERON
WINTER IN AMERICA Arista/1985

PRESTON LOVE
title **PRESTON LOVE'S OMAHA
BAR-B-Q** / *year* **1969** / *label* Kent

MYS35

www.djmys35.com

Mys35 is a DJ and agitator on the Parisian soul and funk scene. An obsessive student and vinyl collector of the soul, funk, and afro cultures, she has been developing notable work spread through the website weGOfunk, which is already an obligatory research reference for black music. Mys35 is one of the founders of this collective and as a DJ she drives the French dance-floors with rare, obscure, classic soul, funk, and afro beat records.

Mys35 ist DJ und gleichzeitig Agitatorin der Pariser Soul- und Funk-Szene. Als obsessive Forscherin und Vinyl-Sammlerin der Soul-, Funk- und Afro-Kulturen entwickelt mys35 ein beachtenswertes Werk. Sie veröffentlicht es auf der Website weGOfunk – bereits jetzt schon eine obligatorische Referenz für Recherchen über schwarze Musik. Mys35 hat das Kollektiv mitbegründet, und als DJ feuert sie rare, obskure und klassische Soul-, Funk- und Afrobeat-Scheiben auf die Dancefloors ab.

Mys35 est DJ et agitatrice sur la scène parisienne du funk et de la soul. Elle étudie avec obsession la soul, le funk et l'afro, dont elle collectionne des vinyles avec tout autant d'obsession. Mys35 a développé une œuvre remarquable qu'elle a diffusée à travers le site web weGOfunk, qui est déjà une référence obligatoire pour les recherches sur la musique noire. Elle fait partie des fondateurs de ce collectif et, en tant que DJ, elle mène les pistes de danse françaises avec des disques rares, obscurs et classiques de soul, funk et afro beat.

1. CLAUDETTE SOARES
CLAUDETTE N°3 Philips/1970

2. HARLEM RIVER DRIVE
HARLEM RIVER DRIVE Roulette/1971

3. SHARON JONES & THE DAP-KINGS
NATURALLY Daptone/2005

4. JAMES BROWN
COLD SWEAT Polydor/1967

5. PRESTON LOVE
PRESTON LOVE'S OMAHA BAR-B-Q Kent/1969

6. OHIO PLAYERS
ECSTASY Westbound/1973

7. MORRIS WILSON
FANTASY ISLAND Mowil/1975

8. LES VIKINGS DE LA GUADELOUPE
VIKINGS GUADELOUPE 3a Productions/1976

9. CRYSTAL WINDS
FIRST FLIGHT Cash Ear/1982

10. NAT DOVE & THE DEVILS – PETEY WHEATSTRAW
THE DEVIL'S SON-IN-LAW Magic Disc/1977

GRANDMASTER FLASH & THE FURIOUS FIVE

title **THE MESSAGE** / *year* **1982** /
label Sugarhill

NICOLAS GODIN

www.aircheology.com

Nicolas Godin is one half of the French group Air. *Moon Safari*, their first album, put the band right in the first row of Pop. The influence of Jazz and Soul behind the sophisticated, cool, and retro sound of Air are easily picked out and clear – in fact black music has always been a part of it and has always been part of Nicolas' education and development as a musician and composer. All you have to do is tune your ears and you'll immediately identify the contribution of black music to Air's art pieces.

Nicolas Godin stellt die eine Hälfte der französischen Gruppe Air. Mit dem Debüt-Album *Moon Safari* landete die Band gleich in der ersten Reihe des Pop. Der Einfluss von Jazz und Soul hinter dem ausgefeilten, coolen Retro-Sound von Air ist klar und unschwer herauszuhören. Schwarze Musik war schon immer ein wichtiger Bestandteil der Band

und prägte auch die Ausbildung und Entwicklung von Nicolas als Musiker und Komponist. Man braucht sich nur ein wenig einzuhören und stellt sofort fest, welchen Beitrag schwarze Musik für die kunstvollen Stücke von Air leistet.

Nicolas Godin est l'un des deux membres du groupe français Air. *Moon Safari*, leur premier album, a propulsé le groupe au premier rang de la pop. L'influence du jazz et de la soul clairement derrière le son rétro cool et sophistiqué d'Air est reconnaissable. En fait, la musique noire en a toujours fait partie et a toujours fait partie de l'éducation de Nicolas et de son évolution en tant que musicien et compositeur. Il vous suffira d'accorder vos oreilles, et vous reconnaîtrez immédiatement la contribution de la musique noire aux œuvres d'art du groupe.

1. SLY & THE FAMILY STONE
FRESH Epic/1973

2. PRINCE
1999 WEA/1982

3. HERBIE HANCOCK
HEAD HUNTERS CBS/1973

4. JAMES BROWN
IN THE JUNGLE GROOVE Polydor/1986

5. SLY & THE FAMILY STONE
THERE'S A RIOT GOIN' ON Epic/1971

6. STEVIE WONDER
TALKING BOOK Motown/1972

7. MICHAEL JACKSON
OFF THE WALL Epic/1979

8. CHIC
C'EST CHIC Atlantic/1978

9. ICE T
POWER Sire/1988

10. GRANDMASTER FLASH & THE FURIOUS FIVE
THE MESSAGE Sugarhill/1982

BRENDA RUSSELL
title **BRENDA RUSSELL** /
year **1979** / *label* A&M

SEAN P

Sean P is an encyclopedic authority on everything relating to black music. His knowledge and music collection of Soul, Funk, and Disco have grown and crystallized through many, many years working in the most important London record shops and clubs. As a result, he's the man behind the extraordinary *Disco Spectrum* compilations on the BBE label.

Sean P ist *die* enzyklopädische Autorität für alles, was mit schwarzer Musik zusammenhängt. Sein Wissen und seine Sammlung mit Soul, Funk und Disco sind im Laufe vieler Jahre immens gewachsen und kristallisierten sich weiter durch seine Arbeit in

den wichtigsten Londoner Plattenläden und Clubs. Er steckt hinter den außergewöhnlichen Compilations, die unter dem Namen *Disco Spectrum* auf dem Label BBE erscheinen.

Sean P est une autorité encyclopédique sur tout ce qui touche à la musique noire. Ses connaissances et sa collection de soul, funk et disco ont grandi et se sont structurées au cours de longues années de travail auprès des plus grands magasins de disques et clubs londoniens. C'est ainsi qu'il est devenu l'homme derrière les extraordinaires compilations *Disco Spectrum* du label BBE.

1. 24-CARAT BLACK
GHETTO: MISFORTUNE'S WEALTH Stax/1973

2. BERNARD WRIGHT
'NARD GRP/1981

3. BRENDA RUSSELL
BRENDA RUSSELL A&M/1979

4. THE IMPRESSIONS
THIS IS MY COUNTRY Curtom/1968

5. THE IMPRESSIONS
THE YOUNG MODS' FORGOTTEN STORY
Curtom/1969

6. KOOL & THE GANG
THE BEST OF KOOL & THE GANG De-Lite/1979

7. LOGG
LOGG Salsoul/1981

8. CURTIS MAYFIELD
CURTIS Curtom/1970

9. P-FUNK ALL STARS
URBAN DANCEFLOOR GUERILLAS CBS/1983

10. PLEASURE
JOYOUS Fantasy/1977

1000 Chairs

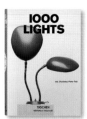

1000 Lights

Decorative Art 50s

Decorative Art 60s

Decorative Art 70s

Design of the 20th Century

domus 1950s

Logo Design

Scandinavian Design

100 All-Time Favorite Movies

The Stanley Kubrick Archives

Bookworm's delight: never bore, always excite!

TASCHEN

Bibliotheca Universalis

20th Century Photography

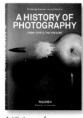

A History of Photography

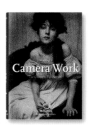

Stieglitz. Camera Work

Curtis. The North American Indian

Eadweard Muybridge

Karl Blossfeldt

Norman Mailer. MoonFire

Photographers A–Z

Dalí. The Paintings

Hiroshige

Leonardo. The Graphic Work

Modern Art

Monet

Alchemy & Mysticism

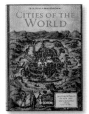

Braun/Hogenberg.
Cities of the World

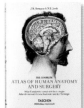

Bourgery. Atlas of
Anatomy & Surgery

D'Hancarville.
Antiquities

Encyclopaedia
Anatomica

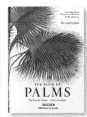

Martius.
The Book of Palms

Seba. Cabinet of
Natural Curiosities

The World
of Ornament

Fashion. A History from
18th–20th Century

100 Contemporary
Fashion Designers

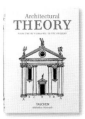

Architectural Theory

The Grand Tour

20th Century
Classic Cars

1000 Record Covers

1000 Tattoos

Funk & Soul Covers

Jazz Covers

Mid-Century Ads

Mailer/Stern.
Marilyn Monroe

Erotica Universalis

Tom of Finland.
Complete Kake Comics

1000 Nudes

Stanton.
Dominant Wives

IMPRINT

To stay informed about TASCHEN and our upcoming titles, please subscribe to our free magazine at www.taschen.com/magazine, follow us on Twitter, Instagram, and Facebook, or e-mail your questions to contact@taschen.com.

© 2016 TASCHEN GmbH
Hohenzollernring 53, D-50672 Köln
www.taschen.com

Original edition: © 2010 TASCHEN GmbH
Editor: Julius Wiedemann
Project Manager: Daniel Siciliano Bretas
& Jascha Kempe
Collaboration: Jutta Hendricks
Design: Birgit Eichwede
Production: Frauke Kaiser

English Revision: Chris Allen
German Translation: Jürgen Dubau
French Translation: Aurélie Daniel

Printed in China
ISBN 978–3–8365–5626–2